THE FIX IS IN

THE SHOWBIZ MANIPULATIONS OF THE NFL, MLB, NBA, NHL AND NASCAR

★

BY BRIAN TUOHY

FERAL HOUSE

ISBN: 978-1-932595-81-9
10 9 8 7 6 5 4 3

Feral House
1240 W. Sims Way
Suite 124
Port Townsend, WA 98368

www.FeralHouse.com

Design by Dana Collins

TABLE OF CONTENTS

CIRCUS FOR THE HORDES

"Pro football provides the circus for the hordes."
— Congressman Emanuel Celler (D-NY 1923 – 1973)

THERE ARE TWO HISTORIES OF PROFESSIONAL SPORTS. THERE is the one fans know and cherish, filled with great players, genius coaches, incredible plays, and dynasty teams. It is the history chronicled in each league's Hall of Fame, the history fans are urged to remember about the games: the moments of struggle, joy, and triumph along with the vast cast of characters that individualized each one of them. Perhaps more than anything, it is this history that has allowed professional sports to mesmerize such a large swath of the population.

There is another history of the sporting world, however, that exists in the shadow created by the glaring spotlight of the sports media. In it the same people exist and the same games take place, yet results are not as pure as most believe them to be. In it Hall of Fame players are criminals, addicts, and gamblers; owners care more about profit than winning; and championships aren't won on the basis of hard work or rising to the occasion, but perhaps because games are outright fixed.

This Hall of Fame history has led sports fans to believe that no game has been fixed since the famed 1919 World Series in which gamblers bribed members of the Chicago White Sox to lose intentionally. Yet, the reality is that gamblers and their Mafia associates have always had a hand in manipulating the outcomes of games. No league has been unaffected by this outside influence, and it continues to seep into each sport today. These stories have been willingly erased not just by the leagues, but also by a sports media apparatus all too willing to bow to its masters' wishes. There is a valid reason for this. If there is a hint of impropriety surrounding the legitimacy of the games, the empire of professional sports could crumble like a proverbial house of cards.

There are many more facets to the world of professional sports than just the franchises that comprise each league. Collateral industries are as much a part of professional sports as players, coaches, and owners. Major sports media outlets like the Entertainment and Sports Programming Network (ESPN), Sports Illustrated, and FOX Sports have a stake in every game played, as do the local beat reporters who cover these events for each hometown newspaper, television, and radio station across the country. If there were no games, there would be nothing to report. And if there were no sports, there would be no baseball hats or hockey jerseys or any of the other sports memorabilia emblazoned with each team's logo for sale. Where would the fortunes of Nike, Reebok and Adidas then lay? How many Foot Lockers, Dick's Sporting Goods, and Champs Sports would continue to do business? Simply put, there are thousands of people who derive hundreds of millions of dollars in income and profit from symbiotic connections with professional sports leagues. In the article "Broadcast Television and the Game of Packaging Sports," author David B. Sullivan stated that at the turn of the 21st century, professional sports became the world's 22nd largest industry because of these vast interconnections.

Therein lays the key to unlocking the hidden history of professional sports. They do not exist solely for personal entertainment. Games are played because there is money to be made. Franchises would not be content to rake in the measly $1.39 profit the Cincinnati Red Stockings, the nation's first professional baseball team, earned in their inaugural 1869 season. Now the leagues are corporations operating under carefully constructed business models and earning billions of dollars each year. Yet this money is not entirely made by selling tickets to the fans lined up outside the stadiums. A majority of each league's income is derived from the major television networks. In fact, it is TV money that actually fuels professional sports.

Without the billions of dollars the television networks pay to broadcast the games, no major sports league would exist today. They simply could not afford to. Because this is true, sports are not really just "sports"; they are show business, and what is passed off onto fans is not as pure as many would like to believe. Is it possible that each league, much like its reality TV counterparts, scripts and manipulates the outcomes of their own games? To do so would in no way violate any law. This would serve to heighten fan interest, drawing more and more viewers to their televisions as the action on the field each week slowly builds to a fevered pitch. Perhaps only that kind of manipulation can ensure the constant ratings that television networks require to provide the leagues with the money they need to operate. It is a seemingly vicious circle, no doubt, but one from which the corporate participants ultimately profit.

Only you, the fan, are led astray. ★

US AND THEM

FANS

ASK YOURSELF A QUESTION: WHY DO YOU CARE ABOUT SPORTS?

That simple question caused an existential meltdown inside me unlike anything Nietzsche or Kierkegaard could have ever dreamed. I grew up both surrounded and consumed by anything and everything sports-related. Then one day it hit me like a vintage Mike Tyson uppercut: Why?

Have you ever stopped and asked yourself why do professional sports matter to you? Why do you care if a bunch of guys who happen to call themselves the New York Yankees win or lose a simple baseball game? You didn't play in the game. You may not have even witnessed it in person or watched it on your television. You probably don't know any of the Yankees personally, nor they you. So why does what they do out on the field affect your life in any way, shape, or form?

In fact, take a brief moment and contemplate your lifetime as it has related to professional sports. How much time have you spent not only watching sports, but reading, researching, blogging, or talking about sports?

Consider your mind as well. How much of your memory is taken up with statistics, player jersey numbers, and the names of insignificant draft picks from the past? Chances are you can explain the pros and cons of the hit-and-run better than you can your own financial investments. Your knowledge of your health insurance plan pales in comparison to what you know about the intricacies of the nickel defense. You can name off, from top to bottom, the batting order of the 1984 Cubs, but you balk when trying to remember the names of your kids' friends. How does that happen? Why do sports take over some people's lives to the point that what should truly be significant and meaningful takes a backseat to something as inane as the name of the pitcher who gave up Duane Kuiper's only major league home run? (It was Steve Stone, by the way.)

The fact that sports can be entertaining is obvious. Baseball has been called the "national pastime" since it became an organized endeavor because it is quite easy to pass time watching a baseball game. Setting this simple idea of a diversion aside, is there something deeper to our need to be fans: something more psychological? What exactly compels one to root, root, root for the home team with such fanatical fervor?

In recent years, researchers have conducted studies seeking answers to these questions. Depending upon how much stock you put into the psychology, some of the causations for sports fandom have been determined.

There are three potential psychological factors that give rise to an individual's identification with a sports team. The first stems from a need for belonging and affiliation. Humans are social creatures. We need to be connected to others, to feel that unity that comes from being in a group. Your family, your friends, your fellow employees are all naturally formed groups you choose to belong to without much thought going into the actual process behind it.

However, as expert Daniel L. Wann of Murray State University wrote, numerous studies in social identity have found that not just any group will do. The second factor deals with belonging to a *distinct* group. You're not just a football fan, you're a *Jets* fan. Your team affiliation becomes a subculture akin to that of a rock and roll fan who identifies more with punk rock than with other types of rock. Doing this will mentally separate you from the masses, yet you still willingly belong to a group. While you may be able to appreciate the league in general as well as some of the other teams, your heart now belongs to just one special team. Wann added that researchers Mlicki and Ellmers claimed that "our desire for group distinctiveness can, in some instances, be more powerful than our desire for a positive group image"[1] which explains Oakland Raiders fans to a T. It's this supposed need to be associated with something unique that makes us choose sides. This newly created identity as a specific team's fan can do more for you than just give you a sense of belonging. It can actually distract you from your own mortality.

This final ingredient involves the "impact of death salience." According to researchers Dechesne, Greenberg, Arndt, & Schimel in 2000, your affiliation with a sports team creates a positive self-image that can act as a buffer between yourself and the realization of your own mortality. While this seems a little outrageous, consider the Boston Red Sox 2004 World Series victory after decades of near misses. Several credible reports in and around the Boston area claimed lifelong Red Sox fans died soon after the title was won. It's not unheard of for people to cling to life to see something significant occur like a graduation or wedding and then pass on soon after it's completed. It comes from an innate need to see something through to the end. The same holds true for sports fans and their teams. This theory also applies to fans of winning teams, such as fans of the Pittsburgh Steelers. Victory breeds distraction it seems, so when the Steelers win yet another title, their fans are happy and not contemplating their own demise.

But what makes one choose to be a Steelers fan? Usually, it comes from a number of factors including your family, friends, where you went to school, and of course, where you live. Regional alliances have existed since the beginning of time, perhaps as an outcropping of tribalism. Choosing to root for the home team is much like joining a sect. There's more than just a common bond formed by the similarity in dress and customs; there's safety in numbers. You're insulated from being an outcast when you conform to those around you.

Deciding to affiliate with the local team can even have health benefits. Research has indicted that "high levels of identification with a local team are related to a variety of psychological health indicators including lower levels of depression, loneliness, alienation, and stress and higher levels of self-esteem, positive affect, and vigor."[2] Mental health aside, other factors can come into play when choosing a favorite team including team colors, logo, specific players, and style of play. But nothing—*nothing*—makes someone choose to follow a team more than winning.

When a person suddenly becomes a fan of a winning team, he is often known as a bandwagon fan. While despised in some circles, most every fan possesses similar traits as those of the bandwagon fan. It is a notion researchers call Basking In Reflected Glory or BIRG for short. Simply put, to BIRG is to attach oneself to the success of another. When you consider yourself a fan of something, you mentally make yourself a part of it. For example, if you're a fan of a local band, and after a few years of struggling, they finally have a hit song, you very may well feel a certain sense of pride from that. You were never directly involved in their success, yet you may still feel some of the joy associated with it. That is the BIRG effect in action.

A person who BIRGs is not only attempting to raise his own self-esteem, he's attempting to elevate his own personal standing in society as well. It's the "we" effect. You can hear this all the time if you listen to sports radio. When fans talk about a team, they say "we" as if they are part of the team (research has also shown that fans do that more often when the team is winning, and conversely, use "they" when the team is losing). A fan's personal sense of failure has something to do with this phenomenon as well. The more perceived failure one has in his own life tends to cause the person to cling to something, anything with a more positive spin on it. "Sports fans use the accomplishments of their team rather than their own actions to derive a sense of accomplishment and a feeling of pride."[3] So when one feels him- or herself failing in life, one BIRGs onto something positive, and suddenly life doesn't seem so bad because "we" have now succeeded.

In essence, when the team wins, the fan wins. This is the main reason we watch, isn't it? "One of the strongest motivations for following sports, in general, is people's desire for achievement and success. The fact that sports usually provide a clear outcome of success and failure reinforces one's desire for achievement. Sports give fans an opportunity for vicarious achievement through specific athletes or teams, every time these athletes or teams compete. Fans see the athletes or teams as extensions of themselves and view the team's victories as personal victories. More importantly, a fan tends to publicize his or her support of the team and bask in the team's victories, even if his or her contributions to the team's success may be minimal or nonexistent."[4]

Watching a sporting event in which the fan has some sort of emotional attachment can actually be beneficial. There is a sort of satisfaction that comes with cheering one's favorite team on to victory. It actually increases a person's self-esteem and confidence. One university study showed that fans wearing the winning team's apparel after a game were more likely to donate to the Salvation Army and in larger amounts than other attendees, and that these same fans were more willing to donate to volunteers who were also dressed in the winning team's apparel. The old saying is true: Everybody likes a winner, especially when it can help you socially.

For all the positives this BIRG effect can give an individual, it can also lead some toward negative consequences. This is the realm of the fanatic. These are the people who have basically given up on their personal identity and handed themselves over to their team's identity. It's theorized by some social identity researchers that this sort of behavior is brought about by the chronic understimulation many people experience in their daily modern lives. Although watching a game and screaming one's lungs out can release plenty of pent-up emotions (both good and bad), these fanatics take this emotional baggage with them home from the game. Fanaticism can and often does destroy all of those beneficial emotions brought on by simple fandom.

You know these people. When the game is on, the world around the fanatic stops. Sometimes, for the best of everyone involved, the fanatic will prefer to watch the game alone. Many of them hold superstitions which they believe actually affect the play on the field or the outcome of a game. Things like a lucky hat or an unwashed jersey become the fanatic's uniform, further creating the illusion of being part of the team. Studies have shown that these fanatical fans' levels of anxiety increased as "important" games approached and maxed out around halftime during those same contests. Besides the stress involved, watching the game leads to a level of arousal in the fanatic. It is the suspenseful nature of the unknown outcome that leads to this hyper-excited state of mind. More often than not, this anxiety and arousal cannot be turned off when the game ends. Like the highs and lows of an addiction, these feelings can linger, sometimes for a week or more.

So what happens to the fanatic when their beloved team loses? "Many highly identified fans report depression, anger, and disappointment (with the game and life in general) after watching their team lose."[5] Those resultant feelings are just the beginning. Because fanatics are so interconnected with the team, they often take the loss personally. "As a result, their collective self-esteem is lowered, resulting in an unpleasant psychological state. These fans will then resort to derogation and aggression toward others (e.g., opposing players and fans, officials) in an attempt to restore their lost self-esteem."[6]

So what is a fan to do when the game and his personal identity is lost? It is then time to CORF. Basically the exact opposite of BIRGing, CORFing is Cutting Off Reflected Failure. Because no one likes to lose, there comes a time in a fan's life to simply cut and run. CORFing is when the fan jumps off the bandwagon. By distancing oneself from a team and its perennial losing ways a person then cuts off all of the perceived negativity against both himself and his self-esteem. I am not a loser—*I can't be*—because I am no longer a Vikings fan (but how 'bout them Cowboys!). That is how a fair-weather fan's mind-set justifies these decisions.

Existing in the gray area between the BIRGing and the CORFing is the die-hard fan. This type of fan cannot binge and purge on a team as easily as the others. They often possess traits not found in other sports fans. For one, die-hard fans have the tendency to be overly optimistic about their team. "Highly identified fans report particularly favorable evaluations of current team performance, predict better futures for their team in general, and expect greater success for individual team members. Interestingly, highly identified fans are able to employ the allegiance bias even after providing rational explanations for potential victory by their team's upcoming opponent."[7] These same fans seem to always remember the good times over the bad. They often overlook losses and remember wins. In fact, numerous studies into "allegiance bias" by Wann and others indicated that fans over-remembered wins, tending to think their team always won more games then they actually had.

The main reason for such die-hard allegiance to a team is that their fandom has become part of their self- and social identity. It's as if someone were to ask such a fan "What are you?" the answer may come back "I'm a Cubs fan" just as easily as "I'm a banker" or "I'm a Sagittarius." It's gang-like in mentality. It goes back to that tribal sense of unity one can feel from being a fan. And it's one not easily shaken by a few or even a few thousand losses.

By attempting to sort through what makes us sports fans, one can see that there are valid, psychological reasons for our love of the game. It is not wrong to be a fan; it can actually be beneficial. Yet knowing even a small slice of what creates a fan can aid in answering the original question: Why do you care about sports?

This is an important question that often goes unasked. But it needs to be posed because the blind faith and devotion many people hand over to teams and leagues leaves us all open as a sort of mark. Suckers to a certain degree, and exploited just as easily.

When the World Series was canceled due to an owner lockout in 1994, many fans said in disgust, "I'm never watching baseball again." How many remained true to that vow? When the National Hockey League (NHL) owners canceled the entire 2004-05 season, how many hockey fans made the same promise? How many kept it?

We willingly give up hard-earned money to purchase hats featuring a team's "new" logo or "alternate third" jerseys, all of which were created simply to up sales profits. We trust owners and management when they tell us a fan favorite has lost a step, only to see that same player succeed on his new team because, in reality, he was let go to save salary cap room. We want to believe an investigation into a player's alleged bad behavior turns up nothing of significance simply because we want to believe his greatness on the field translates to the same off, whether or not that is indeed the reality of the situation. Fans have become the loyal yet gullible dog willing to lap the peanut butter off the league's spoon, failing to recognize the bitter pill hidden inside.

A cynical thought, to be sure. But consider its truth. What kind of thanks do fans get for this devotion to their teams? How are they rewarded by the owners of these franchises that they so religiously follow?

Would you be better off without them?

OWNERS

Many team owners have recently stated that for a team to be "successful," it needs a new and more modernized facility in which to play. On the surface, the argument appears to have some merit. Looking at the list of 2006 National Football League (NFL) playoff teams, half of the 12 teams that made the playoffs—the Baltimore Ravens, the New England Patriots, the Philadelphia Eagles, the Chicago Bears, the New Orleans Saints, and the Seattle Seahawks—played in stadiums that were either brand new or renovated within the past seven years. But the team that won the Super Bowl in 2006, the Indianapolis Colts, played in the RCA Dome, which was built in 1983. However in baseball in 2006, the opposite seemed true as the two World Series teams, the St. Louis Cardinals and the Detroit Tigers, played their 2006 seasons in new stadiums. Yet the other teams with the newest stadiums in baseball—the Milwaukee Brewers, the Seattle Mariners, the Cincinnati Reds, the Pittsburgh Pirates, the San Francisco Giants, and the Philadelphia Phillies—posted a combined record of 461 wins against 510 losses. The fact of the matter is, as nice as it is for the players to have improved training facilities with better medical equipment on site, the basic dimensions of their respective fields/courts don't change from stadium to stadium. And though the physical playing surface may be changed and improved, what's happening on top of it isn't.

It cannot be proved that new stadiums lead to significantly better team performance. As part of the book *Baseball Between the Numbers*, a study was conducted to determine the effect a new stadium had on a team's winning percentage. It found that with the teams that built new stadiums since 1991, their winning percentage went from .486 in the five years prior to the new stadium up to .520 in the five years after moving into their new digs. Those .034 percentage points equate to a difference of about five-and-a-half wins a year.[1] Those are just raw stats, of course, and they don't factor in any player or coaching changes that may have gone along with the "new look" teams. In other words, improvement by those teams was most likely a coincidence.

Owners will also argue that new stadiums don't just benefit the players, but the fans as well. In a certain sense, this cannot be denied. The architecture that goes into many new stadiums is breathtaking. From retractable roof domes to backdrops of statuesque cityscapes, these are truly modern marvels. In these new stadiums, fans are treated to larger spaces, more amenities, and many times, a built-in, falsified history to make them feel as if the stadium has been situated in the city for years. This is wonderful, but consider for a moment the price paid for the pleasure of attending these sporting events.

To pick specifically on baseball owners for a moment, Baltimore Orioles owner Peter Angelos was quoted in the book *The Name of the Game* as saying "Baseball's not a business through which one expects to derive great profits, or maybe any profits at all."[2] That must be why, when the Orioles needed a new stadium in the form of what's now known as The Ballpark at Camden Yards, the public—that is, the taxpayers—had to fork out $226 million of the $235 million it cost to build the stadium. Baltimore isn't the only city this has happened to. Between 1990 and 2006, 18 new baseball stadiums opened at a total combined cost of $5.6 billion. Nearly two-thirds of that money, officially $3.6 billion, was paid by the public.[3] Amazingly during the same approximate time frame (from 1990 to 2004), Major League Baseball (MLB) owners' total revenue went from $1.35 billion to $4.27 billion.[4]

Since we, the fans, are paying billions of dollars to build these fantastic new stadiums, we're getting something in return, right? Perhaps lower ticket prices? Unfortunately, the reverse is true. In 1976 the average MLB ticket was $3.45. By 2005, that average was up to $19.82, which doesn't seem like much, but even when factoring in inflation, it's a 67.5 percent increase.[5] What is even more shocking is what happens to ticket costs when a new stadium opens. Examine the percentage ticket prices rose in one year—just one year—upon the opening of these new baseball stadiums (and this is not including the luxury boxes):

★ Detroit (2000)–increased by 103 percent
★ San Francisco (2000)–increased by 75.2 percent
★ Pittsburgh (2001)–increased by 65.3 percent
★ Philadelphia (2004)–increased by 51.3 percent
★ Houston (2000)–increased by 50.6 percent

- ★ Milwaukee (2001)–increased by 39.2 percent
- ★ Cleveland (1994)–increased by 38.6 percent
- ★ Texas (1994)–increased by 35.2 percent
- ★ Colorado (1995)–increased by 35.2 percent
- ★ San Diego (2004)–increased by 31.9 percent
- ★ Atlanta (1997)–increased by 31.5 percent
- ★ Seattle (1999)–increased by 27.2 percent
  (then another 23.3 percent the next year).[6]

Which fans are paying to see these ballgames? The only demographic segment to attend more games in the 1990s than the 1980s was households earning more than $50,000 a year. Economists John Siegfried and Tim Peterson determined that, excluding corporate tickets and luxury boxes, the average ticket buyers' income was nearly twice the national average.[7] That makes sense, who else could afford, much less be willing to pay for, such incredible increases in cost?

But the fans are getting better seats and "sight lines" for those increased ticket prices, right? Not necessarily. In fact, stadium consultant John Pastier claims that new stadiums actually put most fans further from the field due to space occupied by luxury boxes. Most upper decks are actually higher off the field than they were in the old stadiums. In the new Chicago White Sox stadium, the first row of the current upper deck is further from the field than the *last* row of the upper deck in their previous home.[8]

How about taxes? Surely the fans see some sort of return on their money thanks to the taxes generated by these new stadiums? Not only do federal, state, and local governments allow owners to use their teams as tax shelters, the stadiums generate very little in tax revenues. Johns Hopkins' economists Bruce Hamilton and Peter Kahn figured that the aforementioned Camden Yards in Baltimore cost taxpayers $14 million in 1998 alone while taking in only $3 million in taxes during that same time period.[9] Rutgers stadium lease expert Judith Grant estimates that on average, a typical stadium project costs about 40 percent more than official figures due to unreported costs like free land, property tax breaks, and public operations along with maintenance costs.[10] This was proven true when the city of New York agreed to build two new baseball stadiums. The city donated both the land and infrastructure for each new stadium while at the same time forfeited collecting either rent or property taxes for the teams inhabiting the new homes. Meanwhile, the Yankees and Mets reaped these benefits while being ranked first and second respectively in franchise value in 2007 by *Forbes*.

One cannot argue against the fact that these new stadium projects create jobs, but at what cost? If Detroit created 1,500 jobs with the building of their new stadium, the cost to taxpayers was about $100,000 per job (Detroit's taxpayers paid half the $290 million price tag—$145 million—on Comerica Park). When Arizona built their Bank One Ballpark (now know as Chase Field), it created 340 full-time jobs at the cost of nearly $705,000 per job. One of the proposals for a new stadium in Minneapolis for the Twins would create 168 new jobs at the staggering cost of nearly $2 million per job. Meanwhile, the U.S. Department of Housing and Urban Development requires that the projects they fund create jobs that cost no more than $35,000 per job.[11]

Once all is said and done and the stadium exists in its final form, at very least the fans should get to put a lasting and meaningful name on their stadium. Unfortunately, not even that is true. The team owner can sell the naming rights for the new stadium to the highest bidder. Stadium naming rights can and do defray the costs of the new stadium, however, this rarely has an effect on what taxpayers ultimately pay. This isn't a new tradition. Weegman Park became Wrigley Field because the Wrigley family bought the stadium along with the Chicago Cubs and decided to name it after their popular brand of chewing gum. Same goes with the Busch family and the St. Louis Cardinals' Busch Stadium. Today, franchises earn anywhere from $2 million to $40 million a year in naming rights alone.

Despite these seeming drawbacks to building a new stadium, the thought that always seems to prevail is that at least that new stadium will boost the local economy. It's the typical "win-win" argument. Yet to quote University of Chicago economist Allen Sanderson, "if you want to inject money into the local economy, it would be better to drop it from a helicopter than invest it in a new ballpark."[12]

Many owners as well as city officials will hotly debate this point, but most economists who study the effects of stadiums and sports teams in general state that sports teams do not financially benefit local economies. It seems hard to believe that an industry such as sports, that allegedly is ranked as the 22nd largest industry in the world, can have little effect on an average local economy, but that seems to be the case. It must be remembered that all sports leagues generate the majority of their income from television and radio broadcast rights, not through their local economies via ticket sales. Studies indicate that should a city not have or even lose a sports team, the money that an average person could or would spend on sporting events simply goes to some other form of local entertainment. Certain neighborhoods may feel the boom of having a stadium nearby, but the city as a whole won't feel that fluctuation. Teresa Serata, the city of San Francisco's budget director, stated that when the Giants threatened to leave the city (before they were granted a new stadium), she could document that the city had a $3.1 million annual net gain thanks to the Giants, but that the city's gross economic product was $30 billion or 10,000 times as large as the Giants' contribution to the city. Or as Roger Moll, professor of economics at Stanford University, stated at the time, "Opening a branch of Macy's has a greater economic impact [than the Giants]."[13]

Robert Baade, an economist at Lake Forest College in Illinois, has perhaps done the most study on the subject. He collected 30 years' worth of data from 48 cities to determine the economic impact of sports teams in terms of the citizens of the city's per-capita income. His results were that in the study of 30 cities with new stadiums or arenas built, 27 showed no measurable change and the other three actually appeared to drop. He concluded "Professional sports teams generally have no significant impact on a metropolitan economy [and do] not appear to create a flow of public funds generated by new economic growth. Far from generating new revenues out of which other public projects can be funded, sports 'investments' appear to be an economically unsound use of a community's scarce financial sources."[14] Baade's not the only one with this opinion. In *Sports, Jobs, and Taxes*, authors Roger Noll and Andrew Zimbalist state, "In every case, the conclusions are the same. A new sports facility has an extremely small (perhaps even negative) effect on overall economic activity and employment. No recent facility appears to have earned anything approaching a reasonable return on investment. No recent facility has been self-financing in terms of its impact on net tax revenues."[15]

So what's the owner of a franchise to do when a new stadium "needs" to be built but city officials realize that maybe shelling out hundreds of millions of dollars in taxpayer money for a stadium isn't the wisest use of public funds? Threaten to move, of course. It's an excellent, and for some reason, effective bargaining tool. The Chicago Bears did it. They threatened to move just about everywhere short of the moon when the city of Chicago balked at renovating Soldier Field for them. And the renovation was strictly for the Bears. Soldier Field is used 10 times a year for Bears games and perhaps on two or three other occasions, but otherwise it sits unused for the other 350 days of the year. Chicago city officials felt the city would suffer some sort of image issue, as if Chicago would be looked upon as a "minor league" city, if they couldn't hold on to the Bears. So some $500 million later, the Bears stayed in Chicago and the city was blessed with a semi-new stadium that looks like a UFO crash landed on top of the old one. The Bears did kick in $50 million (that's 10 percent of the total costs) for the renovation. The NFL even paid another $50 million themselves, but the bulk of the money, some $400 million, came either from taxpayers' or out of the fans' pockets in the form of "Personal Seat Licenses."

This subtle form of blackmail doesn't always work. Cleveland Browns' owner Art Modell demanded that the city of Cleveland build his team a new stadium as well. The city of Cleveland said "no." Modell threatened to take his team somewhere else. The city came back and told him they couldn't afford to build yet another new stadium since they were still paying off the Indians' Jacobs Field. Angered, Modell picked up his team and moved to Baltimore where apparently the people there didn't mind building yet another $220 million stadium so soon after building an equally expensive baseball stadium. While the city of Cleveland didn't have to pay for a new stadium, Modell devastated his once rabid Browns fans. Those fans didn't much like the fact that despite all their support and money they had freely given to the Browns' organization over the years, the team left town.

Coincidentally, the Browns left to go to a city, Baltimore, which had gone through the same insult some 15 years earlier when the Colts packed up one night in 1984 and moved to Indianapolis. The reason for the Colts' midnight move was basically the same as the Browns. Colts owner Robert Irsay didn't feel the city of Baltimore was doing enough for his team. So he went out and found someplace that would comply with his wishes. Despite the pleas of the Colts' faithful, the NFL would not step in and stop the Colts' move. Why? Because even before the Colts ditched Baltimore, Oakland Raiders owner Al Davis got fed up with the city of Oakland and moved his team to Los Angeles. When the NFL tried to stop his illegal relocation to L.A., a legal battle ensued which the NFL wound up losing in a U.S. Federal Court (of course, a few years later, the Raiders were back in Oakland with a new stadium deal).

Since the NFL failed to stop the Raiders from moving and turned a blind eye to the Colts' relocation, they decided to step up and finally do something for one of their franchise cities. They promised to award the next expansion franchise to Cleveland. The NFL even went so far as to allow Cleveland to keep the name "Browns" as well as all of the team colors, records, and history their former franchise held. There was a caveat: Cleveland had to build a new stadium for the team the NFL was "giving" them. Remarkably, the city complied, building the $290 million Cleveland Browns Stadium for the latest incarnation of the team.

This relocation business is nothing new in sports. Leagues have always been more than willing to rip popular franchises out of their hometowns despite the cries of their faithful fans. One of the most notable franchise moves in sports history was when baseball's Brooklyn Dodgers packed their bags and traveled across the country to become the Los Angeles Dodgers. The move really had nothing to do with the city of New York or the fans not supporting the team; Major League Baseball (MLB) wanted a West Coast presence. Instead of creating a new team in California, MLB simply took a well-known team and dropped it out there. In doing so, an instant fan base was also created. People in L.A. knew who the Dodgers were, so they were quick to support the team. This was the same reason baseball's New York Giants were moved to San

Francisco. MLB opened up the entire country to its product with these two franchise moves. The National Hockey League (NHL) would mimic this plan of action and expansion a few decades later.

It's a constantly repeating scenario in every league. Baseball's Boston Braves move to become the Milwaukee Braves then turn into the Atlanta Braves. The NFL's Chicago Cardinals move to St. Louis, demand a stadium and then move to Arizona. MLB's Philadelphia Athletics become the Kansas City Athletics then become the Oakland Athletics. The National Basketball Association's (NBA) Charlotte Hornets decided in the immediate aftermath of Hurricane Katrina to move to New Orleans. The strange part in all of this is each of these franchises that abandoned their home cities were backfilled with new teams once they vacated. Milwaukee received the Brewers four years after the Braves left town. St. Louis picked up the Rams from L.A. eight years after the Cardinals split. The people of Kansas City wanted another baseball team, so the Royals appeared two years later. Charlotte had to suffer almost a year before NBA basketball returned.

So what is the real reason these teams are moving around so frequently? Is it that business is so bad in these jerkwater towns that team owners can't turn a profit? If this is the case, then why do teams keep popping up in these same cities? Fan support is clearly present. What isn't always available to these teams and their owners are the cushy deals cities give them. The profit from the stadium deals and the associated tax breaks drive these relocations more than anything. The TV networks maintain that it really doesn't matter to the NFL anymore where teams are located because the majority of the league's revenue is generated from the broadcast rights to their games. The Green Bay Packers could become the Boise Packers and to the NFL and its main revenue stream, it wouldn't matter. Financially, nothing would be lost. In fact, there's more to be gained by these moves as it keeps interest high by energizing a new city full of fans every time a team opens up shop in a new home.

This sort of behavior regarding stadium deals and relocation is but a microcosm of how owners truly feel about their fans. If the leagues really cared about the fans as much as they claim to, these relocations would never occur. The Browns would have never become the Baltimore

Ravens. The Colts would be the NFL's franchise in Baltimore. Brooklyn would still have its beloved Dodgers and New York its Giants. And the list goes on. If owners respected their home towns, then they would pay their fair share of construction costs and property taxes rather than sloughing them off onto the public at large. The fact of the matter is owners care about the fans as long as their pocketbooks remain open. If that cash flow dries up or a team's "favored nation" status ends, so too does the owner's love affair with that city. The fans, the lifeblood of professional sports, have no say in the matter.

Yet it is perhaps only in the world of sports that people bond to the product they purchase. Each fan may subconsciously think of himself as a minority owner, as if he has a direct stake in the team. Though no matter how much money that person spends on tickets, jerseys, etc. the team is independent from the fan. Sports leagues are not fan-friendly. They are massively large and impersonal businesses. Each owner's first and foremost concern is turning a profit which comes directly at the fan's expense. The sooner each fan realizes this, the more one can look at sports in an entirely different light. If owners are not loyal to the fan, why are the fans so loyal to them?

ATHLETES

WHEN THE BIG MONEY OF PLAYING PROFESSIONALLY BECKONS a young athlete, can one ever blame him for chasing after it? Former Marquette basketball coach Al McGuire once said, "I never told a kid not to leave school early for the big dollars after I looked into his refrigerator. I recruited those kids. I knew the environment they had to escape. I would have been a total hypocrite to tell them to stay in school. For what? They only came to play basketball and get noticed."[1]

Though not every player who gets a scholarship to a large college program takes it thinking it is a golden ticket to a pro career, there are plenty who do. Many of these sadly disillusioned student athletes sell out their futures for the hopes and dreams (and in their minds, inevitable certainty) of a future in professional sports. Yet the odds of playing sports professionally are incredibly long. Out of roughly five-and-a-half million high school athletes playing sports in the U.S. in any given year, only about one in 50 will earn a spot on a college team, and then only one in about 1,000 of those college players will ever take the field as a pro. Statistically speaking, it is easier to become an elected member of the U.S. Congress than it is to join the NBA as a player.

For the lucky and supremely talented few who do achieve the dream of playing major league sports, the life of a pro athlete may not be as magical as one had hoped. Once on a pro roster, the athlete will come to find that both the stakes and pressure on him to succeed are higher than ever before. Now something else may be driving that athlete. Not success and the money that comes along with it, but rather something darker: Fear. As former NFL star Bill Romanowski wrote, "When pure passion wasn't driving me, fear and insecurity were...The enemy is always reloading, the roster is always reshuffling, and it's hard surviving, no less thriving. Now I can admit I was afraid a lot."[2]

Success in professional sports can often be fleeting. Every season brings in fresh young athletes while the injured and old are pushed out of the game. Athletes are quite cognizant of this. They realize their time is short and that million-dollar contracts don't come along every day.

Yet this very pressure point could be used against an athlete. For the players often find themselves not just fighting against each other out on the field, but against public opinion, the leagues' ownership, and even the criminal courts. All of these factors threaten finite careers. The question is what are athletes willing to do to extend their playing days?

CRIMINALS

In their 1998 book *Pros and Cons: The Criminals Who Play in the NFL*, authors Jeff Benedict and Don Yaeger investigated the number of criminals playing in the NFL. What they found was that out of a sample of 509 NFL players from the total of nearly 1,600 in the league in 1996–1997, approximately 20 percent of those players (109 from their sample) had been formally charged—arrested or indicted—with a "serious" crime.[1] If their study was extrapolated out from that sample it would mean that on every 53-man roster in the NFL, each team would have nine to 11 charged criminals dressed and ready to take the field on Sunday. Hard to believe, until you see prime examples like nine players from the 2006 Cincinnati Bengals arrested during the course of that single season.

To make matters worse, one of the authors of *Pros and Cons*, Jeff Benedict, took a disturbing look at NBA players in his 2004 book *Out of Bounds: Inside the NBA's Culture of Rape, Violence, & Crime*. In using similar methods as he did with NFL players, Benedict took a sample of 177 out of the 417 non-foreign-born players in the NBA during the 2001–2002 season. The results this time were worse. Approximately 40 percent, that is 71 out of the sample of 177 players, had been "arrested or otherwise recommended by police to prosecuting attorneys for indictment for a serious crime."[2] What makes the statistics so frightening is that Benedict's random sampling, which was based solely on the responses he received through Freedom of Information Act requests, covered nearly half of the NBA.

Rarely spoken about and hardly ever acknowledged is the fact that all of the major sports leagues—the NFL, NBA, NHL, and MLB—have had security departments for many years. Staffed with former and sometimes current members of the FBI, CIA, DEA, and local and state police departments, each league's security department is in charge of policing its respective league's athletes, coaches, and referees. How large and far-reaching these departments are is difficult to gauge, but some information about them is known. For example, outside of the staff housed at league headquarters at least one security member is devoted to each team in its respective league and is stationed in that team's home city. They are charged with monitoring everyone on that team as well as other players and referees when they come to town. These security departments often work and communicate hand-in-hand with the FBI, DEA, the Nevada Gaming Board, Homeland Security, and local police departments, as well as the leagues' home offices and commissioners.

Not once has a league's security division ever initiated an investigation or an arrest against one of its respective members. They do not tip the police or FBI. It is only once an athlete has committed a crime or been arrested that these security departments appear to work. When a league does then investigate itself, new evidence is rarely if ever discovered and made public. The security departments are not proactive in any sense, unless attempting to downplay a crime or cover up some sort of league embarrassment. This is a fact to remember as we go forward.

According to my own research on the NFL, from January 2000 through July of 2007, players had been arrested on approximately 290 different occasions. The most common of these offenses were driving under the influence (DUI) charges that accounted for 105 or just over 36 percent of those arrests. Coming in a close second place were assault or battery charges. They totaled 86 arrests or 30 percent of the tally. The third most common offense was some sort of weapons charge, occurring 25 times and accounting for about another 8 percent of the arrests.

A DUI may seem like a minor offense, unless you know of someone who was unfortunate enough to be in a collision with a drunk driver. Most sporting events will make a public service announcement about the dangers of drinking and driving, yet alcohol and sports have always seemed to mix. Beer flows freely in the stands, championships are celebrated with champagne, and many players have been alcoholics. Some, like baseball's Mike "King" Kelly, Grover Cleveland Alexander, and Mickey Mantle, managed to parlay their addiction into induction into the Hall of Fame. The world of professional sports has been rather lucky though. Despite over 100 years of mixing young athletes with alcohol and automobiles, very few DUI-related accidents or deaths have cut short careers. Perhaps the most notable was the death of former Yankees player and manager Billy Martin who, though suffering from alcoholism himself, died while a passenger with another drunk driver in 1989. A much more recent case occurred in 2007, when, less than 12 hours after pitching in a game against the Cubs, St. Louis Cardinals reliever Josh Hancock was killed in a single-car accident while driving drunk.

Whether Hancock had a drinking problem or not was unknown, but if he did actually have a problem, it's doubtful anyone in baseball would have helped him. Major League Baseball sure wouldn't have punished him. MLB punishes *no one* in any way for a DUI arrest. Neither does the NFL, the NBA, or the NHL. No fines. No suspensions. Nothing. I can find no record of a player being punished by his league for such an offense. Instead, they choose to handle the matters internally, or more accurately, they sweep all these reports under the rug and ignore them.

Major League Baseball did eventually ban alcohol from team clubhouses as a reaction to Hancock's death. However, this new rule was nothing more than a knee-jerk reaction to the problem. Especially when one considers that drinking in the clubhouse had nothing to do with the accident which spawned this decision.

Neither was drinking in the clubhouse to blame when Hancock's manager, Tony LaRussa, was charged with a DUI during spring training of the 2007 season. LaRussa was found asleep at the wheel at an intersection at 4 a.m. Police reported that LaRussa's car sat through two cycles of green lights and that the vehicle behind his had to drive around his car to get through the intersection. Reportedly, LaRussa didn't wake up until an officer knocked on his window. Here was an instance where baseball had a high-profile case, the manager of the defending world champions arrested for a DUI, which they could have used to make a statement with regards to drinking and driving. Yet MLB did nothing. LaRussa has missed more innings for arguing with umpires than he has for breaking the law. A message well sent.

Yet baseball isn't alone in ignoring its members' drinking and driving habits. The NFL is just as guilty. Case in point, former 2001 first-round draft pick of the Seattle Seahawks' Koren Robinson. Robinson was suspended by the NFL for four games in 2004 for an unspecified violation of the league's substance abuse policy. In 2005, Robinson was arrested for a DUI. Though the arrest did not lead to another league-mandated suspension, the Seahawks cut Robinson. After emerging from rehab, Robinson was picked up by the Minnesota Vikings. He played one full season with the Vikings until he was arrested for another DUI during training camp in 2006. As promptly as he was cut by the Vikings, the Green Bay Packers swooped in and picked up Robinson. He managed to play in four games for the Packers until the NFL stepped in and suspended him for the remainder of the '06 season. As soon as he was eligible to do so in 2007, Robinson was back out on the field wrapped in the Packers' familiar green and gold. He had served his time away from the NFL, but was welcomed right back into the fold in time for the Packers' playoff run. The question remains, will Robinson remain clean and sober? If he doesn't, how many more teams like the Packers will give him a fourth or fifth chance?

Keith Law, a former special assistant to the general manager of the Toronto Blue Jays, wrote in an article for ESPN.com, "We were offered a pitcher in trade—someone still in the major leagues—and the GM making the offer acknowledged that the pitcher was a serious alcoholic who had been stopped four times for driving under the influence since joining the organization."[3] Law didn't further elaborate to say whether the trade was made, but one has to wonder why repeat offenders get second or third or fourth chances? Is it because while getting a DUI is a crime, drinking is not?

How many of these DUI cases go unreported? How often has a

professional athlete been pulled over for what should have led to an arrest, but not been cited for a DUI because the player's "Don't you know who I am?" excuse actually worked on a star-struck police officer? What would be a night in the drunk tank for the average citizen becomes just another autograph signing for the player because of his celebrity. Could the number of DUI arrests for pro athletes actually be doubled or tripled if this sort of "wink, wink" treatment didn't come into play?

When you have people at every level of an organization from players to coaches to even the team owners cited for DUIs (the 74-year-old Los Angeles Lakers owner Jerry Buss was arrested for a DUI in May 2007 when he was found driving the wrong way down a one-way street), it makes you wonder how big of a problem drinking actually is in sports. For the NFL, the problem may be much larger than publicly acknowledged. Author Mike Freeman wrote in his book *Bloody Sundays*, "Privately, [NFL] players and team officials have claimed for years that alcohol abuse is far more of a problem than illicit drug use. But no union or league official has ever made such a statement publicly."[4]

That unstated problem may suddenly become a chief concern for the NFL. In March 2009, Cleveland Browns wide receiver Donte Stallworth hit and killed a pedestrian while driving drunk. Charged with DUI manslaughter, he faced a maximum of 15 years in prison, yet in a plea deal reached with both the victim's family and the state, Stallworth was sentenced to just 30 days behind bars with house arrest and several years of probation thrown in for good measure. Even though all of this occurred in the off-season, the NFL, as usual, took their sweet time to hand down any sort of punishment against Stallworth. When they finally did act, it was simply to indefinitely suspend him, meaning the league knew he should be suspended since a person was killed, but for how long, the NFL wasn't sure. Stallworth will likely play in the NFL again.

Will this sad case, regardless of what becomes of Donte Stallworth, be a wake-up call for the NFL and the rest of professional sports in regards to the dangers of alcohol? It's doubtful. In 1998, Leonard Little of the St. Louis Rams was involved in a car accident when driving while intoxicated. The crash killed a woman in the other vehicle. Little served 90 days in jail and was suspended for the first eight games of the 1999 season. After the suspension ended, he was right back in the NFL where he has played 12 seasons in the league.

Alcohol affects one's judgment not only behind the wheel of a car, but out at the bar as well. Out of the aforementioned 86 NFL arrests for assault and/or battery in my research, a quarter (22 to be exact) of the offenses occurred in or around bars and nightclubs. Now I cannot say with certainty if any of the offending parties were inebriated at the time of their arrests, but it's quite easy to make the stretch that alcohol may have had a hand in causing many, if not all, of those unfortunate incidents.

What was the cause of the majority of those assault and/or battery arrests was domestic violence. A whopping 45 of the 86 arrests (52 percent) were cases of abuse against women. The sad truth to the situation is that many women never even press charges against their attacker. Some fear of not being believed when it's their word against a celebrity athlete's. Others fear the publicity that inevitably goes along with such proceedings. Even when there is clear evidence of violence, women tend to shy away from pressing charges, almost empowering the athlete to continue the abuse. Without any repercussions, what compels one to stop? Especially when one already has a heightened sense of self, what's a woman to a player other than a plaything? Women are constantly throwing themselves at professional athletes (the stories about "sports groupies" are endless), so they unwittingly render themselves disposable. And why treat something you're just going to throw away with any care or respect? Even when an abused woman stands up and presses charges against her attacker, athletes usually have enough money to hire lawyers able to work the system to spare the player any real trouble. So again we're presented with a constantly reoccurring crime on which we cannot get the true numbers because athletes are able to slip through any sort of prosecution.

Not all of these repulsive stories go unreported however. Michael Pittman has already had an 11-year career as a running back in the NFL. In June of 2001, Pittman was arrested after an argument with his estranged wife Melissa at her apartment. Seemingly not content with the outcome of the argument, Pittman returned two weeks later to his wife's apartment and was again arrested. This time the charges were harsher, including domestic violence, criminal damage, and criminal trespassing. Pittman served five days in jail for the offenses while the NFL suspended him for one game. Two years later and still married to Melissa, Pittman was arrested yet again for attacking his wife. This time, however, Pittman was charged with two felony counts of aggravated assault for ramming his Hummer into a car carrying Melissa, their two-year-old son, and a babysitter. Pittman pleaded guilty to one count of assault and was jailed for 14 days. The NFL suspended him again, this time for three games. In the past six seasons, the only four games Pittman has missed have come as a result of the league's imposed suspensions. Yet despite twice serving time in jail for domestic violence, Pittman was allowed to continue to play in the NFL.

The Kansas City Chiefs' Larry Johnson is another NFL running back who has a history of abusing women. Johnson was first arrested during his rookie year in December 2003 with a felony aggravated assault charge as well as a misdemeanor charge for brandishing a handgun during an argument with his then girlfriend. As a result, he entered a diversion program, underwent anger management, and had to serve 120 hours of community service. Not two years later, in September of 2005, Johnson was again arrested for a domestic abuse assault against another girlfriend. This woman refused to press charges against Johnson, but instead simply wanted to have the incident recorded. Johnson wasn't finished. In October of 2008, he was arrested again, this time for battery when he threatened to kill a woman's boyfriend at a nightclub. After making the threat, Johnson allegedly spit his drink on the woman in question. Despite this recorded history of violence and arrests, all the NFL has done to Johnson is to promote his accomplishments on the field.

Perhaps the most prominent case of domestic violence involves NBA all-star Jason Kidd. In January of 2001, Kidd was arrested on a misdemeanor domestic abuse charge stemming from hitting his wife Joumana in the presence of their two-year-old son. The argument developed over Kidd taking a French fry from his child's plate. According to the police report, Kidd spit the French fry at his wife, and then struck her. She ran to the bedroom and locked the door. Kidd kicked the door down. She then ran to the bathroom and locked that door. Joumana then called 911.

During an ensuing press conference, where Kidd was seated alongside Phoenix Suns chairman, CEO and managing general partner Jerry Colangelo, the first question asked of Kidd was whether this was the first time anything like this had ever happened. Kidd's response was, "At this point I really can't answer any more questions in detail. This is not appropriate." But Kidd's wife Joumana had already answered this question during her 911 call saying, "There's just a bad history here. I told him [Kidd] this would be the last time, and he popped me right in the mouth." The very next question posed to Kidd was whether this incident would cause him to miss any playing time because really, nothing is more important to society than a regular season NBA game.

Kidd would end up missing one game, not because of some NBA action, but "due to the circumstances at hand." He would eventually strike a deal with the court that included counseling and anger management for this offense. Kidd twice represented the United States—in 2000 and again in 2008—as a member of the men's Olympic basketball "Dream Team."

What will it take for the major sport leagues to crack down on their players for domestic violence? The NFL's stated policy on domestic violence is that any of the players accused of it must enter counseling. A conviction for such a crime *can* result in suspension and a second conviction *can* result in being banned from the game. Since "can" doesn't equate to "will," players like Pittman who have twice been jailed for such offenses are free to play on. I cannot find a single instance of a player being kicked out of their sport for domestic violence offenses despite the large number of arrests made due to the crime.

However, there are a few scattered incidents of players being cut from their team due to such conduct. Of course, even within a single franchise there can be a double standard. In early 2008, Pittsburgh Steelers wide receiver Cedrick Wilson was arrested and charged with assaulting his ex-girlfriend at a Pittsburgh area restaurant. When word of this reached the Steelers, the team immediately cut Wilson from the roster. While that may make the Steelers franchise appear responsible, less than two weeks prior to Wilson's arrest, another member of the Steelers—starting linebacker James Harrison—was arrested for a similar incident. What happened to Harrison? Harrison's girlfriend dropped the charges against him. And even though Harrison had already undergone anger management in the past, the court only mandated that he enter domestic abuse counseling. As for the Steelers' franchise, they did nothing to punish their linebacker. Worse yet, team owner Dan Rooney actually tried to cover for Harrison saying, "What Jimmy Harrison was doing and how the incident occurred, what he was trying to do was really well worth it. He was doing something that was good, wanted to take his son to get baptized where he lived and things like that. She said she didn't want to do it."[5] Rooney later realized the idiocy of his comment and backpedaled from that seemingly pro-abuse stance, yet the non-action the team took on Harrison speaks louder than any words can. A year after this incident, Harrison would be hailed as a hero for his 100-yard interception return in Super Bowl XLIII and be rewarded with a multimillion-dollar contract extension.

Perhaps it would take the death of a woman at the hands of an athlete for the leagues to take notice, similar to the drunken driving death of Josh Hancock that was needed to spur baseball into (limited) action. But perhaps not: Rae Carruth was a wide receiver for the Carolina Panthers when he stopped his car in front of his girlfriend's car, blocking Cherica Adams from moving her vehicle. Another car pulled alongside hers, and the passenger in that car shot her four times, killing her. Why? Because Adams was pregnant with Carruth's child at the time and refused to get an abortion. Carruth would eventually be found guilty of conspiracy to commit murder among other felony counts and was sentenced to serve 18 to 24 years in prison. Yet nothing is publicly done by any of the leagues to address the problem of domestic violence.

The major sports leagues don't seem to have too much of a problem with athletes arming themselves, either. While not alone, the NFL has seen a major spike in gun-related incidents recently.

Chicago Bears defensive lineman Terry "Tank" Johnson was arrested in December of 2006 after approximately 20 police officers raided his home. Johnson was charged with six counts of possessing an unlicensed firearm.

According to reports, he had two assault-style rifles (an AR-15 and a .223 caliber), three powerful handguns (a .44 Magnum, a .50 caliber, and a .45 caliber), and one .308 Winchester hunting rifle. At the time of his 2006 arrest, Johnson was already on probation from another weapons-related charge. This came in June of 2005, when he was arrested on a felony gun charge for having a loaded 9mm handgun in his car. Between these two arrests, Johnson was arrested a third time for two misdemeanors, aggravated assault and resisting arrest, but both charges were later dropped.

What did all these arrests add up to for Tank? He was serving an 18-month probation sentence resulting from his original gun charge, so when arrested for the second time in 2006, Johnson was given four months in jail and a $2,500 fine. The NFL, always willing to dish out their own severe form of justice in these matters, suspended Johnson a grand total of one game, albeit a playoff game. However, since the Bears were marching their way to the Super Bowl in 2006, both law enforcement and the NFL made sure that Johnson didn't miss a play in the big game.

These types of incidents are on the rise in the NFL. In June 2008, New England Patriots defensive back Willie Andrews was arrested twice within two months. On the second occasion, it was for pointing a handgun at his girlfriend's head after an argument. He was charged with illegal possession of a "large capacity firearm" and assault with a dangerous weapon. Late in November 2008, New York Giants wide receiver Plaxico Burress accidentally shot himself in the leg inside a nightclub when attempting to place a loaded handgun into the waistband of his pants. While the resultant wound cost Burress the rest of the season, the NFL still decided to suspend Burress for four games due to the incident, even though his injury prevented him from playing. Burress was then arrested on two criminal gun charges and later sentenced to two years in prison. In early 2009, Buffalo Bills running back Marshawn Lynch was arrested and charged with three misdemeanor gun charges—possession of a concealed firearm, a loaded firearm, and an unregistered firearm—when police sensed the smell of marijuana coming from inside his car. (Lynch did not have a drug charge added to the incident.) He was suspended for the first three games of the 2009 season for conduct unbecoming to the league.

Due to the sports leagues' unwillingness to significantly punish their own players, athletes seem to have little concern for the effect an arrest may have on their careers. In certain situations, suspensions are handed out, but that is almost the exception rather than the rule. And is suspension really an effective deterrent? The leagues would argue it is, but it is clearly not stopping players from getting arrested.

NBA players Ron Artest and Stephen Jackson were involved in a memorably massive fight (or riot, depending on your perspective) in Detroit with fans in November 2004. Both were punished harshly by the NBA for their actions, receiving suspensions of 73 and 30 games respectively. Then come the 2007–2008 NBA season, both players began the season suspended for seven games due to criminal arrests in the preceding off-season. Artest's seven games stemmed from a domestic violence charge while Jackson's were for a felony count of criminal recklessness for firing a gun outside a strip club. Yet, NBA player union director Billy Hunter said in a statement at that time, "Based on prior precedent, we think the [seven game] suspensions are excessive. We plan to confer with the players and their representatives to consider all of our options for appeal."

Unfortunately, this is often the role of the players' union in each major league. They act as a protectorate for criminal athletes, enabling them to continue careers that many would prefer to see immediately end. The leagues, for their part, rarely put up much of a fight. In the NFL alone, several such incidents have recently occurred.

Just prior to his rookie year in 2000, Jamal Lewis of the Cleveland Browns used a cell phone to set up a drug deal. He was subsequently charged with conspiring to possess cocaine with the intent to distribute to which he pleaded guilty and served four months in prison. The NFL suspended him for two games.

Baltimore Ravens all-pro linebacker Ray Lewis was arrested on murder charges in 2000 following a Super Bowl party he attended. Since little to no evidence could show that Lewis committed any overt acts against the victims, Lewis was allowed to plea-bargain his case down to a misdemeanor charge of obstruction of justice. The NFL did not suspend him, but fined him a record amount of $250,000.

Dominic Rhodes of the Indianapolis Colts and Oakland Raiders pleaded guilty to a domestic abuse charge in 2002, a reckless driving charge in 2007, and tested positive for a banned substance prior to the 2007 season thus violating the NFL's substance abuse policy. He was suspended four games only due to the positive drug test.

Former Seattle Seahawks and current Tampa Bay Buccaneers tight end Jerramy Stevens was arrested for a DUI in March 2007, a reckless driving charge in 2003 for which he served two days in jail, and for driving into a nursing home while in college in 2000 for which he served five days in jail because he was already on probation at the time. He has never been disciplined by the NFL.

Chris Henry of the Cincinnati Bengals was arrested on five separate occasions in a time span of just over two years. He was twice suspended by the NFL for those arrests and was ultimately released by the Bengals; however, when the Bengals were desperate for wide receiver help, Henry was re-signed by the team.

Adam "Pacman" Jones was suspended for an entire season by the NFL due to multiple arrests, yet the Dallas Cowboys actively sought Jones out and made a trade with the Tennessee Titans for his services. Jones became the first player in the NFL's history to ever be traded while under suspension.

Denver Broncos star wide receiver Brandon Marshall was arrested on three separate occasions in the year between March 2007 and 2008. His three-game suspension for violating the league's personal conduct code was lowered to just one game.

Atlanta Falcons quarterback Michael Vick was a NFL superstar when he was convicted on various charges of dog fighting. He served nearly two years in prison for his crimes. Even before Vick was released, media outlets were wondering for whom Vick would suit up upon his return to the league. It wound up being the Philadelphia Eagles. NFL commissioner Roger Goodell, who vowed to take a "hard line" against this sort of off-the-field behavior, issued a "conditional" suspension in Vick's case, meaning he could have missed anywhere from one to six games. The final decision was two.

Why are multiple and repeat offenders always allowed back into their sport, and often with little or no discipline from the league? Is it because special athletes, those who can perform at the very high levels professional sports demand, are really that rare? The answer to that appears to be yes. There are only so many baseball players who can hit .300, only so many basketball players who can score over 20 points a game, and only so many 1,000-yard rushers. History has proven that. On the other hand, these sports haven't ever run out of star players. Every time a star athlete is injured or retires, another is there to step in and fill that void, which makes the talent pool seem pretty deep.

Many times, the criminal athlete in question isn't even the star player. Though the examples I've given are often notable names, for every known player arrested probably 20 or 30 unknown players are also put in handcuffs. Despite that, such players often retain their status as pro athletes as well. Why?

When the average businessman is arrested for a DUI, he isn't fired from his job. So why should a player arrested for a similar charge lose his? Just because one is charged in an isolated incident doesn't mean it's a lifestyle. Ron LeFlore learned to play the game of baseball in a prison yard while serving time for armed robbery. He went on to have a successful nine-year career in MLB. Green Bay Packers wide receiver Donald Driver admitted to dealing drugs and stealing cars in his youth, yet he too changed his life around and became a great athlete and model citizen. So leeway in some cases seems warranted, but shouldn't some line in the sand be drawn?

These leagues always claim to be "acting in the best interest" of their sport, yet they seem to do the exact opposite when it comes to their athletes and crime. As part of the league's collective bargaining agreement, written into every NFL player's contract is a phrase about "conduct detrimental to the integrity of, or the public confidence in, the game of professional football." Why is no action taken on it? Certainly players being arrested and serving time in prison are detrimental to the integrity of the league. So why is a two- or four-game suspension the best the NFL, or any league, can do to rid their sport of criminal behavior?

Regardless of what players' unions call for to "protect" these criminal athletes, a stand could be made by owners and league officials to clean up their sports, if that is what they truly desire.

DRUGS

"In the old days, 24 of the 25 guys on every team were drunk. Today nobody hardly drinks anymore, and very, very few take drugs."—Detroit Tigers manager Sparky Anderson in 1984

On April 29, 1993, the Boston Celtics were engaged in a heated playoff game against the Charlotte Hornets in the Boston Garden. Midway through the first half, Celtics star Reggie Lewis collapsed while running up the court. Examined during halftime, Lewis was allowed back into the game for the second half. However, after a short period of time on the court, he pulled himself from the game, saying he felt faint.

The next day, doctors did a battery of tests on Lewis and discovered Lewis' heart was scarred, showing three "dead spots" on his left ventricle. Lewis wouldn't play in any more games that season. Not that it would matter as the Celtics were quickly knocked out of the playoffs by the Hornets.

Though not medically cleared by his doctor, Lewis took part in some off-season practice sessions at Brandeis University in Massachusetts. During one of those sessions on July 27, 1993, Lewis would again collapse, this time suffering a heart attack that would claim his life at the age of 27.

The preliminary autopsy results showed his heart was "abnormal, enlarged, and extensively scarred." Before Lewis' burial, his heart was preserved for further study. Nearly four months after dying, the official cause of death was reported. "It listed the cause of death as adenovirus 2—a common virus that causes the common cold—that led to inflammation of Mr. Lewis' heart, widespread scarring of tissue and, ultimately, a fatal cardiac arrest."[1]

As sad as Lewis' early passing is, this official story of his death overlooks one very important fact—most of the doctors involved with the case felt Reggie Lewis' heart was damaged by cocaine abuse. After his death, the two pathologists that first studied Lewis' heart agreed that the damage was consistent with cocaine cardiomyopathy[2] though cocaine was never found in his system.

After Lewis' passing, the Celtics collected $5 million from the insurance policy on Lewis' contract. Had Lewis ever tested positive for drugs before or after his death, that policy would have been null and void. But for the Celtics that $5 million was chump change when considering the problems they and the NBA would have had to face if Lewis' death was officially ruled as a case of drug abuse.

Just one year prior to Lewis joining the Celtics, the team snatched up University of Maryland star Len Bias with the number two overall pick in the 1986 NBA draft. Bias had all the potential in the world. Yet within 48 hours of his selection by the Celtics and less than 24 hours after signing a multimillion-dollar deal with Adidas, he would be dead. Bias died in the early morning hours in his dorm room from a cardiac arrhythmia brought on by a cocaine overdose.

Having learned a lesson from Bias' untimely passing, both the NBA and the Celtics knew the questions and controversy that would have surrounded everyone involved had Reggie Lewis' death been attributed to cocaine. If it became widely known that had Lewis allowed himself to be tested for drugs he may still be alive today; the NBA could've been seen as being almost an accomplice in Lewis' death. Because the fact of the matter is, the NBA's newly adopted drug-testing policy most likely scared Lewis into forbidding those crucial tests to be performed.

The NBA wasn't always the highly-rated sport it is today. During the late 1970s and early 1980s, the league was struggling to get fans in the seats. Part of the reason is that the NBA had a perceived drug problem. Although there are no definitive numbers on drug use in the NBA at that time, a 1982 *Los Angeles Times* article claimed that 75 percent of the NBA's players were on drugs. Tom McMillen, an NBA player at the time (and later a congressman), wrote in his book, "Our coach on the [Atlanta] Hawks was the hard-charging Hubie Brown, who was convinced that the performance of several players was suffering from drug use."[3] He wasn't the only one. Greg Ballard, who played in the NBA from 1977–1989 and later worked as an assistant coach in the NBA, told the *Minneapolis Star-Tribune* in 2001 that the reported 75 percent of players on drugs statistic from the *Los Angeles Times* article was accurate in his opinion for at least one of the teams for which he played.[4]

The NBA's only option to clean up their sport was to begin some sort of a drug policy. It had to have some teeth to prove to its potential fans that the league was tough on drugs. So beginning in 1984, the NBA became the first professional sport to implement a drug policy. Aimed at stopping the use of "hard" drugs, the league would suspend a player for a minimum of two years if they tested positive for these types of drugs. Clearly, the NBA sent the message it wasn't fooling around anymore. At least, publicly it did.

Privately, the NBA's policy was a bit of a joke. The league needed "reasonable cause" to test players. What constituted "reasonable cause"? Reggie Lewis' doctors believed based on his test results that he had a cocaine habit, but this wasn't "reasonable cause" enough for the NBA to test him. How does the NBA then define "reasonable cause"? Basically, the process is like this: If the league or the players' association receives information regarding a player's use, possession, or distribution of drugs, the NBA can request a hearing within 24 hours of obtaining this potentially damning information. In other words, someone—a coach, a teammate, an opposing player—has to rat out the offending player for this process to even begin. During this fact-finding hearing, an independent expert will determine whether reasonable cause actually exists based on all the evidence that can be gathered in that short period of time. If there is sufficient evidence, the expert will then authorize further testing of the player in question. As this shows, the NBA's policy was created not to stop its players from using drugs, but simply to convince the public this was the case. It was simply a great public relations (PR) move.

In the first 10 years of its drug-testing policy, a grand total of six players were suspended by the NBA. This seems to belie the notion that 75 percent of the league was taking drugs. Of course, testing records were never made public, so who's to say how many tests did come back positive for drugs and were covered up? The numbers could've been astronomical because there was one thing the NBA forgot to inform the public: It wasn't testing for marijuana.

The NBA knew the drug of choice for most of its players was marijuana. They also were wise enough not to fight the players' union over testing for the drug the first time they put drug testing into their collective bargaining agreement. The players simply would not have gone along with it. For all the testing the league was doing then, it overlooked the drug most likely to register a positive result.

For 15 years, the NBA's policy was mocked for its lack of marijuana testing. But all that changed in the 1999–2000 season. A new league agreement allowed for testing not only the players, but coaches, trainers, and other team personnel as well for all illegal drugs, including marijuana. Every player would be tested once in the preseason. Rookies were then subjected to three more random tests during the regular season. But for veterans, that one time would be it, unless the NBA had "reasonable cause" to test the player again.

Charles Oakley, a 17-year veteran of the league, called the NBA's testing policy "a joke." He stated in 2001 that when he joined the NBA "there might have been one out of six" players using marijuana. "Now it's six out of 12."[5] Oakley went on to explain that a veteran player with any brains to go along with his drug habit realized that the only time the NBA was going to test a player was during training camp. Players recognized the obvious loophole in the system and were exploiting it. At the same time, the NBA claimed the lack of positive tests indicated there was no longer a drug problem within the league. Everyone was off the hook.

Clearly, there were drug users within the NBA slipping through the system. The most obvious example was of Damon Stoudamire. Between 2002 and 2003, Stoudamire was arrested three times for marijuana. The first would come after police officers searched his home in response to a burglar alarm that went off while Stoudamire's Portland Trailblazers were on a road trip and officers stumbled across a bag filled with 150 grams of marijuana. Stoudamire was released from these charges as the search was later deemed "illegal." About nine months later, Stoudamire and teammate Rasheed Wallace were pulled over and arrested for marijuana possession, but again the charges were dropped. Stoudamire was arrested yet again for marijuana in July 2003 when he attempted to sneak about an ounce of marijuana through airport security wrapped in aluminum foil. Based on these arrests, Stoudamire was obviously a user, yet the NBA never caught him with their supposedly stringent testing policy. It wasn't until Stoudamire's third arrest that the NBA decided to punish him, handing out a three-month suspension and fining him $250,000.

Another example of the strength of the NBA's drug policy in action involved Shawn Kemp. Kemp missed the last eight games of the 2000–01 season after voluntarily entering the substance abuse program for an admitted cocaine addiction. Because Kemp did this of his own accord and seemingly hadn't failed a NBA test, the league could/would not punish him in any way. Upon returning in 2002, Kemp was suspended "indefinitely" and without pay by the NBA for violating its substance abuse policy. Just five games later, Kemp was back in the Orlando Magic's lineup. The very next season, Kemp was suspended yet again for violating the NBA's substance abuse policy even though testing positive for cocaine was supposed to mean an instant two-year banishment from the NBA. Kemp instead retired, but attempted a comeback for the 2006–2007 season. This was allowed despite the fact that Kemp was arrested on marijuana and cocaine possession charges while out of the league in April 2005.

Since Stanley Roberts in 1999, only one player, Chris "The Birdman" Andersen in 2006, has ever been given a two-year suspension for violating the NBA's substance abuse policy.

Despite its poor history, during his "state of the NBA" address given during the league's All-Star break in 2009, NBA Commissioner David Stern felt the league's testing policy was fine as implemented. Stern was quoted as saying, "Could we improve it? Sure…You could hound your players completely, but you do something that you think is rational compared to where you are, and I think we're almost at the right place. There may be ways we can improve it and we'll talk to Billy [Hunter, the NBA Players' Union Director] and the union about it, but we're pretty comfortable that our system is working."[6]

While the NBA has had its fair share of players with drug problems, they aren't alone. Major League Baseball has its own history of players using illegal drugs. One that's older, longer, and much richer than the NBA's recent trials and tribulations.

If there ever was a poster boy for how many times a player can get busted for drugs and still have a major league career, it's Steve Howe. Howe stitched together a 12-year major league career in a 16-year span, the gaps brought on by suspensions and perhaps even a hint of blackballing.

Howe broke into the bigs in 1980 with the L.A. Dodgers already having a taste for cocaine dating back to his college days. He was named the National League (NL) Rookie of the Year in 1980, despite later admitting to getting high two or three times a week. During the off-season, he would sometimes go missing for days while out on a binge. After the 1982 season, Howe entered rehab. The day after he was released, he found the stash of cocaine he hid in his home and was right back at it. He entered rehab again midway through the 1983 season, and was required to pay a record-setting fine of over $50,000 based on the time he was unavailable to the Dodgers. After that month-long stint, Howe was back out on the mound, posting an incredible 1.44 ERA in 33 total appearances in 1983. His habit was still uncontrollable and something he couldn't hide.

Baseball had reached its breaking point and suspended Howe in December of 1983 for the entire 1984 season. The Dodgers were also fed up with Howe and refused to bring him back in 1985. In fact, no team would bring Howe back for the '85 season, leading him to believe he was being blackballed by the league spurred on by MLB commissioner Peter Ueberroth. The fact was, Howe could still pitch and spent time in the minors, in the Mexican League, and in Japan. In 1987, the Texas Rangers brought Howe back to the majors even though the team incurred a $250,000 fine because Commissioner Ueberroth didn't approve Howe's return. For once, a commissioner may have been right. Howe failed a drug test early in 1988 and was suspended yet again.

Despite serving six suspensions for drugs in less than 10 years, Howe made yet another comeback, this time with the Yankees in 1991 at the age of 31. However, just a year later, Howe was again suspended. This time, Howe was "banned for life" by the league for testing positive for drugs. I guess in this instance, though, "banned for life" simply meant the rest of the year as an arbitrator reinstated Howe for the 1993 season. Howe continued his career completely uninterrupted by suspensions until the Yankees tired of his 6.45 ERA in 1996 and released him.

Steve Howe died in 2006 in a single-car crash with methamphetamine in his system. Upon his passing, MLB commissioner Bud Selig said, "In the

'80s, this sport had a very serious cocaine problem—and that was a pretty consistent pattern."[7]   Selig knew of what he spoke.

The 1980s started off with a bang for baseball when Ferguson Jenkins of the Texas Rangers was busted in Canada for possession of marijuana, hashish, and cocaine. Just 14 days later, Jenkins would be the first baseball player "banned for life" for drugs by the league. Not one month later, an arbitrator would let Jenkins back into baseball. He would be elected to the Hall of Fame in 1991.

Three years later, four members of the Kansas City Royals served time for drug charges. Willie Aikens, Vida Blue, Jerry Martin, and the 1982 American League (AL) batting champion Willie Wilson were all arrested in 1983 for attempting to purchase cocaine. All four pleaded guilty to misdemeanor charges and were sentenced to one year in jail. Of course, since they were athletes, nine of the 12 months they were supposed to serve were suspended. As for the other three months, the players were allowed to wait until the off-season before entering jail.

But all of this was nothing compared to what happened in 1985. In the early part of that year, Philadelphia Phillies catcher Curtis Strong was indicted along with six other drug dealers by a federal grand jury for various cocaine dealing charges. All of the dealing, it seems, was done with various professional baseball players and many times inside Pittsburgh's Three Rivers Stadium itself. The "Pittsburgh Drug Trial" brought in a slew of major leaguers to testify under grants of immunity. What fans got an earful of then is almost hard to believe.

Tim Raines, who would put together a 23-year-long career, testified that he was a habitual cocaine user (though he did go through rehab in 1982, prompting the Montreal Expos president John McHale to tell the *New York Times* that he believed "at least eight of the Expos" at the time were on cocaine). Raines would claim that he took cocaine before, after, and even during games, keeping a small vial in the back pocket of his uniform. He even said that his patented head-first slide was performed not to get to the base faster, but to protect the cocaine stashed in the seat of his pants. But by the time of the trial, Raines was a reformed user. Others were not.

Some believe that Keith Hernandez's trade from the St. Louis

Cardinals to the New York Mets in 1983 was based in part on his cocaine habit. Hernandez threatened to sue a member of the Players Association over the allegations, but changed his tune when he took the stand in 1985. Hernandez admitted to a having a huge cocaine habit that led him to losing 10 pounds, waking up with nosebleeds, and having the shakes. He testified that it was his belief that 40 percent of the players in baseball were cocaine users.

Several other players also testified during the trail. Two of the Royals who served time in 1983, Willie Aikens and Vida Blue, testified along with Jeffrey Leonard, Lonnie Smith, Lee Mazzilli, and Dave Parker. Names were named and fingers were pointed. Parker supposedly bragged about smuggling drugs into the U.S. in a catcher's mitt and sold some of it to the Astros' J.R. Richard. Dusty Baker, Bernie Carbo, Gary Matthews, and even the Pittsburgh Pirates' mascot were implicated during the trial as being cocaine users .

In the end, Strong and the other six dealers were found guilty on 11 counts of distributing cocaine. In February of 1986, seven players—Keith Hernandez, Dave Parker, Joaquin Andujar, Dale Berra (Yogi Berra's son), Enos Cabell, Lonnie Smith, and Jeffrey Leonard—each received a one-year suspension from the league while four others—Lee Lacy, Claudell Washington, Lary Sorensen and Al Holland—received 60-day suspensions. Though the commissioner seemingly came down hard, none of the 11 players missed a single game. Each of the seven facing a year-long ban agreed to donate 10 percent of their 1986 salary to various drug causes and to serve 100 hours of community service, while the other four agreed to donate 5 percent of their salary and serve 50 hours of community service. One of the suspended players, Lonnie Smith, claimed that the league's punishment was nothing more than "a joke" and that he never paid the entire fine or served any of the community service time because no one bothered to check on him.

Not long after that scandal, the New York Mets would field a team with not one but two troubled athletes who had drug problems. Dwight "Doc" Gooden had a live fastball and a livelier cocaine habit. Even so, Gooden himself insisted on a drug testing clause in his contract and even filmed a "Just Say No to drugs" commercial. In 1987, before the start of his fourth season, Gooden tested positive for cocaine. He entered rehab for 28 days, and then returned to the Mets. But he wasn't clean. In 1994, Gooden would again test positive and be suspended for the entire 1995 season.

Gooden's teammate in those early seasons was Darryl Strawberry. Early on, Strawberry had problems with alcohol and entered rehab for a drinking problem in 1990. After the stint in rehab, Strawberry moved to Los Angeles to join the Dodgers. In 1994, Strawberry was placed on the disabled list by the team while again undergoing rehab. Then in 1995, he was suspended 60 days for testing positive for cocaine. Four years later, Strawberry was arrested for cocaine possession and soliciting a prostitute. The next year, MLB suspended him a third time for drugs, this time for the entire season, effectively ending his career.

Something akin to the NBA's amazing ability to make drug problems disappear on their rosters, MLB hasn't had much of a public drug problem since these heydays in the 1980s. Why? Most likely, baseball had a few other problems—like strikes, lockouts, Pete Rose, and drugs of another sort (steroids)—to deal with, therefore they turned a blind eye to the issue, masking it with PR-ready drug testing programs designed to find potential troublemakers before they made more negative headlines. In this way, the league could control any potential embarrassment before it got out of hand, as it had in the past.

The NHL isn't as clean as the ice they skate on either. One of the first NHL drug suspensions occurred in 1983, when Montreal Canadiens defenseman Ric Nattress received a year-long suspension for possession of marijuana and hashish. In reality, it amounted to only 40 games as he was reinstated before season's end. Three years later, Toronto Maple Leafs forward Borje Salming was suspended for the season for admitting to using cocaine "five, six years ago" in a newspaper article. He missed eight games and was later inducted into the Hall of Fame. Skip ahead to 1989, and the NHL suspends its first player "for life" when Detroit Red Wings goon Bob Probert was arrested for smuggling about 14 grams of cocaine into the U.S. Probert was back in the league the following year. Probert's troubles weren't over, though, because as a member of the Chicago Blackhawks, he was suspended again for drugs and entered rehab. In 2000, New York Rangers forward Kevin Stevens was arrested for possession of crack cocaine while in the company of a prostitute. He admitted to having only an alcohol problem, and was sent through the NHL's substance abuse program. He was not suspended.

The NHL has a standing drug policy which suspends a player for 20 games for the first offense, 60 games for a second, and a lifetime ban for a third. Of course, should someone actually "strike out" in the NHL, like the NBA, there's a chance for reinstatement after two years. A penalty of this nature has yet to occur.

In June 2009, a question of whether an athlete was taking illegal drugs surfaced in an unlikely sport—The National Association for Stock Car Auto Racing (NASCAR). Driver Jeremy Mayfield reportedly tested positive for methamphetamine and was suspended by the circuit. However, Mayfield vehemently denied ever using the substance and sued NASCAR to keep racing. Mayfield claimed the positive result was from a mixture of the allergy medication Claritin-D and another prescribed medication, Adderall XR, used to combat attention deficit hyperactivity disorder (ADHD). Mayfield went as far as claiming NASCAR tampered with his test results, stating, "I don't trust anything NASCAR does…never have, never will."[8] His lawyers added in writing, "NASCAR is absolutely corrupted by power."[9] As of this writing, the battle between NASCAR and its driver continues.

NASCAR's chairman Brian France declared its drug testing policy as the toughest in all of professional sports. In a very real sense, it should be. France said, "It's our responsibility to protect the drivers, the fans, other participants within the events. We have a very unique challenge relative to all sports, which is the inherent danger of somebody impaired on the racetrack."[10] NASCAR doesn't just test its drivers, either. They test everyone on a race team, from crew chiefs down to the pit crew. However, some of NASCAR's drivers openly wonder about the league's testing policy because they claim that NASCAR doesn't provide anyone with the complete lists of banned substances. So in essence, no one being tested by NASCAR knows what is or isn't allowed by the racing league. All that seems to be clearly known about NASCAR's secret list of banned substances came from driver Jeff Burton in an ESPN.com article. He told reporter David Newton that "the list is three inches thick and close to 500 pages" in length.

While routine testing for such a laundry list of banned substances should make one feel safe about going to the track, NASCAR chairman French told the Associated Press, "People frequently test positive for one thing or another. It happens very, very frequently. It's very rare, though, that we do a suspension, because that's a very serious matter. We realize the seriousness and implications that has to an individual, to a race team, to their careers. It's why the policy has some built-in flexibilities."[11] So NASCAR has a hard line against drugs, yet it's flexible, too? Is NASCAR's policy really that stringent then?

The NFL has a history of looking the other way when it comes to its players taking illegal drugs. Baltimore Colts all-pro defensive tackle Eugene "Big Daddy" Lipscomb died from a heroin overdose in the off-season of 1963. Ten years later, in a widely forgotten fact, the U.S. House Commerce Committee investigated drug use by professional athletes. Its recommendation, made some 35 years ago, was for leagues to test their athletes for illegal drugs and attach harsh penalties for those caught via testing. Every professional league ignored these congressional suggestions. NFL Commissioner Pete Rozelle went only so far as to institute a "reporting program" in which teams were to rat out their own players. Not surprisingly, this program was an utter failure.

The poster boy for the NFL's inability to combat drug-abusing players was clearly Lawrence "LT" Taylor. Taylor began using cocaine in his second season. Was this a secret habit? Hardly. As New York Giants offensive lineman Karl Nelson is quoted as saying in LT's own book, "He [Taylor] was standing on top of the hill watching practice one day. Harry Carson saw him and got down on his hands and knees and started snorting the white lines on the practice field. LT just laughed it off."[12] By 1984, Taylor was addicted, regularly smoking the drug. "I went from using about half a gram every two to four weeks to an eighth or more in one night. I used to buy a gram, then all of a sudden I was buying an eightball—that's three grams. Then I stopped buying eightballs and I'd buy a couple of ounces a week. Go through an ounce in a day or two. It got to the point where there would be times when I'd be standing in the huddle and instead of thinking about what defense we were playing, I would be thinking about smoking cocaine after the game."[13]

LT wrote that the first time his urine turned up "dirty" was before the 1985 season. Yet he didn't receive "strike one" in the NFL's drug testing program until 1987, three years after he started using the drug because he was able to fool the NFL's drug testers with urine that wasn't his. Somehow LT coasted along using and abusing until 1988 when he tested positive a second time. He was hit with a four-game suspension. Realizing that "strike three" meant he was out of the NFL, Taylor stopped his cocaine habit cold until he retired from the game.

That was the 1980s. Today, the NFL's drug program isn't much better. In the 2007 NFL draft, three of the top prospects in the country—WR Calvin Johnson, DE Gaines Adams, and DT Amobi Okoye—all admitted to using marijuana when asked during interviews at the NFL combine. How did this surprising honesty affect their positions in the draft? Not in the least, as Johnson was selected third overall by the Lions, Adams went fourth to the Buccaneers, and Okoye was taken 10th by the Texans. In July 2008, Jacksonville Jaguars wide receiver Matt Jones and two others were arrested when caught cutting up cocaine with a credit card inside a parked car. Jones was charged with felony possession of a controlled substance. What did the NFL do in response? Nothing. He had apparently never tested positive. When Jones was allowed to enter a drug rehabilitation program in October that would erase the charge against him if completed, did the NFL act to punish Jones? No. It took the NFL another week to respond to an arrest that occurred three months earlier, and then the league simply handed down a three-game suspension. Jacksonville later released Jones after the 2008 season.

Does any professional sports league have a drug policy that works? Seemingly, fewer and fewer athletes are testing positive for drugs because of more and more testing. At the same time, every league's policy has clear and open loopholes that players can walk through. In his book

You're Okay, It's Just A Bruise, former Oakland Raiders team doctor Rob Huizenga, M.D. tells of one player who tested positive for cocaine *10 times* with no action taken by the league.[14] He also recounts the story of an unnamed member of the Denver Broncos who was going to be suspended because of a second positive drug test. Yet he never was. In fact, he was in the lineup the following week. According to Huizenga, "I knew then that something was wrong with the new drug penalty system. Either the fix was in at the commissioner's office or some major legal roadblock had been thrown up."[15]

Part of the blame again rests in each league's players' union which assists their athletes by limiting most of the constraints leagues may try to impose. It was the unions that bargained down the amount of testing while keeping punishments from being too harsh. And it is this lack of serious punishment that is keeping any testing policy from being truly effective. If a "lifetime" ban winds up being a five- or 10-game suspension thanks to appeal processes and arbitration, where does responsibility go? As long as the unions consider that protecting their members from drugs means sparing them from any lost playing time and the money associated with it rather than helping these players avoid the actual use of drugs, no relief is in sight.

In the book *Bloody Sundays*, author Mike Freeman details a video he witnessed taken during an NFL players' union meeting in 1999. The most frightening revelation was when the union's assistant executive director Doug Allen tells those assembled that "the union was informed by the NFL that a significant number of players had failed drug tests and faced suspensions....Because of a private agreement with the league office, the players would not be suspended."[16] Freeman related that a source told him the "significant number" in fact totaled 16 players who were given free rides by the league in cahoots with the union. How many other secret, under-the-table deals between the leagues and their players take place? The knowledge that just *one* took place should destroy any faith held that these tests make any athletes accountable for their actions. Truly, how can anyone believe that drug testing in professional sports actually works as advertised?

PERFORMANCE ENHANCERS

"Do you want to know the terrifying truth, or do you want to see me sock a few dingers?" — Mark McGwire on *The Simpsons*

In October of 2005, an article appeared on the *New York Times* website entitled "Drug testing in the NFL appears to be working well." As the title suggested, the NFL's testing program seemed to be working properly. However, like the NBA and its failure to test for marijuana, the NFL had a secret, too. It hadn't been testing its players for amphetamines.

"Frankly, we didn't see amphetamines and methamphetamines as a big issue, as a big problem in the league," said the NFL Executive Vice President of Labor Relations Harold Henderson in a June, 2006 article. He added, "Now we've come to learn that at least in other sports, and maybe in our sport, too, people believe it is a performance-enhancer."[1] Clearly, Mr. Henderson didn't know his league's history, as amphetamines have long been used as a NFL player's performance enhancer of choice.

Bernie Parrish played eight years in the NFL in the 1960s as a member of the Cleveland Browns. Once out of football, he wrote one of the first negative and damning books against the NFL entitled *They Call it a Game*. In the book, Parrish documents his and other players' use of amphetamines. He wrote, "Despite the claims of doctors and trainers to the contrary, it [Dexedrine, a stimulant] did improve my performance."[2] At the end of his career, Parrish claimed he was "taking 10 or 15 5-milligram tablets of Dexedrine" before each game.[3]

In 1973, Washington Redskins center George Burman made a startling revelation to *Newsday*. He claimed that one third of his teammates regularly took amphetamines before games. He never named names, but this opened a NFL investigation into the subject. Nothing ever came out of it publicly.

Flash forward 10 years, and amphetamines were still in regular usage. Lawrence Taylor, on top of his cocaine and drinking habits, utilized amphetamines to get "up" for games. "Many times I'd be out all night, and then have to take a lot of that over-the-counter speed truck drivers take to stay up."[4]

A drug user of a different sort, Bill Romanowski treated his body like a chemical testing laboratory, taking anything and everything he could to stay on top of his game, including amphetamines. He wrote in his book *Romo: My Life on the Edge* how he, in the midst of the 1989 season (his second season in the league), discovered Phentermine. The drug is an appetite suppressant yet it increases the amount of adrenaline in one's system which, according to Romanowski, "is why Phentermine was so popular [in the NFL] before it was banned."[5] Romanowski loved the stuff so much, he nearly went to jail for fraudulently obtaining it. It was only once he made headlines for his and his wife's drug-related arrest that the NFL banned the substance in 2001. So apparently the NFL *did* realize its players might be taking forms of speed, regardless of Mr. Henderson's claim.

Despite the fact that various forms of amphetamines were being taken by its players throughout the league's history, it took the NFL until the start of the 2007 season to add amphetamines and methamphetamines to its list of banned substances.

The NHL, however, doesn't feel it needs to test its athletes for such substances at all. Stephane Quintal, a 17-year veteran of the NHL, begged to differ. He claimed shortly after he retired in 2004 that over 40 percent of the players he encountered used stimulants. World Anti Doping Agency (WADA) chairman Richard Pound said that stimulants were the "drug of choice" for hockey players and that the league's testing policy was riddled with loopholes.[6] Pound seemed incensed that the NHL wouldn't adopt WADA's stringent anti-drug code which includes a ban on certain stimulants, considering how the NHL sends its top athlete to play in the World Cup and the Olympics. In November 2005 Islanders defenseman Bryan Berard and Colorado Avalanche goalie Jose Theodore both failed tests administered by their respective national anti-doping agencies prior to international competition, yet neither player received any disciplinary action from the NHL, and to date the league stands pat on its policy.

Major League Baseball stepped up to the plate against amphetamines, but not until 2006, again long after a problem was recognizable. Stories have been told of baseball clubhouses having jars full of "greenies" out for players to indulge as needed. John Milner, a 12-year veteran who testified in the 1985 Pittsburgh drug trial, stated under oath that Willie Mays took amphetamines in the form of "the red juice." During that same trial, both

Dave Parker and Dale Berra testified that Willie Stargell had handed out amphetamines to his Pittsburgh Pirates teammates. It was just the way baseball was played.

What drove the "greenie" jar underground was most likely the story of the 1980 World Champion Philadelphia Phillies. A doctor on Philadelphia's AA team in Reading was charged with 23 counts of illegally prescribing amphetamines to clients. Who were among the good doctor's clientele? None other than the Phillies' Tim McCarver, Larry Bowa, Steve Carlton, Greg Luzinski, and Pete Rose. During the doctor's trial, Rose claimed he didn't even know what a "greenie" was, even though he had admitted in an earlier interview in *Playboy* magazine that he had taken them in the past. Steve Carlton magically disappeared and couldn't even be served with a subpoena to show up in court. McCarver claimed he never asked for or received any such pills. Only one Phillies player implicated in the case, pitcher Randy Lerch, admitted to requesting and receiving the drugs. In his testimony, he called his teammates liars and claimed that all of those named used the drugs regularly. Lerch was traded to Milwaukee after the trial ended.

Amphetamines didn't disappear from major league locker rooms. Some 25 years later in the *Congressional Report on the Investigation into Rafael Palmerio's Testimony* (which we'll get to later), tales of amphetamine use were buried in the report. The first involved former Texas Rangers head trainer Dan Wheat, who worked for the Rangers from 1985 through 2002. He claimed that amphetamine use was "rampant" in the league. He would often hear players asking each other for them before games. Once, he asked a player, "Of the nine players on the field, how many took greenies today?" The response from the player was "eight." Also in the report was an interview with an unnamed player concerning amphetamines. This player claimed amphetamine use "is part of the baseball world." As frightening as it sounds, he even claimed he couldn't drink the coffee in the clubhouse because players would sometimes spike it with speed. "I can guarantee you there has [sic] been players, when a team is struggling or a team is going through a bad streak, they will spike the coffee."

Perhaps this report provided some motivation to the league to finally include amphetamines on its banned substance list. A second influence came directly from the league's doctors and trainers. In an address to the Baseball Writers of America, Commissioner Bud Selig told the audience, "They said, 'If you don't do something about this, somebody's going to die.'"[7] What I want to know is, was this warning acted upon out of the players' best interest, or out of fear of the PR nightmare that would ensue from a player's death linked to amphetamine use?

With the new policy in place to battle the rampant use of amphetamines, how many players did MLB ensnare? Officially, through 2008, one middle-infielder, Neifi Perez, has been caught. Perez, a 12-year veteran of the league, was in fact caught three times. Perez received an 80-game suspension in August of 2007 for a third positive test for a banned stimulant. Neifi's first positive result, according to the league's policy, was to be kept confidential. Though no news has appeared identifying any other players that tested positive, somehow another player's first positive test leaked out and made headlines. That was baseball's all-time home run king Barry Bonds, who according to a *New York Daily News* report, tested positive for amphetamines sometime in 2006. The *New York Daily News'* sources informed the paper that having tested positive and due to MLB policy, Bonds had to undergo treatment and counseling as well as be subjected to six further tests a year. But it wasn't amphetamines that many fans wanted Bonds to get busted for; it was steroids.

Though steroids have been around since the mid-1960s, baseball players seemed to shy away from them. Players felt they didn't need the muscle mass of weightlifters to hit a baseball, they simply needed a good eye and quick wrists to make contact. When Jose Canseco made his major league debut in 1985 all that changed. Because of his instant success in the game, along with the fact that he credited it to steroids, Canseco very well may have single-handedly changed the face of the baseball.

The self-titled "godfather of steroids in baseball," Canseco won the AL Rookie of the Year award in 1986 and was named baseball's Most Valuable Player in 1988. When other players inquired about his training regimen, Canseco was happy to oblige by sharing the secret of steroids. As Canseco wrote, "I was the first to educate other players about how to use them, the first to experiment and pass on what I'd learned, and the first to get contacts on where to get them. I taught the other players which steroid has which effect on the body, and how to mix or 'stack' certain steroids to get a desired effect."[8]

Canseco was fingered in *Sports Illustrated* for using steroids in 1988. Baseball did nothing. When Canseco was traded to the Texas Rangers (which he felt had something to do with his steroid usage), his boss became George W. Bush, managing general partner of the team. As Canseco wrote, "It was understood then that teams knew all about steroids in the game. There was no question that George W. Bush knew my name was connected with steroids…but he decided to make the deal to trade for me anyway."[9] Bush didn't do anything about steroids in baseball until 15 years later when he was president of the country.

Fay Vincent, who was baseball's commissioner from 1989–1992, was quoted in *Newsweek* in 2008 as saying, "Look, I was there, I was part of the problem. I never thought steroids was going to be as big an issue as it became because I thought it was a muscle-building drug. I looked at [Hank] Aaron and [Willie] Mays and they weren't muscle guys. It was all about quickness. I thought it was a football problem. I thought Jose Canseco was an anomaly."[10] Vincent was not just wrong, but incredibly naive.

Baseball considered implementing a program that tested for steroid usage, but the players' union managed to delay its approval until 2005. "The Players Association was as complicit as the owners in the explosion of steroids in the game. They knew as much about it as anyone, because they dealt with the players all the time. To those of us on the inside, there was no mystery over why the union took such a hard line against steroid testing, for example. Their concern was always making money for the players, and if the players were remaking their bodies using steroids to do so, the MBPA never lifted a finger to stop it."[11]

Baseball's most in-depth examination of steroids occurred in 2003. The league ran some 1,400 semi-anonymous tests (players were given coded numbers instead of names) secretly during the 2003 season to see just how prevalent steroid usage was in the league. Reportedly,

104 of these tests came back positive. The results of that testing were never meant to be released to the public, but once the government became involved in the controversy the names of players who tested positive began to leak to the press.

With the situation spinning out of baseball's control, in 2007 the league conducted an official investigation into the steroid situation within the game. Two months prior to receiving the investigation's findings, MLB Commissioner Bud Selig said, "There's nothing to be afraid of. Whatever comes out comes out. I have no concern."[12] He was right. What was officially known as the "Report to the Commissioner of Baseball of an Independent Investigation into the Illegal Use of Steroids and Other Performance Enhancing Substances by Players in Major League Baseball" but was dubbed "The Mitchell Report" was nothing but a gigantic PR whitewash condoned by the league. The investigation was led by former Senate Majority Leader George Mitchell of Maine who was hardly an unbiased investigator. At the time, he was a director of the Boston Red Sox and a former chairman of the Walt Disney Company, which owned ESPN, which partially funded MLB by broadcasting its games. Ultimately, little of significance resulted from Mitchell's work, though he suggested that the players named in his report were just the tip of the iceberg and that steroid usage had been widespread throughout the game for years, touching every team in the league.

Mitchell was correct in that declaration. One could field a virtual All-Star team with players connected to steroids:

★ C – Ivan Rodriguez (named by Jose Canseco in his book as a user)
★ 1B – Mark McGwire (named by Jose Canseco, also caught with Androstenedione in his locker in 1998); Rafael Palmeiro (a positive test for Stanozolol ended his career)
★ 2B – Brian Roberts (named in The Mitchell Report, admitted to "trying" steroids once)
★ SS – Miguel Tejada (named in The Mitchell Report, pleaded guilty to a misdemeanor for lying to Congress about a teammate's steroid usage)
★ 3B – Alex Rodriguez (name leaked out as one of the 104 positives in the 2003 anonymous test. Afterwards, A-Rod claimed he "didn't

think they were steroids," but he knew "I wasn't taking Tic Tacs. I knew it was something that could perhaps be wrong."[13])

★ OF – Manny Ramirez (named leaked from 2003 MLB test, also tested positive for the drug hCG in 2009 and was suspended for 50 games); Jason Giambi (named by Canseco and admitted to grand jury he used both steroids and HGH. In May 2007 stated, "I was wrong for doing that stuff. ...What we should have done a long time ago was stand up—players, ownership, everybody—and said: 'We made a mistake.'"[14]); Barry Bonds (entire case against Bonds is laid out in the book *Game of Shadows*. He is currently under indictment for perjury for lying to grand jury about steroid usage.)

★ DH – David Ortiz (name leaked from 2003 MLB test)

★ P – Andy Pettitte (named in The Mitchell Report, claimed to have used HGH "twice"); Roger Clemens (named in The Mitchell Report, currently under investigation for lying to Congress about his past steroid usage.)

Since The Mitchell Report was released, baseball has altered its testing program. In April 2008 the league added 600 more tests, raising the yearly total conducted to 3,600. Still, MLB's testing plan leaves much to be desired. For one thing, much like the NBA's drug testing plan, players are tested within five days of arriving at spring training. Thus every "dirty" player has ample time to get clean prior to that scheduled test. Following that, players are subjected to one more random test during the season that could take place at any time including during the playoffs. However, as reported by the *New York Times* in October of 2007, these tests aren't as surprising or random as they should be. The testers routinely contacted the teams they were about to visit 24- to 48-hours prior to their arrival in order to gain access to both their parking areas and stadiums. According to many anti-doping experts, this 24 to 48 hour window is more than enough time for suspect players to either clean out their systems, use a masking agent, or even replace dirty urine with a clean sample.

Though baseball is the league most picked on for its steroid problem, the NFL has had its recent issues with steroids as well. It is possible that several members of the Carolina Panthers used steroids during their run to the Super Bowl in 2003–2004. This story only broke because federal prosecutors arrested and charged Dr. James Shortt with writing illegal steroid prescriptions. Among his clients were Panthers offensive linemen Todd Stuessie and Jeff Mitchell. According to CBS' *60 Minutes*, both Stuessie and Mitchell refilled steroid prescriptions a total of 10 or more times each. The *Charlotte Observer* reported both players filled prescriptions for a combined *five* NFL banned substances less than a week before the players left with the team for the Super Bowl. Four other members of the Panthers were also reported as the doctor's clients—tight end Wesley Walls, punter Todd Sauerbrun, defensive lineman John Milem, and offensive lineman Kevin Donnalley (making three of the Panthers' starting five offensive linemen users). The *Charlotte Observer* stated, "Several of [the players] were using disturbing, particularly alarmingly high amounts with high dosages for long durations—some in combinations. This wasn't just a passing flirtation with these prohibited substances."[15] For all the ballyhoo surrounding the NFL's testing policy, the league caught exactly zero of these Panthers players red-handed. Dr. Shortt later claimed in an interview on HBO's *CostasNow* that he treated 18 different NFL players with steroids and growth hormone.

Shawne "Lights Out" Merriman was named the NFL defensive rookie of the year in 2005. The next season Merriman tested positive for the anabolic steroid nandrolone and was slapped with a four-game suspension. He immediately appealed that suspension. Why? First, his team, the San Diego Chargers, was playoff -bound. Second, Merriman claimed the positive result was from a supplement he had been taking which unknowingly contained the steroid. ESPN's Chris Mortensen reported that a source with knowledge of the case said that Merriman's positive test was "definitely for steroids...not one of those supplement deals."[16] A week later, Merriman dropped his appeal and served the suspension. Despite this suspension, at the end of the season the NFL nominated Merriman for Defensive Player of the Year. Merriman didn't win.

The NFL recently updated their testing policy for performance-enhancing drugs. They now test for the blood-boosting substance EPO (being the only pro sports league to do so) and they increased the number of random tests on each team from seven players to 10 from each team each week. The NFL even upped the penalties for positive tests: not only does the player miss four games with a suspension (which is a quarter of the regular season) for a first positive, but the player also forfeits a prorated portion of his signing bonus. This is all well and good, but there are still loopholes.

For instance, recently deceased NFL Players' Association executive director Gene Upshaw stated he considered blood tests "unreliable and overly intrusive."[17] Since the NFL only uses urine tests for detection of illegal substances and there is no current urine test able to detect Human Growth Hormone, players are still free to use HGH. In 2008, the players union changed their tune ever so slightly as the NFLPA stated its players would agree to HGH testing once there was an acceptable urine test for it. As Upshaw stated, "Until a test is developed for HGH, there's really not an awful lot to talk about. And when that test is developed, we really believe it should be a urine test. No one is interested in a blood test. We got a lot of big tough guys, but they don't even like to be pricked on the finger to give blood."[18]

HGH aside, there are other drugs available to players that the NFL and every other league does not and cannot test for. Tetrahydrogestrinone or THG was better known as "The Clear." Former NFL linebacker Bill Romanowski used it knowing how the steroid got its name—it didn't show up on any tests. In fact, it wasn't until a used syringe of THG was passed from an anonymous track coach to officials that the U.S. Anti-Doping Agency (USADA) even became aware of it. Once the USADA released a report on THG, use of the drug effectively stopped because it became a known and testable substance. Romanowski wrote, "It wasn't about illegal; I was taking performance-enhancing substances they couldn't test for, like THG. As soon as I found out something could be tested for, I stopped taking it."[19] Romanowski claimed to have spent over $1 million during his career on whatever substances he thought would keep him playing in the NFL. "I clearly pushed the envelope ethically and morally, because if I could take something that would help me perform better and it wasn't banned, then hell, I was going to take it."[20]

And that's what the NFL and the rest of the professional sports leagues can't test for. They cannot and will not stop players from taking substances that either physically or even psychologically give players an edge over their opponents. Regardless of how often they test players or what kind of penalties are handed out, chemists are out there cooking up new and better performance-enhancing substances every day. And players seeking that edge will seek out those chemists.

What will the professional sports leagues do when they are faced with the looming menace that is gene doping? When scientists can actually alter players' genes as they currently do with mice, making them twice as strong or fast as they originally were? What then? Barry Bonds' 762 home runs may pale in comparison to the kid who can hit 100 home runs a season because his physical makeup was altered at a genetic level before he even entered the league. Test for that. Prove it beyond a reasonable doubt. It won't be possible. The first gene-doping wunderkind that enters the league and achieves monstrous success will open the door to players who perform like supercharged video game creations, less human than creature.

Major corporations have drug testing policies to ensure that they don't hire or employ drug addicts because they feel having such employees will negatively affect the company's overall performance or image. It's not done out of the concern for an employee's well-being; it's about the bottom line. But should some miracle drug emerge that would boost a businessman's output or profit by say some 20 percent, yet is later deemed illegal by the powers that be, you better believe no employer would test for it unless mandated by a higher power to do so. Even then, perhaps only so many employees would be tested. "Random" testing would only be so random. Some employees would never take the drug, able to succeed on their own accord. Testing only these known "clean" employees would make testing results always look impressive. But some employees would need to use the drug to achieve their quotas and stay with the company. And some "clean" employees may want to enhance ability, to move up the corporate ladder, and use the drug to go above and beyond their current position. So testing would be required of every employee, even if just once a year. To ensure that their biggest earners, though violating the law with their drug usage, are never caught and embarrass the corporation, these employees are warned of the looming "random" test. Amazingly, known users test clean. The corporation looks good to Wall Street investors. Everyone profits as the law is skirted. Professional sports could never operate in such a way, right? They couldn't possibly be profiting from illegal drug usage, could they?

There is a monstrous "catch-22" in each league's drug testing policies: the leagues oversee their own tests, results, and punishments. They have complete control without any oversight. The players don't want to be caught, the unions don't want players to be caught, and the leagues don't want to see their players test positive. Yet the idea behind testing is to ensure the integrity of the game.

GAMBLING

APPROXIMATELY 15 MILLION AMERICANS BET "REGULARLY AND often heavily" on football, basketball, baseball, prizefights, and horse racing.[1] These gamblers mostly book their bets through the 250,000-plus illegal bookies operating across the country. Estimates indicate that upwards of $200 billion is wagered yearly in the U.S. on sporting events, a total that is continually rising. The NFL is the most wagered-upon sport, with over $1 billion being bet on its games each week of its season. All of these numbers are mere guesses because the vast majority of the money bet on sports is wagered illegally. No one knows the true numbers.

What these numbers clearly indicate, however, is the dirty and little-discussed secret of professional sports. Plain and simple, gambling is the driving force behind the popularity of sports. Fans often have a direct financial investment in what's happening on the field. The added interest of one's own money in the form of a wager ensures that even a matchup between two lastplace teams will garner spectators. Though the game may be meaningless to the players, hundreds of thousands or possibly millions of dollars is at stake for gamblers nationwide who perceive an edge in such contests. Gambling keeps things interesting for fans even when all indications should say otherwise. So are sports really keeping that many fans intrigued in the game? Or are many fans betting on the games in order to force that interest? If these fans didn't or couldn't bet, would they completely stop caring about sports?

The history of professional sports is tied directly to the money gambled upon it. Baseball was the undisputed national pastime for the first half of the 1900s. It was also the most widely wagered-upon team sport. From its very advent, people were gambling on baseball. "Betting on baseball was an integral part of the game, especially in cities, since the inception of organized professional leagues in the 1870s. Baseball team owners were active gamblers who apparently bet heavily on their own teams."[2] Without gambling, would baseball have survived into the 1900s? Possibly not, as professional teams and leagues were formed in part to legitimize the sport as a gambling endeavor. The baseball men of that era did nothing to discourage the practice for they realized a gambling fan was an interested fan. When the U.S. entered World War I in 1917, the federal government shut down horse racing nationwide. That move pushed thousands of gamblers out of racetracks and into baseball stadiums for their action. Gambling was known to take place openly in the bleachers of Boston's Fenway Park and Chicago's Wrigley Field well into the late 1930s, often under signs declaring "No Gambling."

Gambling on baseball games was problematic for bookmakers. Bookies make a living off of what's known as "the vig" or vigorish. This is the "juice" or what bookmakers charge gamblers to place their bets. Most gambling takes place on an 11/10 proposition. This means that a gambler has to bet $11 to win $10, with the bookie keeping the $1 (or 10 percent) for booking the bet. The casino sports books in Las Vegas utilize this system to operate and profit also. What a bookmaker would like more than anything is to see equal action on every game bet. If a bookie receives half of the bets on one team and an equal half on the other, regardless of the outcome, the bookie stands to profit because of the vigorish. What happens in baseball because of lopsided pitching matchups is that bookies and casinos often have to alter those 11 to 10 odds. In hopes of keeping the influx of wagers equal on both teams, the odds on a team with the good pitcher will drop while the odds on the team with the lousy hurler will rise. This is offered only as an attempt by the bookmaker to not "bust out" from one-sided bets on a particular game.

Thanks to the rise in popularity of college basketball in the late 1930s and early 1940s, a solution to the bookie's problem was invented—the point spread. The name of the genius who invented the point spread has been lost to history, but it was refined and first offered as a betting option by one Charles McNeil in Chicago around the late 1930s.[3]

It works like this: Let's say the Boston Celtics are playing the Los Angeles Lakers, and the Celtics have a great team while the Lakers are floundering. Originally, bookies would've had to offer odds on the game, paying off more should the underdog Lakers win and less if the favored Celtics did. But chances are an equal share of money would not have been wagered on both teams. For the bookie, this meant a certain outcome would have been more beneficial than another. Hence, the bookmaker stood to lose if the game went the wrong way for him. But armed with the point spread, all advantage returns to the bookie. Instead of offering odds, the bookmaker now offers a number, say nine points on the game. The Celtics, as the favored team, are listed as minus nine points (-9) or said to be giving nine points to the Lakers. It means that the Celtics would have to win by more than nine points for a gambler to win his bet on the Celtics. The reverse is also available, with a bet on the Lakers getting +9 points, meaning if the Lakers lose by less than nine points (or win the game outright), the gambler would win his bet. If the game ended with the Celtics winning exactly by nine points, it's considered a "push" and all money is returned. All bets, whether for the Celtics or the Lakers in this scenario, would pay the 11 to 10, meaning the bookie was guaranteed his 10 percent take. The genius in the point spread is it evens out all contests, rarely leaving a game lopsided from a betting standpoint.

The point spread did undergo some development along the way. Originally, it was known as the split line. Using the previous example between the Celtics and Lakers, the split line would have been set as 10/8, which means to bet the Celtics, you'd have to believe they would win by 10 points or more. If you were putting money down on the Lakers, they would have had to lose by eight points or less. A very subtle difference to be sure. So, what happened if the Celtics won by nine? When split lines were used that result would not have been a push, and the bookmaker would have won all bets. No money would have been returned. Needless to say, as the line became set more accurately and more games ended in the middle of the split line's numbers, bettors began to shy away from it. That loss of business led to the creation of the modern point spread system.

The slow destruction of the split line shows how accurately that number could be developed. Just as it is today the line was originally set by gamblers, bookies, and numbers crunchers who knew exactly what they were doing. It was precisely determined based upon numerous calculations and perceptions. A man named Leo Hirschfield set what was known as the "Minneapolis Line" from the late '40s through the early '60s. He and his staff created and sold the line to bookies nationwide. Ironically, Hirschfield also sold tip sheets to gamblers offering ways to beat the very line he set, and profited from both ends of the spectrum.

In 1975, the nation's first casino sports book opened in the Union Plaza hotel in Las Vegas. Upon its opening, the nation's leading bookmaker of the time, Bobby Martin, went to work for the hotel. From there, Martin's "outlaw" line was distributed to other legal and illegal bookies nationwide. One of the first casinos to pick up on Martin's line was the Stardust which opened its own sports book later in 1975, run by Frank "Lefty" Rosenthal.[4] Rosenthal was a notorious lifelong gambler who not only had tight Mafia connections, but allegedly participated in fixing numerous sporting events. Robert DeNiro's character Sam "Ace" Rothstein in the Martin Scorsese film *Casino* was based on Rosenthal.

Not nearly as underground as it was then, today's "Las Vegas" line is set by several different line-making services as well as many casino sports books. These line-makers devise and debate what the numbers should be, based upon numerous stats, trends, and injuries. Once set, these early lines are then released and bet into by select and respected gamblers. Based on these initial wagers, the line may be adjusted up or down depending on the early action. Then these numbers make their way out to all the illegal bookmakers nationwide. Subtle variations can be seen in the number set on a game because not just one person or place sets an official line. Shrewd gamblers take advantage of these differences, shopping around to find the best prices before laying their money down. With the illegal bookies, often the lines on teams within the bookmaker's home city will be slightly different than those in Las Vegas because most gamblers are homers and bet accordingly.

What's interesting to note about the point spread is that it has no direct relationship to which team the bookmaker thinks will actually win a game. It is created simply to even out the betting, in hopes of ensuring the bookmaker's 10 percent vig. This fact is often overlooked by gamblers. A team is often favored simply because the line-makers observe the gambling public's likes and dislikes, and set the line based on those perceptions.

Though the point spread never really had any effectiveness on baseball betting, it opened up a whole new world for football. The rise and refinement of the point spread format ties directly to the growth of professional football. In the 1920s and '30s, the NFL clearly trailed in popularity to college football. Even through the 1940s when the point spread was in its infancy, the NFL wasn't a highly regarded league. But after World War II, three key factors opened the nation up for the NFL. First was the birth of television. As TV exposed the nation to pro football, more fans picked up on the game. Second was the amount of disposable income available to the average person. That allowed more people the wherewithal to gamble. Finally, the idea and availability of the point spread reached a national level. With the ever-growing intrigue in the NFL, a larger percentage of gamblers became willing to lay their money down on pro football. The clear linking these three elements—football, television, and the point spread—are often overlooked by sports historians, yet it is no coincidence that the growths of all three are closely tied together.

The NFL is rated as the number one sport today because it offers a perfect format for gambling. Besides the usefulness of the point spread in evening out every game, unlike the other major pro sports, each NFL team only plays one game a week. That not only heightens the importance of each game, it allows the casual fan plenty of time to examine the upcoming contest and then place an informed wager on the game. The NFL isn't oblivious to that fact. For decades, they have had direct ties and relationships to line- and bookmakers in and outside of Las Vegas. They constantly monitor the lines for their games and are supposedly notified of any unusual fluctuations or betting that may occur (of course, this should never happen since the NFL has never admitted that any of their games have been fixed). At the same time, somewhere in the neighborhood of $35 billion is wagered illegally on the NFL alone each year. This guesstimated number is approximately six to eight times more than the annual profit of all 32 NFL teams combined. Yet the NFL would never publicly admit their need for illegal gambling to maintain fan interest.

Oddly enough, for all the money wagered, most sports gamblers are not winners. The point spread is a tough monster to beat. To be a profitable sports gambler, statistically speaking, one needs to win more than 52.4 percent of wagers to overcome those 11 to 10 odds. This is much more difficult than it sounds. True professional sports gamblers rarely win 60 percent of their bets over the course of a season with selective wagering. Winning in the 54–58 percent range is more likely, yet even the pros have losing years.

The legal casino sports books don't fare that much better. Booking sports bets is the only game casinos offer in which they don't have any built-in advantage. The sports books must survive off that 10 percent vig. However, their profit is usually much less than that. Between 1980 and 2000, the legal Nevada sports books only had a four percent take off all the bets placed over the course of those 20 years. In 1999 alone, out of the over $2.5 billion bet, the 75 Nevada sports books split a profit of about $100 million.[5]

So if the pros struggle to beat the spread while the legal sports books barely eke out a profit, what's that say about the chances of the average, every-so-often gambler out there? "In a routine NFL season, fewer than one bettor in 12 turns a profit. Over the course of a large number of seasons, the percentage of bettors who turn a profit is minuscule. Bob Martin, former head linesmaker for the NFL, once [said] that the number of bettors who win betting pro football is so small that 'it is virtually the same as if no one won.'"[6]

Oftentimes, these armchair gamblers' bets are made based on the false or over-hyped opinions of experts. Tout services are people or companies a gambler pays to provide them with winners. Yet more often than not, touts are just as unsuccessful at predicting outcomes as the general public is. They operate much like palm readers, simply telling you what you want to believe. Touts often inflate their true winning percentages by massaging their statistics to lure the gullible out of their money. Touts will hype their 70 percent or 80 percent win rates, yet as the pros know, these percentages are outright lies.

Sports reporters and prognosticators are just as ill-informed as the touts. Dan Gordon is widely recognized as one of the top three sports handicappers in the country and has made a living gambling on sports for over 20 years. He worked as a columnist handicapping NFL games for several major newspapers. Yet as he later wrote, "I had come to see that competence in handicapping had nothing to do with getting published."[7]

Backing up Gordon's opinion is the work of Gregg Easterbrook who writes a column titled "Tuesday Morning Quarterback" for ESPN.com's *Page 2*. Easterbrook publishes an annual list of horrible NFL predictions made by sportswriters and sportscasters. For his recap of 2008, he laid out some damning evidence of this incompetence. For preseason Super Bowl predictions, which eventually was played between the Pittsburgh Steelers and the Arizona Cardinals, five analysts for FOX Sports, six from *USA Today*, four from *Sports Illustrated*, eight from *Pro Football Weekly*, and two from ESPN's "Sunday NFL Countdown" all chose the Dallas Cowboys as the NFC's representative. Dallas didn't make the playoffs. Fourteen of these combined NFL experts chose the New England Patriots as the AFC's representative. They, too, failed to reach the playoffs. Four others, including ESPN's Chris Berman, thought the Seattle Seahawks would reach the Super Bowl. The Seahawks finished the season 4–12. None of the 38 predictions Easterbrook tracked included either the Steelers or the Cardinals. FOX Sports' Alex Marvez called the eventual Super Bowl champion Steelers "the most overrated team" in the NFL (he was also foolish enough to call the Detroit Lions "the most underrated" ; The Lions didn't win a game all season).

While predicting either of the two Super Bowl teams may be a tough call prior to the season's opening kickoff, these fellows don't do much better once the games are in progress. Consider the following from Easterbrook's column: "In its regular issues, *Pro Football Weekly* (PFW) publishes two or three 'best bets' to entice readers to sign up for an online 'Handicapping Inner Circle' product that costs $59.95 annually. In 2006, the PFW Best Bets went 31-34-2; in 2007, 32-36; in 2008, 35-32-1. That's a three-year total of 98-102-3, meaning when *Pro Football Weekly* pundits are certain they are right, they are usually wrong."[8] Prior to the 2008 season, Easterbrook quoted Hub Arkush, publisher of *Pro Football Weekly,* as saying, "Pittsburgh looks to me like a club headed in the wrong direction." Pittsburgh won the Super Bowl. Easterbrook himself wasn't immune from foolish predictions regarding the 2008 NFL season. He wrote in early December, more than halfway through the season, "The Chargers and Eagles are all but mathematically eliminated [from the playoffs]." Both eventually proved him wrong on that point.

Of course, this begs the question why any—newspapers, ESPN, etc.—report the lines for sporting events in the first place. If no one living outside the Nevada desert can bet these games, why bother to publicize such information? Just like the leagues themselves, the newspapers and their ilk are aware that millions of people out there are gambling illegally, so why not give them what they want? The lines in the newspaper are published the same way how-to-make-a-bomb books are—"for informational purposes only."

The same rules apply for the NFL's injury report. Though the NFL would never admit as much, the injury report is released by the league strictly for gambling purposes. The reason is that early in the NFL's history inside information regarding key player injuries were a boon to gamblers and often led to payoffs from gamblers to the players willing to share such knowledge. To stop that, the NFL made all teams list their injuries publicly. It does very little to benefit actual NFL teams, but to the gambling public the injury report saves valuable time and energy that can be devoted elsewhere.

The only one who really profits from all this gambling is the bookie. Yet despite funneling some $200 billion through the nation's economy, the bookie's operation is outright illegal. Some have thought that turning this illegal empire into a legal one and then taxing it would benefit not just the gamblers, but everyone. Earlier attempts at this proved disastrous. In 1977, the state of Delaware started a state-run NFL gambling lottery. It lasted a total of three weeks. Despite heavy sales, numerous protests regarding who the favored teams were and where the state set the line on those games brought a quick end to the adventure.

Amazingly, one of the biggest protestors to this legalizing of sports gambling was and remains the NFL itself. When Delaware and another

14 states were considering forms of legal sports wagering in 1976, NFL commissioner Pete Rozelle argued that the league feared "fans" would be replaced by "gamblers" and that the numerical outcomes of games would become more important than which teams won. Thirty years later, when Roger Goodell stepped into the NFL commissioner's shoes, he continued to spout the same hypocritical party line, stating, "I don't think it is in the best interest of the NFL to have any association with sports betting."[9]

But all of this talk hasn't stopped the spunky state of Delaware from giving sports gambling a second go-around. Congress passed a law to make sports gambling illegal in the nation in 1992, yet it grandfathered in the four states which had previously allowed it in one form or another—Nevada, Delaware, Oregon, and Montana. When Delaware's beleaguered economy was under pressure in 2009, the state decided to once again legalize sports gambling in an attempt to raise revenue to fund its "core government services." While the original attempt at doing this in 1977 was in the form of a "lottery" which utilized NFL parlay cards, this more modern take on the endeavor would allow single-game betting on all the major sports leagues as well as National Collegiate Athletic Association (NCAA) games. In effect, Delaware would become a state-sponsored sports book. And it hoped to have the entire operation up and running by the kickoff of the 2009 NFL season.

Led by the NFL, the four major sports leagues—the NFL, NBA, NHL, and MLB—and the NCAA filed a lawsuit in July 2009 to stop Delaware in its tracks. Why? According to the suit filed in federal court, Delaware's sports betting plan "would irreparably harm professional and amateur sports by fostering suspicion and skepticism that individual plays and final scores of games may have been influenced by factors other than honest athletic competition." The suit went on to contend that Congress' 1992 ruling would only allow a state to reintroduce whatever form of gambling it had previously allowed. In the case of Delaware, this would have meant the state could only offer up parlay cards on NFL games; not single game betting on all games and in all sports. The sports leagues won their suit, and Delaware settled for a gambling system similar to the one that failed originally.

Yet even if the NFL publicly fights the good fight against gambling and won't admit how beneficial such action really is to its survival, the league openly promotes another form of gambling which is mutating the game in exactly the way former NFL commissioner Pete Rozelle feared possible. It is known as fantasy football.

A "fantasy" team is created out of real players and uses real game statistics to simulate a game. Rarely is there a fantasy football (or baseball or basketball or hockey) league created in which the participants don't throw money into a pot to pay to their championship-winning owner. By definition, it is gambling, and it's big business, openly publicized and supported by numerous corporate websites including CBS, ESPN, and the NFL itself. The truth is that the leagues endorse fantasy sports because just like illegal gambling, it adds more interest to their sport, thus increasing their ultimate profits.

What else are professional sports endorsing by ignoring the vast amount of money being wagered on their games? Organized crime. Financial backing for the big illegal bookmakers comes straight from the pockets of the not-quite-so-goodfellas. Many gamblers, even professional ones, like to argue this point, maybe not wanting to believe that their gambling finances the Mafia's illegal operations. They either don't like to believe the Mafia exists or they assume that organized crime's involvement in bookmaking is limited. Neither is true. For over a century, the Mafia has had its hooks deep into bookmaking operations. Author Dan Moldea has spent decades researching the Mafia. In his 1989 book *Interference: How Organized Crime Influences Professional Football*, Moldea makes distinct and clear connections between organized crime, bookmakers, and members of the NFL.

What should be most worrisome for the professional sports leagues is the obvious notion that with all this illegal money involved, games can be fixed. It's not that actual wins and losses are likely to be at stake in a fix. Today, it's mostly a matter of the point spread. Because as much as the invention of the point spread has helped professional sports, the spread has also cursed them. A player not wanting to outright lose a contest can simply shave points to ensure his team wins, yet doesn't win by enough to cover the spread.

The idea that today's modern athlete earns too much money to fall victim to a fix is ridiculous. Leading NFL handicapper Dan Gordon argued that because of today's athletes' inflated salaries, too much money would need to be bet to cover bribes to the fixing player(s). According to Gordon, Las Vegas sports books report any bets over $10,000 to the IRS while illegal bookies won't book bets over $25,000 unless the person is known to them. Hence, too much "unnatural" money would show up on a certain game leading to that game being taken off the boards (all bets canceled). Yet with a billion dollars being wagered weekly on football games, how obvious would that extra million or so really be? If spread around, would it stick out enough to be noticed? As another counterpoint to Gordon's argument, Dan Moldea details several instances of this happening in his book—often with the questionable game *not* taken off the boards—even when leading bookies smelled something fishy.

What's more likely to facilitate a fix is that a certain player gets in trouble with the wrong sort of people and needs an easy way out. As detailed earlier, athletes aren't ones to shy away from crime or drugs. Say an addicted athlete burns through his ready cash buying drugs, but still craves more. Well, not only does the Mafia deal drugs, it books bets. How easy would it be for an athlete to throw a game or two to sustain his habit? Or what if an athlete already has a gambling problem, and needs a win to cover his losses? Think the bookie who is owed this money wouldn't be willing to let it all ride in trade on a sure thing involving said athlete? These types of scenarios can happen and have. How can I be so sure? A wise guy told me so.

Michael Franzese was one of the Mafia's biggest money earners since Al Capone. During his heyday as a captain with the Colombo crime family, Franzese claims to have been making $6–8 million a week. *Forbes* ranked him as number 18 in the top 50 mob bosses in 1986. A percentage of that came directly from his illegal gambling operations. Since leaving the mob, and after having spent seven years in prison with a supposed Mafia death warrant hanging over his head, Franzese now tours the country lecturing college and pro athletes on the dangers of gambling. So if anyone knows the true inner workings and connections between the Mafia, bookmakers, and athletes, it's him.

Franzese is well aware of how members of the mob are constantly looking for an edge. He nearly took advantage of one himself back in his Colombo days. As detailed in Chris Mortensen's 1991 book *Playing for Keeps*, Franzese helped finance a newly formed sports agency, giving $50,000 to Norby Walters to open up World Sports and Entertainment, Inc. in exchange for a 25 percent ownership in the firm. Walters had made a name for himself managing several leading black entertainment acts including Michael Jackson, Rick James, and Kool and the Gang. Now with Franzese's help, he attempted to become an agent for athletes. Walters had early success, signing the likes of future NFL players Cris Carter, Jerry Ball, Maurice Douglass, Ronnie Harmon, Mark Ingram, and Rod Woodson as clients. But Walters made a huge mistake in signing many of these players to agent deals prior to their becoming eligible. In the end, Franzese, already in prison after facing his own 28-count indictment, testified against Walters in the ensuing case regarding the agency. Walters was found guilty and convicted of mail fraud.

For his part in the agency, Franzese later saw the possibilities available to him. "There's no question in my mind had Norby been successful, and both my associates and I realized we had somewhat control over a number of major league ballplayers, that at some point in time we'd try and use this to our advantage....I mean, the mob lives to gamble. The mob is built upon it...almost everybody is a gambler. It's a major mob enterprise. I saw that as a tremendous possibility. Just establishing a line, throwing the bets the right way, making the bets tilt the right way. That would have been a tremendous advantage."[10] Franzese went on to tell Mortensen, "I think if he [Walters] had maintained control, he could've spoken to them, 'let's make some money this way.' There would have been things that if he wanted continued support from the family, which he always got, then he would have been obligated to deal."[11]

Several years later when Franzese was out of the mob, he appeared as a guest on the Jim Rome radio show in February 2006. Rome asked him what would happen should an athlete get in trouble with a bookie and can't pay. How exactly does an athlete get compromised? Franzese's response: "Well, it's real easy. If they're gambling with a bookmaker, you understand, and they lose money, I mean, they gotta pay. If they can't come up with the money some way, shape, or form, you explain to them, listen, if you're in a game, okay, and you have a meaningful position in that game, you're going to help us win. If you guys are favored by 10, you're gonna shave points. You're gonna win by seven. You're not gonna cover the spread. Get some of your teammates, tell them you're in deep trouble, and then do whatever you gotta do to help us out and we'll cover the debt in that way. The problem with that is normally they'll go along. They don't know what else to do. They're scared. But if they do it once, they're done. I mean, then they're gonna do it forever or until they're told to stop."[12]

Rome pressed him further on the matter. And the conversation became more enlightening.

Jim Rome: "When you were in the business, did you ever fix a game?"

Michael Franzese: "Yes. Well, when I say 'fix a game' we had an athlete compromise the outcome of a game. Yes. Absolutely."

Jim Rome: "Professional?"

Michael Franzese: "Professional and college."

Jim Rome: "They looked the other way or purposefully missed a shot or did something to lose a team a game?"

Michael Franzese: "Purposefully did something to compromise the outcome of a game. Yes."

Jim Rome: "It happens obviously, right, still?"

Michael Franzese: "Without a doubt."

Jim Rome: "How often?"

Michael Franzese: "Well, I gotta tell you, Jim. The NCAA, on a college level, there are recent studies showed that approximately one percent of 21,000 players admitted to being asked to compromise the outcome of a game because of a gambling debt. And I believe 2.3 percent admitted to actually compromising the outcome of a game because of a gambling debt. These are anonymous studies, but it's going on right now."

Jim Rome: "Not to be salacious, but did anybody ever tell you 'no' in that situation? Where you said 'you're going to make this right and you're going to fix that game?'"

Michael Franzese: "No. They have no choice. At that point, they're going to do it or they're going to pay."

A few moments later, they progressed to this point in the conversation:

Jim Rome: "How many times were you involved in fixing a game?"

Michael Franzese: "Several times."

Jim Rome: "How do we know what we see is legitimate?"

Michael Franzese: "Well, you don't know for sure. And I tell people, look, you can't assume that every bad call or every game that doesn't go your way is fixed."[13]

However, when Jim Rome asked him whether the fix could be in on a big game such as a Super Bowl and when bad calls seem to be obviously made, if someone could've gotten to "those guys" in that game, Franzese had this answer: "Jim, nobody is immune. I mean, I'll be honest with you. Because of my experience in the street, whenever I see a call that's, you know, outrageous, I'm cynical immediately. I'm cynical all the time, but that's based upon my experience…the leagues know no one's immune to this."[14]

Of course the leagues know no one is immune to the lure of gambling and fixing games. Sports history is littered with tales of game fixing and point shaving. What follows is the litany of gambling athletes, rumors of point shaving, and true fixes that have occurred over the years in professional sports, presented in chronological order.

1865 – On September 28th of that year, three members of the New York Mutuals—shortstop Thomas Devyr, third baseman Ed Duffy, and catcher William Wansley—all agreed to accept $100 to throw that day's game against the Brooklyn Eckfords. The Mutuals lost 23–11 (or 28–10 depending on your source). Wansley was charged with six passed balls in the game. All three were subsequently banished from baseball; however, in keeping with baseball tradition, all three were allowed back into the game by 1870.

1877 – Just one year into its existence, the National League faced a gambling scandal. Three members of the Louisville Grays accepted bribes ranging from $10 to $150 from a New York City gambler to throw games at the end of the season. The games they intentionally lost cost the team the pennant as they dropped from first to second behind the Boston Red Caps. Newspaper owner and team president Charles Chase smelled a rat. An investigation into the matter revealed that infielder Al Nichols had received telegrams regarding the fixes. Nichols, outfielder George Hall, and pitcher Jim Devlin all admitted to being in on the scheme. Subsequently,

National League president William Hulbert banished the three players for life. However, it was claimed by the three that they only took the bribes because the team had failed to pay their salaries. Shortstop Bill Craver was also banned along with the other three for failure to cooperate with the investigation. It's not known if he was involved with the others or not. The next season, the Louisville Grays disbanded.

1882 – Richard Higham was a former player and manager before he turned to umpiring in 1881. When too many calls seemingly went against the NL's Detroit Wolverines in 1882, team owner (and mayor of Detroit) William Thompson became suspicious of Higham. Thompson hired an investigator who discovered letters written from Higham to a gambler informing him when to bet against Detroit. The NL owners agreed on the situation and forever banned Higham from the game.

1903 – Baseball's first World Series. Along with it came rumors of its attempted fixing. Twenty years after the Series had taken place, Boston Red Sox catcher Lou Criger, believing he was on his deathbed, confessed to American League president Ban Johnson in 1923 that he was approached by a gambler before the Series and offered $12,000 to throw it. Criger made three errors during the course of the eight-game Series that Boston eventually won five games to three. Criger went on to live another 11 years after his deathbed confession.

1905 – Pitcher George "Rube" Waddell very well may have been mentally handicapped. Easily distracted with stuffed animals and shiny objects, Waddell was also known to love fire engines and would literally run from the field to chase one if he heard it drive past the stadium. Waddell had a great season in 1905 going 26–11 with a 1.48 Earned Run Average (ERA) for the Philadelphia Athletics. They were set to face off against the New York Giants when a group of gamblers offered Rube $17,000 to sit out the series. Waddell indeed did not pitch in the World Series, claiming he tripped over some luggage at the train station injuring his arm just prior to the Series' start. Without Waddell, the Athletics lost the Series four games to one. Waddell was subsequently suckered out of the $17,000, receiving maybe only $500 of the total. He was inducted into the Hall of Fame in 1946.

John McGraw, a future Hall of Famer himself, was the manager of the Giants in that 1905 World Series. McGraw reportedly placed and collected a $400 wager on his own team against the Athletics. It wasn't the first time he'd done that. McGraw was arrested in 1904 for unsolicited public gambling. McGraw was never disciplined for either transgression.

1908 – Philadelphia Phillies weak-hitting catcher Charles "Red" Dooin alleged that three unnamed pitchers on the team had been offered $150,000 by gamblers to throw the last seven games of the season against the New York Giants in hopes of giving the Giants the 1908 pennant. The pitchers refused. Dooin himself was then approached with a similar offer. He, too, refused. The Phillies managed to win enough games against the Giants to force the Giants into a tie-breaking game against the Chicago Cubs to determine who would win the pennant.

The umpire for that fateful playoff game between the Cubs and Giants was Bill Klem. Before walking out onto the field for the game, the Giants' team doctor Joseph Creamer offered Klem a deal which would keep him "set for life" if the Giants won. Creamer even forced $2,500 into Klem's hand. He refused the generous offer. The Cubs wound up winning the game (well, not exactly *that* game), thanks mainly to the immortal play of one Fred "Bonehead" Merkle for the Giants. With the game tied, the Giants had a runner on third while Merkle sat at first. A base hit knocked in the winning run, but Merkle never reached second base. In the ensuing craziness of the Giants' apparent win, Cubs second baseman Johnny Evers got the ball back (that is *a* ball, maybe not *the* ball) and tagged Merkle out. The game was ruled a tie, thanks in part to Klem calling Merkle out. (Was the call made to counter Creamer's offer?) Another playoff game the following day resulted in the Cubs winning their only world championship ever. Creamer was banished from baseball in 1909.

1908 – Hal Chase was known as one of the best first basemen in baseball. Two baseball immortals, Walter Johnson and Babe Ruth, agreed with that assessment. Yet for all the praise lavished on Chase for his glove work, he led the league in errors seven times, committing a grand total of 402 in a little over 1,800 games played. Of course, this very well may have had something to do with Chase's career-long love of fixing ball games.

Chase's scandalous career may have had just as much of a hand in the rise of an overlording baseball commissioner as the 1919 Black Sox.

Chase was first accused by his New York Highlanders manager of fixing games in 1908. Highlander management didn't look too closely into the accusations because Chase was their marquee attraction. Instead, a new manager was hired. Chase felt the job was rightfully his and he (most likely) laid down in a few games to get his new skipper fired. The ruse worked. Even though the Highlanders finished in second place in 1910, Chase was named player-manager in 1911. The team plummeted to sixth place in Chase's sole year at the helm. In 1913, the Highlanders changed their name to the Yankees and ex-Cub Frank Chance was brought in to manage. Chance, too, felt Chase was throwing ball games, and brought it to the attention of Yankees management. Apparently they had had enough of Chase's shenanigans and traded Chase to the Chicago White Sox. But Chase opted to jump to the rival Federal League and play in Buffalo for the Buffeds. There, he led the league in home runs. However, after the 1915 season, the Federal League collapsed. In 1916 Chase couldn't find an American League team that would take him, so he jumped to the National League and joined the Cincinnati Reds. Chase kept out of trouble until the stout Christ Mathewson became his manager in 1918. Mathewson didn't take kindly to gamblers, and when one of the Reds' pitchers told Mathewson that Chase had tried to bribe him into throwing a game, Mathewson suspended Chase for the last part of the 1918 season. Chase was then shipped from the Reds to the New York Giants in 1919. There, he recruited third baseman Heinie Zimmerman to help throw ballgames and bribe other players into doing likewise.

Through all those years of accusations including rumors that Chase was *doubling* his baseball salary by throwing games, not a shred of evidence ever got him into hot water. That is, until a check in Chase's name for the amount of $500 from a known Boston gambler came to light in 1919. Finally armed with something substantial, National League president John Heydler banned the 38-year-old Chase from the game for life. Heinie Zimmerman was also shown the door for his cooperation with Chase.

1912 – One of the most obviously fixed games that received little attention was Game Seven of the 1912 World Series. The Boston Red Sox led the New York Giants three games to two with their ace due to pitch Game Seven (Game Two was called due to darkness and ruled a tie after 11 innings). Set to clinch the Series at home in Fenway Park that day, the Red Sox sent their ace "Smoky" Joe Wood, who posted a 34–5 record that season, to the mound. He lasted an inning. Wood lobbed in pitches and gave up a quick six runs on seven hits. Wood even pitched out of a full windup with runners on base, allowing the Giants to pull off an easy double steal. But Wood wasn't alone in the fix. Hall of Fame outfielder Tris Speaker was in on the con as well. Wood threw an errant pickoff throw to second base into center field, and somehow the ball managed to get past Speaker in center. The right fielder had to track the ball down while Giants runners circled the bases. The Red Sox lost the game 11-4.

1919–1921 – There are a few interesting things to know about the 1919 fix of the World Series. First, even though the White Sox were heavy betting favorites to win, the Cincinnati Reds had a better record (96–44) than the Chicago White Sox (88–52). Second, in truth, the White Sox as a team weren't *that* underpaid when compared to other players and teams of that era. What stood out was owner Charles Comiskey's "fat cat" nature. He made it clear to his players that not only did he own them like farm animals, (which was true thanks to baseball's reserve clause which contractually bound players to teams for life prior to the advent of free agency in the 1970s) but that he was and would always be much richer than any of them could dream of becoming. Third, the fix was an open secret among other ball players, as several bet on the Series, with the aforementioned Hal Chase winning a reported $40,000 on the eventual outcome. Fourth, through the course of the Series, the Reds as a team committed as many fielding errors as the White Sox did, leaving a few to think that players on the Reds also attempted to fix at least a game or two, if not the entire Series themselves. And finally, had the players of the White Sox really needed the money that badly, they could've just gone out and won the damn thing without all the controversy. The winner's share was $5,000 apiece—more than what most of the crooked players earned for their part in the fix.

The 1919 World Series is an excellent case to study and recommended to those who don't believe gambling conspiracies can happen. Eliot Asinof's *Eight Men Out* chronicles all the sordid details. Besides the eight White Sox players—"Shoeless" Joe Jackson, Buck Weaver, "Lefty" Williams, Ed Cicotte, Chick Gandil, "Happy" Felsch, Swede Risberg, and Fred McMullin—at least nine others outside baseball contributed to setting up the fix. Also, Comiskey and both league presidents were made aware of the potential existence of the fix immediately following the end of the first game. Even armed with this damning information in the midst of the Series itself, baseball didn't get around to investigating the matter until nearly a year after the Series was over.

The strange part is how the Black Sox fix eventually came to light. In August 1920, a Kansas City gambler by the name of Frog Thompson received a telegram from a Chicago Cubs pitcher Claude Hendrix telling Frog to bet $5,000 on the Cubs' opponent that day, the last-place Phillies. At the same time, another telegram (from a different source than Frog's) arrived for Chicago Cubs president William Veeck, Sr. detailing the possibility that day's game against the Phillies was being rigged. It was followed by five more telegrams relating the same information. The Cubs altered their pitching rotation, benching Hendrix in favor of their best pitcher, Grover Cleveland Alexander. The Cubs still dropped the game to the Phillies 3–0.

But the alert flags had been raised. Frog's telegram eventually wound up on the desk of sportswriter Otto Floto. Floto published a story detailing baseball's gambling issues based in part on Frog's telegram. Soon afterwards, as rumors and innuendo swirled, Chicago sportswriter Hugh Fullerton further broke the story in the *New York World*. Why was a Chicago sportswriter published in a New York newspaper? Because Fullerton's employers at the *Chicago Herald and Examiner* refused to run his story on the alleged fix of the 1919 Series. The thought was that Fullerton wrote the anti-White Sox story simply because he had predicted them to win and wanted to save his own reputation. With these and other stories circulating nationwide, an actual investigation into baseball's gambling problem finally began.

In September of 1920, a grand jury convened to look into the allegations behind the Cubs-Phillies game in question—not the 1919 World Series. The grand jury took testimony from owners, managers, and players regarding gambling in baseball. Somehow during the grand jury's questioning, the whole scheme behind the White Sox fix unexpectedly spilled out for the world to hear. White Sox pitcher Ed Cicotte confessed to taking the $10,000 bribe to throw games, and "Shoeless" Joe Jackson signed a confession admitting to taking part as well. (For all you apologists out there, Jackson did indeed pocket $5,000 to participate in the fix.) Suddenly all focus shifted away from the Cubs-Phillies game to the previous year's World Series, and eight of the White Sox found themselves indicted.

Meanwhile, out on the playing field, those same White Sox—led by seven of the indicted eight from the previous year (Chick Gandil retired after the 1919 season, perhaps thanks to the extra $35,000 he pocketed from the fix)—were again winning the American League pennant. Under intense scrutiny and pressure, Comiskey finally took a belatedly hard stand and suspended those players until their names were cleared. The White Sox lost the 1920 pennant by just two games to the Indians.

It was not until July of 1921 that the eight White Sox players stood trial. Amazingly, the players' signed confessions disappeared from the Illinois state attorney's office in the midst of the trial. It was rumored that gambler Arnold Rothstein (the mastermind behind the fix) paid $10,000 for the written confessions to disappear. Later, under oath, these same players claimed that they never signed such a confession. Also surprising is that the players' defense was funded by none other than Charles Comiskey himself. Why would Comiskey do such a thing? In the ensuing attempt to clean up the game since the scandal erupted, the owners hired a commissioner to rule over the game, with his judgments being absolute and final. The newly appointed Kenesaw Mountain Landis promptly placed all eight White Sox on the ineligible list. Therefore, Comiskey stood to lose nearly his entire team if the eight White Sox were convicted.

During the trial, Comiskey must have wondered what he got himself into. Part of the defense's argument was that the players never signed a contract that obligated them to attempt to actually *win* ballgames, but just to show up and play (which, sadly, is as true then as it is today). The jurors were then instructed to find the players guilty not only if they threw ballgames, but if they had attempted to defraud the public in the process.

The jurors took a whole two hours to find the eight White Sox not guilty. The jurors then proceeded to carry the players around the courtroom on their shoulders. However, Commissioner Landis cut the celebration short two days later as he banned the eight White Sox from baseball for life with the words, "They can't come back. The doors are closed to them for good. The most scandalous chapter in the game's history is closed." Landis went further with his ruling, basically spelling out baseball's current anti-gambling rule, "No player who throws a ball game, no player that undertakes or promises to throw a ball game, no player that sits in confidence with a bunch of crooked players and gamblers where the ways and means of throwing a ball game are discussed and does not promptly tell his club about it, will ever play professional baseball."

Not forgotten in this whole mess was Claude Hendrix, the Cubs pitcher whose foolish telegram launched the whole affair off the ground. Hendrix was released by the Cubs after the 1920 season, and as a result of the ensuing investigation both he and another Cubs pitcher, Paul Carter, were found to have been involved in fixing games during that 1920 season. Commissioner Landis banned them for life as well.

As harshly as Landis came down on the eight White Sox and two Cubs, he looked the other way when another gambling scandal took place in 1919. This one involved two of baseball's legends, Ty Cobb and Tris Speaker.

The story didn't surface until some years later, when a former teammate of Cobb's sought revenge against the Georgia Peach. "Dutch" Leonard was a pitcher for Cobb's Detroit Tigers in 1919. Late in the season, the Tigers were set to face the second-place Cleveland Indians in what seemed to be a meaningless game. Yet, if the Tigers won, they would finish third, giving all their players a $500 salary boost. So player-manager Cobb and Leonard met with player-manager Tris Speaker and pitcher "Smoky" Joe Wood of the Indians (who were former teammates on the Red Sox in 1912 when they allegedly threw Game Seven of the World Series) under the stands in Detroit to work out a deal. The four agreed to throw the game in the Tigers' favor, plus put some money down on the game with a gambler to boot. Indeed, the Tigers triumphed over the Indians that day

9–5. After the season ended, the players sent each other letters to settle up the agreement that was reached before the game.

In ensuing years, Leonard came to despise Cobb. To seek some measure of revenge against him, in 1926, Leonard attempted to sell the letters regarding the final payouts from the fix to the press. He found no takers. So he took the letters to AL president Ban Johnson. Johnson, not wanting to cause another gambling scandal, met with Speaker and Cobb confidentially and convinced them both to "retire" from their player-manager positions. In exchange, the whole thing would be forgotten. The two agreed and stepped down, thinking that was the end of that. But it wasn't.

Commissioner Landis got wind of the whole affair. Since as commissioner he felt he ruled over Johnson and should've been consulted in the matter, Landis brought Leonard's accusations to the press, publicly opening up the whole affair. Johnson quickly changed his mild-mannered tune and announced that both Cobb and Speaker would never return to the American League because of their actions. Needless to say, this didn't sit well with Cobb or Speaker. They had been betrayed, and now had to deal with Commissioner Landis.

Landis held a hearing on the matter in which everyone—Cobb, Speaker, and Wood—admitted to nothing. Armed with only the seething words of Leonard and the letters, Landis then sat on his final ruling for two months. Why so long? It was because Cobb threatened to really blow the lid off of gambling in baseball if Landis decided to banish him from the game. Knowing Cobb was a vengeful prick and knowledgeable enough to do so, Landis safely ruled that Cobb, Speaker, and Wood were not guilty of gambling on or fixing a ballgame. As perhaps an added slap to baseball's face, both Cobb and Speaker then returned to the field for the 1927 and 1928 seasons. After retiring, neither was offered another job in baseball.

Remarkably, even with baseball's hard and fast anti-gambling rule now in place, trouble was still brewing out on the diamond throughout the 1920s.

1921 – New York Yankees pitcher Carl Mays is best known for having killed the Cleveland Indians Ray Chapman with a fastball to the head in 1920—the only player death to have occurred in a major league game. While Mays is often remembered for that, few recall that Mays might have fixed a few World Series games in the early 1920s. While the top pitcher for the rising 1920s Yankees dynasty, Mays' reputation came into question during the 1921 World Series. In Game Four, he blew an eighth-inning shutout, as well as the game, 4–2 to the rival New York Giants. Then Mays dropped Game Seven by the score of 2–1 (even though only one of the Giants' runs were earned and Mays failed to walk a batter). New York sports reporter Fred Lieb got wind that Mays may have dumped Game Four, taking the complaint all the way up to Commissioner Landis' office. The resulting investigation turned up nothing of note. In the 1922 World Series, again against the New York Giants, Mays took the hill only once and lost 4–3 in Game Four. Perhaps even Yankees officials were themselves beginning to wonder about Mays as in 1923, though healthy, Mays didn't make a single appearance in the 1923 World Series. After the season, Mays was cut by the Yankees only to be picked up by the Reds where he posted a 20–9 record in 1924. No solid evidence outside of Lieb's story ever came to light regarding Mays tanking games.

1922 – Just as the Yankees may have had their issues with pitcher Carl Mays, their crosstown rivals the Giants soon found that they had their fill of pitcher Phil Douglas. "Shufflin' Phil" was a decent pitcher but an even better drunk. However, in 1922, he had managed to stitch together an 11–3 record before his career went drastically south. After dropping a game to bring his record to 11–4, Douglas took the loss personally and went out on a bender, disappearing for several days to both his wife's and his team's dismay. Giants' detectives finally located Douglas and relegated him to a sanitarium to dry out. Once sober(ish) and free to go, Douglas wasn't happy to find that the Giants had sent him a bill to cover his stay in the hospital. On top of that, the team had fined him for missing so many games. Douglas fired off a letter to St. Louis Cardinals outfielder Leslie Mann saying with the right encouragement, he'd disappear again, thus hurting his team while helping the then second-place Cardinals beat the Giants out for the pennant. Mann, for his part, apparently didn't find Douglas' offer too appealing and turned the letter over to the commissioner. It only took a short time for Commissioner Landis to give Shufflin' Phil the old heave-ho out of baseball for good.

1924 – Prior to that day's game, Jimmy O'Connell of the New York Giants sauntered up to Philadelphia Phillies shortstop Heinie Sand to offer him a $500 bribe to go easy on the Giants. The Giants needed the win to stay atop Brooklyn for the NL pennant, and O'Connell thought $500 was enough to buy Sand's loyalty, if for only nine innings. Sand refused the offer and went to manager Art Fletcher with the story. Fletcher in turn went to the commissioner. Soon, O'Connell found himself in hot water and promptly started pointing fingers at one of his coaches, Cozy Dolan, as well as teammates Frankie Frisch, George Kelly, and Ross Youngs whom O'Connell claimed were all in cahoots together in offering Sand the $500 payoff. Upon hearing all the evidence (including Dolan's persistent answer of "I don't remember" to every question asked of him) and just prior to the start of the 1924 World Series between the Giants and the Washington Senators, Landis banned both O'Connell and coach Dolan from the game for life. The Giants went on to lose the Series to the Senators four games to three.

1927 – Rogers "Rajah" Hornsby posted a lifetime .358 batting average by collecting more hits in his career than games played, but he was also a notorious horse race enthusiast. Apparently, Hornsby liked to play the ponies, but he wasn't one for ponying up the cash when his horse didn't come in the money. In 1927, a gambler sued Hornsby for not paying the nearly $100,000 owed from horse racing wagers. The gambler lost the suit, but Hornsby lost his job with the New York Giants. He was shipped to Boston for a season, then on to the Chicago Cubs for a couple, then back to the St. Louis Cardinals for one, and finally on to the St. Louis Browns where he finished up his career. So why did the Hall of Famer get shipped to five different teams in ten years? Hornsby couldn't stay away from the track. And while there was no rule preventing him from betting on the horses, teams and even the commissioner worried that Hornsby was gambling on more than just horses. Though no evidence ever surfaced of Hornsby betting on baseball, the fear that he may have kept him constantly on the move for the last half of his career.

1940 – Another legendary Hall of Fame member, "Joltin' Joe" DiMaggio may have had some unsavory gambling connections. Prior to the days of sports agents, players were mostly on their own to work out their contracts.

When DiMaggio's came up in 1940, he decided to talk to Joe Gould about the negotiatio ns. The problem was, at least for baseball and the then paranoid Commissioner Landis, Gould was a boxing manager who was also well-known as a baseball gambler. Whether Landis was more concerned about Gould's gambling history or DiMaggio's attempt to acquire an agent, no one can say, but the investigation into DiMaggio's connections to Gould went away as soon as the commissioner's office learned that Gould wasn't about to get a cut of DiMaggio's salary.

Though Joltin' Joe reveled in his clean and wholesome image, perhaps it was more of a façade than reality. Joe's celebrity status and New York baseball roots brought him into contact with many disreputable men of the "goodfella" sort. After his playing days ended, the FBI interviewed DiMaggio regarding his connections with Albert "The Mad Hatter" Anastasia, a member of the Mafia's "Murder, Inc." DiMaggio claimed he was just introduced to Anastasia a mere two weeks before Anastasia was shot to death in a barbershop. But during that FBI interview, DiMaggio admitted to befriending two well-known gamblers including one who was a partner of mob boss Santo Trafficante. This gambler, Joseph Silesi, offered DiMaggio a chance to front a Cuban gambling operation, but DiMaggio told the FBI he turned the job offer down because he didn't want it to tarnish his image with the youth of the nation.

1920–1950 – At the time of the Black Sox scandal, the small four- to six-team version of the NHL was the only other established major sports league in existence. The NBA wasn't created yet, and the NFL was in its infancy. With baseball's new anti-gambling rules attached to Commissioner Landis's heavy-handed dictatorship over the game, MLB seemed to keep its nose clean of gambling scandals throughout the 1930s. Yet, it's not as if gamblers stopped betting and avoided sports. In fact, many gamblers "legitimized" themselves through sports—as NFL team owners.

The NHL is not often viewed as a gambler's sport, yet its early ownership built the league with gambling revenues. The Norris family, whose patriarch James, Sr. owned the Detroit Red Wings while son James, Jr. owned the Chicago Blackhawks, was investigated by the U.S. Senate in the 1950s for their ties to several Mafia dons, particularly Frankie Carbo.

In 1925 the New York Americans were purchased by "Big" Bill Dwyer, a mobster and bootlegger.

Conn Smythe built the Toronto Maple Leafs franchise, along with the Maple Leaf Gardens arena, out of his racetrack winnings. Smythe's understudy was Frank Selke who shared not just his boss' love of gambling but later became the kingpin of the Montreal Canadiens dynasty in the 1950s. The Canadiens, too, saw its ownership evolve from gambling money. In the 1920s through the mid-1930s, the three men who owned the team— Leo Dandurand, Joe Cattarinch, and Louis Letourneau—also owned a casino in Cleveland, OH and were frequent visitors at area racetracks.

While some of its history is ignored by the NHL, many of these names are not forgotten within the league. At the end of each season, the NHL awards its players trophies emblazoned with the names of James Norris (best defenseman), Conn Smythe (playoff MVP), and Frank Selke (best defensive forward).

A pertinent fact the NFL blatantly overlooks as part of its historical development is that several of its early team owners were well-known gamblers. The New York Giants' original owner Tim Mara (whose family still owns the team) had a history as a bookmaker before and even during his ownership of the team. He wasn't alone.

Another original owner whose family still has control of its franchise, Charles Bidwell bought the Chicago Cardinals (now the Arizona Cardinals) after relinquishing his share in George Halas' Chicago Bears. Bidwell was not just a gambler and a racetrack owner; he was a known associate of Al Capone (they shared the same lawyer, Ed O'Hare) and a bootlegger.

Beloved Pittsburgh Steelers owner Art Rooney, Sr. was another big-time gambler who reportedly won over $250,000 over a two-day span at the racetrack. Rooney would also own pieces in several horse and dog racing tracks and reportedly hired head coach Joe Bach to work off a gambling debt he couldn't immediately pay off.

George "Dick" Richards was known to be a heavy gambler outside of his car dealership when he purchased an NFL team, moving them to Detroit to become the Lions. In letters he had foolishly written, Richards detailed how he bet on his own team's games, including upwards of $50,000 on a single contest prior to selling the Lions in 1940.

DeBenneville "Bert" Bell was another heavy gambler with known Mafia friends when he purchased the Philadelphia Eagles in 1933. Bell would later serve as the NFL commissioner after World War II. Another Eagles owner, Leonard Tose, had a suit brought against him by his wife asking for control over the family's estate in part because of Tose's heavy gambling habits.

Mickey McBride was the sole owner of the Continental wire service which was widely used for bookmaking operations in the 1940s. Together with Paul Brown, the pair formed the Cleveland Browns. When McBride sold his portion of the team, it went directly to Saul Silberman, a gambler known to wager upwards of $2 million a year while he owned Tropical Park racetrack in Florida and another racetrack in Cleveland. Silberman would later sell out to Art Modell who was a well-known sports gambler in and around New York City at the time. Modell owned the team, now known as the Baltimore Ravens, up until 2004.

1943 – Slingin' Sammy Baugh is a Washington Redskins legend and a Hall of Fa me member. He also was perhaps the first NFL player to be investigated by the league for gambling and possibly throwing a game. At one point in the 1943 season, the Redskins were 6-0-1 having notched that lone tie against the "Steagles," a team comprised of half of each the Pittsburgh Steelers and the Philadelphia Eagles. When the two teams met a second time, the 4-3-1 Steagles dropped the Redskins 27–14 thanks in part to a Baugh interception and an attempted punt by Baugh that was blocked. After the game, two Washington sportswriters reported on rumors that members of the Redskins had fixed the game, causing Redskins owner George Marshall to respond, "Anyone connected with professional football who is gambling or has gambled on a game in our league should be thrown out immediately."[15] It was mighty bold talk for a former gambler. In fact, Marshall had only recently reformed his gambling ways upon moving the team from Boston to Washington, D.C. in the '30s. But he meant what he said as Marshall then offered up a $5,000 reward to anyone who could prove the allegations made in the article as true (no one—not even the reporters themselves—ever collected).

Despite Marshall's threatening words, he knew there were kernels of truth in the reported gambling story. Baugh was admittedly a known associate of Pete Gianaris. Gianaris was a convicted bookmaker and reportedly won big on the 4-to-1 underdog Steagles in the game in question. Also, Marshall himself secretly hired an investigator who recorded conversations between Baugh and bookmakers the very week the story broke in the newspaper. So did Baugh fix the game? NFL commissioner Elmer Layden and Marshall issued a joint statement declaring their investigation turned up nothing noteworthy. Baugh remained adamant that he never gambled or fixed a game in his life.

1943 – Not to be outdone by its growing rival the NFL, baseball, too, had a gambling scandal to deal with at the end of 1943. Only this one didn't involve a player. William Cox was the owner of the Philadelphia Phillies. Just one year after purchasing the team, Cox came under scrutiny after it was alleged that Cox had placed around 20 bets on the Phillies during the course of the 1943 season. Cox first claimed not to have made any bets on his Phillies. Then he claimed he didn't know gambling on baseball was against league rules. Then he found himself kicked out of the game for life by Commissioner Landis. It was never discovered if Cox ever made large wagers on his team, but even the $100 wagers he made were too much for baseball's liking.

Strange as it may seem, Cox wasn't the first Phillies owner to be stripped of his ownership and kicked out of baseball. That honor goes to Horace Fogel, who was a sportswriter for the *Sporting News* prior to his ownership of the Phillies from 1909–1912. Fogel felt the National League and its umpires were favoring the New York Giants and made his accusations public, claiming the 1912 pennant race was "crooked." He must not have felt the league and the umps were against his team, as the Phillies finished 30½ games back of the Giants. Either way, the league wouldn't stand for that sort of talk and ushered Fogel out of the game for good.

1946 – Just prior to the kickoff of the 1946 NFL Championship game between the Chicago Bears and New York Giants, New York district attorney Frank Hogan announced that there had been an attempt to fix the game. Hogan reported that during surveillance of gambler Alvin Paris, a wiretap revealed that Paris and three others had attempted to bribe Giants running back Merle Hapes and quarterback Frank Filchock. The offer made to both players was an immediate $2,500 payoff with another $2,000 wagered for each player on the game. Unfortunately for Hapes, only he was called by name on the wiretap, so commissioner Bert Bell ordered the Giants to bench only him for the game. As for his part, Filchock denied being approached and was subsequently allowed to play. That was too bad for Giants fans. Though he did throw two touchdown passes in the game, Filchock racked up six interceptions as the Bears went on to win 24–14. Filchock later admitted to being offered the bribe, but claimed he refused to take it. Commissioner Bell suspended Hapes and Filchock indefinitely immediately following the conviction of the four gamblers who attempted to bribe the Giants players. Both Hapes and Filchock went on to play in the Canadian Football League. Filchock would later return to American football as a coach with the AFL Denver Broncos in 1963.

1946 – The NHL's first gambling scandal hits. Walter "Babe" Pratt, a longtime member of the New York Rangers, had recently become a member of the Toronto Maple Leafs when he was caught gambling on hockey games. Luckily for Pratt, those weren't Maple Leaf games his money was on. Initially suspended for life, Pratt admitted his mistake and was reinstated in just 16 days. After this incident, the NHL decided to make gambling on hockey an illegal activity among its players. Despite being busted and banned for gambling, Pratt was inducted into the Hall of Fame in 1966.

1947 – Famed manager Leo Durocher's one-year banishment from baseball for consorting with gamblers was a little questionable. It was during his stint as manager of the Brooklyn Dodgers that Durocher apparently irked former senator and newly appointed baseball commissioner Albert "Happy" Chandler into action. One of Durocher's closest friends was actor George Raft who happened to be tight with mobster "Bugsy" Siegel as well as a few other underworld and gambling figures. Commissioner Chandler got wind of Durocher's acquaintances and sternly warned him to stay away from these shady characters, noting baseball's anti-gambling rules. Durocher did as instructed until he saw Yankees' co-owner Larry MacPhail hosting two known gamblers in his private box during a spring training game. Durocher pointed out the fact to both MacPhail and Commissioner Chandler, questioning why it was okay for MacPhail to do exactly as Durocher was instructed not to do. In turn, Chandler promptly held a hearing on the state of baseball and gambling, questioning several witnesses including Durocher. After the meeting, Chandler decided on just one thing—kicking Durocher out of baseball for "conduct detrimental to the game."

Durocher never gambled on a game, nor was he accused of it. Apparently, he just ran with the wrong crowd, although a team owner doing the same resulted in no punishment at all. It might have helped in MacPhail's favor that he was largely responsible for getting Chandler named commissioner. Durocher went on to manage for other teams into the 1970s. But his suspension for "gambling" most likely kept him from being inducted into the Hall of Fame. After his death, his will demanded that any posthumous induction into the Hall be denied.

1947–1948 – Despite "Babe" Pratt's bust just a year before, the NHL rooted out two more players gambling on hockey. However, this time, at least one of the players—Boston Bruins' Don Gallinger—was betting on the games in which he played.

Gallinger was caught red-handed. He associated with a Detroit area gambler and racketeer by the name of James Tamer. The police were well aware of Tamer's criminal background and had tapped Tamer's phone when they happened to record a conversation between the pair. During the call, Gallinger told Tamer "not to worry about the game tonight" because two key Bruins would be out and Gallinger "don't intend to do so good." Gallinger then told Tamer to bet $500 for him against the Bruins. Tamer promptly hung up and placed a call to New York City to make the bet. Less than a week later, Tamer was in police custody.

It was soon discovered that Tamer also had a tie to former Boston Bruins center Billy "The Kid" Taylor. Taylor had placed at least one $500 bet through Tamer, quite possibly on the same game Gallinger had given Tamer the skinny on. However, before that was discovered, Taylor was traded from Boston to the Rangers. New York didn't get much out of the deal. Taylor played two games for them, and then was banned for life for his gambling.

NHL president Clarence Campbell, who was both a Rhodes scholar and an ex-hockey referee, investigated the incident. He promptly announced, "Nobody fixed anything anywhere." An odd statement considering, after the seven-month investigation of Gallinger, it was discovered that he had placed several bets on Bruins games ranging from $250 to $1,000. In at least one of the games, he had bet against the Bruins, taking the Blackhawks to beat his team. Perhaps Campbell's saving grace on the game in question against the Blackhawks was that Gallinger scored a game-tying goal in that contest, and the Bruins went on to win, costing Gallinger his wager. Nonetheless, at the age of 22, Gallinger was suspended for life. Both players, however, had those lifetime bans lifted in 1970.

1951 – Though not a gambling incident that directly affected professional sports, the great college basketball point-shaving scandal that hit the front pages in 1951 merits mentioning.

It's interesting to note that even though the scandal didn't erupt until 1951, there was enough evidence to indicate that college basketball players in the New York City area had been participating in fixing games/point shaving back well into the 1930s. Yet no one did anything public or privately about the problem for 20 years. When the scandal did finally break, some 33 players—including several All-Americans and the 1951 "Sporting News Player of the Year" Sherman White—were implicated. Officials believed 80 or more games in 23 different cities had been fixed by 33 players from more than seven universities. It had a wide-ranging effect on the college game, perhaps most notably in ending the National Invitation Tournament's (NIT) prominence. Prior to the scandal, the NIT tournament received more coverage than the NCAA's Final Four tournament that now reigns over the month of March.

Two legendary coaches also found themselves in the center of the scandal. "Mr. Basketball" Nat Holman, a member of the Basketball Hall of Fame, was the head coach of one of the most heavily implicated teams, City College of New York, which had just pulled off the incredible feat of winning both the NIT and the NCAA basketball tournaments in 1950. Though seven of his players were ultimately charged in the case, Holman escaped any embarrassment by repeatedly claiming he knew nothing throughout his questioning. Makes you wonder how much "Mr. Basketball" really knew about the game if he couldn't tell over half his team was shaving points.

Another member of the Basketball Hall of Fame, legendary University of Kentucky coach Adolph Rupp also found himself in the middle of the scandal. Rupp's team included three of the accused, including Ralph Beard who had led the American men's basketball team to the gold medal in the 1948 Olympics. "At the time of the scandal, one of Rupp's closest friends was Ed Curd of Lexington who was a nationally recognized big-time gambler, handicapper, oddsmaker, and horse wire entrepreneur who spent time in federal prison for tax evasion."[16] The focus of the scandal was not on the coaches, just the players. Rupp, in trying to help his boys out, was quoted as saying, "The Chicago Black Sox threw ball games, but these kids only shaved points. My boys were the inexperienced victims of an unscrupulous syndicate."[17] Nonetheless, Rupp and University of Kentucky's men's team were barred from playing in the 1952–1953 season as a result of the gambling scandal.

In the end, only two college players served jail time. Most of the 33 players involved received either probation, suspended sentences, or were outright acquitted. A few were even allowed to enter the military to avoid jail time. The gamblers behind the scheme all served one to four years behind bars with the ringmaster, Salvatore Sollazzo, sentenced to 16 years in prison.

Two players, Ralph Beard and his UK teammate Alex Groza, managed to slip out of the NCAA and on to the courts of the NBA prior to the point-shaving investigations. Both suited up for the Indianapolis Olympians during the 1949–1950 and 1950–1951 seasons. As a result of their participation in the college basketball point-shaving ring, both Beard and Groza were suspended by the NBA for life. Just when the NBA thought it had eliminated a potential problem in Beard and Groza, a real gambling menace arrived on the court two years later.

1953 – Reportedly possessing a 175 IQ, Jack Molinas survived the 1951 investigations into college basketball's point shaving while playing as an All-American for the Ivy League's Columbia University. Yet Molinas was already waist-deep in fixing basketball games, dating back to his high school days. He graduated to the Fort Wayne Pistons of the NBA and as a rookie in the 1953–1954 season was named to the All-Star team. Molinas' love of the lifestyle and the easy money gambling brought led him to rig nearly half of the games in which he played. Caught betting with bookies in New York, the NBA wisely banned Molinas for life after just the one season in the league.

Out of the NBA, Molinas earned a law degree then went to work with all five of the main New York Mafia families as one of their leading bookmakers. In 1961, yet another large point-shaving scandal hit college basketball. Again, over 30 players were involved. Who was at the center of it? Jack Molinas, who personally fixed the outcome of over 40 games using a mixture of cash and prostitutes as bait for the greedy and gullible collegiate players. Among the careers ruined by Molinas, Connie Hawkins was the most promising to fall under Molinas' spell. Hawkins met Molinas just prior to his entering the University of Iowa. Regrettably for Hawkins, the connection to Molinas derailed his career before it even started. Hawkins never played a game for Iowa and was banned from the NBA even before he had an opportunity to sign with a team. Hawkins would star, yet languish, in the American Basketball Association (ABA) until a court ruling allowed him to join the NBA in 1969.

Meanwhile, Molinas was brash enough to serve as attorney for one of the implicated players in the 1961 scandal, Bowling Green's Billy Reed. Reed cut a deal and wore a wire while meeting with Molinas, with prosecutors hoping to ensnare Molinas for his role in the scandal. They got more than they bargained for. Molinas went so far as to instruct Reed how to lie to the grand jury. Caught red-handed, Molinas was eventually convicted of conspiracy, bribery, and subornation of perjury and given 10 to 15 years in prison. He served five before getting paroled. Back on the streets, Molinas hooked up with his Mafia buddies and got into producing pornography, but apparently Molinas was in a little too deep with the mob. In 1975, he was shot dead in his backyard.

1956–1960 – It's interesting to note that even the Pro Football Hall of Fame's website states that "there is no question [Bobby Layne] did not always subscribe to the general rules of team behavior."[18] What the website fails to mention is that one of those rules Layne broke was gambling on football, including perhaps fixing games. In an interview in the book *Interference*, Detroit-area gambler Donald "Dice" Dawson claimed, "It was Bobby Layne who was the bettor, who I bet for. I knew him better than my own brothers. And he did plenty. He'd be playing in his own game, and he'd be betting all over the board. He'd bet five, six, seven games on a Sunday."[19] Dawson claimed that Layne fixed games or shaved points in at least seven games that he knew of, but the total may have actually been higher.

That's not the only evidence against Layne. In the book *They Call It a Game* written by former Cleveland Browns player Bernie Parrish, he also relates the story of Layne potentially fixing games. Howard "Hopalong" Cassady was a former teammate of Layne's on the Lions and later of Parrish's with the Browns. He told Parrish that a 1956 game between Layne's Lions and the Chicago Bears was fixed. According to Cassady, Layne faked an injury in that December game, even though the loss cost the Lions the 1956 Western Division title to the Bears. Another likely fixed game was the meaningless 1958 All-Star game which Layne's West team lost to the East 28–21.

"Bobby gambled more than anyone who ever played football, period,"[20] stated legendary Green Bay Packer Paul Hornung in his book *Golden Boy*. That's a mighty bold statement coming from one of the few players ever to be suspended by the NFL for gambling (more on that in a moment). But Hornung backed up his claim with some proof. He wrote that in 1958, Layne had bet down on the Lions to cover the -3½-point spread against Hornung's Green Bay Packers. With the score tied late in the fourth quarter, Layne (who called his own plays) waved the kicker off the field and attempted to force the Lions into the end zone for the win—both on the scoreboard and over the spread. Layne overthrew a sure touchdown pass, and the game ended in a tie, costing Layne his wager.

Interesting to note is that Bobby Layne has a direct link to the NFL's publication of a weekly injury list. Rumor had it that the Lions shipped Layne off to the Pittsburgh Steelers midway through the 1958 season because of his gambling problems. It didn't seem to alter Layne's ways in the least. In a 1960 game against the Washington Redskins, Layne was up to his old antics as the signal caller for the Steelers. During the week leading up to kickoff, the line on the game dropped from Steelers -7 down to Steelers -1. Eventually with the funny shift in the line, bookmakers took the game off the boards. What caused the dramatic drop? A newspaper published a photograph of Layne holding his "injured" passing arm. Layne still played, but the game ended in a

27–27 tie. From that point onward, NFL teams were required to submit injury reports for their players, using the same "probable, questionable, doubtful, and out" delineations as they do today.

1958 – The 1958 NFL Championship game between the New York Giants and the Baltimore Colts has been called the greatest game ever played. This game, broadcast nationwide by NBC, perhaps did more for the rise of the league than any other single NFL game played. It featured 12 players and three coaches that later made their way into the football Hall of Fame including Johnny Unitas, Frank Gifford, and coaches Vince Lombardi and Tom Landry. The game was also the first-ever NFL game to go into sudden death overtime with the Colts beating the Giants 23–17 on a one-yard Alan Ameche run. That's what the NFL history books will tell you. Here's what went on behind the scenes.

The Colts were the favorites in the game, with the line set on them anywhere from -3½ points up to -5 or -5½. Earlier in the week, Colts owner Carroll Rosenbloom laid down $1 million on his Colts to win the game, perhaps confident in his boys' ability or perhaps just because he was a degenerate gambler. But Rosenbloom had more than just faith going into the game. He sent Colts staff assistant Bob Shaw to Yankee Stadium to spy on the Giants' workouts. He even guaranteed Shaw a "job for life" should he get caught during his subterfuge. Rosenbloom's confidence must've soared when game time finally arrived. The Giants didn't start their regular quarterback Charlie Conerly, instead using backup Don Heinrich supposedly to get a feel for what sort of defense the Colts were going to run (why Conerly couldn't do that remains a question). Then as the game wore on, Giants star running back Frank Gifford fumbled three times, leading to a 14–3 Colts lead at halftime.

These early gaffes and questionable decisions may have led one to think the Giants were attempting to shave points or throw the game themselves, yet they came roaring back in the second half and took the lead 17–14. Down three with just 2:20 left in the game, Rosenbloom must've been sweating bullets as the Colts started their final drive from their own 15-yard line. But thanks to the lethal combination of Unitas to Berry, the Colts quickly drove deep into Giants territory. A 20-yard field goal by Colts kicker Steve Myhra with just seven seconds left in regulation forced the game into the NFL's first-ever overtime.

The Giants won the game's second coin toss and elected to receive the opening overtime kickoff. They went nowhere, making it a quick three and out, and punted possession back to the Colts. Led by the great Johnny U, the Colts again marched straight down the field, driving 70-plus yards in just 10 plays. But here's the rub. As the ball sat first and goal on the Giants' eight-yard line, kicker Myhra—the one whose kick sent the game into overtime—wasn't called in to finish off the game. Supposedly Colts head coach Weeb Ewbank was too concerned that Myhra would miss the kick (something he had done once earlier in the game) and opted to push the ball into the end zone for the win. But Ewbank's memory must've been rather selective, forgetting that the Colts were stuffed four straight times from the Giants' four-yard line earlier in the third quarter. That series culminated with a five-yard loss on a fourth-and-one call. But perhaps something else influenced Ewbank's decision-making: the $1 million bet his boss had down for his team to cover the spread.

A field goal would have won the game, yet with the spread at -3½, Rosenbloom stood to lose his money. It's a good possibility that Rosenbloom sent word down to the sidelines ordering coach Ewbank to get six points or else. How? With the ball at the Giants' eight, a fan ran out onto the field, temporarily halting play. Rumors have since circulated that the "fan" was an employee of NBC sent out to stall the game because the network lost their camera feed at exactly that critical juncture in the game. For whatever reason that man ran onto the field, the pause gave Rosenbloom plenty of time to get word down to Coach Ewbank. When the game resumed, on first down fullback Alan Ameche ran for two yards. Then Unitas dangerously threw the ball to tight end Jim Mutscheller in the flat, gaining five more yards. Finally, on third and goal from the one, Ameche scored the game-winning and spread-covering touchdown.

What isn't in question is that Rosenbloom did indeed bet on the game. Investigator Dan Moldea found confirmation of it, both from legendary bookmaker Bobby Martin and an unnamed NFL official that told Moldea "[NFL commissioner] Bert Bell knew about the bet and had scolded Rosenbloom for his gambling activities."[21] The $1 million bet wasn't Rosenbloom's first. In fact, various sources have reported that Rosenbloom often bet heavily on football throughout the course of his ownership of the Colts. Sometimes for and sometimes against the team he owned. Rosenbloom would later trade (yes, trade) ownership of the Colts for the Los Angeles Rams. When the team moved to St. Louis and later won the Super Bowl in 1999, Rosenbloom's widowed wife, Georgia Frontere, still owned the franchise.

1963 – Just five years after what, on the surface, appeared to be the NFL's brightest moment, Alex Karras (that's Mongo for you *Blazing Saddles* fans) derailed it with an ill-timed comment. During an interview on *The Huntley-Brinkley Report* in January of 1963, Karras, then a defensive lineman for the Detroit Lions, was asked, "Have you ever bet on a game in which you were playing?" Karras responded, "Yes, I have."[22]

This incident was just the public face on an investigation that the NFL had tried to keep private for some time. During the 1962 season, both the NFL and law enforcement officials were investigating the entire Detroit Lions team as gambling rumors and accusations were flying. It seems more Lions players than just Karras were buddy-buddy with known gamblers and Mafia types, and many of them were openly placing bets on football. How bad was the gambling problem among the Lions at the time? It was alleged that many Lions players disliked quarterback Milt Plum simply because he didn't care about the point spread like their former quarterback Bobby Layne did. Plum played to win games, and would sit on the ball to ensure a win rather than drive the score up to cover the spread.

Yet the Lions weren't the only club being examined. Both the Chicago Bears and Green Bay Packers had problem players as well. For the Bears, George Halas' headache came in the form of running back Rick Casares. Casares often found his way out to Las Vegas to gamble legally, but he also had close ties to known Chicago gamblers. He also may have actually been Mafia don Santos Trafficante's godson. Casares was twice given polygraph tests regarding his gambling and ties to gamblers, managing to pass both.

The Packers' "Golden Boy" Paul Hornung was just as troublesome. Hornung loved living life in the fast lane. In doing so, he was often found in some unsavory company, including his buddy Rick Casares. Hornung's behavior raised enough eyebrows around the league to lead the NFL to follow him for about 10 months, and, according to Hornung, even tap his phone. This surveillance eventually led to a meeting with new NFL commissioner Pete Rozelle.

Around the time of Karras' foolish admission, Papa Bear George Halas told *The Chicago Tribune* that the NFL was investigating gambling accusations against a member of a Midwestern team—just one guy on one team. But that really wasn't the case. In fact, the NFL was actually looking into several players from the Bears *alone*, along with members of four other NFL franchises. What kind of investigation was Rozelle leading? It was one that kept everything very, very quiet.

Karras detailed a meeting between himself and Rozelle in his book *Even Big Guys Cry*. Just two weeks prior to the airdate of Karras' interview on *The Huntley-Brinkley Report* and literally just hours before kickoff of the Detroit Lions-Pittsburgh Steelers 1962 Playoff Bowl game (to determine which team came in third and fourth place, held a day after the NFL Championship game), Rozelle met with Karras in Miami. According to Karras, this was the exchange that took place between the two:

Rozelle asked, "Have you ever bet on league games?" Karras didn't answer, so Rozelle pressed on, "How many games have you bet on, Alex?"

Karras responded, "I don't know...a few."

Rozelle then asked him, "Did you bet on the championship game yesterday?"

Karras answered honestly. "Yeah, I bet on it."

This must've taken Rozelle back. He shook his head and told Karras, "You could be in a lot of trouble. There's an investigation going on."[23]

No kidding. Karras was already aware the FBI was looking into his connections with some "business associates" he'd made in Detroit. In the spring of 1963, Rozelle called upon Karras again, this time bringing him to New York City. But Rozelle purposefully didn't hold the meeting at league headquarters in an attempt to keep everything hush-hush. Rozelle, brought in to be commissioner based in part on his extensive public relations knowledge, knew even back in the early '60s how to handle the league's damage control. During this meeting, Rozelle asked Karras to take a lie detector test like Casares, implying that if he hadn't fixed any games, all would be forgiven. Karras refused.

Rozelle then moved on to interview Paul Hornung. Trying to intimidate Hornung a bit, Rozelle threatened to drag Hornung to Washington, D.C. to testify before a senate subcommittee that had convened to investigate gambling. Hornung promptly turned the threat around on Rozelle telling him, "If I go to Washington and raise my right hand, this whole league is in trouble."[24]

Rozelle didn't take too kindly to threats, especially when he was holding all the cards. On April 17, 1963 Rozelle acted. He suspended Alex Karras and Paul Hornung indefinitely. That actually cost each player just one full season. Also taken down by the league were five other Lions players—John Gordy, Gary Lowe, Joe Schmidt, Wayne Walker, and Sam Williams—who had bet on the 1962 championship game between the Green Bay Packers and New York Giants. They were each fined $2,000. The Detroit Lions organization was hit with a $4,000 penalty for minimizing information concerning the "undesirable associations" of their players as well as allowing unauthorized personnel on the sidelines during games. Rozelle also added that other unnamed players had been gambling on football (by playing parlay cards) and that those players had been reprimanded, but not fined. How many others? Who knows? But in the final report on the matter, Rozelle had the audacity to write, "There is no evidence that any NFL player has given less than his best in playing any game. There is no evidence that any player has ever bet against his own team."

For the Lions' part, the front office seemingly thought this was all a bit excessive. Though the *Detroit News* reported at the time that written into every player's contract was the phrase "players must not enter drinking or gambling resorts or associate with gamblers or other notorious characters," Lions team president and owner of the Ford Motor Company William Ford claimed in the same article that the phrase in the contract was "a pretty vague term to throw at people" and "things have been blown out of proportion."[25]

Today, Alex Karras denies he ever bet on football. In interview after interview, he claims he was "railroaded" and that his words on *The Huntley-Brinkley Report* were taken out of context. Yet, in his book, *Even*

Big Guys Cry, Karras wrote, "In the previous months (1962) on four or five occasions I had dug into my pocket and come up with a $50 bill to bet on the football games. I remember losing more times than I won."[26] Don't blame the guy. Football can be hell on the memory.

Paul Hornung seemed to have gotten away with more than anyone. In his rather mixed-up book *Golden Boy*, Hornung claimed to have never bet more than $800 on a game and never won more than $2,000 gambling during a season.[27] Yet in that same book, Hornung details how in 1960 he met up with Barry Shapiro, a "millionaire bachelor" whom he had known since college. After talking about the upcoming game Hornung and the Packers were playing against the San Francisco 49ers, Shapiro told him he'd put down $5,000 for Hornung on the game. The Packers were six-and-a-half-point favorites and won the game 13–0 with Hornung scoring all 13 points himself.[28] So, since Hornung didn't put the $5,000 down *himself*, that clears him of not personally betting more than $800 a game. Maybe 1960 was rough on the guy, so the $5,000 win didn't increase his profits beyond that $2,000 benchmark.

Hornung went on to write that later in life he told the likes of Joe Montana and Jerry Rice, "Hell, I had to gamble. That was the only way I could make any money."[29] During his playing days with Green Bay, Hornung, by his own admission, was making $100,000 as a spokesman for Chevrolet and another $75,000 doing the same for Marlboro cigarettes. He also endorsed other products including Jantzen leisure wear and various shaving products. So how hard up for cash was he?

Hornung even went as far as to implicate Rick Casares as a gambler, even though Casares weaseled his way through the NFL's investigation and got off scot-free. Hornung recounted the story of how he and Casares called a bet in from Los Angeles to an unnamed friend in Las Vegas on the 1959 All-Star game in which they were both playing, hoping the bet would cover the expenses they racked up at the hotel they were partying in during the week leading up to the game. Together, they won the game and the bet.[30] Hornung's story aside, Casares most likely was as guilty as Karras and Hornung for gambling on games. His was the first name to come up in the NFL's investigation and he admitted to befriending a known Chicago gambler. His saving grace may have only come in the form of Bears owner and head coach George Halas who, though suspicious of Casares at first, stood by him after both lie detector tests failed to turn up anything to the contrary.

But Casares clearly wasn't alone in getting away with gambling. There were the unnamed multitudes Rozelle had simply "reprimanded." And then there's Hornung who again graciously served up another former player as a gambler, this one a teammate. Though he never calls the player out by name, Hornung wrote that another member of the Packers gambled along with him, but "got away with it."[31] Of course Hornung can't really complain. Had he and Karras been members of the rival American Football League (AFL), both players would've been kicked out of the game for life. Written into the AFL's constitution was a rule strictly forbidding players from gambling on the game with the punishment for such behavior being banishment, something the NFL's rules did not state at the time. But despite Hornung's admission of guilt and the NFL's subsequent suspension, he was still inducted into the Hall of Fame in 1986.

1964–1969(?) – In 1973, Larry Merchant wrote a book titled *The National Football Lottery* detailing his own betting habits during the 1972 football season. In that book, he interviewed an unnamed NFL player who played in the league prior to the merger with the AFL. This player admitted to Merchant that he participated in fixing six or seven games during his career. Four or five of the fixed games were with his first team, where this player worked alongside both a running back and a cornerback who were also involved with him. The player personally bet anywhere from $350 to $1,000 on the fixed games. Then the player in question was traded. Working with another player on this new team, he again participated in a fix. When traded to a third team which was a "contender," the player stopped and focused on actually winning football games. Yet he related the story of a cornerback on this contending team who asked him if he knew where he could put $500 down on the opposition prior to a crucial game. His team lost that game, costing them the playoffs.

1966–1970 – The AFL's biggest gambling pariah, someone who would later infuriate the NFL as well after the leagues' merger, came in the form of Kansas City Chiefs quarterback Len Dawson. Dawson has been called by some as the most controversial man ever to play professional football.

If Dawson really did fix games may never be known. But he was associated with some of the gambling underworld's biggest names of the late 1960s.

One was Donald "Dice" Dawson (no relation) who, as previously mentioned, had been connected to Bobby Layne. Dice admitted to investigator Dan Moldea, "I was involved with players in at least 32 NFL games that were dumped or where points were shaved."[32] The second was Gil Beckley, one of the nation's leading bookmakers of the time, who was tied to the Kansas City Mafia (which may sound like small potatoes, but Kansas City was the central meeting point for most of the Midwestern crime families. As detailed in both the book and film *Casino*, Kansas City was also where the Mafia divvied up the money skimmed from the Las Vegas casinos they controlled). Beckley actually worked with the NFL at times, giving them inside information from the gambling world. At the same time, the FBI believed Beckley had been involved fixing the outcomes of several NFL games. The third was Jimmy "The Greek" Snyder. Snyder wasn't just some buffoon CBS hired years later to handicap football games on TV. He was a convicted bookmaker with his own shady ties to the Mafia.

For his part, Len Dawson didn't seem to do anything wrong. He was named an All-Pro in 1966, '67, '68, and '69. During those four years, the Chiefs posted a 43-12-1 record. Yet during this same period, several of the Chiefs games were taken off the boards by bookmakers. "According to FBI records, nearly 20 games played by the Kansas City Chiefs over a period of two and a half seasons, 1966–1968, were the targets of unnatural money. In a vast majority of these games, the side where the unnatural money turned up was the winner."[33] Games that weren't taken down by bookmakers tended to unfold oddly, including one game in 1968 where the Chiefs attempted a total of three passes and won, beating the Oakland Raiders 24–10. Consequently, the FBI opened a sports bribery investigation on the Chiefs, focusing mainly on Len Dawson.

Then in 1969, the Internal Revenue Service (IRS) opened an investigation into "Dice" Dawson during which Len Dawson's name inevitably turned up. Telephone records showed Dice had called not only Len Dawson, but Lions quarterback Bill Munson, Rams quarterback Karl

Sweetan, and other big-name NFL players. But to some of the investigators, this wasn't much of a surprise as Dice had contact with numerous players in every major sports league.

Rumors continued unabated that Dawson, defensive back Johnny Robinson and even head coach Hank Stram were in on the fixes. Head Las Vegas linesmaker Bobby Martin confirmed something fishy indeed was occurring in Kansas City. Larry Merchant wrote, "Martin said two or more players were involved in a point-shaving conspiracy. He said they had an acquaintance bet $1,500 for each of them against themselves."[34] With all these government investigations running concurrently, no one could pin down anything, including the suspicions about Len Dawson. However, the government was closing in on Dice. Jimmy The Greek, for his part, felt that Dice wasn't using Len to fix games directly, but was using the rumors surrounding him to manipulate the lines in an attempt to middle many of the games in question.[35] However, Dice might have been just a bit player in the whole scheme with Gil Beckley and the Kansas City mob actually running the show controlling the point spreads.

By the end of the 1969 season, the Chiefs were set to face the Minnesota Vikings in Super Bowl IV. The line for the game fluctuated wildly, starting with the Vikings -3 and moving up to the Vikings -9, which as history had proven wasn't too unusual for a Kansas City Chiefs game. Just prior to the Super Bowl, NBC was set to release the story of a Detroit grand jury that was prepared to convene regarding the investigation into Dice Dawson. The grand jury was ready to subpoena several NFL players including Len Dawson due to their relationship with Dice. To counter the claims, the NFL wrote up a statement for Dawson. Wisely, he signed it without quarrel. The following day at a press conference, Dawson read the statement in which he admitted to both knowing Dice Dawson and speaking to him on several occasions. Len then went out and quieted any critics by leading the Chiefs to a 23-7 win over the Vikings. Dawson was named the game's Most Valuable Player.

Perhaps the controversy surrounding Dawson finally put a little scare into him and his cronies. From Super Bowl IV onwards, gamblers and bookmakers would have no issues with Chiefs games. Dawson played another six seasons and was inducted into the Hall of Fame in 1987.

1966–1969 – Wilt "The Stilt" Chamberlain is known for scoring 100 points in a single basketball game as well as scoring with 20,000 women during his lifetime. Starting out as a member of the Harlem Globetrotters in 1958, Wilt played a historic and record-shattering 14 years in the NBA. Also, during the years in question, Wilt most likely gambled on basketball games.

Author Robert Cherry wrote in his 2004 book *Wilt: Larger Than Life*, "Because there is no evidence that he ever did so [gamble on basketball games], it was, and is, a calumny for the FBI or anyone else to say or speculate otherwise."[36] Wilt loved to gamble. On just about everything. This wasn't a secret as he often visited Las Vegas and was known to bet on horse races. One of Wilt's former teammates, Al Attles, wrote in his book *Tall Tales* a typical exchange Wilt and he would have. Once when the team plane was flying over a city, Wilt wanted to bet Attles on the population. Attles agreed to bet Wilt $2 on the number. Wilt wanted to lay down $2,000. Whether it was just childish bravado or a real wager, Attles wasn't sure, but it ended their conversation on the subject. Apparently Wilt was also fond of cheating. That was a truth even author Cherry reported (though he gently labeled it "deception"), writing "every one of Wilt's friends" acknowledged he cheated at cards and tennis. So I guess it was cool for Wilt to cheat, just as long as he was swindling his friends out of money. But for heaven's sake, he'd never consider doing such a thing on the basketball court, where he physically dominated, right? Wilt's sister Barbara Lewis was quoted in Cherry's book having said Wilt couldn't have bet on basketball because he was "way too honest" and had he gotten caught, it would've embarrassed the family too much. But Wilt's claim of sleeping with 20,000 women didn't damage the family's reputation at all, did it?

The fact is the FBI took a hard look at Wilt's gambling habits beginning in 1966. In his FBI file, the feds examined two Boston Celtics-Philadelphia 76ers games played in November of 1966. The first of the two games was taken off the boards after the line dropped two or three points based on an injury to Wilt's leg. He still took the court and played. Interestingly, both games that an unnamed FBI informant claimed Wilt gambled on with a bookie in New York resulted in losses for the big man, as the informant claimed Wilt bet on his own team. But the FBI was also looking at the gambling habits of an unnamed Boston Celtics player at the same time and in the same game. In actuality, neither the informant nor the Celtics player are unnamed, they are just both still redacted (blacked out). Later in that same month, the FBI looked at yet another 76ers game Wilt reportedly bet on, this time in a game against the Bulls. In the FBI report regarding this game, the FBI appeared to also be curious about the gambling habits of an unidentified Philadelphia Eagles player as well.

Skip ahead to 1968 and the feds were still keeping an eye on Wilt. In a February game against the Knicks, the 76ers not only lost big, but Wilt hurt his knee. After the game, he told reporters he wouldn't be able to play in the next game against the St. Louis Hawks. As a result, the 76ers were huge underdogs to the Hawks. But lo and behold, Wilt started the game and helped crush the Hawks by 20. Even the FBI reported this incident as "suspicious."

The FBI's final look into Wilt's gambling came during the 1969 NBA Finals when Wilt's L.A. Lakers matched up against the Celtics. The game of interest for the feds was Game Six in Boston. The line again moved a couple of points in Boston's favor supposedly based on Lakers star Jerry West's groin injury. The FBI received information that Wilt reportedly again bet on his Lakers, but they lost "by 12 or 13" according to the FBI (when in reality they lost by nine). It's interesting to note that the Lakers lost the Finals in Game Seven after Wilt injured his ankle, was taken out of the game, then desperately tried to re-enter the game, but Lakers coach Butch van Breda Kloff refused to let him back in. The Lakers lost by two. It seems odd that a Wilt Chamberlain injury seemed to crop up and play a role in all these instances.

The claim of the Chamberlain apologists is if the FBI was really on to something, why didn't they pursue it further? As the FBI wrote in its own 1966 report, "As you know, the fact that players bet on a game or games in which they are involved, does not itself constitute a violation of the Sports Bribery statute." In other words, the FBI couldn't care less if a player was betting; their only concern came if a player was being offered money or taking a dive to alter the outcome of a game. It's an important idea to remember in all of these reported gambling cases. Per the Federal Sports Bribery Act of 1964, gambling in and of itself wasn't a real issue for the feds, it was fixing games that was the crime. Because every report they had on Wilt claimed he was betting on his own team to win, they didn't care because he wasn't breaking the law (outside of gambling illegally, that is). What did the NBA think about it? In 2000, after Wilt's FBI files were made public, the NBA claimed they were never informed of such an investigation during his career nor did the league investigate Chamberlain itself.

1967-1968 – During a federal investigation, two former Washington Redskins—quarterback Ralph Guglielmi and defensive tackle Fran O'Brien—were called to testify before a grand jury regarding their affiliations with various D.C. Mafia/gambling figures. Five more NFL players including the Redskins' other quarterback Sonny Jurgensen were also to be subpoenaed, but suddenly the whole thing was squashed. Messing with football in the nation's capital just doesn't happen.

Though during this brief time frame a few Redskins games were taken off the boards by bookmakers due to suspicious betting, no one really wanted any questions asked about it. The NFL pulled some strings with their buddies in the Justice Department and was able to keep their players' names out of the whole ordeal. The mobsters that were the focus of the case eventually were convicted of racketeering charges, yet all of the NFL players associated with them conveniently avoided any public scrutiny.

1967-1970 – In 1968, Denny McLain put together one of the best pitching performances in the modern era of baseball, recording a 31-8 record with a 1.96 ERA for the Detroit Tigers. Yet the trouble for McLain and baseball started toward the end of the 1967 season. At that time, McLain invested about $6,000 in a bookmaking operation. He and his partners took bets on horse races and other sports, the lone exception being baseball. McLain was even brash enough to book bets right in the Tigers' clubhouse. Then a gambler won $46,000 on an $8,000 bet in a horse race. McLain and partners couldn't cover it. Though McLain denied it in his autobiography, the jilted gambler went to a Detroit area Mafia enforcer who convinced McLain to pay up by crushing two of his toes. To explain away the injury, McLain offered up three alternate stories to the press. He kicked his locker after a bad outing, stubbed his toes while watching TV, or injured himself chasing raccoons. The truth of the matter aside, he missed a chunk of the 1967 season with the injured toes.

McLain made his return to the mound on the last day of the 1967 season, taking the hill in a must-win game that would've propelled the Tigers into the post season. McLain didn't make it through the third inning, dropping the game to the Angels and costing the Tigers the pennant to the Red Sox. In a 1970 *Sports Illustrated* article, it was reported that the Mafia enforcer's brother had bet heavily against the Tigers in that game. (Also, McLain never had to pay off the $46,000 as the gambler in question died in a single-car accident prior to pocketing his winnings.)

Major League Baseball, as usual, was slow to react. In fact, they didn't seem to know anything about McLain's activities until the *Sports Illustrated* article hit the newsstands in February 1970. Only then did MLB suspend McLain. But despite being suspended for his gambling activities, McLain wasn't banished for life or even a season. After just three months, he was back on the hill for the Tigers, posting a weak 3–5 record. After several odd incidents that included dumping a bucket of ice water on two reporters and carrying a gun onto a plane, MLB commissioner Bowie Kuhn suspended McLain for the rest of the 1970 season. And thus began his downward spiral. Reinstated, McLain returned in 1971 on the Senators but was horrible, losing 22 games. He somehow secured a pitching gig in 1972 with the A's, then moved to the Braves later in the season which wound up being McLain's last. From there, McLain declared bankruptcy, was busted for carrying cocaine, and subsequently sentenced to 23 years in prison.

1970 – Remember Len Dawson's acquaintance Don "Dice" Dawson? After Len snuck his way out of trouble with the feds and the NFL, Dice still had to face the music. Another sports figure's name cropped up in that investigation, Jay "Dizzy" Dean, the St. Louis Cardinals' Hall of Fame pitcher. It appeared that Dizzy had a friend by the name of Howard Sober who was a high–stakes gambler and an associate of Dice Dawson. For his part, Dizzy would eventually be named as an unindicted co-conspirator, meaning the grand jury felt Dizzy was involved, yet not enough evidence existed to nail him to the wall. Meanwhile, Dice, Sober, and eight others were sent to jail.

While this occurred over 20 years after Dizzy's playing days, it is worth mentioning because he had been examined previously by baseball for gambling well before this incident. Just a year out of the game, Dizzy was called before

MLB Commissioner Chandler in 1948. Rumors of his gambling were rampant, so Dizzy had to confess to Chandler that he was indeed gambling, but of course, not on baseball. When it was brought up that he had contacted bookmakers asking for odds on baseball games, Dizzy claimed he did that for "friends" in Texas who I guess were incapable of picking up a phone themselves. Dizzy was given a free pass to the Hall of Fame in 1953.

1977 – The Miami Dolphins found themselves in hot water when it was revealed that "team booster" J. Lance Cooper had been arrested and charged along with four other bookmakers for illegal gambling. In the years leading up to his arrest, Cooper enjoyed free access to the Dolphins' locker room and practice field, and had even supplied the team with the carpeting for their clubhouse. After Cooper's arrest at the end of 1976, Coach Don Shula went to the NFL and let it be known that several of his players were associates of Cooper including quarterback Bob Griese. The NFL promptly launched an investigation into the matter, focusing on 10 of the Dolphins' players. The names of Griese, backup quarterback Earl Morrall, and defensive lineman Bill Stanfill were found in Cooper's address book. Though under a polygraph test Cooper admitted passing inside information about the Dolphins on to gamblers, the NFL found none of the players guilty of any wrongdoing.

1979 – Ed DeBartolo, Sr. bought the San Francisco 49ers in 1977. At the time, he also owned the NHL's Pittsburgh Penguins. Prior to gaining control of the 49ers, DeBartolo attempted but failed on several occasions to buy a MLB team mainly because of baseball's fear of his connection to gambling. His exclusion from MLB didn't bother the NFL, nor did the fact that DeBartolo owned racetracks. DeBartolo also liked to gamble on football while he was an owner, which, again, apparently didn't bother the NFL. Thanks to Paul Hornung, who again strung out an unknowing co-conspirator, we know that both he and DeBartolo, Sr. bet on the 1979 Super Bowl. The pair won the bet which should have kicked DeBartolo out of the league, yet members of his family still own the 49ers.

1979 – While not known to gamble during their playing days, two Hall of Famers were kicked out of baseball for their gambling affiliations. Both Mickey Mantle and Willie Mays needed jobs. Just three months after getting his Hall of Fame nod, Mays took a job with the Park Place casino in Atlantic City basically serving as a meet-and-greet guy. Not to be outdone, the Claridge Casino across the street from the Park Place hired Mickey Mantle to do the same. Given baseball's ugly gambling history, commissioner Bowie Kuhn didn't like the open association between baseball and gambling. He gave both an ultimatum—the casino job or a future in baseball. Both Mays and Mantle decided the casino paid better and kept their jobs. They were promptly expelled from the game (though they didn't lose their Hall of Fame status). In 1985, Kuhn lost his commissionership and his ruling to new commissioner Peter Ueberroth who welcomed the two legends back to baseball with open arms.

1979 – On his personal website (www.moldea.com) and in his book *Interference*, investigator Dan Moldea related the story of how two NFL referees were betting on and fixing games in which they participated during the 1979 season. He detailed how both the FBI and IRS were investigating the claims while national bookmakers had similar suspicions regarding the refs in question. The most damaging information came from an informant who told the IRS not only the names of the refs, but gave them the outcomes of the games prior to their taking place. Why didn't this make headlines? Though it seemed that both the FBI and the IRS had it cold that fixes were occurring, the heads of each department involved refused to push the investigation any further. According to Moldea and the FBI reports, these were the games fixed:

★ 9/9/79 – Cleveland vs. Kansas City. Cleveland, a one-point favorite, won 27–24.

★ 9/17/79 – N.Y. Giants vs. Washington. Washington, a six-point favorite, won 27–0.

★ 9/24/79 – Dallas vs. Cleveland. Cleveland, a three-point underdog, won 26–7.

★ 10/29/79 – Seattle vs. Atlanta. Seattle, a one-point underdog, won 31-28.

★ 10/15/79 – Minnesota vs. N.Y. Jets. New York, a five-point favorite, won 14–7.

★ 10/8/79 – Miami vs. Oakland. Oakland, a one-point underdog, won 13–3.

★ 10/25/79 – San Diego vs. Oakland. Oakland, a one-point underdog, won 45–22.

★ 12/10/79 – Pittsburgh vs. Houston. Houston, a three-point underdog, won 20–17.

Even with this sort of evidence, questions abound. Primarily, as handicapper Dan Gordon pointed out, how did the same two referees manage to officiate four Monday night games and one Thursday night game in the same season? Indeed, it would be highly unusual for the same refereeing crew to be assigned to so many high-profile games during the course of a single season. If this was such an open-and-shut case as Moldea claimed it was, why did both the FBI and IRS completely drop it? Did a handshake deal between former members of the FBI now employed by the NFL's security department and current members of the FBI manage to hush it all up, or wasn't the evidence as strong as it seemed to be? Something didn't, and still doesn't, add up on both sides of this case. Of course, this was neither the first nor the last time referees would come under scrutiny for potentially fixing games.

1982 – Art Schlichter is the type of player the NFL outright fears. Despite all of the background checks teams supposedly do on the players they draft, Schlichter and his gambling habits managed to slip through the cracks. There's no doubt he had the talent to be a starting NFL quarterback, but for all the testing of his athletic skills, no one seemed to notice that while still at Ohio State Schlichter was gambling hundreds of dollars on sporting events.

Drafted as a first-round pick by the Baltimore Colts in 1982, Schlichter gambled away his $350,000 signing bonus and his $140,000 salary before his rookie season was over. In fact, during that strike-shortened season he managed to get himself some $700,000 in debt with bookies. While supposedly charting plays as a backup on the sidelines, he'd instead work on his bets. When he did manage to get into a game, he'd become distracted lining up behind the center because he'd be checking the scoreboard to see how his bets were doing. He had such an overt problem the NFL actually caught and suspended him for the 1983 season. Unlike what happens in baseball, Schlichter wasn't banned for life because of his gambling habits. He was suspended "indefinitely," meaning in this case, one season. In 1984 and even 1985, he returned to the Colts before they caught wind of his still unabashed gambling and released him. He still managed to make the Buffalo Bills training camp in 1986, but lasted through only one preseason game. He never made another NFL roster after that.

Note that though the NFL forbids players from gambling on any sporting events, which Schlichter did in spades, Schlichter's career did not end by suspension. In 1987, he was arrested for his part in a multimillion dollar sports betting operation and only then did Commissioner Rozelle refuse to allow him to sign with another team. Even then he wasn't officially suspended, only blackballed. But Schlichter's football career didn't end there. He made it into the Arena Football League where he won the league's MVP award in 1990 while leading the Detroit Drive to the championship. But once he left the Arena league in 1993, things went south as Schlichter's gambling problems consumed his life, leading him to robbery and several stints in prison. Somehow, amazingly, Schlichter never gambled on his own team.

1987 – The book *Money Players* details a point-shaving incident in the NBA brought about via players' associations with drug dealers. It seemed as though the mid-1980s Phoenix Suns had a bit of a drug problem. In April of 1987, three active members of the Suns—James Edwards, Jay Humphries, and Grant Gondrezick, along with two retired Suns, Mike Bratz and Garfield Heard—were indicted along with four others on 21 counts of felony drug charges. At least five other then-current and former members of the Suns were also linked to the case. At the same time, two Phoenix area men were arrested for running a million-dollar bookmaking operation. All of these paths apparently crossed in a February 1987 game between the Suns and the Milwaukee Bucks. The game had a posted over/under total line of 226. Informed bettors were told to let it all ride on the under. The game ended with the Suns losing at home 115–107, just barely under that 226 mark. When the assistant DA in the drug case was asked about whether or not there was point shaving occurring in that game, he responded in the affirmative with, "We received information to that effect."[37]

1989–1990 – While a member of the Detroit Pistons, Isiah Thomas often attended and even hosted illegal high-stakes craps games. Of course when this news broke in 1990, Thomas was quick to deny it, saying "I'm mad and I'm angry. I don't even know how this happened. I don't believe you should gamble. I think gambling is one of the stupidest things you can do. You always lose."[38]

What put Thomas in the FBI's crosshairs wasn't the fact that he was at these craps games with other Detroit Pistons and various big-time Detroit gamblers, but it was the thousands of dollars in checks he wrote to his neighbor (and godfather to his son Joshua), Imad "Emmet" Denha. On the surface, Denha was just a grocery store owner. But the FBI linked Denha to Henry Allen Hilf who was the FBI's prime target in a racketeering investigation. Hilf was also the biggest bookmaker in Michigan with direct ties to organized crime, and Denha was caught laundering $6 million for Hilf. Now Thomas claimed that the questionable checks were just his "monthly allowance" and he cashed them through Denha rather than going to the bank. But in fact, they were written to cover his losses at the craps table. According to various sources in the book *Money Players*, Thomas was losing hundreds of thousands of dollars in these dice games, falling deeply into debt with exactly the wrong sort of people. This made Thomas a perfect target for the unscrupulous gamblers surrounding him to exploit. The question is, did they?

The NBA wasn't ignorant of these facts. They performed a cursory investigation into the claims that members of the Detroit Pistons, including Thomas and forward-center James Edwards (who often joined him at the illegal craps games), were shaving points. Two December 1989 games were scrutinized—one against the Golden State Warriors and another versus the Milwaukee Bucks. The day prior to the questionable game against the Warriors, the Pistons played the Utah Jazz. Thomas had been injured, getting bloodied from an elbow thrown by Jazz guard John Stockton. He briefly went to the locker room, and then returned to finish the game. Neither the NBA nor the bookmakers in Vegas realized that Thomas was too injured to play the following game against the Warriors because the West Coast game finished so late his injury went unreported. As a result, the Pistons were favored by three, but without Thomas, they lost 104–92. The thought after Thomas' injury was finally reported was that he'd miss a week to 10 days. In fact, he missed only that one game against the Warriors. In the other questionable game against the Bucks, the Pistons were favored by 10 as the game was played in Detroit. The game was tied at the end of the third quarter, but the visiting Bucks went on a 27–13 tear in the fourth to win 99–85. In that game, Thomas tallied two whole points on a one-for-eight shooting performance.

Amazingly, all of this—the dice games, the FBI investigation, the allegations of point shaving/game fixing—occurred during the Pistons' championship season of 1989-1990. Ten years later, Thomas would be elected to the Basketball Hall of Fame.

1989

"Before [Pete] Rose was even halfway to Cobb's hit record, the office of baseball commissioner Bowie Kuhn had identified him as a problem gambler, and a probable violator of the game's rules against gambling 'associations.'"[39] While that was certainly true, Rose had actually been known as a gambler since his rookie year in 1963. Originally he wagered only on horse races, often catching the matinee prior to playing a night game, but soon he was betting with bookies on various sports, against baseball's well-established anti-gambling rules. According to the book *Hustle*, Rose had the dangerous habit of losing his bets and then not paying off his debts. He'd pay off maybe half and let the rest hang on the bookie because, you know, he was Pete Rose. As a former Cincinnati Reds general manager was once quoted as having said, "Pete's legs may get broken when his playing days are over."[40]

So as "The Big Red Machine" of the 1970s was steamrolling through the majors, both the Reds and Major League Baseball knew Pete Rose was gambling. The Reds, not wanting to lose just a great ball player but a fan favorite in Rose, simply stuck their collective heads in the sand and let Pete be Pete. MLB, slightly to its credit, went a step further. It actually investigated Rose starting around 1970, just after Denny McLain was suspended.

Baseball's lead investigator at this point was Henry Fitzgibbon. Straight out of the FBI, Fitzgibbon was hand-picked by J. Edgar Hoover himself to head baseball's security office. Yet as quoted in *Hustle*, perhaps his loyalty to the game went a little too deep, having said, "We would try, if possible, to avoid giving the game a black eye."[41] Fitzgibbon met separately with both Rose and Commissioner Kuhn on several occasions regarding Rose's gambling throughout the early 1970s. Because Rose often bet through "beards," a third party who would actually place the bet with the bookie but in Rose's name, Fitzgibbon didn't have enough solid evidence to urge Commissioner Kuhn to press things further. When Fitzgibbon met with Rose, in a habit that would stretch over another 25 years, Rose would outright lie to him. After 10 years of this back-and-forth, eventually the investigation faded away, yet it would never completely close.

Come 1989, baseball was *still* keeping a watchful eye on Rose. Yet it wasn't an unpaid bookie that brought Rose down, it was a steroid dealer. Rose had a buddy who was a lousy drug dealer. He was subsequently picked up by the feds and turned informant. During that investigation, baseball was alerted that Rose's name came up repeatedly. When baseball dug into it for itself, it realized Rose was gambling through the dealer, and using him as a beard to place bets. Commissioner Ueberroth and soon-to-be new commissioner Giamatti brought Rose in for another sit-down. They asked Rose, now manager of the Cincinnati Reds, if he'd been gambling on baseball. Rose, as usual, lied and said "no." But baseball had the goods on him this time. Besides informants, they had telephone records, betting sheets, fingerprints, banking records, everything needed to take him down. And surprisingly, they did. As MLB's special counsel to the Commissioner of Baseball John Dowd wrote in his report, "The testimony and the documentary evidence gathered in the course of the investigation demonstrates that Pete Rose bet on baseball, and in particular, on games of the Cincinnati Reds Baseball Club during the 1985, 1986 and 1987 seasons." Rose, backed into a corner by the mountain of evidence against him, agreed to sign the paper that would ban him from the game for his gambling.

Foolishly, Commissioner Giamatti had given Rose two outs in that signed agreement. The first was the chance to apply for reinstatement after one year. Needless to say, Rose has never been reinstated (nor should he be). The second was a line that read, in part, that nothing in the agreement "shall be deemed an admission or a denial" that Rose bet on baseball games. But immediately after both sides signed that agreement, Commissioner Giamatti turned around and told the press that, as far as he was concerned, Rose had indeed bet on baseball. Suddenly stung by the league that made him a highly-regarded superstar. Rose quickly claimed Major League Baseball had jobbed him. Thanks to the wording of the agreement, he was free to do so.

Unfortunately for the fans, they were now subjected to nearly 20 years' worth of denials and lies. Rose would claim he never bet on baseball. Then he would make the dramatic statement, accompanied by the spotlight and interviews, that yes, he did bet on baseball, but never on his team, the Reds. In 2007, perhaps in a desperate attempt to save himself and his reputation while clinging to hopes of still being elected to the Hall of Fame, Rose came clean and admitted he bet on the Reds while he was their manager—to win, of course—every night. All of which was printed in plain and clear English in the Dowd Report. So it took Rose almost 20 years before he could publicly admit the obvious, and for many people to believe it. And yet, to this day, Cincinnati still has the street outside its baseball stadium named Pete Rose Way.

1990 – Less than a year after purchasing the Yankees in 1973, George Steinbrenner pleaded guilty to 14 felony counts of illegal contributions to then President Nixon's reelection campaign. Commissioner Kuhn suspended Steinbrenner from baseball for two years for his behavior. He was allowed back in after nine months.

Steinbrenner's second suspension from baseball came about when he was caught red-handed having written a $40,000 check to a gambler. The gambler in question was named Howard Spira, and he had dirt on one of Big Stein's newest acquisitions, Dave Winfield. As part of Winfield's contract with the Yankees, Steinbrenner had agreed to give a yearly contribution to Winfield's personal charity foundation. According to Spira's story, Winfield was skimming funds from that charity. Yet after Steinbrenner handed the $40,000 check over to Spira for the scoop, Spira turned around and demanded more cash. Steinbrenner scoffed at the demand and went to the feds crying blackmail.

For Steinbrenner, that move wound up being a double-edged sword. Spira's home was raided by the feds and he eventually was tried and convicted on extortion charges. Yet for Steinbrenner, the case raised the collective eyebrows of those in MLB's front office. In meeting with new commissioner Vincent, Steinbrenner faced the music. Baseball had the $40,000 check and Spira was a known gambler. The biggest problem was Steinbrenner kept changing his story regarding the payoff, thus making the deal between the two seem ever the more suspicious. Commissioner Vincent felt he had little choice, and the two hammered out an agreement. Steinbrenner would admit to his indiscretion, not file suit against MLB for its decision, give up majority ownership of the Yankees, and accept a lifetime ban from dealing with the new majority owner of the Yankees which was to be his son, Hank. Steinbrenner signed his name to the agreement and was out of baseball on July 30, 1990. He agreed to this deal because he and his lawyers were allowed to control the wording of the agreement. Two years later, Steinbrenner was back in baseball and once again lording over the Yankees.

Who might have really slipped the noose in all of this was future Hall of Fame member Dave Winfield. MLB never investigated him for his role in the whole affair, which is strange considering Winfield had a closer association to Spira than Steinbrenner ever did. Spira worked for Winfield and even received a questionable $15,000 loan from him. On top of that, Spira was right about Winfield and his charity. Steinbrenner later sued Winfield for mismanagement of his charity. The case was settled out of court.

1990 – Philadelphia 76ers' Charles Barkley and New York Knicks' Mark Jackson decided during a January 1990 game that the action on the court simply wasn't enough for the two of them. They decided to make wagers against each other during the game. With only about 23 seconds left in the game, Barkley bet Jackson $1,000 that he'd make the two free throws he had just been awarded. Barkley then promptly sunk them both. But their betting wasn't finished. Literally seconds later the two bet that Jackson couldn't sink a game-tying three-pointer. He did.

During a post-game interview, Barkley related the story that occurred out on the court. Barkley then added that this evened the two of them up as Barkley had lost a bet to Jackson over the playoff game between the two teams the season before saying, "We bet $500 in the playoffs and I won it back tonight. I want my money." Amazingly, Jackson confirmed the whole to-do by saying, "He owes me from the playoffs and he never paid me, so we're even."

On the surface, it appeared to be good-natured fun, until the NBA caught wind of it. Commissioner Stern promptly fined both players $5,000. The 76ers' general manager John Nash was quoted as saying, "Charles says outlandish things all the time…but my suspicions are that neither guy intended to pay the other. When players play the game of Horse they often make references to 'I'll bet you $1' or 'I'll bet you $1,000.' No one ever pays off; they are more statements than bets. I don't think money ever changes hands." Sounds an awful lot like the claims about Wilt Chamberlain, doesn't it?

What was perhaps just a friendly wager with no real substance turned out to be something more for Sir Charles. In 2007, Barkley admitted to having a gambling "habit"—one that once cost him $2.5 million in about six hours. One that he claimed cost him some $10 million since leaving the game. But it's not really a "problem" Barkley has because "The problem is when you can't afford it. I can afford to gamble. I didn't kill myself when I lost two and half million dollars…I like to gamble and I'm not going to quit." And being somewhat true to that word, Barkley got into a little hot water in early 2008 when the Las Vegas casino The Wynn called in a $400,000 marker Barkley "forgot" to pay back. Ultimately Barkley did settle up with the casino, but it took the threat of a criminal complaint being filed to spur him into action. Afterwards, Barkley vowed not to gamble for "the next year or two."

1991 – Lenny "Nails" Dykstra not only played center field for the Philadelphia Phillies, but played in several high-stakes poker games that got him in trouble with MLB. Commissioner Vincent assigned investigator John Dowd (of Pete Rose fame) to Dykstra's case. Dowd would find that Dykstra was "drowning in debt"[42] at the time that he wrote some $78,000 in checks to cover his poker losses. Dykstra was forthcoming with baseball, admitted his wrongdoing, and never bet on baseball. He was given a one-year probation by MLB for the incident.

However, Dykstra's name wasn't quite cleared. In 2005, a civil suit was brought against Dykstra by a former business partner. This partner alleged that Dykstra told him to bet thousands of dollars with a bookmaker on several Phillies games during the 1993 season. Coincidently, in 1992 both Commissioner Vincent stepped down from his post and Dykstra's probation period came to an end. 1993 happened to be the year the Phillies won the National League pennant, but lost the World Series to the Toronto Blue Jays four games to two. Dykstra denied the allegations against him and MLB reportedly never investigated the former business partner's claims. Dykstra filed for Chapter 11 bankruptcy in 2009 reportedly having no more than $50,000 in assets against anywhere from $10 to $50 million in liabilities.

1991-1993 – Michael Jordan once said "I'm no Pete Rose." By that I think he meant Pete Rose could hit a curve ball while Jordan couldn't, because Jordan surely couldn't have meant that he didn't have a love of gambling.

Michael Jordan always craved competition. That is what drove him to be the tremendous player he was on the court. But it was also that passion that fueled his compulsive gambling. He gambled on just about anything (much like Wilt Chamberlain). While at North Carolina, he used to bet fellow players sodas or small amounts of money on free throws or games of Horse. Although definitely not sanctioned by the team, it went largely ignored. Those activities carried on into his time with the Chicago Bulls, and with the huge influx of money, the stakes steadily increased. He played poker with his teammates on road trips and was known to be quite the shark. Bulls coaches would warn the younger players not to play poker with him. He was that good. He even gambled on the outcome of video games.[43] It was golf, however, his second passion, which proved to be his downfall.

He began betting small, maybe $100 on a hole or a putt. As his confidence on the golf course grew, so did the amounts wagered. In 1991, Jordan and a group of friends went on a week-long gambling spree at his Hilton Head home in North Carolina, golfing all day and playing poker all night. By the time it ended, Jordan was into James "Slim" Bouler for $57,000 and Eddie Dow for $108,000. This in and of itself wouldn't have been such a big deal except for the fact that Bouler was a convicted cocaine dealer and had two probation violations for carrying semiautomatic weapons. On

October 21, 1991, Jordan paid the $57,000 to Bouler who turned around and placed the money in an account for the "Golf-Tech Driving Range." The IRS quickly seized it, believing the funds may have been ill-gotten since Bouler was again under investigation for dealing cocaine.

Now the trouble really began for Jordan. In the wake of these dealings coming to light, Jordan told the press that the $57,000 was merely a loan to a friend to start a golf range. That lie carried a lot of weight. So much so that U.S. District Court Judge Graham C. Mullen ruled that the IRS violated Bouler's rights in seizing the $57,000 check. Judge Mullen admitted that he based his ruling on Jordan's claims that the money was a loan even though he never actually questioned Jordan.[44]

That seemed to suffice, for a while. Then in February of 1992, Jordan's gambling associate Eddie Dow was robbed of $20,000 and murdered just outside his home. In Dow's belongings they found photocopies of three checks that totaled $108,000, the exact amount Jordan had lost to him months earlier. Two of the checks were from Jordan's personal account. The third was a cashier's check made out by Jordan.

Then, almost one year to the day after originally paying Bouler the $57,000, Michael Jordan was in court at Bouler's trial for drug and money-laundering charges. Under oath, during a nine-minute testimony, Michael Jordan admitted that the $57,000 was not a loan but indeed a gambling debt. Maybe Jordan *is* more like Pete Rose than he'd like to imagine. With the trial of Bouler over and done with, it should've put an end to the public side of Jordan's gambling.

In June of 1993, another Michael Jordan gambling story broke. This one hovered around the book *Michael & Me: Our Gambling Addiction...My Cry for Help!*, written by San Diego businessman Richard Esquinas. In that book, Esquinas claimed that during a 10-day period in 1991, Jordan had lost $1.25 million to him gambling on golf. No one initially believed his story until Esquinas produced the correspondences with Jordan and the canceled checks to back it.

Starting in early 1992, Esquinas contacted Jordan several times asking Jordan to pay off the bet. After a few token payments (some sent to Esquinas by Jordan's wife at the time, Juanita) and many broken promises, Esquinas offered Jordan an out. Jordan agreed to settle his debt with a

$300,000 payoff. In March of 1993 Jordan had Chicago attorney Wayne A. McCoy send Esquinas $100,000. Then in May of that same year, McCoy sent Esquinas another $100,000. By then, Esquinas had lost his patience waiting for his money and he published the book.

Jordan didn't lie this time. Instead, he issued a statement. "I have played golf with Richard Esquinas with wagers made between us. Because I did not keep records, I cannot verify how much I won or lost. I can assure you the level of our wagers was substantially less than the preposterous amounts that have been reported."[45]

Even with that admission of guilt, Jordan managed to deny any sort of problem. He told playerfriendly NBC reporter Ahmad Rashad "If I had a [gambling] problem, I'd be starving. I'd be hocking this watch, my championship rings, I would sell my house. My kids would be starving. I do not have a problem. I enjoy gambling."[46] For a man who made hundreds of millions of dollars to claim that "if" he had a gambling problem he'd be "starving" is quite laughable. He went on to say to Rashad, "My wife, if I had a problem, would have left me or certainly would have come and said seek help...my wife never said anything, and she's the chief of finances in our household." It's obvious she must have known something since she's the one who originally paid Esquinas. And later, she did divorce MJ.

During the time this story broke, Jordan decided to make an ill-advised trip to Atlantic City right in the middle of the 1993 playoff series against the New York Knicks. Jordan claimed to the media that he was gone before midnight the night before Game Two in New York; however, he was seen in the casino well past midnight and into the wee hours of the morning. That was the last time Jordan would do that during the playoffs. It has been reported on more that one occasion that when Jordan played in New York or New Jersey he'd venture down to Atlantic City, or if he were in Los Angeles or Utah he'd likely make a pit stop in Las Vegas.

The day after this new gambling story broke about Jordan and Atlantic City, NBC announcer Bob Costas had a halftime interview with NBA commissioner David Stern. During that interview, Costas badgered Stern about the story much to the disdain of NBA Sports president Dick Ebersol who was screaming in Costas' earpiece to lay off and switch subjects.[47] Costas, much to his credit, did not back down and asked the tough questions that should have been asked, but to little avail. NBC muffled the story from that point onward. Jordan became quite tight-lipped as well. He stopped talking to the media. Even though such silence, especially during the playoffs, is a fineable offense in the NBA, Jordan never received a single fine. For Stern and the NBA, Jordan's silence might have been a blessing in disguise.

Even so, by now the NBA had had enough. They had been through this once before in 1992 with the Bouler ordeal. That two-week "investigation" ended with commissioner David Stern announcing, "This situation has been investigated with complete cooperation of Michael and his attorneys and [the head of the NBA investigation] Judge Lacey has assured us that there appears to be no reason for the NBA to take action against Michael."[48] In reality, the "two-week investigation" consisted of a two-and-a-half-hour meeting between Jordan, his attorneys, and top NBA officials. The NBA never questioned either Bouler or any of the local or federal investigating officers in the case, and never asked to see the records from Bouler's trial. It's no wonder there appeared to be no reason to take action against Jordan.

Jordan was merely given a slap on the wrist and told to watch who he associates with. He himself claimed to *Chicago Tribune* writer Bob Greene, "Was I gambling with goons who had bad reputations? Yeah, I was. Should I not gamble with goons anymore? Yeah, I shouldn't gamble with goons."

But now, in 1993, Jordan was on strike two-and-one-half. During this second, and much more thorough investigation, the league was to discover that not only were the amounts of money involved larger, but also that the accusations were much more damning. According to the book *Money Players: Days and Nights Inside the New NBA*, in July 1993 the NBA interviewed Esquinas in its New York offices. During that interview, Esquinas told the investigators that in March of 1992, he had overheard a telephone conversation Jordan was having with an unknown person. During that phone call, Jordan talked about a betting line, saying "So you say the line is seven points."[49] Of what game, it is unknown. But this was a serious accusation. If Jordan was indeed gambling on sports, then the rules of the investigation should have changed.

The question is, how credible did the NBA think this allegation was? I believe they took it as quite credible. They most definitely did not want Jordan to become the NBA's version of Pete Rose, who was a certain Hall of Famer until he was banned for life over his gambling addiction. What was potentially even more threatening to the league than MJ's gambling was the fact that he was consistently associating with unseemly types. He was putting himself in a position where he could easily be blackmailed, perhaps into doing something on the court like shaving points or worse, throwing games. I think at this point the NBA and Commissioner David Stern stepped in and talked to Michael Jordan about "retirement."

Though I will get into Jordan's first "retirement" later, what's interesting to note here is that a mere two days after Jordan retired in October 1993, the NBA concluded its five-month investigation into Jordan's gambling. Curiously, it found nothing of significance.

But there were obvious omissions. Take the story Magic Johnson related in the book *When Nothing Else Matters*. While MJ's teammate on the Olympic "Dream Team" in Barcelona in 1992, Magic claimed that Jordan spent more time there playing all-night poker games or round after round of golf rather than practicing. He was constantly racing around from his basketball obligations to his gambling interests. Yet none of this was ever reported.

Once retired from playing basketball, Jordan became part owner of the Washington Bullets/Wizards. Even then, he still gambled like a freak. Author Michael Leahy details a MJ escapade at the Mohegan Sun casino when Jordan spent all night playing blackjack "losing what for most people would have been their life savings."[50] According to Leahy, Jordan played all night, down some $500,000 at one point before managing to leave the casino around 8 a.m. up nearly $800,000. In 2006, Jordan made local headlines when he won a No-Limit Texas Hold'em charity poker tournament. He beat some 120 other players to win the event.

When interviewed by Ed Bradley on *60 Minutes* in 2005, Jordan would talk about his gambling, saying, "Yeah, I've gotten myself into situations where I would not walk away and I've pushed the envelope. Is that compulsive?

Yeah, it depends on how you look at it. If you're willing to jeopardize your livelihood and your family, then yeah."[51]

1993–2005 – During this period, stories of professional athletes associating with gamblers or gambling themselves dried up. Considering the time it took for many of these other gambling stories and allegations to come to the surface, it's not surprising that more modern-day tales have yet to be heard. When a constant pattern of behavior from pro athletes stretches back 100 years, it is most likely that something of note occurred during that 12-year span. What exactly, and by whom, remains a question for which answers are still sought.

Though stories about the pros dried up during this period, on the college level, point-shaving incidents continued and are still occurring. Two members of Arizona State's basketball team were busted for point shaving during the 1993–1994 season. In 1995, two starting players for the Northwestern Wildcats basketball team were charged for the same offense. Then in 1996, 13 members of Boston College's football team were suspended for point shaving (amazingly, it was BC's second point-shaving scandal; the first came in 1978–1979 thanks to their basketball team and *Goodfellas* real-life mobster Henry Hill). Even in 2006, the University of Toledo's football and basketball team were both under investigation for point shaving. One of Toledo's football players was officially charged at the beginning of 2007.

Perhaps even more frightening is the following fact from the book *Bloody Sundays*. According to author Mike Freeman, "A 1999 survey by sports agent Ralph Cindrich of 75 draft-rated college football players found that 56 percent of the respondents believed that there were college athletes who had bet on the outcome of a game in which they participated, while 11 percent said they were aware of at least one incident in which a college football player bet against his own team on the outcome of a game in which he participated."[52] That meant eight of the 75 players knew another player that had bet against his own team. Why would a player do that unless he was certain of the outcome? If he was certain his team was going to lose (or not cover the spread), how much less than 100 percent was that player putting forth on the field? An even bigger question to ask then is, if we extrapolate those numbers beyond 75 players to the entire draft class, does that 11 percent number hold true? If it does, how many college players might be out there shaving points?

If so many college players are gambling on their own sport and games, where are the pro athletes that are doing the same? Since only the NFL completely bans gambling on any pro sports (the other leagues simply disallow gambling on their own sport), gambling athletes most likely exist everywhere. Amazingly, the ones catching the most heat play in the NHL.

Philadelphia Flyers' Mike Knuble told the *Delaware County Daily Times* newspaper, "We can't bet on hockey. That's grounds for getting kicked out of the league. Some club rules say you're not allowed to bet on any sports, but it's a dirty little secret everybody has." One such player was former NHL All-Star Jaromir Jagr. While a member of the Washington Capitals, Jagr admitted to owing the offshore gambling website CaribSports some $500,000 in losses. The story supposedly only leaked to the media because Jagr stopped making the scheduled payments to the website to settle up the debt. Jagr's lawyers claimed Jagr himself didn't make all of the bets; an unnamed friend had access to his internet account and was responsible for some of the losses. CaribSports owner William Caesar, who was the likely source of the leak, told *Sports Illustrated* that Jagr's account was specially set up so that he could not bet on NHL games. Even so, Jagr wasn't one to immediately settle up his debts. Twice the NHLer had liens issued against him by the IRS for failing to pay his taxes. In 1999 he was hit for $350,000, and in 2003 for another $3.3 million. It was not surprising to see Jagr flee both the NHL and North America in 2008 to play hockey in Russia. Another NHL All-Star gambling during his playing days was Jeremy Roenick who reportedly bet $100,000 with a sports tout service. Roenick took the Barkley approach, saying "I'm not a poor man. I can go out and afford to spend a couple thousand dollars I want to put on a hockey game, I mean, a football game or basketball game, something like that. That's my God-given right."[53] And yes, he really let slip that "hockey game" bit.

Perhaps the NHL escaped an even bigger scandal when its Director of Officiating and Hall of Fame referee Andy Van Hellemond resigned in 2004. It was reported by various sources within the Canadian press that Van Hellemond was borrowing money from numerous NHL officials in order to pay off debts believed to be from gambling. He would request various amounts from the refs he lorded over, asking for anywhere from $100 to $10,000. One former NHL referee quoted in *The National Post* made it sound as if Van Hellemond was practically begging for cash, asking for a $500 loan prior to a game. The NHL looked into the allegations and of course, found nothing of note. But because of his post within the NHL, it raises some suspicions. Van Hellemond had not just access but direct control over the NHL's entire officiating staff. What kind of sway could such a person have over a referee? What sort of deals could have been made? Especially considering Van Hellemond was in charge of handing out the lucrative playoff assignments for referees.

2006 – The NHL wasn't off the hook just yet. Early in 2006, it was revealed that former NHL star and then-current Phoenix Coyotes assistant coach Rock Tocchet was operating a sport gambling ring. Apparently Tocchet understood that it was more profitable to book bets rather than to make them. Working with a New Jersey state trooper and a New Jersey businessman, Tocchet and company took in over $1.7 million in a 40-day period booking some 1,000 wagers. The scary part was, more than a dozen unnamed NHL players were placing bets, which of course were on everything *but* hockey games. This even included hockey god Wayne Gretzky's wife who plunked down a reported $500,000, including $75,000 alone on the Super Bowl, through Tocchet. When asked about his wife's betting habits, Gretzky responded, "Oh really, I don't know. You'd have to ask her that."[54] Gretzky managed to play dumb rather well, once quoted as saying "I'm trying to figure it all out."[55] Gretzky needed to. He was the Coyotes' managing partner, head coach, and Tocchet's boss at the time this story made headlines.

Named "Operation Slap Shot," the investigation into Tocchet also included a search to see if any NHL players were passing along inside information regarding NHL games. Never mind that Tocchet was an active coach and former player who knew more than enough to pass along inside info to whoever wanted it. That end of the investigation seemed to turn up nothing, perhaps, in part, because hockey isn't a heavily gambled sport. Nonetheless, none of the players who were gambling illegally through

Tocchet have yet to be named or publicly disciplined by the NHL.

When asked if he'd ever bet on hockey, Tocchet stated simply "no." His lawyer, Kevin Marino, was more direct. Prior to Tocchet's arraignment, Marino stated, "allegations that Rick Tocchet financed an illegal gambling operation with organized crime is categorically false and irresponsible...Mr. Tocchet will fight false charges with the same grit and resolve he displayed during his illustrious playing career."[56] That he did, until May 2007 when Tocchet pleaded guilty to financing a sports gambling ring. Tocchet's relatively quick plea may have saved the NHL loads of trouble. Sans a trial, no testimony would ever be heard and the depths of the case never needed to be probed.

In August 2007, Tocchet received two years' probation for his role in the gambling ring. As for Tocchet's two partners, the New Jersey area businessman received the same sentence while the New Jersey state trooper was sentenced to five years in prison. At this time, Tocchet's lawyer, Kevin Marino, again made a bold blanket statement in his client's honor saying, "Mr. Tocchet never placed a bet on professional hockey. Mr. Tocchet never took a bet on professional hockey. He in no way compromised the integrity of the game of hockey or the National Hockey League."[57] Yet the criminal investigation of Tocchet and company covered less than two months of wagers. It's never been reported exactly how long Tocchet was running this ring (years, maybe?); to say hockey was never bet upon wasn't completely provable.

Meanwhile, the NHL hired Robert Cleary, who was the lead prosecutor in the Unabomber case, to run their side of the gambling investigation on Tocchet. As soon as Tocchet was sentenced, the NHL released a statement that read, in part, "In light of today's events, Mr. Cleary is now in a position to conclude his independent investigation."[58] Was Cleary aware of that? It is rather amazing that Mr. Cleary's investigation ended precisely when Tocchet was officially sentenced by the state. And just like the unnamed NHL players who were gambling through Tocchet, the public has yet to hear what the NHL's lead investigator discovered in his somewhat truncated search through the NHL's gambling underworld.

Remarkably, by November 2008 Tocchet was back coaching behind a NHL bench. Tampa Bay Lightning head coach Barry Melrose, who had left his job as a "talking head" for ESPN to join the team, was fired just 16 games into the 2008–09 season. Who did the Lightning decide was the best replacement? Rick Tocchet. He was back in the league with zero discipline from the NHL and little to no protest from fans or the media. Originally just named the "interim" head coach through the end of the 2008–2009 season, Tocchet was signed to a three-year deal in May of 2009 to be the team's long-term solution behind the bench.

2007 – "I can't believe it's happening to us," said NBA Commissioner David Stern during the press conference that confirmed 13-year veteran referee Tim Donaghy had been busted by the FBI for gambling on NBA games. Perhaps Stern had a right to be shocked. Despite "subject[ing] our referees to extensive security checks, to the limit provided by the law," as Stern stated, no one within the league saw this coming.

The NBA, like every other major league, had indeed conducted background checks on its referees. The league used the Arkin Group, which was led by the former head of the CIA's worldwide operations, as the agency to run these checks. They can be incredibly invasive. In his book *Inside the Meat Grinder*, former NFL umpire Chad Brown described the process he had to endure to move up from the college ranks to become a member of a NFL officiating crew. Though the NFL and NBA are different entities, considering Commissioner Stern's words it is doubtful the workup they do on a prospective referee recruit varies by much in either league. As Brown detailed, he first received a letter informing him he was a "candidate" for the NFL. He went for an interview during which he was in his own words "interrogated" by NFL supervisor Jack O'Cain for about two hours. He was then subjected to both written intelligence and psychological examinations which lasted another hour. Succeeding there, he was then deemed a "finalist" for the NFL which opened him up to a background check. As a NFL representative explained this process to him, "We call current employers, past employers, friends, relatives. We do a detailed financial history, interview neighbors, and do an extensive education history. We will often interview a former teacher. In your case, we've decided to interview your second-grade teacher." A private detective was indeed sent out by the NFL to interview Brown's neighbor. He knew that only because the misdirected investigator rang Brown's doorbell instead of his neighbor's by mistake.[59] According to the NFL, it subjects all of its referees to this sort of background check every three to four years.

Major League Baseball also subjects its umpires to background checks. In the wake of the Donaghy story breaking into the national spotlight, MLB stepped up its program only to find that some of its umpires weren't too happy with the types of questions being asked. According to an article published on SportsIllustrated.com in January 2008, MLB investigators were asking neighbors of some umpires whether the umpire in question was living outside his means, throwing wild parties, beating his wife, growing marijuana plants, or belonging to a group such as the Ku Klux Klan. As umpire union spokesman Lamell McMorris said, "To try to link our umpires to the Ku Klux Klan is highly offensive. It is essentially defaming the umpires in their communities by conducting a very strange and poorly executed investigation. It resembles a kind of secret police in some kind of despotic nation."[60] MLB had asked the umpires' union to allow the league the right to conduct financial background checks on each of its umpires, but the union wouldn't allow it.

The bad apple that was Tim Donaghy somehow slipped through this exact sort of intense scrutiny *for 13 years*. The amazing thing about Donaghy is that he got roped into this gambling scandal in exactly the manner former Mafia member Michael Franzese described as possible. Donaghy ran up a gambling debt he couldn't pay. To make good, he started providing inside information on games (only some of which he officiated) so both he and the Mafia boys he was indebted to could profit immensely. What this little group didn't realize was that the FBI was listening.

What is extremely interesting in Donaghy's case is the fact that for a supposed "addicted gambler," Donaghy never once placed a bet himself. He only provided inside information to first Jack Concannon, who was never arrested by the FBI for his association with Donaghy, and later to former high school chums James Battista and Thomas Martino. While the others may have been acting as beards for Donaghy, the FBI did not prosecute Donaghy and his cohorts for their actions.

What the FBI did arrest Donaghy for was providing this inside information to gamblers on about 30 to 40 NBA games a season since 2003.

This included over 100 games that Donaghy officiated. A large majority of those games were actually bet on by Concannon, not Battista and Martino who were the two arrested along with Donaghy. Why and how Concannon avoided this trouble remains a mystery.

What was this precious inside information Donaghy relayed to his associates? Some of it included details on which crews would be officiating certain games (which was not known outside the league's inner circle), how those officials tended to interact with the players, and up-to-the-minute player injury status. If Donaghy's information proved to be accurate, he collected $2,000 to $5,000 per game. If the bet didn't cover, he lost nothing (because he had not made a bet). Amazingly, even with wagering on games Donaghy was not directly involved in, his group managed a reported 80 percent success rate, something a career gambler would kill for, considering that even the top-level professional sports gamblers struggle to win 60 percent of their wagers.

While the FBI concluded that Donaghy "compromised his objectivity as a referee because of his personal financial interest in the outcome of NBA games," they concluded Donaghy did not—repeat—*did not* intentionally fix a single game. That is remarkable. The FBI (and, of course, the NBA) said that even though Donaghy had a financial stake in the outcome of several of the games he officiated, he remained an impartial judge while on the court. Donaghy himself told the FBI that if he did influence the outcome of a game he officiated, he did so only "unconsciously." That seems unlikely. Since Donaghy didn't admit to fixing games, it was up to the FBI to prove that he did if they doubted his story. That is no small task. Determining which fouls should and should not have been called is incredibly difficult given the speed of the game. Donaghy was forthright with everything else, and perhaps to save the Bureau some grief, the FBI might have taken Donaghy at his word and let the fixing side of the scandal slide. They still had their man dead to rights.

Donaghy's case blows apart many point-shaving/game-fixing myths: (1.) Despite claims that both Vegas bookmakers and underground bookies would and could sniff out a fix because of the large amount of "unnatural" money that would inevitably show up; none of them caught wind of

Donaghy. The FBI was investigating Donaghy's group for that very behavior for two years. While it's supposedly true that the games Donaghy was involved with were not fixed, with his gambling crew riding an 80 percent success rate, they might as well have been. Any gambler would take the odds of winning a 50/50 proposition 80 percent of the time. (2.) The idea that too much money would be needed to buy someone off? Not in the case of a referee with a gambling habit. Even earning in the neighborhood of $200,000 a year, Donaghy was living over and above his means. Apparently he needed the extra income that providing inside information gave him. (3.) The belief that conspiracies such as these can't be kept quiet? No one outside the mobsters' closed circle heard or recognized the deal they had worked out with Donaghy, and they were making money hand over fist using him. Even the NBA and its vast security department claimed it was clueless until made aware of the FBI's investigation on June 20, 2007, nearly a month after Donaghy's last refereed game.

Suddenly armed with some 20-20 hindsight, everyone could figure out Donaghy was in on the take. Interviewed by Wayne Drehs for ESPN. com, noted sports gambling expert R.J. Bell laid out some convincing stats regarding Donaghy's guilt. In examining the two years the FBI alleged Donaghy was involved with gambling on these games, he found that Donaghy's games achieved the "over" 57 percent of the time. In the two years before the FBI was involved, Donaghy's games went "over" just 44 percent of the time. The average for totals results in Vegas is darn near perfect at between 49–51 percent. Something was amiss. Bell dug a little further and found that in Donaghy's games, the two teams involved scored an average of 201.4 points per game compared to an over/under number that averaged 188. A difference of over 13 points a game. As Bell stated, "Vegas is too good for that to happen."[61] Perhaps worse, Bell found 10 straight games Donaghy was involved in where the point spread would move one-and-a-half points or more prior to tipoff, due to big money being wagered. In each case, the big money was correct. Again, Bell noted, "When the money is right 10 straight times, something is going on. To me, that's the gavel clicking down."[62] Still, the authorities stated Donaghy was not influencing the games he officiated.

As for the NBA, according to Commissioner Stern, despite having a "consultant" in Las Vegas "whose job it is to inform us whether there are any movements or unusual movements in betting on the NBA about which we should be concerned" as well as direct contact with the Nevada Gaming Board (NGB), the NBA was completely unaware of the Donaghy problem.

Fox Sports did some digging themselves. They found that over the two seasons in question, Donaghy led NBA officials in technical fouls, foul outs, and free throws awarded per game. Somehow the NBA either didn't notice this, or they didn't care that Donaghy was first on all three lists. But the truth is that once a referee makes the big leagues in any professional sport, the scrutiny started during the initial background check doesn't stop. All leagues continue to monitor their officials closely. The NFL, for example, evaluates their referees four times each week during the season. An observer will sit in the press box watching the game, keeping tabs on the referees' position on the field, their movement during game play, and the infractions that are called. A report and game films are sent to NFL headquarters where they are reviewed and catalogued. The NFL grades every official on every play within a game, using multi-angled game film to make these determinations. Once the league is finished, the information is shipped back to the referee crew for their own analysis. Like the players, referees are required to watch the game film and critique each other's performance with the hopes that seeing their mistakes will refine their technique.

The NBA probes even further. The NBA reviews and collects data on all its referees, partially in hopes of catching some sort of shenanigans well before they hit the front pages. As Commissioner Stern liked to boast, his referees were the most ranked, rated, reviewed, statistically analyzed and mentored group in the world. Stern stated, "We have, since the beginning of 2003–2004, been implementing a system that is designed to capture every call that a referee makes, and every non-call that is deemed by observers to be incorrect." The NBA employs 30 observers, one for each team in the league, which monitors each and every game. Yet, the NBA never discovered what Fox Sports reported: that Donaghy was leading the league in about every foul-assessed category there is. Was Stern's statement just good PR that blew up in his face, or was it real? Were Donaghy's methods too subtle to be noticed by the various ex-federal agents that make up the NBA's security office?

The question needs to be asked, where exactly was the NBA during Donaghy's apparent gambling years? Reported rumors had it that the NBA was aware of Donaghy's gambling habits for quite some time. It was against league rules for referees to gamble *at all,* yet Donaghy was seen frequenting Atlantic City casinos. The *New York Times* reported that the NBA had hired an outside firm (which Stern stated was the aforementioned Arkin Group) to investigate Donaghy sometime back in 2005. But, again to quote Stern, "We checked not only the Borgata [casino in Atlantic City], but every casino in Atlantic City and in Las Vegas to determine whether he had any presence in any of those places, and all of our investigation came up negative." Donaghy was free to continue refereeing not just regular season games, but was awarded playoff duties, something that is handed down from the league office as a sort of reward for a job well done during the regular season. All these rumors of casino-hopping coupled with the statistics that showed Donaghy was issuing fouls at the highest rate in the league, and the NBA still considered him to be one of their top officials?

Perhaps the NBA's biggest fear was that Donaghy wasn't alone in having a gambling habit. In May 2008, Donaghy's attorney, John Lauro, filed a letter in U.S. District Court on his client's behalf that said in part, "Tim [Donaghy] described the gambling activities of NBA officials, which were contrary to league rules. He also furnished information concerning circumstances that favored certain players or teams over others." It went on to claim that the NBA "allowed an environment to exist that made inside information, including knowledge of the particular officials who would work a game, valuable in connection with predicting the outcome of games" and added "particular relationships between officials and coaches or players affected the outcome of games, and other practices prevented games from being played on a level playing field." In other words, Donaghy's attorney said the NBA was dirty from front to back.

The NBA, of course, was quick to denounce everything Donaghy and that letter claimed. Joel Litvin, the NBA president of league and basketball operations, said, "The letter filed today on Mr. Donaghy's behalf contains an assortment of lies, unfounded allegations, and facts that have been previously acknowledged, such as the fact that certain NBA referees engaged in casino gambling in violation of NBA rules."[63] Litvin added, "The letter is the desperate act of a convicted felon who is hoping to avoid prison time. The only thing it proves is that Mr. Donaghy is no more trustworthy today than he was when he was breaking the law by betting on NBA games."[64] Of course, much of the best and damning information the feds get on organized crime come straight from former members who get busted and come clean to shorten their prison time, just like Donaghy attempted to do.

In the end, Donaghy was sentenced to two 15-month prison terms that were served concurrently. This was less than the 33 months he originally faced. So perhaps his revelations about the NBA did indeed help him. As for Donaghy's betting partners, Battista and Martino, they were sentenced to 15 and 12 months respectively. However, Donaghy's revelations didn't protect him while in prison. According to Pat Zaranek of Executive Prison Consultants ,of whom Donaghy was a client, Donaghy was assaulted and threatened while behind bars in November 2008 by another inmate with ties to the "New York mob." The attack damaged Donaghy's knee to the point of requiring surgery. Whether this was just another prison feud being played out or an actual message sent by the mob for Donaghy to keep quiet remains unknown.

The FBI may ultimately leave no stone unturned in its investigation, if only to make sure there wasn't a wider conspiracy involved. Any "wink, wink" deals the NBA has had with law enforcement might be set aside for this case. But it's not like the NBA is just sitting back and letting the FBI have free rein over the case. According to Lauro, the NBA might have "pressured" the attorney's office "into shutting down this prosecution to avoid the disclosure of information unrelated to Tim's [Donaghy] conduct."[65]

All of this has to be rather unsettling for the NBA and Commissioner Stern. In his initial press conference regarding the Donaghy situation, Commissioner Stern testily repeated the fact that this was an "isolated case," almost belaboring the point. Yet by 2007, Stern would state that the NBA's internal review of the situation, known as the Pedowitz Report, had in fact found other instances of referees engaging in gambling "policy violations" but, to quote Stern, "they are not hanging crimes." Then in a subsequent press conference later in the month, Commissioner Stern admitted that "*every single current NBA referee* has gambled in some form" while "more than half" of the league's 56 referees had broken the NBA's anti-casino policies.[66] Of course, Stern was quick to add that these trips to the casinos involved "No sports books. No bookmakers."[67] At the same time, according to an ESPN.com article, the referees did bet with their colleagues on college basketball games, football pools, and NCAA tournament pools. While attorney Lawrence Pedowitz, who led the NBA's investigation into its referees and gambling, interviewed all of the league's referees to discover this shocking information, the truth is no referee needed to admit to anything damning because no one was under oath. Perhaps they gave up minor infractions to alleviate the fear of, or keep hidden, bigger crimes. Because what referee would be foolish enough to 'fess up to gambling with a bookie without a threat forcing them into such an admission? How dumb could the NBA believe its own referees to be?

What kind of punishment was doled out by the league for these numerous infractions, all of which broke the policies set forth in the referees' collective bargaining agreement with the NBA? None. And none will be forthcoming. Instead, *NBA policies are to be rewritten* because according to Stern the policy was "too harsh and was not particularly well-enforced over the years."[68] This, among other things related to the Donaghy case, should create a credibility gap within the league that should worry every NBA fan.

Stern would love to downplay all of these gambling issues, not just to save his league and its referees' collective faces, but because the NBA is taking a good, hard look at expanding into Las Vegas. They held the 2006–2007 All-Star game in Las Vegas and the NBA's Summer League takes place there as well. Talks have been in the works for some time to either move a franchise into Las Vegas, or once again expand the league to include a team in the nation's gambling capital. The NBA can't attempt such a move if gambling allegations are constantly hanging over the league's head. How far can the NBA spin this story to get their way?

2009 – Having won a national college championship as a member of the University of Kentucky in 1996 and a NBA Championship as a member of the Miami Heat in 2006, three-time All-Star Antoine Walker ended his 12-year NBA career in 2008. By mid-2009, Walker had an arrest warrant out for him for writing 10 bad checks totaling $1 million to three Las Vegas casinos. Six were written to Caesars Palace with the other four split evenly between Planet Hollywood and the Red Rock Resort. Each of the bad checks was written for $100,000 and was dated between July 27, 2008 and January 19, 2009. Walker had paid back $178,000 of the debt, but there was still an outstanding balance of $882,500 when the warrant for his arrest was requested. While on the surface this appears to be the actions of an addicted gambler, one cannot say this with any certainty. It begs the question that if Walker ran up over $1 million in losses in a year's time since leaving the NBA, was he gambling—and on what—during his playing days? The question remains valid as Walker still wishes to play in the NBA.

So there you have it, over 140 years of professional athletes and officials gambling. Note that all of these cases (with the exception of the Mickey Mantle and Willie Mays banishment) involved people active within their respective sport. This list is as complete as I could make it. Yet chances are there are several incidents and cases I missed, not for lack of looking, but because they never came to light.

In researching this book, I discovered that not only does the FBI have its own file designation for the crime of sports bribery—the actual or attempted act of fixing the outcome of a sporting event—but it possesses over 450 different files directly related to the crime dating back to the crime's inception in the early 1960s. Not all of these deal with the four major professional sports; some pertain to college sports and known gambling sports such as horse racing, yet the fact that the FBI has averaged over 10 investigations into the crime each year is frightening. And that was prior to the FBI canceling the designation around the year 2000. Now most of these investigations are difficult to research as they have been spread into at least six separate designations, most of which involve organized crime. These types of reports are not the kind of thing the leagues want to be made public. Because they realize that nothing strikes deeper into the integrity of their games than the knowledge that their athletes are gambling on them.

Gambling can be a harmless activity. It can also become an addiction. The National Council on Problem Gambling released a report in 2006 that stated one percent of the U.S. population could be considered pathological gamblers while another two to three percent are simply problem gamblers. That equates to some six to 10 million adults with a gambling problem. The top three characteristics Gamblers Anonymous claim a compulsive gambler possesses are an inability and unwillingness to accept reality, emotional insecurity, and immaturity. How many coddled young athletes may embody those character traits? To believe that not one of these millions of addicted gamblers is currently suiting up or working for a major professional sports league is ludicrous.

What is worrisome is that when an athlete is caught gambling a fix is possible. As history has proven, it's not a far stretch of the imagination to believe that to be the case. How easy is it to fix a game? Thanks to the point spread, very easy. A team can still win the contest on the score board but lose the game in the sports book. Because of that, numerous professional games have been fixed. Points have been shaved, and no one outside of the conspirators is completely aware of the full truth.

The key is in not making such actions overt. Arizona State Sun Devils basketball player Stevin Smith was busted for point shaving in the mid-1990s As he said, "It's not what most people think it is, you know? Most people think you have to, uh, don't score, miss a shot, throw the ball in the stands. That's obvious. That's things that make it look obvious."[69] An outfielder plays ever-so-slightly out of position to allow a fly out to become a double. An offensive lineman misses a blocking assignment, costing the team a drive-sustaining first down. A small forward gets picked during a set play giving his man just enough space to hit a jumper. All of these are subtle actions, all unnoticed, all costly. When are they the results of fatigue or loss of concentration, when are they something more sinister? Most likely, we will never know.

TELEVISION

"Television is not the truth. Television's a goddamn amusement park. Television is a circus, a carnival, a traveling troupe of acrobats, storytellers, dancers, singers, jugglers, sideshow freaks, lion tamers, and football players. We're in the boredom-killing business. So if you want the truth, go to God. Go to your gurus. Go to yourselves. Because that's the only place you're ever going to find any real truth. The Man...you're never going to get any real truth from us." – Howard Beale (as portrayed by Peter Finch) in the motion picture *Network*

ALMOST EVERY SPORTS ENTHUSIAST WATCHES SIGNIFICANT ly more sporting events on television than they do in person. Some have no choice. What's a sports fan in Montana or Maine or Nebraska going to do without a professional sports team located within a reasonable driving distance? Even people who aren't sports fans are more than willing to watch at least a portion of big events like the Super Bowl on TV, if to do nothing more than watch the commercials. When you consider that even the largest stadium holds a maximum of 100,000 people per game, while tens of millions may be watching the same game from home or at the local pub, it is easy to realize which group of fans the leagues are more eager to please. Former Atlanta Braves and Atlanta Hawks owner Ted Turner once remarked that he wouldn't need a live audience to make his sports ventures profitable, and in the not-so-distant future, could foresee *hiring* spectators to provide local color and to cheer on cue, as if acting like a laugh track for a television sitcom.[1]

The influence of television is so powerful it has caused each of the major sports leagues to actually alter the play on the field to make their games more TV-friendly. Every sport has built-in TV timeouts so more commercials can be aired for the folks at home while boring the poor saps in the stands. NFL referees consult with the TV network representatives prior to kickoff to work out the signals and timing for such breaks in the action. Football's two-minute warning was strictly a TV invention, meant to halt play at a critical juncture in the game so that when the spectator at home was at his most heightened emotional and physical state, he could be hit with an advertisement. Rules have been changed and altered, such as the adding of the three-point basket in the NBA, in hopes of making the game more exciting to the fans at home. Instant replay rules, available in all leagues today, wouldn't exist if they weren't so widely used in the televised coverage of their games. The outcry from fans over "bad" calls that seemed obvious on instant replays led the leagues to resort to delays in action to check replays to ensure the calls on the field were made correctly. Playing fields have been made brighter and more photogenic (and covered with more advertisements) for television. Jerseys had TV numbers added to the sleeves to make players more identifiable to broadcasters. Schedules have been changed to fit television ideals, with the adding of *Monday Night Football* and later *Sunday Night Football,* and "flex" scheduling that allows both the NFL and NBC to change any Sunday day game into a prime-time night game at their very whim, being the most obvious. Even the scheduling of playoff games is built around what works best for the television networks and their viewers.

Roone Arledge, former president of ABC Sports and the mastermind behind *Monday Night Football* once said, "Most of what TV does wrong is done to generate more dollars for [team] owners. If we cram 18 commercials into a football game it's because the owners and the leagues are so damned greedy in what they ask for in rights."[2] His comment begs two questions. The first is, only 18 commercials there, Roone? Maybe that's all there were in the 1970s, but not today.

A study was conducted in 2003 to see what exactly was broadcast during a typical NFL game. The game used was a CBS broadcast of a regular season contest between the Indianapolis Colts and Denver Broncos. The game featured 133 replays, 141 graphics, 107 shots of coaches, and 80 shots of fans. As for commercials, the couch potato watching at home had to endure 29 commercial breaks featuring 78 ads on top of 34 promos for other CBS broadcasts. During another examination of an NFL game, this time an ABC broadcast of a 2003 playoff game between the Tennessee Titans and Baltimore Ravens, there were 108 replays, 56 shots of coaches, and some 67 commercials as well as 29 promos for ABC's other programs. For the ABC broadcast, which lasted approximately three hours, only 16 minutes and 48 seconds was actual game play with an average play lasting all of 6.9 seconds.[3] This realization should've hit anyone owning a VCR or a digital video recorder some time ago. If you just watch the action and skip all the related junk that fills the spaces between it, you can take in just about any sporting event in much less than half the time period in which it was broadcast.

The second and more important question Arledge's statement brings to mind is just how much money is involved in TV broadcast rights to sporting events? The frightening answer is literally billions of dollars every year.

Television didn't have an impact on professional sports until after World War II. The first World Series broadcast nationally was in 1949. According to the book *Baseball and Billions*, author Andrew Zimbalist states that less than 12 percent of households in the United States had televisions at the time of NBC's broadcast of the 1949 World Series. But by 1953, 15 of the 16 MLB teams in existence had local TV contracts while during that same year ABC introduced the national MLB "Game of the Week." Just three years later, according to Zimbalist, approximately 17 percent of all money earned by MLB teams came directly from broadcast television rights.

It took time and some convincing on the part of baseball owners to package their television rights and sell them as a single unit. Mostly, MLB broadcast rights were sold independently and on a team-by-team basis with the Yankees being the first to do so in 1946. Football saw the folly in this. The NFL, too, had originally sold its television rights on a team-by-team basis since the 1940s, but by 1960 they recognized the entertainment value of their product and decided to market it as such. However, in order to sell its rights as a unit, the NFL needed help to avoid any antitrust issues. As a result of a little deal-making in congress, the NFL got its wish. Proposed by Congressman Emanuel Celler, the bill that allowed the NFL and the rest of the professional sports leagues to package and sell their broadcast rights while maintaining their antitrust status was signed into law by President Kennedy in 1961.

CBS promptly gobbled up the rights to NFL games in 1962. They paid the NFL approximately $9 million for the first two seasons. By the time its contract ran out in 1964, CBS had some competition. The resultant bidding war forced CBS to spend just over $28 million to renew its two-year deal with the NFL.

Meanwhile the NFL's rival, the AFL, was floundering. Having made its debut in 1960, the AFL didn't seem likely to be in operation in 1965. Luckily for them NBC, which had failed in its bid to steal the NFL away from CBS, was still in the market for professional football. NBC promptly forgot about the NFL and gave the AFL $42 million for the next five seasons' worth of games. That money saved the AFL. Thanks to that much-needed cash injection, the AFL was able to lure better talent to its league and make itself a viable rival to the NFL. In fact, without that deal with NBC, the NFL today might be a much smaller league as the 10 AFL teams that joined the league in the 1970 merger probably would not have survived without NBC's money.

The growing rivalry between the competing football leagues was both profitable and infuriating. Both made a good deal of cash from their respective TV deals, but they were treading on each other's turf. The NFL had a longstanding rule that blacked out a team's home games, whether a sellout or not, within a 75-mile radius of the stadium. If you wanted to see a Packers home game, either you bought a ticket or moved yourself 75 miles away from Lambeau Field. In fact, the NFL felt so strongly about keeping fans in the seats in those early days, no other games were broadcast into those blacked-out areas. NBC and the AFL didn't impose such a restriction. They promptly began broadcasting their games nationally, even into areas the NFL had blacked out. Fans now had a choice. And the NFL didn't like it. Soon they began broadcasting rival, non-home games into areas that would have previously been blacked out. Then the NFL began adding doubleheaders to their schedules, trying anything to maintain its popularity over the AFL. Amazingly, the NFL's 75-mile blackout radius remained in effect until 1973 when congressmen in and around Washington, D.C. became fed up with not being able to watch Redskins home games. They forced the NFL's hand into what is today a league standard in which home games are only blacked out if the game isn't a sellout in the stadium within 72 hours of kickoff.

For these and other financial reasons, both leagues decided they had butted heads long enough. They struck a deal to merge into one unified league. Because of each league's prior television commitments, the merger did not take place officially until 1970. That is why both CBS and NBC simultaneously broadcast the first Super Bowl in 1967.

Perhaps the biggest addition to the new NFL's package was the advent of *Monday Night Football (MNF)*. What seems like a tradition of sorts today was in fact a huge gamble when first aired in 1966 by CBS. The league feared oversaturation would cause fan apathy. As an experiment, the NFL and CBS aired four Monday night games between 1966 and 1969. Those first trial Monday night games earned great ratings. They paved the way for ABC's official weekly *Monday Night Football* telecasts that began in 1970. What is most important about this is the fact that sports were not seen as "prime time" material in the early 1970s. Sports were a fine afternoon diversion, but were not judged capable of competing with true television programs. *Monday Night Football* changed that line of thought by making each game a spectacle, a type of must-see TV. With the consistently huge audiences *MNF* pulled in, spurred in part by gamblers wanting to recoup Sunday's losses on Monday's game, the networks began to realize the potential for prime-time sports programming that blurred the line between sports and entertainment. They grabbed that baton and have never looked back. By the time of its 1977 deal with the three NFL network partners, each of the 28 NFL teams was earning $6 million from broadcast rights alone, more than each team's individual gate receipts from tickets sold.[4]

However, it wasn't always sunshine and roses for the NFL and its friends in television. In the early and mid-1980s, the NFL saw its popularity take a hit. Ratings dropped. In 1985, the TV networks *lost* an estimated $50 million on their investment in the NFL.[5] That was just the beginning.

In 1990, CBS was responsible for approximately 50 percent of all sports coverage available on TV including the Super Bowl, the NCAA Final Four tournament, Major League Baseball's Division Championship Series and the World Series, and NASCAR's Daytona 500. All of that didn't amount to a hill of beans for the network. They continued to trail both NBC and ABC in the ratings war. Plus, the network lost somewhere between $55 and $100 million on its deal with MLB *alone*.[6] That led CBS to practically beg MLB to restructure the $1 billion deal the two had just recently signed. The debacle led CBS Sports president Neal Pilson to ask, "How far can free TV go to support the major sports leagues?"[7] Apparently, much further than anyone expected. The very next year, the NFL's new broadcast rights contract cost the networks $3.6 billion. Factored into that was $260 million in *losses*.[8] Meanwhile, the revenues from that same TV deal accounted for 64 percent of each NFL team's annual income.[9] The NFL wasn't alone in reaping massive TV profits.

The NBA's sweetheart deals with NBC brought in truckloads of cash the league desperately desired. It wasn't long ago that the NBA was considered to be adjunct programming. In the 1970s, the NBA had a paltry $74 million contract for four years with CBS. CBS in turn focused primarily on the four big-market NBA teams it thought were worth broadcasting. It didn't help raise the ratings as NBA games barely registered on the Nielsen charts. It was so bad the 1981–1982 NBA Finals were broadcast by CBS... when they felt like it. Game Six, the deciding game of the series between the Los Angeles Lakers and the Philadelphia 76ers wasn't broadcast live. CBS refused to interrupt their normal broadcast schedule (which was showing a rerun of *Dallas*) for the game. Instead, it aired the game tape-delayed starting at nearly midnight on the East Coast. But once NBC got its mitts on the NBA, the two worked hand-in-hand massaging the league into a ratings powerhouse. It didn't come cheap. By 1989, NBC was paying the NBA $600 million for four years. In 1993, they re-upped for another four-year deal tallying $750 million. Plus, the NBA received an additional $275 million for four years from the TNT cable network. Some NBA teams also supplemented their income by producing their own TV broadcasts, raising their collective incomes from an estimated combined total of $63 million a year in 1987–1988 to some $130 million by the 1992-1993 season.[10]

Baseball wasn't doing too shabby for itself at this time, either. By 1990, approximately half of the money a MLB team earned came directly from broadcast rights. In 1996, MLB signed deals with FOX, NBC, and ESPN tallying a grand total of $1.7 billion for four years. Through that contract, MLB teams received about $28 million apiece, an amount equal to the average MLB team's payroll at the time.[11]

Despite that early to mid-1980s hiccup in televised sports' ratings, the numbers for sports on TV continued to rise throughout the 1990s and into the new millennium. With that came a ridiculous increase in revenue that each league raked in with each new TV contract. For example, here are the numbers the NBA took in with each successive television revenue deal: In 1994, NBC and TNT paid the NBA a combined $1.1 billion. Four years later, with their next contract in 1998, that amount doubled to $2.64 billion. When that deal expired in 2002, ESPN, ABC, and Time Warner stole NBC's thunder, gobbling up the rights to televise the NBA's games for an amazing $4.6 billion. The new contract signed between ABC/ESPN and the NBA in 2007 will bring $930 million *a year* to the NBA for the next eight years. This latest deal also includes the NBA's digital media rights, the first sale of this sort for a professional sports league.

Amazingly, to the NFL, that $1 billion a year is chump change. They've been making that since their 1994 contract with the TV networks. In 1998, the new TV deal brought the NFL $17.6 billion, which equated to $2.2 billion a year for eight years. With that, the average NFL team earned $73 million alone in broadcast rights fees.[12] The NFL's salary cap—the maximum amount any team was allowed to spend on its roster—was $85.5 million in 2005. With the new TV contract for 2005, the NFL took in $11.5 billion from CBS, FOX, and DirecTV. Seems like less, but when you factor in another $1.1 billion a year alone from ESPN for *Monday Night Football* (which is bizarre since ABC was reportedly losing $150 million a year on *MNF*) and some $600 million a year more from NBC for *Sunday Night Football (SNF)*, in reality, both CBS and FOX are paying 25 percent more for the NFL with this contract while DirecTV is paying a whopping 75 percent increase in its fee—mainly so DirecTV can maintain solitary control of its NFL "Sunday Ticket" package.[13] In 2009, DirecTV again upped its ante to maintain control of that "Sunday Ticket" package, promising to pay the NFL $1 billion a year for its rights. CBS, too, re-upped with the NFL in 2009 to maintain control over AFC games through 2013 while obtaining broadcast rights to Super Bowl XLVII in the process. Terms of the new CBS deal were not disclosed, but it is believed to be a new record price.

While MLB doesn't command such lofty numbers, it isn't lacking. In 2001, FOX dropped some $2.5 billion for five years worth of MLB. Oddly enough, FOX declared a $909 million loss on that deal, while at the same time, MLB teams profited nearly an additional $700 million from the sale of local TV rights.[14] Surprisingly FOX re-signed a seven-year deal with MLB in 2007 to the tune of another $3 billion.

The primary reason TV networks are so willing to dish out billions of dollars is because they can make that money back and more through advertising. Granted, having the rights to certain major events like the Super Bowl or World Series is a feather in any network's cap. These events bring in a certain amount of added viewers along with a short, but massive ratings boost for the broadcast. TV networks can't survive billion-dollar hits just to use professional sports as promotional tools for other programs. Especially when the money laid out to buy the rights for those athletic contests is greater than the money spent on the entire network's other scripted programming content combined. The only way to recoup those costs is through ad revenue (for Super Bowl XLIII played in 2009, NBC raked in a reported $260 million in ad revenue on that day alone).

Advertising dominates sports programming, and these days it's not just the typical commercials to which the average viewer is subjected. Games will be "brought to you by" certain companies. Halftime shows are "sponsored by" other companies. Pregame shows will have certain facts and stats highlighted "courtesy of" even other corporations. Heck, if you watch an episode of ESPN's *SportsCenter* these days, it's hard to tell the commercials apart from the actual show thanks to such segments as the "Budweiser Hot Seat" or the "Coors' Cold Hard Facts." The obtrusiveness of these advertisements and sponsorships exists because the networks need to get their money's worth from every second of broadcast time.

There are many more revenue gimmicks that the networks and leagues use to get money out of their advertisers. Certain companies are willing to pay more for an "official product" designation. In 2007, Coors was the "official" beer of the NFL even though Coors hasn't always been the NFL's beer of choice. They had to pay for that honor. Many other companies are more than willing to do likewise. Look at NASCAR. The racing league is the ultimate advertising sell-out with their drivers appearing as walking billboards for their sponsors while eager fans, wanting to look like their driving heroes, do likewise. NASCAR was even willing to change the name of their championship title for a few extra bucks. What was once the Winston Cup became the Nextel Cup, then the Sprint Cup. They are willing to slap an advertiser's sticker anywhere there is space to fit one (and anywhere a camera can film one) while their drivers are obligated to mention and thank sponsors' names during interviews. How long will it be before other leagues take NASCAR's lead and have their victorious athletes thanking Nike, Budweiser, and Chevy for helping them achieve their lifelong dreams? We've already had to endure years of newly crowned champions exclaiming to the nation, "I'm going to Disney World!" What's next?

While watching a game, you may have noticed that certain ads are more repetitive than others. Corporations are willing to pay extra money to the networks to ensure theirs is the only such product type shown during a game. Sometimes purchased for a quarter, a half, or even an entire game, such exclusive ad time will guarantee a corporation like the Ford Motor Company that theirs is the only car company advertised for that time period. So when you're starting to get hungry before the first half is over, McDonald's may have been the only food commercials you've been subjected to, and really, doesn't a Big Mac sound pretty good right about now? There is no democracy when it comes to selling ad time, just money and the greed for more.

The reason advertisers are so willing to shell out the extra loot for sporting events is that sports consistently bring in a certain key demographic group, males aged 18–49. No other TV program can boast of catering to and holding the attention of men better than sports programming. This is why so many commercials during these events are directed squarely at men. Specific types of advertisers thrive upon the male population and can only be certain that their tailored message is seen and absorbed by their target audience during sporting events. This is partially why the NFL can command such a price from the networks. The NFL draws a guaranteed 20 percent of the TV audience on Sunday afternoon,[15] and a vast majority of it is male.

Because of sports' consistent ability to pull in viewers, networks are willing to go out on a limb and will guarantee certain sponsors specific ratings for their sports programming content. For larger corporations, the ones willing to buy the most ad time, networks will give advertisers an insurance policy of sorts. They will promise certain ratings numbers and pay refunds for the ads that fail to reach a targeted number of people. There is substantial risk involved. While the Super Bowl is one of the most-watched events televised every year, the NFL's weekly numbers can wax and wane from season to season. The NBA Finals, their usual blue -hip product, endured its lowest ratings in years in 2007. Every league has endured a downturn in the recent past, the powerhouse NFL included, and the NHL nearly fell completely off the face of the earth (well, at least American TV) just four years ago. What can make both the networks and the leagues so confident that the numbers they are used to remain at or surpass the usual levels? How do they ensure that they don't lose their devoted followers? How do they expand their audience?

The answer is simple. They take absolute control of the message.

Don't for a second think that any of the TV networks took their investment into the professional sports leagues lightly. From the very beginning, television established its presence in sports, all the way down to the locker room. Former NFL player Bernie Parrish described CBS's invasion of the NFL in 1964 thusly: "Players complained about the intrusion of TV technical crews and the pompous interviews demanded by the pseudo-experts in the crested sports coats. When CBS executives paid $14.1 million to televise the NFL games, they acted as if they had bought the sport, including the people who played it."[16] Though the money the networks spent on sports clearly gave them the right to act as they did, it didn't mean the leagues relinquished control of their respective sport.

Instead, the two homogenized, forming symbiotic relationships.

The most overt and blatant blurring of the line between league and network came in the form of the NBA's deal with NBC in the early and mid-1990s. CBS, which had broadcast the NBA without much success, wasn't ready to pay the kind of numbers the NBA suddenly wanted in 1989 so they, and later ABC, passed on the league. That left just NBC which eagerly snapped up the NBA's rights. But something more was in the works between the league and the network. NBA commissioner David Stern and NBC Sports president Dick Ebersol began working hand-in-hand, day in, day out developing not just the relationship between the two entities, but the very fabric of the league itself. Amazingly, Stern seemed to be the one calling the shots as to what NBC should and shouldn't do when covering the NBA. Ebersol is quoted in the book *Money Players* describing the weekly meetings the NBA would have with people at NBC, saying, "Twelve to 14 of us for lunch, once our season starts up, to discuss how we're promoting, how we're producing, what we're doing with features in the pregame, at halftime, what *Inside Stuff* [the weekly NBA show the league demanded NBC air as part of their deal] is doing, our thoughts about the previous weekend. And if he [Stern] feels that something may have been lightly treated or not enough… he'll go right in the face of the producer or director or promo person and it will be a tough one minute."[17] Who was running what, exactly?

The ties between the TV networks and the leagues run even deeper today. When NBC paid the NFL some $600 million a year for the rights to *Sunday Night Football*, as part of the deal, the NFL agreed that all 32 of its franchises would be required to use General Electric products including such things as financial services, stadium lights, and medical equipment. Did I mention GE just happens to own NBC? So in giving the NFL $600 million a year, GE stood to receive some $300 to $500 million a year *back* from the NFL, not to mention the exclusiveness the pair would now share with each other.

With the huge amounts of money involved in such sweetheart deals between the leagues and the networks, it's as if the leagues have been given a green light to run roughshod over the networks. For instance, ESPN aired a scripted show called *Playmakers* that was a fictional account of a professional football team. The show dealt with many controversial subjects within sports including drugs, gambling, and homosexuality. Despite garnering good ratings, ESPN canceled the program. Why? It's rumored that the NFL didn't appreciate the light the fictional show shined on its practices (even though the show's team was fictional and the league wasn't named the NFL) and threatened to bar ESPN from carrying NFL games. ESPN was wise enough to side with the NFL on the matter. This shows the near absolute control a league can have over a network concerning the message being broadcast.

The NFL appears to have the most control over its broadcasting partners. Recently, it has tightened the noose around its local affiliates, most notably in Cleveland. In the summer of 2006, the Browns faced a lawsuit for breaking a contract with local Cleveland TV station WOIO. Why? Because WOIO aired a 911 call involving the team owner's relatives. Although the call was a public record, Browns ownership believed WOIO was "irresponsible" in its reporting, therefore they yanked away the station's broadcast rights, breaking a contract that allowed them to air preseason games and other Browns-related programming.[18] The case was later settled with the end result being that WOIO lost its ability to air any Browns programming.

That's not all on the local front. Without much fanfare, the NFL began a new policy in 2006 which effectively kicked all local affiliated camera crews off its sidelines, barring them from a field which more often than not was paid for with public funds. The Radio and Television News Directors Association (RTNDA) has accused the NFL of "subverting the American tradition of free press" through this newly implemented policy."[19] Why would the NFL do such a thing? Control. As a NFL spokesman told *Daily Variety* in regards to the new policy, the local news footage often ends up portraying the NFL unfavorably.[20]

But just how far down will a network stoop to accommodate the NFL? Try censorship. CBS broadcast Super Bowl XLI in 2007, yet it didn't have complete control over the ads broadcast during the game. The NFL refused to allow CBS to air a recruitment commercial for the U.S. Border Patrol. The ad in question was no problem for the NBA which allowed the same commercial to be shown during the *NBA All-Star Game* nor did the

NCAA have a problem, which allowed CBS to broadcast the ad throughout the course of the Final Four basketball tournament. So what did the NFL find so offensive with the TV spot? According to NFL spokesman Greg Aiello, "The ad that the department submitted was specific to Border Patrol, and it mentioned terrorism. We were not comfortable with that. The borders, the immigration debate is a very controversial issue, and we were sensitive to any perception we were injecting ourselves into that."[21] Instead, the NFL proposed a "more generic recruiting ad for the department that didn't highlight the borders." Why did this matter to the NFL? The ad in question might have upset the NFL's latest target audience, Latinos. The NFL has gone to great lengths to appeal to this specific segment of the population. In an attempt to widen their North American appeal beyond the United States, the NFL has held a regular season game in Mexico City in 2005, launched the NFLatino.com website, and celebrated Hispanic Heritage Month during the 2007 season with their own set of ads aimed squarely at the Latino market. Apparently a single 30-second commercial that mentioned both "terrorism" and the "securing of America's borders" would have ruined all of the NFL's hard work.

Even with all of this factored into the equation, the primary way any league controls its message is through the very people that should be informing the fans of the leagues' abuses, the sports reporters. It is rare, very rare, to see a sports reporter do an ounce of true investigative reporting. Like the leagues themselves, sports insiders only discuss such negative instances *after* they've come to light. Have you ever heard a local or even national sports reporter make a statement like "Through my investigative leads and contacts within the league I've been able to discover that so-and-so on such-and-such team is a major drug addict, criminal, or gambler?" No. Even supposed "hard-hitting" sports programs like HBO's *RealSports* or ESPN's *Outside the Lines* fail to stir the pot enough to actually uncover dirt within the sports world that's not already known.

Sports reporters break no significant stories because truth be told, they can't. Or won't. They're not just handcuffed by the teams and players they cover, they're beholden to them. And everyone involved knows it. Even former Detroit Lions player Alex Karras wrote, "Reporters who presented a favorable image of club policy were taken care of. Those who reported flaws in the system usually found themselves on the outside looking in."[22]

The NFL realized a long time ago that the way to the fans' hearts was through positive sports reporting. Don Weiss was the NFL's director of information during the late '60s and early '70s who wrote in his book *The Making of the Super Bowl*: "[NFL commissioner] Pete Rozelle was unwavering in his insistence that the league level with the press and help them do their job. Moreover, by our providing them with information that helped them better perform their jobs, he reasoned, writers would follow pro football more intently and naturally tend to look with favor on the NFL—or at least be less inclined to go out of their way to criticize [the NFL]."[23] It was during Rozelle's tenure as NFL commissioner that the league began to realize the power of public relations. Of course, it didn't hurt that Rozelle's background was in PR. A significant part of the NFL's public relations machine was focused squarely on reporters covering the NFL. As Weiss wrote, "Almost overnight, these public relations people gained a status throughout the league they had never enjoyed before…High school students were hired to clip everything that was written about the NFL in the hundred-odd daily papers to which the NFL subscribed. The clips were used to build hundreds of files on players, coaches, and every conceivable football topic. The best—and occasionally the worst—were distributed throughout the league to keep clubs apprised of what various writers were thinking. When the tone of a columnist indicated that some friendly guidance was needed, he'd get a phone call offering it."[24] Weiss' use of the phrase "friendly guidance" hints at something darker. Who exactly needed those phone calls from the league office? The writers presenting favorable stories about the NFL or the ones commenting negatively on the league? Probably the latter since former player Bernie Parrish, who was familiar with Weiss during those days, wrote, "Rozelle gets whatever he wants released through the wire services. The moral and, perhaps, legal question is how much is stopped or restricted to local areas to please him and the people he represents."[25]

The NFL's Big Brother-like behavior was not a new phenomenon, merely an updated version of a policy that had been in place in sports reporting for decades. "By the end of the decade [the 1920s], the American people had a new type of hero, the exceptional athlete whose exploits quickly became the stuff of legend, thanks to star-struck sportswriters who covered up their human weaknesses and exaggerated their athletic achievements."[26] How true is that statement? How many fans today know the reality of Babe Ruth? That he was a serial adulterer who would bed multiple women in a night and whose famous "stomachache" wasn't caused by too many hot dogs and soda pops but was most likely a bout of the clap? That wasn't reported back in the day because any sportswriter who knew the truth simply couldn't print it because he would instantly lose access to Ruth, if not the entire Yankees organization. In the 80-plus years since Ruth's heyday, not a single thing has changed about the dynamic between sports reporters, star athletes, and their leagues.

For example, look at the idol worship that existed between Michael Jordan and his minions, the so-called sports reporters. Do you want to know why MJ's gambling issues were as hushed up as they were? Why the fans never heard more than what MJ or the NBA begrudgingly told us? It's because no one had the guts to dig deeper and tell the full story. As author Michael Leahy wrote in his book about Michael Jordan, *When Nothing Else Matters*, "Michael Jordan offered them [sports reporters] the celebrity's form of friendship: small morsels of self-serving information in exchange for the tacit understanding that they'd never write or say anything critical about him."[27] That's exactly what fans got, year in, year out. No one dared besmirch MJ in Chicago during the Bulls' six championship runs for fear of losing access not to just the biggest sports story in Chicago, but the biggest sporting star in any league in the entire world. Today, many of those same sports reporters in the Chicago area will now talk openly about MJ and his known gambling habits during those championship days. Why didn't any of them step up back then and break the story? They were too busy kissing his butt to get their puff pieces written to keep their jobs.

When you dig further into the sports broadcasting world, you realize that the behavior of these sports reporters is just the tip of the iceberg. All leagues have control over whom the networks hire as broadcasters to discuss and analyze their games. As controversial a choice both Rush Limbaugh and

Dennis Miller were in their brief stints as commentators for the NFL, both were allowed in by the league. Because all of the network commentators have to bend to the wishes of not just the networks, but also to the leagues, they find themselves having to toe the league-mandated line whether they like it or not.

Of course, for many of the commentators this isn't too difficult since they once played for the very league they are now covering. All pro sports coverage is inundated with ex-players and coaches who now act as commentators. A cursory look at just the NFL will find that in 2008, pregame shows featured ex-players Terry Bradshaw, Howie Long, Dan Marino, Boomer Esiason, Shannon Sharpe, Tom Jackson, Keyshawn Johnson, Emmitt Smith, Steve Young, Cris Collinsworth, Jerome Bettis, Tiki Barber as well as ex-coaches Jimmy Johnson, Barry Switzer, Bill Cower, and Mike Dikta. Most of the NFL's color announcers, guys like Troy Aikman, Ron Jaworski, Phil Simms, and John Madden, cut their teeth in the NFL. Fans trust them because they've played or coached the game. They understand the nuances, the preparation, and the strategy involved.

Now they are simply broadcasters and act as nothing more than shills. In fact, who better to spread league propaganda than commentators like these? It can't be easy to criticize something that not only made you rich and famous but continues to keep you in the limelight. They may be considered dumb jocks, but they know better than to bite the hand that feeds. There's no reason to rock the boat. If the league wants something pushed, a new rule or product, these guys do it without any coercion. And if the same league demands something be downplayed, hey, these guys know how the game's played, on all levels. So how can we trust the opinions of these commentators to be their own and not something that's been league-approved and mandated? Truth be told, we cannot.

Even though roughly 98 percent of what these network sports commentators say is nothing more than opinionated bunk, occasionally they are forced to discuss real off-the-field issues. Often avoided or brushed aside, current news such as Michael Vick's federal dog-fighting case and NBA referee Tim Donaghy's federal gambling probe cannot be completely ignored. The leagues use their commentators to belittle these incidents while pushing league-mandated ideas, not to dig deeper into such things as the root causes behind them. It happens because those discussions do not produce profit. In fact, "as co-promoter of pro leagues…broadcast television tends not to take an adversarial approach to lapses in integrity by leagues, teams, and players."[28] The networks can't afford to. They have too much invested in these leagues to turn around and hammer them on their potential improprieties. Because of this, "even when network sportscasters do attempt adversarial reporting, the results are often limpid…when assessed from normative standards of journalism, such as those advocated by the Society of Professional Journalists."[29] Which should come as no shock since we're not dealing with trained journalists, we're dealing with ex-jocks.

What this leaves us with then is something that very well may not be what it appears to be. "[TV] coverage may obscure the reality of competitive sports, particularly at the highest levels: Playing fields are not always level; victory is sometimes secured by the athlete who best bends the rules, not to the most able or to the best trained athlete; the star isn't necessarily clean; and very few college standouts ever make a living at sports."[30] Even above and beyond that, the major sports leagues are masters of their own realities. They create the sport you see, they package and sell that as a product, and then control everything that is said or written about it. It is their game. This realization makes one wonder what sports are anymore. Are "sports" something played in backyards and on little league fields? Have professional sports been transformed into something unidentifiable?

Legendary quarterback Joe Namath related the following story on the television program *America's Game: The Story of the 1968 Jets*: "I remember one time at a table with [New York Jets owner] Mr. and Mrs. Werblin at the Four Seasons and I was so upset because something had been written about our team, about me, and I was just ready to call it. And you know, I said, 'This is ridiculous!' And Mrs. Werblin just chuckled and she said, 'Joseph, it's show business.' I said, 'No, it's not! It's football! This is football! This is not show business!' She said, 'Joe, it's show business.' And, you know, that's stayed with me since."[31] Perhaps no truer statement has ever been made about the NFL or any other professional sports league.

It's show business.

If, as we've seen, the fans in the stadium seats no longer matter compared to the millions out there in TV land, then what can professional sports be beyond a televised production? The athletes are the actors while the game is the story. Professional sports becomes a never-ending soap opera with characters constantly coming and going while a similar storyline is played out with subtle variations ad nauseam season after season. Televised games need to always cultivate high ratings, and to ensure those ratings, productions are subject to tinkering. Certain story lines and characters deemed more interesting or important need to be pushed while the less desirable are killed off. How can that manipulation happen when what we see is supposed to be actual reality?

In show business, what is deemed "reality" often times is not. For centuries, magicians have fascinated intelligent people with their illusions. Mediums and spiritualists continue to convince sound-minded people into believing they have the power to communicate with the dead.

The advent of radio further blurred the lines between what was factual information and what was simple entertainment. Orson Welles' famous broadcast of *War of the Worlds* seemed so real to its mesmerized radio audience that some chose refuge in suicide because they believed that aliens from Mars were actually invading the Earth. Disk jockeys, bribed into popularizing certain songs and artists through payola schemes, scandalized the music industry in the late 1950s. In 2006, several music companies including Sony, Warner Music Group, and Universal Music Group all had to pay millions of dollars in fines for their participation in modern-day payola schemes. These companies even attempted to influence what was aired on MTV knowing the power the network had on CD sales. Yet more proof that popularity is bought and sold.

The music industry has even more secrets they don't like to reveal. What you hear when you attend a recording artist's "live" concert may not actually be the performers at work. Ashlee Simpson's infamous appearance on *Saturday Night Live*, during which her band played one song while her recorded voice sang another, was a gaffe that revealed how live performances are sometimes enhanced. Music artists may seem to be rocking on stage, but sometimes they're simply faking it. Other artists employ hi-tech pitch-shifters that allow tone-deaf vocalists to seem to sing in perfect pitch. These devices can work instantaneously to alter one's voice, raising or lowering it to the correct pitch while the artist "sings." Even with such systems available, an artist like Britney Spears can still charge her fans exorbitant ticket prices to witness her lip-sync to her own songs. Yet she still plays to packed arenas.

Television is no better. Game shows in the 1950s were wildly popular. What seemed to be a test of intelligence on programs like *TwentyOne* turned out to be nothing more than a battle to see which contestant was the better actor. The producers of the programs would give their contestants the answers to the questions to be asked on the show prior to the live broadcasts. Then the contestants would do their best to act as if they were struggling to come up with the answers during the show, all the while having had plenty of time to memorize the answers. The producers would also designate which contestants had overstayed their welcome and ask them to take a dive, and they usually did without protest. When one such contestant felt he was screwed over by the producers, his allegations against the program led to congressional investigations that revealed the truth everyone involved had originally denied: that the shows were rigged with the most popular contestants allowed to linger on air for longer periods of time because they brought in higher ratings.

While these high-minded game shows are no longer in vogue as they were in the '50s, TV viewers are now subjected to "reality" television shows. Just how "real" these reality shows are remains a very interesting question. One of the most popular reality shows, *Survivor*, has admitted to "re-staging" certain scenes with body doubles, meaning nothing you saw during those segments was, in fact, real. Criticisms about the "survival expert" host of *Man Vs. Wild*, alleged that he preferred staying in hotels rather than living off the land as the program suggested. One of MTV's recent hit reality shows, *The Hills*, was discovered to be filming scripted scenes rather than the unrehearsed, actual dialogue between the stars of the show. More than one former contestant on *American Idol* claimed that the voting system was rigged. So what else in the world of "reality television" has been an outright lie? Who's to say, with the strictly enforced non-disclosure contracts that must be signed by everyone participating in these programs? Without a doubt, situations on all reality programs are intentionally manufactured, manipulated, and edited to make the shows as riveting as possible.

So why couldn't the same be true for professional sports? I am not the first, nor most likely the last to equate sports with being nothing more than show business. Former MLB player Jose Canseco wrote, "I always saw myself as more of an entertainer than a baseball player, and I was always very up-front about it. Some people didn't like to hear that back then, but now I think most people have accepted that baseball is as much an entertainment business as a game. I never had a problem with thinking of baseball as entertainment. Actually, I always enjoyed that part of it."[32] Former NFL player and current TV commentator for the NFL Tim Green wrote, "If you think that the players in an NFL game aren't only aware, but affected by the television cameras and microphones, you're wrong. Players often know when the cameras are on them, whether they can see the little red lights or not, and they play to them as if they were on a Hollywood movie set."[33] Perhaps more to the point is author Mike Freeman who wrote, "Football stopped being simply a game long ago. It is as big a business as Microsoft or American Express, complete with all of the corporate trimmings: backstabbing, manipulation, and power plays. And despite wisely investing in revenue sharing and a salary cap, most football players are beginning to realize for the first time that the sports world is an entertainment medium in which everyone acts out of his own self-interest."[34]

So, let's assume for a moment that professional sports leagues are not just sports entities, but are mere cogs in the greater show business machine. What does that mean? It forces each league to concern itself with increasing market share while maintaining popularity with its original fan base. How can a league do this, especially when the audience has seen and heard it all before?

The how is that the leagues script the outcomes of their own games. Not *every* game, just key games. At certain critical junctures, storylines become more important than the purity of the contest. So, the storylines during the course of a season, or during the playoffs, that compel fans to keep watching even once their beloved teams are out of the running for a championship, are artificially extended. Certain matchups undoubtably offer more built-in intrigue across the nation than others. It is at this point that the league may see substantial profit in extending that one particular team's run over and beyond its actual, and natural, existence.

A manipulation of this sort may seem like a shocking and unnecessary step for any league to undertake because any sporting contest naturally lends itself to the randomness of its outcomes. The idea that any team can win today's game normally prevails. Even so, such randomness won't guarantee an increase in audience size. Wise businessmen minimize risk especially when billions of dollars are at stake. So, it makes sense that leagues and owners do what they can to minimize the effect of the randomness factor while increasing their fans' emotional connection, thus wringing out as much audience perpetuation as possible.

TV networks manipulate viewers into feeling that if they do not watch they're missing out on something special. They pinpoint who their stars are, craft storylines featuring them, and then hype these programs to the point where viewers feel they must watch to remain informed. The networks succeed because they know how to captivate and control the audience. Every professional sports league has learned to do likewise.

Manipulation has to be subtle lest it be perceived. Sports leagues found to be fixing games run the risk of losing their loyal fan base by betraying its trust. Remarkably, fans seem to have a lot of tolerance. Remember two facts: One, that every major league has faced a crisis within their sport including work stoppages that led to the canceling of the World Series and Stanley Cup, but survived and managed to lure fans back to their game. Two, the sport of professional wrestling has been known to be a scripted athletic event for decades, yet it still remains a hugely popular diversion for millions of people. The fact that the outcomes are determined prior to anyone stepping into the ring hasn't deterred people from tuning in to see what happens. Fans shell out their hard-earned money to buy the T-shirts, the tickets, and the pay-per-view events. Fans boo the villains and cheer for their heroes, as if it made a difference in that predetermined result. That's how good the storytelling can be. Fans don't care that it's fake.

Is the idea of leagues fixing games really so absurd that it couldn't possibly happen? Because billions of dollars at stake, and because fixing doesn't seem all that hard to do, and keeping in mind that it is hard to find a time in sports history when games *weren't* being purposefully thrown by someone, it seems not only plausible but probable. To fix a game, all one needs is control. And as we've seen, each sports league has complete control over itself.

Fans need to identify their emotional attachments to professional sports and what causes them in order to determine what is real from what is not. Do professional sports thrive purely on the happy little accidents known as coincidence? Coincidence is really a rare commodity. When profit motive and market share become joined to what appear to be many unlikely outcomes, is the result really coincidental, or something else? Therein lays the fix.

THE GREAT HIPPODROME

Hippodroming: slang – from late 1800s-early 1900s. Definition: To arrange contests with predetermined winners.

THE BEGINNING

JANUARY 12TH, 1969. NOT THE MOST MEMORABLE OF DATES, YET it was perhaps the single most pivotal day in NFL history, if not the history of modern professional sports. On that day, the New York Jets defeated the Baltimore Colts 16 to 7 in Super Bowl III. Doesn't seem all that important, does it? Most good football fans already know the gist of the game. They know about Joe Namath and his famous guarantee that the underdog Jets would win. They've repeatedly seen the footage of Namath jogging victoriously off the field, wagging his finger in the air, declaring himself and the Jets number one. What more is there to know?

Tons.

During the raucous mid-1960s, the NFL and the AFL fiercely battled head to head attempting to sign the top college players. With two competing leagues, there were two competing drafts. Players were free to choose which league to join. Highly sought-after college players were lavishly wined and dined at a prospective team's expense. Though unconfirmed, rumors abound that teams would even provide players with women "free of charge" as an extra incentive to sign. During this courting period, teams would actually resort to sneaking a player out the window of his hotel room while executives from the rival league knocked on the player's door, ready to give that same player their own version of this star treatment. Every tactic was employed to sign the best players in these wild and unregulated days. Valuable high-draft choices were at stake, and there was no compensation if a team's pick jumped ship and joined the other league. This player signing war soon spilled over and began to involve the wooing of veteran players as well, using the very same tools of bribery, and, if need be, blackmail to ensure the player signed his name on the line. The expenses of doing this year in and year out for both the NFL and AFL were spinning recklessly out of control.

Then along came Joe Namath. Namath was an exceptional as well as controversial athlete even in his college days. While a quarterback for Alabama, Namath was once arrested for directing traffic in downtown Tuscaloosa while drunk. He also had a tremendous upside, posting a 29–4 record with the Crimson Tide and leading them to a National Championship in 1964. He was drafted in the first round of both leagues' drafts, going 12th overall to the St. Louis Cardinals of the NFL while being picked third overall by the New York Jets of the AFL. The Jets' new owner, Sonny Werblin, recognized his team needed a star to draw some needed attention away from the rival NFL Giants, so he spared no expense in chasing after Namath. Soon, Namath signed the largest contract in football history—$427,000 plus a signing bonus. Werblin's actions pushed both leagues over the edge. Soon afterwards, talks for a merger began.

The upstart AFL didn't possess the power to demand such a merger, but the stalwart NFL owners did. In a closed meeting, the top NFL powers, including Cowboys owner Tex Schramm, Giants owner Wellington Mara, Browns' Owner Art Modell, and Cardinals owner Stormy Bidwell, decided a merger between the two leagues was in their best interest. Oddly enough, the owners met their biggest opposition from their own commissioner, Pete Rozelle. Despite NBC saving the AFL with its $40 million TV contract, Rozelle firmly believed the AFL would eventually fail. He felt the NFL owners just needed to weather the storm and they'd come out on top. The owners failed to see it that way. Instead, they actually gave Rozelle an ultimatum: "The league would pursue the merger under Pete's direction. But if he chose not to lead it, then NFL owners would pursue the merger without him."[1] Not wanting to lose his position within the league, Rozelle begrudgingly agreed to help the owners hammer out a merger deal with the AFL.

By the summer of 1966, the merger was officially announced, but not every detail had been worked out by then. For one, the two leagues wouldn't be able to completely merge until 1970 when each of their respective television contracts had expired. The AFL, whose owners worked behind the back of their own commissioner Al Davis (who was himself the owner of the AFL's Oakland Raiders) to finalize the deal, had to fork over $18 million to the NFL for having to "share" the city of New York and the San Francisco Bay area. (That is most likely why Davis was kept primarily in the dark about the deal.) Another point of contention was stadium size. The NFL had more fans and also played in much larger stadiums, so the agreement stipulated that every stadium in the new version of the NFL needed to accommodate at least 50,000 fans to ensure the growth of every team's gate receipts.

The biggest blockade to the merger was getting around the federal antitrust laws. Congressman Emanuel Celler, who was most responsible for helping the NFL skirt the antitrust regulations when it originally sold its packaged TV rights, suddenly turned on the league. Celler was a leading congressional antitrust expert who came to despise the fact that Major League Baseball was exempted from those laws. Celler became determined not to allow football to get away with the same thing. The businessmen owners of the NFL knew how to work around such a roadblock. Rozelle testified before a congressional panel that should the NFL be given this exemption, no team would leave its current city (though later the Rams, Raiders, Colts, Browns, Oilers, and Cardinals all would break that vow). The owners also leveraged a few deals with the likes of future President Gerald Ford and two Louisiana congressmen, Russell Long and Hale Boggs. Once the merger's antitrust status passed through Congress while attached to an investment tax credit bill, President Johnson signed it into law. It should come as no surprise that the very next NFL franchise that was created was awarded to the city of New Orleans. That gesture was the NFL saying "thank you" to congressmen Long and Boggs, no doubt about it.

With the legal aspect of the merger complete, the owners had to turn their attention to both the fans' reaction and the quality of play on the field. There was no doubt that fans saw the NFL as the superior product. Not only did it have 40-odd years of history, but with its deeper pockets, the NFL had the better talent and coaches. The AFL, in its first five-plus years, had proven little beyond its ability to play free-flowing, high-scoring games. However, as part of the merger deal, both leagues agreed to play a "World Championship" game at the end of the 1966 season, in which the NFL's best would square off against the AFL's top team. Initially an afterthought of the merger, it would be a few years before this game would come to be known as the Super Bowl.

The first two Super Bowls did little to allay the fears of both the leagues and the fans. Right from the start of this Super Bowl era, the old guard of the NFL established themselves as the kings of this new-look NFL. As if to hammer this point home, the NFL took utter control of that first Super Bowl. To solve the issue of which league's official would be the head referee for the game, a coin toss was used. According to former NFL executive Don Weiss, "we [the NFL] 'influenced' that first flip."[2] Once the NFL had its referee in charge of that first game, it made sure that from that point on, games would be played with the NFL's interpretation of football rules, not by the seemingly lax version that the AFL often employed. That included the elimination of the AFL's collegiate-like two-point conversion following a touchdown. The NFL dictated the referees' uniforms, doing away with the AFL's red-and-white striped versions for the NFL's long-used black-and-white "zebra" look. The NFL even went so far as to determine which team would wear which uniform for the game. According to Weiss, "We resorted to a little more subterfuge again sometime later to ensure that Green Bay wore its patented green and gold home uniforms, with Kansas City wearing white. We simply thought they looked better, especially with the game's being televised in color."[3] Those give-and-take decisions, which were more like take-and-take orders, may not seem like much, but they ensured the NFL's rightful control over the game.

Out on the playing field, the NFL continued to have its way with the AFL. Represented by the Green Bay Packers, the NFL's team ripped apart its AFL opponents the Kansas City Chiefs 35–10 in that inaugural Super Bowl. The following year, the Packers again took it to their AFL rivals, pounding the Oakland Raiders 33–14 in Super Bowl II. This was great for the NFL as the league seemed to prove its dominance over its rival with these two lopsided victories. It did not help the looming merger very much. How were fans supposed to accept the AFL into the NFL's fold as true representative franchises if they couldn't beat a NFL team? If competition was lame, fan interest would wane, and ratings would drop. The NFL knew it had to negotiate a new television deal once the merger was completely in place. What kind of bargaining chip did it have with a weakened league that no one was interested in watching?

These were the extremely important questions that loomed large for the league as it approached Super Bowl III. Imagine what would have happened if the short-lived NFL rival, the X Football League—the X didn't stand for anything—(which like the AFL was funded in part by NBC), managed to survive that tumultuous first year and actually began to thrive. Had it earned good ratings and made a profit, the XFL could've then tempted some of the better talent coming out of college. Some might believe that to be unlikely, but recall that another short-lived rival to the NFL that existed in the mid-1980s, the United States Football League (USFL), was able to recruit future Hall of Fame members Steve Young, Reggie White, and Jim Kelly straight out of college, and briefly sign Lawrence Taylor away from the Giants. As the XFL gained more star power, more advertisers and co-sponsors would step up and work with the league. Then the XFL might have gained enough momentum, excitement, and word-of-mouth to actually impact the competition between itself and the NFL. Would fans have ever accepted a merger of the two?

The match-up for Super Bowl III didn't appear to be offering a solution to any of those problems. The representatives for the NFL were the Baltimore Colts. Simply put, the 1968 version of the Colts was one of the best teams in NFL history. That year the Colts averaged an 18-point margin of victory, a Super Bowl-era record that stood until the 2007 New England Patriots topped it. With its Hall of Fame quarterback Johnny Unitas injured for most of the season, the Colts were led by 12-year veteran backup Earl Morrall who put together his best season ever, tossing 26 TDs in nearly 3,000 yards of passing. For his efforts, he was named the NFL's Most Valuable Player. Coached by future Hall of Fame member Don Shula, the Colts went 13-1, losing only to the Cleveland Browns in a midseason 30 to 20 defeat. The two teams met again in the 1968 NFL Championship game, but in that game the Colts crushed the Browns 34–0.

As for the AFL, its champion team was the New York Jets led by none other than Joe Namath. Namath was the brightest star in the high-flying AFL and made the Jets the second highest scoring team in the league. Along with a defense that ranked fourth in points allowed, the Jets were tough enough to post an 11°3 record under Head Coach Weeb Ewbanks, who was previously the Colts' head coach during the 1958 NFL Championship game. Two of the Jets losses had resulted directly from Namath's passing. He threw 17 interceptions in 1968, and 10 of them happened in just two games. (It is interesting to note that in those two games, the Jets were heavily favored over their opponents, leading some to wonder if Namath was involved in fixing them. Those suspicions may have been justified as Namath would later have run-ins with NFL Commissioner Rozelle over his ownership in a bar with known members of the gambling underworld. Those "discussions" about the bar actually led Namath to "retire" from football for a brief time.) Despite all of this, Namath was named the AFL's MVP that year. With a 27–23 come-from-behind victory over the Oakland Raiders in the AFL's Championship game, the Jets were in the Super Bowl.

Even though the Jets looked good on paper, no one believed they could actually beat the Colts. Bookmakers made the Colts anywhere from 17- to 22-point favorites in the game. Even legendary Green Bay Packers coach Vince Lombardi, who had just won the previous two Super Bowls, called the Jets' chances "infinitesimal." Nearly all of the nation's sportswriters saw it the same way, with *Sports Illustrated* predicting a Colts win by the score of 43–0. The league was faced with a potential disaster. If the game went the way everyone expected it to, fans would be treated to more evidence that the NFL was way too good to accept the AFL into its midst.

On top of that, the very idea of even playing a "Super Bowl" was in doubt. As Don Weiss wrote, "That NFL championship games were far more competitive than the Super Bowl game was equally undeniable, while the NFL's overall superiority over the AFL was difficult to dispute. Had the Colts defeated the Jets with anything approaching the ease with which the Packers had routed Kansas City and Oakland in the first two games, the Super Bowl's viability would have come under a dark cloud and prompted serious discussions about how much longer this apparent mismatch could continue beyond the 1970 expiration date of the original television contract with NBC and CBS."[4] What would that have meant to the future of the NFL if the Super Bowl wasn't the "Super Bowl" and instead paled to the likes of the World Series or the Stanley Cup?

With everything on the line in Super Bowl III, from the fate of the actual Super Bowl game to, more importantly, the future of the NFL and the success of its looming merger, an amazing thing happened. Joe Namath guaranteed the Jets would beat the Colts. How and where he made this fabled prediction seems to be lost in the myth surrounding the moment in time, but the fact that Namath guaranteed a win is undeniable. As brash and bold as the prediction was, it was an even better turn of events for the NFL. According to NFL executive Don Weiss, "Joe was our dream, too. We loved every syllable, even if our NFL roots caused us to think he was a little misled. We couldn't have promoted the game better had we written our own script. Literally overnight, Namath's guarantee of a Jets victory turned a colossal mismatch into a must-see event and twisted Baltimore's 18-point spread into a promotional advantage."[5]

It seems very plausible that the NFL *did* write a script for that game. Former Baltimore Colts defensive lineman Bubba Smith, who played in Super Bowl III, once said that the game was "set up" for the Jets to win.[6]

Taking an objective look at the game itself, it definitely seems to have played out strangely. A member of that New York Jets team, defensive end Gerry Philbin said, "They should've been very upset Joe guaranteed the game. If they were as good as what they said they were they should've came [sic] out and beat the shit out of us. They didn't do it."[7] In fact, the Colts did the exact opposite.

On five different occasions in the first half, the Colts threatened to score and yet each time they failed to put points on the board. The Colts missed an easy field goal, fumbled, and league MVP Earl Morrall tossed three drive-killing interceptions, the worst of which came on the fabled "flea flicker" play. The flea flicker, a play in which the quarterback hands off to the running back who fakes a run and then tosses the ball back to the quarterback so he can pass, was put into the playbook specifically for Morrall who had utilized it for years as a member of the New York Giants. He knew the play as well as anyone and knew his intended target that day was Colts wide receiver Jimmy Orr. Yet although the play unfolded perfectly—so perfectly in fact that Orr was wide open, alone in the end zone, waving his arms for Morrall (and everyone in the stadium) to see—Morrall chose not to throw the ball to Orr. Instead of heaving the ball in Orr's direction, Morrall floated the ball over the middle where it hung in the air long enough to be intercepted by one of the Jets' defensive backs. To go along with those three interceptions, Morrall would complete a total of six passes for 71 yards in that first half. Despite all of this, the score at halftime was only New York 7, Baltimore 0.

Morrall shouldn't take all of the blame. Colts head coach Don Shula's actions need to be examined as well. The then 27-year-old head coach was managing to turn the NFL's most dominant team into a bunch of semi-pros. The Colts' running game was working that day against the mediocre Jets' defense. In fact, it had worked all season long. Despite not having a star running back to shoulder the load, the Colts averaged over 100 yards a game rushing during the regular season. In the Super Bowl, Tom Matte alone rushed for 116 yards on just 11 carries, including a dash of over 50 yards that Morrall squandered with an interception near the goal line. As a team, the Colts would finish the game with 143 yards rushing on just 23 carries for a 6.2-yard-per-carry average (which included three rushes for a net two-yard loss from the Colts' quarterbacks, meaning the Colts' running backs were actually averaging over seven yards per attempt).

Trailing for most of the game, yet keeping the score within reach, Shula ignored the running game. Whatever his reasoning, he must have believed the Colts needed to throw to win. Shula kept Morrall in as the second half began even though his first-half performance showed him to be completely inept. Morrall's struggles continued in the second half. He was unable to complete another pass during his time on the field. Before the end of the third quarter,

Shula finally benched Morrall and sent in Colts legendary quarterback Johnny Unitas to attempt to lead a Colts' comeback. Amazingly, the Colts were still in the game with the score 13–0 at the start of the fourth quarter.

For his part, Unitas tried to make up for lost opportunities. Supposedly too injured to start the game, Unitas still let 'er rip 24 times in his limited playing time, but could complete just 11 passes for 110 yards. However, he did march the Colts some 80 yards on a touchdown drive, bringing the Colts to within nine points as the score stood at 16–7 late in the fourth quarter. But when Unitas got the ball back and again pushed the Colts down near the Jets' end zone, the interception curse caught up with him, too. Attempting to complete a simple crossing route, Johnny U tossed the Colts' fourth interception.

Game over.

Unitas would later lament that had he been given more time, he could've done more out on the field. Of course he could have. The idea that one of the best teams in NFL history, one that beat its opponents by an average of 18 points, would score only seven points and lose to a defense ranked fourth in the lowly AFL is preposterous. It was an unthinkable outcome prior to kickoff and just as absurd when the final gun sounded. Yet that is exactly what happened on the field.

For his part in this incredible upset, Namath was named the MVP even though statistically his performance didn't amount to much. Awarding the MVP to Namath did more than just further cement his star status; it also lent credence to his pregame guarantee of a win which, in retrospect, was perhaps more important to the league than his play. At that moment, the skyrocketing star of Joe Namath looked to be the future of the league.

The important question remains, was the game truly "set up" for the Jets to win? Colts defensive lineman Bubba Smith thought so. He told *Playboy* magazine, "That Super Bowl game, which we lost by nine points, was the critical year. The game just seemed odd to me. Everything was out of place. I tried to rationalize that our coach, Don Shula, got out-coached, but that wasn't the case. I don't know if any of my teammates were in on the fix."[8] Was his quote just the angry ramblings of a sore loser? Or from an informed source who recognized the importance of the game to the league and saw how he was subsequently screwed on the deal?

Bubba wasn't alone in questioning the outcome of Super Bowl III. Former NFL player Bernie Parrish wrote, "Namath and his teammates' performance secured the two leagues at the very least $100,000,000 in future TV revenue. The game was almost too good to be true. Considering other devices imposed by TV's needs to lift fan interest and raise the advertisers' prices, perhaps it *was* too good to be true."[9] Parrish, too, had an axe to grind with the league, but only because he knew the NFL was a business first. Having played the game, and feeling as though he, too, was screwed in many ways by the league, Parrish was the first ex-player to step up and call the league on their actions. He knew what the NFL owners were capable of doing and saw how all the pieces fit together in the outcome of Super Bowl III.

If the game was indeed fixed, then how did the NFL profit? One, it gave the AFL the credibility it sorely lacked in the eyes of NFL fans. The Jets winning the game proved the AFL could not just compete against, but beat the very best the NFL had to offer. As former NFL executive Don Weiss wrote, "The Jets' astounding 16–7 victory on January 12, 1969, did more than any other event in the history of the Super Bowl to establish the game's credibility...or save it, even if NFL blue bloods didn't feel that way at the time."[10] Fans now believed the AFL was worthy of inclusion in the NFL.

Two, because of this, the merger solidified itself not just to the game's fan base, but to the TV networks that brought an enormous amount of money to the NFL's coffers. If the fans were now willing to believe that the AFL was as good as the NFL, then they were willing to watch. If they wanted to watch, then the NFL was going to profit immensely in their next round of contract talks with the TV networks.

Three, it made football's championship game, the Super Bowl, a true TV event. Of course, it didn't hurt that this Jets "team of destiny" that won the game hailed from the nation's largest television market and featured the AFL's biggest star in Joe Namath. Plus, Namath's simple quote guaranteeing the game taught the league everything it needed to know about how to market matchups in the future.

Four, this "David vs. Goliath" upset was national news. It was the type of feel-good Cinderella-style story that people love, and it heaped more attention on Namath, the Jets, and the game as well as the league. It was the sort of advertising the NFL couldn't buy, and it made the selling of the merger to the general public all the more easy.

Could all of this been just a coincidence? The happiest, luckiest coincidence the ownership of both the NFL and AFL could have possibly been blessed with?

The opposite outcome, where the Colts beat the Jets' by some huge margin, would have been devastating. There was no positive spin to put on a Colts victory, which by everyone's estimation was the most likely outcome of the game. Simply put, there was just too much at stake for the Colts to win.

Fixing Super Bowl III to achieve this desired result would have been easy to accomplish. Perhaps by the ownership's line of thinking, it was quite necessary to ensure not just the merger, but that the money backing it wasn't lost. It is at this juncture in the NFL's history that mere coincidence, which is what we're supposed to believe led to the Jets' unlikely victory, cannot fully explain the dramatic results brought about by its outcome.

It wasn't just the league that benefited from the Jets miraculous win. Namath's popularity went through the roof thanks to Super Bowl III, and the resulting endorsement deals continue to this day. The owner of the Jets was able to get back a significant slice of the New York pie that he was forced to pay to the Giants in order to share the city, and the rest of the Jets players got championship rings as their reward for a job well done.

What did the Colts get out of the loss? Its rewards were perhaps even larger, and were paid back just as quickly. Longtime Colts owner Carroll Rosenbloom (he of the $1 million bet in 1958) would see the once-inept Earl Morrall lead his team again to the Super Bowl in just two years time. By then, ironically, the Colts were members of the newly formed American Football Conference (AFC), the NFL's new conference of teams comprised primarily of the former AFL teams. Not many owners were willing to drop their long-standing affiliations and rivalries with their former NFL counterparts that existed in the newly christened National Football Conference (NFC), but Rosenbloom was one of the three owners who willingly swapped divisions and joined the AFC. Was it a coincidence that the Colts and Morrall then triumphed in Super Bowl V, thanks to two late interceptions that led to the Colts' final 10 points in a 16–13 game? Was it a reward for all Rosenbloom had sacrificed for the NFL?

As for head coach Don Shula, Super Bowl III was the last game in which he'd ever call plays for the Colts. In the immediate off-season, Shula would sign a lucrative deal with the Miami Dolphins. In just four years' time, Shula would lead them to wins in both Super Bowls VII and VIII. One of these teams, the 1972 version of the Dolphins, went undefeated, being the only team in the Super Bowl era to do so. Was Shula paid off by the league through the Dolphins for his poor coaching decisions that led to the Jets' dramatic victory? Was he, too, rewarded for a job well done?

For all the positive effects Super Bowl III had on the NFL, perhaps it wasn't enough to secure everything that the league had hoped for, but if the league did get away with rigging Super Bowl III, it forever enabled the NFL to do the same to nearly any game it pleased. It is also why many believe that Super Bowl IV, too, was fixed.

The 1969 season was the final season played with the NFL and AFL existing as separate entities. At the end of this season, after Super Bowl IV, the new NFL would officially arrive. A new television deal would need to be worked out with the networks, and that hinged on the fans' belief that the two leagues could co-exist as one superior product. Since the leagues weren't yet integrated, the only game that pitted an AFL team against a NFL team was the Super Bowl. Thus, it was in the league's best interest that an AFL team won that matchup.

The NFL's number one team in 1969 was the Minnesota Vikings. Posting a dominant 12–2 record, the Vikings were the NFL top offensive and defensive team, ranking first in both points scored and points allowed. Most impressive was the Vikings defense nicknamed "The Purple People Eaters" which featured Hall of Fame members Carl Eller and Alan Page. As a unit, they allowed a miserly average of just 9.5 points per game. Their two losses bookended their season, losing 24–23 to the New York Giants on opening day, and later dropping a meaningless game to the Atlanta Falcons 10–3 in the last game of the year. In the first round of the playoffs, the Vikings beat the Los Angeles Rams 23–20, then they steamrolled the Cleveland Browns 27–7 in the NFL Championship game to reach the Super Bowl.

Their opponents would be the AFL's Kansas City Chiefs. The Chiefs had an impressive 11–3 record in the AFL, possessing the league's best-ranked defense, and the second best overall scoring offense. Despite that, the Chiefs finished the season in second place behind the Oakland Raiders. In fact, two of the Chiefs' three losses came thanks to the Raiders during the regular season with scores of 27–24 and 10–6. However, when the two met again in the AFL Championship game, the Chief prevailed 17–7, leading them to face off against the Vikings in Super Bowl IV.

Both the Chiefs and the NFL had a problem leading up to the big game—the gambling accusations against Chiefs quarterback Len Dawson. It was during that 1969 season that many of the Chiefs' games were taken off the boards by bookmakers because of the unusual money coming in on its games. Several of the Chiefs looked dirty, but all of the heat was on Dawson. In the week leading up to the game, the NFL discovered that a federal investigation had linked Dawson to organized gambling. Worse yet, NBC (which was not broadcasting the Super Bowl that year) was set to air a report saying as much to the entire nation. Panicked by the situation, the NFL quickly set its damage-control machine in motion.

Though it was true that Dawson had a relationship with gambler "Dice" Dawson and that Chiefs games were routinely taken off the boards by bookmakers, the NFL's two- to-three-day investigation found Dawson to be innocent. He was allowed to play, but only after signing a written statement which was prepared for him by the league. Dawson read the statement to the media during a press conference and refused to elaborate in any way beyond that. Later that week, NFL commissioner Rozelle stated that the league had given Dawson a lie detector test *the previous year* regarding his links to gambling, but he had passed without issue. For his part, Dawson held his tongue until kickoff.

The Vikings were favored to win by 12 to 13 points in Super Bowl IV. They were the best team in the NFL facing a second-place AFL team led by a quarterback who, whether guilty or not, had just suffered through a week in the national media's wringer for his ties to gamblers. By all accounts, the game should have gone the Vikings' way.

It didn't. The Chiefs drubbed the Vikings 23–7. Dawson, apparently unfazed by the controversy surrounding him, completed 17 of 22 attempts for 142 yards and a touchdown. He was named the game's MVP. The Chiefs win also got Len Dawson, and the NFL, off the hook for his gambling associations. Poor play by Dawson, or perhaps even just a Chiefs loss, could've raised a cloud of speculation over the league that hadn't been seen since 1963, when Alex Karras and Paul Hornung were suspended for their gambling habits. Yet again, the fans' interest, if not their respect for the league, could've gone up in smoke should the Chiefs have lost under such suspicious circumstances. As soon as the game was over and Dawson was named the hero for the day, all the allegations against him vanished.

Meanwhile, just like the Colts, the Vikings juggernaut completely broke down on the national stage. The Purple People Eaters were quite un-monsterlike, allowing 151 rushing yards on top of Dawson's MVP performance while giving up 13 points more than their season average. On offense, a Vikings team that averaged nearly 125 yards rushing per game during the regular season posted just 67 yards for the day. They fumbled the ball away twice while Vikings' quarterback Joe Kapp tossed a Morrall-like three interceptions, despite throwing only 13 during the entire regular season.

Yet again, the unlikely AFL underdog whooped the dominant NFL team in the Super Bowl. The Chiefs' win allowed the AFL to fold on a high note, rewarding both its owners and fans for the previous 10 years. But most importantly, it reinforced the unstated meaning behind the AFL's victory. Perhaps former NFL executive Don Weiss summed it up best when he wrote, "Kansas City's convincing victory did more than ratify the Jets' victory and the quality of AFL football. It gave credence to the new structure of pro football and single-league play that were coming in September…Fans' tongues were wagging…We couldn't have had it any better if we had written a script."[11] By the way, that's twice now the former NFL executive wrote that "it couldn't have been better had we written a script" when describing a Super Bowl's outcome.

He was correct. Both the Jets' and the Chiefs' victories in Super Bowls III and IV firmly established the AFL, the merger, and the Super Bowl game itself for football fans everywhere. Super Bowl IV's ratings were through the roof. According to CBS, 69 percent of the televisions in use—which equated to 23 million U.S. households—were tuned to the Super Bowl. That was more Americans than had tuned in to watch Neil Armstrong become the first man to step foot on the moon just six months earlier.

The NFL was now set up to become the ratings-hungry, money-making monster it is today.

MAJOR LEAGUE BASEBALL

In 1969, a researcher and mathematician by the name of Robert Helmbold wrote a research paper for the Rand Corporation titled *Have the World Series Been Fixed?* Helmbold wasn't discussing the fabled 1919 World Series featuring the Black Sox. No, he was considering the situation surrounding the games being played at that time in the 1960s. It was Helmbold's contention that the longer the duration of the World Series, the more everyone involved, from players and owners to mass media and even the gamblers, profited. He felt it might be necessary to monitor the league to ensure the outcomes weren't prearranged.

His research begged two important questions. The first being, could one, using mathematics and statistics, determine if the World Series was being intentionally lengthened? Helmbold's "fix" wasn't concerned with who won or lost. To him, that was unimportant. He was interested in figuring out whether the World Series was reaching the maximum length, seven games, more often than it should statistically. The equations, graphs, and reasoning that Helmbold used to reach his conclusions were designed to determine how often a seventh and deciding game should actually be needed in a seven-game series.

The second question regarding Helmbold's work is, why bother? It seems doubtful that someone like Helmbold would just randomly think, geez, maybe I should work out a mathematical formula to see if the World Series has been fixed without feeling that something was wrong. His work wasn't on a conundrum screaming for a solution. In fact, it is probable that not too many people felt that a problem even existed. Yet Helmbold went out of his way to determine an answer to a question no one seemed to be asking. Did the Rand Corporation see something strange afoot? His paper never mentions why he undertook the project, it simply presents the idea that a longer World Series benefits everyone involved.

Despite his work, Helmbold oddly never offered a clearcut, definitive answer. It very well may be in part because of the rather small sample of numbers with which Helmbold had to work. When he wrote this paper, there had only been 64 World Series played, which in mathematical terms makes it difficult to find true anomalies within a sample. What Helmbold did instead was present a hypothetical situation involving a fictional law enforcement-like agency created to monitor baseball and the World Series. Using a Bayesian probability model, the agency tracked the number of times a World Series went seven games, and then determined if that occurred often enough to be outside the baseline norm. In Helmbold's theoretical model, both the 1967 and 1968 World Series, which reached seven games, merited investigation. Perhaps to avoid any libel cases, Helmbold didn't flat out claim that his mathematical findings meant the Series were rigged.

Setting aside Helmbold's high-minded math, take a gander at what the plain old numbers do show. The first World Series televised to a nationwide audience was in 1949. Between 1950 and 1969 (when Helmbold's paper was released), 11 of the 20 World Series played between those dates went the full seven games. That's 55 percent. Compare that against four four-game sweeps, two five-game Series, and three six-game Series (or 45 percent) that occurred during that same time span. Perhaps it was those sorts of numbers that spurred Helmbold into action in the first place. Even more interesting is that in the 20 years following Helmbold's study, very little changed. From 1970 through 1989, the World Series reached seven games on nine more occasions (45 percent). This means that in the 40 years between 1950 and 1989, the World Series went the maximum number of game half (50 percent) of the time. Compare that against the number of four-game sweeps (15 percent), five-game Series (17.5 percent), and six-game Series (also 17.5 percent), and it becomes apparent you don't need to be a mathematician to see something odd may have occurred.

What's happened since 1989? Between 1990 and 2008, the numbers have leveled out. In those 18 World Series played (remember, no Series in 1994), it went the full seven games only on four occasions. Meanwhile, there were more four-game sweeps, six, than anything else. Does this blow the notion that MLB was altering its own outcomes out of the water? Not exactly, if you remember that, prior to the release of Helmbold's study in 1969, there were no playoffs. The divisional championship series began in 1969, with each league having a best-of-five-game playoff between division winners to determine which team went on to the World Series. That format was expanded to seven games in 1985. Then in 1995, MLB added a third division to each league which necessitated the adding of a "wild card" team to the playoffs. That added four additional best-of-five-game series to the playoff schedule each year. Amazingly, as MLB added playoffs and then increased the length of those playoffs, the number of seven-game World Series steadily declined from five in the '70s, to four in the '80s, to just two in both the '90s and thus far though the 2000s.

What we're left with is the fact that if baseball had artificially lengthened the World Series in the past, it would no longer need to do so today. As baseball has increased the potential number of post-season games played, thus lengthening its playoff schedule, the expanded MLB playoff format has eaten up more and more television time no matter the results. Even a three-game sweep in the division series, followed by a four-game sweep in the league championship series, followed again by another four-game sweep in the World Series equals more in terms of TV coverage and time than any single seven-game-long World Series could. What both baseball and television needed to get out of the World Series in terms of ratings and advertising in the '60s and '70s in such a limited number of games could now be squeezed out of the divisional and league championship series. Though still important to baseball from a business perspective, the World Series became little more than the icing on the cake for everyone involved.

Of course this would presuppose the idea that the owners could gather together and prearrange such an agreement. One that would force the World Series to run the full seven games without knowing which two teams would eventually be battling for the championship. The nature of such a deal would risk the outcome for both teams involved because each team by necessity would have to knowingly dump a game or two to force the Series to go the distance. That would be quite a chance to take. Plus the question is raised: which is more important, the TV ratings and revenues (total profits) from a seven-game World Series, or the glory of being crowned baseball's best? It's hard to believe that owners would be willing to lose the World Series just to make a couple extra bucks. We all know, team owners, players, and managers, want to win more than anything, right?

Major League Baseball's biggest, yet now mostly forgotten, conspiratorial scandal occurred in the mid-1980s. It is known as collusion. Actually, in MLB's case, Collusion I, II, and III because the owners of Major League Baseball were bold enough to try it three times.

Baseball lost its precious reserve clause which bound players to teams as long as the team decided to keep the player and began to deal with free agency in the 1970s. With players now free to shop their wares around to any team willing to pay for the player's service, players' salaries began to escalate rapidly. Baseball owners began to experience the same financial headaches that the NFL and AFL had in the mid-'60s when competing over players. The bidding wars went out of control.

Baseball's new commissioner at that time, Peter Ueberroth, had an epiphany. Without actually saying the words, Ueberroth implied to owners that they were morons to fight amongst themselves over the players. No one ever told a player that if he became a free agent, other teams were obligated to sign him to a bigger and better deal. Maybe, no other team would be interested in a free agent. Maybe, then, a free agent would have little choice but to sign with his former team.

Now you wouldn't think these baseball owners, businessmen one and all, could actually believe such a plan could work, but damn if they still didn't try it anyway. Every single one of them was in on the plan. Because the league had just reached a five-year collective bargaining agreement with the players, the idea was to keep new contracts to a minimum—no more than three years for hitters and two for pitchers; stay away from the big-name players; and keep salaries to a bare minimum. That was the plan.

In the off-season between 1985 and 1986, 33 players filed for free agency thinking it was payday. Were they in for a surprise. Kirk Gibson was coming off a season in which he hit 29 home runs while driving in 97 runners for the Tigers. No one wanted him. Gibson's teammate, pitcher Jack Morris, coming off a 16–11 season with a 3.33 ERA and 191 strike outs received no offers. Chicago White Sox catcher and future Hall of Famer Carlton Fisk's 37 home runs and 107 RBIs were enough to entice Yankee owner George Steinbrenner to offer him a deal, but after a phone call from White Sox owner Jerry Reinsdorf, Big Stein pulled the deal off the table. Other notables from that season's crop of free agents that went without offers included Tommy John, Donnie Moore, and both of the Niekro brothers. Of those 33 free agents, only four signed with new teams, and mostly because their old teams no longer wanted their services.

The players realized that this just didn't seem right. By early 1986, the players' union filed a grievance against the league. This would become known as Collusion I. Commissioner Ueberroth, covering for himself and the owners said that "they [the owners] aren't capable of colluding" and that "it's just a trend" that owners are showing some "fiscal restraint." But what owners were truly doing was avoiding the best possible players simply to save some cash. Without a doubt, the baseball owners' actions or lack thereof proved that money was more important to them than wins.

Collusion II began following the 1986 season. That free-agent crop of players included the likes of Ron Guidry, Andre Dawson, Rich Gedman, Lance Parrish, Tim Raines, Bob Boone, and Bob Horner. Dawson, clearly wanting out of the Montreal Expos organization, signed a blank contract with the Chicago Cubs that nearly halved his salary for the one-year deal. Other big-name players also took pay cuts, and were forced to re-sign with their current clubs at reduced prices because it seemed as if no other team wanted their services. Bob Horner decided to cut and run all the way to Japan, signing with the Yakult Swallows rather than re-upping with the Atlanta Braves. As baseball's revenue went up some 15 percent during the year, the free-agent market's salary *declined* by roughly 16 percent. Meanwhile, nearly three quarters of all the free agent signings between the end of the 1986 season and the start of the 1987 season were just one-year deals.

Yet again, the players' union filed a grievance against the league for collusion in February of 1987. As work began on Collusion II, arbitrator Thomas Roberts reached his decision in Collusion I. On September 22,

1987, Roberts ruled that the owners had indeed colluded against the free agents in the 1985–1986 market. Eventually Roberts would award $10.5 million to the shunned players, but before that was totaled and announced, the 1987–1988 free agent players had to outwit Collusion III.

Seeing as how the owners blatantly disregarded the rules they themselves had created some 20 years before when Don Drysdale and Sandy Koufax attempted to work together through an agent to increase both of their salaries, the owners decided to alter their game plan. Not willing to concede the idea of keeping player salaries to a minimum, the owners created an "information bank." Deposited into the "bank" was nothing more than the current offers teams were making to free agents. For example, if a team was considering offering a contract to 1987 free-agent Paul Molitor, it could go to the bank and see what other owners had already offered him. Then the team could decide whether or not to make an offer based on that known figure. It was collusion of a different sort, but just as effective. For the first time in years, the aggregate of players' salaries actually went *down* some two percent in 1988. Though the two percent may not seem like much, compare that against the average *increase* of 10 percent by which salaries usually rose, and you can understand the owners' joy at instituting their new bank. In fact, prior to Ueberroth taking the commissioner's post at the end of 1984, reportedly 21 of MLB's 26 teams were operating at a loss. By the end of 1987, all teams were operating solidly in the black. Ueberroth's orchestrated collusion was paying dividends.

The enthusiasm over the information bank and collusion in general was short-lived. In January of 1988, the Collusion III grievance was filed over the owner's new tactic. Shortly thereafter, Roberts released his awarded figure of $10.5 million in the Collusion I case. Along with his ruling came a second chance at free agency for all the remaining active players that were screwed in Collusion I. Kirk Gibson was the primary recipient of this good news, signing a $4.5 million, three-year deal with the Los Angeles Dodgers. Immediately thereafter, Gibson won the 1988 National League MVP and in the ensuing World Series, hit one of the most famous home runs in baseball history.

A different arbitrator, George Nicolau, ruled over Collusion II and III. The results were similar. Nicolau again found for the players in both cases, allowed the players affected immediate free agency, and awarded $38 million in damages in Collusion II and $64.5 million in Collusion III. Nicolau further stuck it to the owners by forcing them to compensate the players for losses relating to multi-year contracts and signing bonuses that were never offered.

In the end, Major League Baseball settled with the players union for $280 million for its three years' worth of collusion against the players. Commissioner Ueberroth stepped down from his post in 1989, a full season before his contract was to end.

What must not be forgotten in this collusion scandal is how many different levels of baseball's upper echelon were involved. Commission Ueberroth basically convinced the owners that to become profitable again, they needed to ease off their spending on players. All of the owners agreed with his assessment. Not one owner reneged on the unwritten agreement or signed a major free agent in three years, a period which might have been longer had the players union not immediately recognized the problem. That action trickled down through each organization in the game, including all team general managers and club officials. No member of upper management in baseball came forward and blew the whistle on the players' behalf. Not one, and clearly every team played a part in the scam.

During at least those three years in question, no team wanted to win badly enough to significantly alter their rosters. Winning, or the attempt to field a winning team, was secondary to profit margins. In other words, the outcomes of those seasons were clearly and purposefully tainted by the league's owners. If the available free agents had shuffled around the league as they should have in a truly open market, the results of the 1986, 1987, and 1988 seasons would have been completely different. No team was even trying to improve its product and, therefore, if a team posted a winning season, it was more by happenstance than intent. At the same time, however, every team, winners and losers, saw their profits rise. It was no accident.

Chances are that if the owners weren't so blatant and didn't stop signing free agents cold turkey but more gradually, the tactic might have worked for much longer. Paradoxically, as soon as the owners were punished for their wrongdoing, they performed a complete 180-degree turn and began spending money at ridiculous rates. Despite that, all was still not hunky-dory between owners and players. The idea of collusion continued to hang in the air. In 2006, the players and owners reached a little-known agreement in their new collective bargaining agreement to settle what was considered a fourth collusion case that supposedly affected the free-agent markets in both 2002 and 2003. The owners shelled out $12 million from their "luxury tax" to pay for the damages done. The settlement came with the agreement that there would be no admission of guilt on the owners' part.

Meanwhile, the owners' wild spending had pushed the marketplace to a near breaking point by the offseason between 2007 and 2008. Because some teams act rather skittish in courting free agents, players and their agents are again wondering if owners are colluding with one another. One free agent in particular, Alex Rodriguez, might become a new focal point for the resurrection of the owners' illegal behavior. Rodriguez, opting out of his $252 million deal with the New York Yankees, became a free agent after the 2007 season. Reportedly he was seeking somewhere around $300 million in his next deal, which was more than the value of some entire MLB franchises. Because that $300 million number leaked out to the press (shades of the information bank) and there weren't many teams willing to sit down and talk to A-Rod, rumors of collusion again began to circulate. Though he eventually signed a $275 million incentive-laden deal to remain with the Yankees, A-Rod's salary may not exactly lead to the level of collusion seen in the mid-1980s, but simply to the necessary step of fiscal restraint Commissioner Ueberroth sought some 20 years ago.

What should come as no surprise to any fan is that the owners' collusion against players led to a significant amount of distrust between the two factions. Not that players in any time period of baseball's history ever trusted their paymasters, but collusion in the 1980s exasperated an already bad situation. Since 1972, baseball had experienced six labor-related work stoppages prior to the owners' institution of their collusion plans (1972, 1973, 1976, 1980, 1981, and 1985). All of baseball's labor disputes occurred because the two sides couldn't agree on how to split the hundreds of millions of dollars MLB generated. As the years went by and the stakes increased, the animosity between players and owners intensified. In 1990,

MLB owners locked out the players from spring training in hopes of forcing them to accept a radical restructuring of their collective bargaining agreement. The owners' plans failed as commissioner Fay Vincent stepped in and publicized the owners' new scheme. Vincent brought in the media, and the owners backed off their initial hard-line stance. Vincent's direct involvement in the negotiations brought a quick end to the lockout and created a new compromise between both sides.

Just two years later, baseball would find itself without a commissioner. In 1992, the owners found themselves back in total control of their league, and they seemed bound and determined to get some of what they lost back from their laborers. The owners reopened negotiations with the players, but waited some 18 months to officially propose anything. When they again asked players to accept radical changes to their collective bargaining agreement, the players union balked. Thus began the players' strike of 1994 that, for the first time in 90 years, caused the cancellation of the World Series.

The reason the players waited so late into the season to strike was fourfold. First, because the owners didn't put an offer onto the table until mid-June of 1994, the players had little time to react to the new proposals. They were already in the midst of playing the season, and had little chance to gather together and discuss the offer. That was an intentional move on the owners' part. Reason two, if the players' union didn't reach a conclusion on the owners' new offer by the end of 1994, the owners could declare an impasse and effectively put whatever they wanted into place, and they wanted a salary cap. However, the players saw this looming. For the previous four years, the players' union had been stockpiling its cash reserves from its licensing revenue, just in case. Now the union had enough money to pay every player with at least four years' experience $150,000 to survive the work stoppage. Plus, having already played two-thirds of the season prior to striking, every player had received the majority of his season's pay. With that money in their pocket, the players could fight back and hurt the owners financially. Striking at that late date in the season (officially on August 12, 1994) threatened not just the post-season, but, more importantly, the owners' beloved television revenue. Every owner stood to lose millions as nearly 75 percent of the national TV revenue earned by baseball comes directly from post-season play. No post-season, no post-season money.

The strike would cancel the 1994 World Series, survive mediation imposed by President Bill Clinton, ignore the Congressional threat of baseball losing its precious antitrust status, and not see an end until the National Labor Relations Board filed an injunction against the owners in the spring of 1995. Baseball resumed play in late April of that year. As Paul Staudohar wrote for the Bureau of Labor Statistics in 1997, "Nothing was settled by the strike, because the old contract provisions continued to apply, which has to make the strike one of the most eventful, but unproductive, ever."[12] The strike did affect the immediate profitability of baseball. Owners claimed to have lost $1 billion because of the strike. Players' salaries dropped some five percent in 1995. In the season immediately following the strike, fan attendance fell nearly 20 percent. Major League Baseball was not quick to recoup those losses.

Baseball needed to get the fans back on their side. What baseball craved more than anything was a national story, one that could be played out in every ballpark across the league, something that could capture every fan's attention, both young and old. As Jose Canseco wrote, "If the owners were asking themselves, *How could we bring baseball back?* they finally hit on the simple answer: home runs. So how could you pump up the sport and get an exciting home run race going? The players knew the answer to that: steroids."[13]

Every fan loves a home run. You can argue that a great pitching duel makes for spectacular baseball, but nothing brings the entire stadium to its collective feet like a home run. The baseball owners are no dummies. They, too, know chicks (and dudes as well) dig the long ball, and that is exactly why they turned a blind eye to the steroid problem for so long.

There is no good way to judge just how widely used steroids were in MLB. The most obvious gauge, however, is to use home runs. It seems the larger the hitters become, the farther the ball will fly. Therefore, more home runs should be hit. If fans take the word of both MLB and Rawlings, the league's official manufacturer of baseballs, that the balls themselves are not juiced, then the only reason home run numbers drastically rose must be because the players were juiced up. As "the Typhoid Mary of steroids in baseball" Jose Canseco wrote, "The powers you gain [from taking steroids] can feel almost superhuman. Besides the boost to your strength and confidence level, you start running faster. Your hand-eye coordination and muscle-twitch fibers get faster. Your bat speed increases. You feel more powerful, and you can use a heavier bat without sacrificing any bat speed, which is the most important thing."[14] Canseco reckoned that, if a player could hit a dinger or two before taking steroids, juicing would clearly boost his season home run (HR) total to new heights.

Home run numbers definitely rose immediately after the strike. By averaging the number of home runs hit by the top 20 players in the few years before and after 1994 (without including that strike-shortened season), the difference becomes apparent:

★ 1990 – top 20 players hit 651 HRs – 32.5 HR average per player
★ 1991 – top 20 players hit 640 HRs – 32 HR average per player
★ 1992 – top 20 players hit 614 HRs – 30.7 HR average per player
★ 1993 – top 20 players hit 730 HRs – 36.5 HR average per player
★ 1994 – Strike
★ 1995 – top 20 players hit 715 HRs – 35.7 HR average per player
★ 1996 – top 20 players hit 860 HRs – 43 HR average per player
★ 1997 – top 20 players hit 783 HRs – 39.1 HR average per player
★ 1998 – top 20 players hit 901 HRs – 45.1 HR average per player
★ 1999 – top 20 players hit 875 HRs – 43.75 HR average per player

That is a significant increase, no? Sure, the averages for 1995 are less than those of 1993, but remember the fact that the 1995 season was a mere 144 games long, rather than the usual 162. Without a doubt, those 18 games would've added to each hitter's season HRs totals. Also, what would have been a top 20 performance in 1993 (30 HRs) would not have cracked the top 20 in any of the years since 1994 including the strike-shortened 1995 season. Since the end of the 1994–95 strike through the 2008 season, baseball has seen its players hit more than the milestone mark of 50 home runs in a season 23 times. In the 100-plus years prior to that, a player had hit 50 or more home runs in a season only 18 times.

Despite this increase in the number of home runs hit each year, some would argue baseball has yet to regain the popularity it had prior to that 1994–1995 strike. While this may be true, there is no doubt that during the 1998 season and the dramatic home run chase attached to it, baseball was more than happy to have the national spotlight shining on itself.

What happened during that magical season was nothing short of a godsend for MLB. At one point during the season, not one but three players, Mark McGwire, Sammy Sosa, and Ken Griffey, Jr., all appeared to have a chance at breaking the single-season home run record of 61 set by Roger Maris in 1961. Most of the media's focus was set on McGwire and Sosa who seemed to consistently one-up each other in this historic chase while their teams battled for the final playoff spot in the National League. McGwire would be the first to break Maris' record, hitting his 62nd home run of the season at home in St. Louis remarkably while facing Sosa's Chicago Cubs. It caused a media feeding frenzy. The moment was national headline news that MLB soaked up for all it was worth. Better still, just a few days after McGwire broke the record, Sosa, too, would surpass Maris' mark. Now the focus became which of these two titans would finish the season on top? Sosa would stall at 66 home runs while McGwire would finish the season as the new record-holder with an amazing 70 home runs. Ken Griffey, Jr. would not be able to keep up with those two monsters, topping out at 56 HRs for the season.

From this, baseball in 1998 was revitalized. Coupled with the addition of two expansion teams, the Arizona Diamondbacks and the Tampa Bay Devil Rays, the home run record chase brought out the fans in droves. The attendance levels in stadiums across the country were also up over 10 percent, with nearly 7.5 million more people going out to see a ballgame. On top of that, TV ratings jumped over 10 percent in a single season. The nationwide hysteria regarding McGwire's and Sosa's slugfest reached a pinnacle late in the season. When FOX aired the game in which McGwire finally broke Roger Maris' long standing 61-home-run mark, it captured nearly 43 million viewers.

A pair of dark clouds hung over the proceedings, however. One was public, and the other was kept quite private. As much as MLB wanted to ignore it, the fact was McGwire was caught red-handed with steroids during that record-breaking 1998 season. Steve Wilstein, a reporter working for the Associated Press, spotted a bottle of the over-the-counter supplement Androstenedione in McGwire's locker during an interview session midway through the season. The substance was not banned by MLB nor was it illegal at the time (it became illegal in 2005); however, more than a few eyebrows were raised. Jose Canseco, who claims to have introduced McGwire to steroids some 10 years before he shattered the single-season home run record, thought McGwire's andro usage was just "a ploy." He wrote, "There were two big advantages for Mark in having his name associated with andro. One, it was a distraction from the real issue, which was steroids…Two, if he'd ever been required to take a steroid test, and he failed it, it would have been easy for him to say: That was just the andro. I didn't do anything illegal."[15]

Using andro gave McGwire a perfect (and legal) excuse to stop questions before they were asked, and thanks to the cozy relationship between reporters and the players they need to cover, the andro issue was conveniently put on the back burner while McGwire chased Maris' record. No one at the time dared call McGwire's use of the substance into question and no one even attempted to infer that McGwire's new record might be tainted. The only one who suffered in the "andro incident" was Wilstein who first mentioned McGwire using the supplement. The Cardinals organization attempted to ban him from their locker room. Meanwhile, Wilstein's peers outcast him faster and further than McGwire ever was at the time. As Canseco wrote, "McGwire was untouchable. He was so protected by the powers that be in the game, it was incredible. No media outlet would even think of calling him into question, because there's no way they'd ever get an inside source."[16]

McGwire continued to get a free pass from both reporters and the league during the 1999 season when he blasted another 65 home runs. Again, McGwire had competition from Sammy Sosa who hit another 63 HRs himself that year. But the shock and awe of their 1998 campaign gave rise to questions at least in the fans' minds with their continued assault on the pitchers in the National League. Yet in the media, all was kept hush-hush.

According to Canseco, "The steroid spectacle was making money for them [the owners]. It brought the game back to life....Everybody was profiting, and they never even had to answer difficult questions, since no one wanted to ask them. There's a name for that kind of thing: good business."[17]

The owners were fine with players taking steroids as long as they didn't get caught, they kept hitting home runs, and fans remained interested in baseball. Yet again, baseball owners showed that wins and losses, which were being affected by the players' willingness to take steroids, didn't matter as much as the overall profitability of the game. They were as complicit in the steroid era as the players who used the drugs.

Owners had warnings well before the steroid issue exploded on the front pages of newspapers around the country. In fact, right after McGwire and Sosa breathed new life into the league, one player was willing to stand up and point a knowing finger at those involved. Rick Helling, then a 27-year-old pitcher and the players' representative to the union for the Texas Rangers, spoke up at the 1998 winter meetings. Helling simply stated that steroids were being used, it was an open secret, and those not using were feeling pressured to join in because they were falling behind the performance level of the others who were. He said he didn't know exactly how many were using, but it was far more than anyone suspected. After Helling spoke his piece, the union and the league did nothing to address the problem, much less even attempt to correct it. Over the course of the next three years, Helling would make this same speech at each successive winter meeting. The results within the league were the same as well. No one in baseball cared to heed his warnings.

With each successive spring training, players would show up bigger and stronger than they were the year before. Players with warning track power were now hitting home runs while pitchers whose fastballs normally topped out at 90 mph were suddenly reaching 95 mph with regularity. These improvements were overtly visible, yet no one bothered to question it. While obvious drug-influenced improvements were overlooked within the tight-knit unit of players and coaches with a knowing wink, the media, who should have broken the story surrounding steroid usage, also remained completely complacent. Perhaps as culpable as anyone were the hallowed Baseball Writers of America (BWA). Afraid to bite the hand that feeds them, no one within that community raised a stink as numbers and players inflated with each passing season. While they patted themselves on the back for keeping Pete Rose out of the Hall of Fame because of his gambling, the Baseball Writers of America sat back and happily watched as the game was hijacked by a bunch of drug pushers. Had the situation not made a complete U-turn during the 2001 season, most likely, steroids would still be corrupting baseball.

Barry Bonds destroyed the goodwill that baseball built back up through McGwire and Sosa. The problem with Bonds was that most fans thought he was a jerk. Had he been the All-American boy McGwire was promoted as, or as loveable as Sosa seemed to be, perhaps fans would not have had a problem with Bonds. If we're to believe the authors of *Game of Shadows*, Bonds became upset over the hype the McGwire/Sosa affair was receiving when he believed the pair was using steroids. Bonds set out to be the new home run king no matter what he had to do (steroids included) to achieve that mark.

By the time he smashed McGwire's single-season record by smacking 73 HRs during the 2001 season, most fans had become tired of the spectacle surrounding the chase. Part of it was their personal dislike of Bonds' inflated attitude. Another aspect was the unnatural growth Bonds, then 36 years old, seemed to undergo prior to his record-breaking season. Many fans weren't buying it, no matter how hard MLB and their media outlets like ESPN tried to sell it. With Bonds' 73 HR season, and his subsequent overtaking of Hank Aaron's all-time home run record in 2007, the steroid issue blew up in the owners' faces. And that wasn't good business.

Major League Baseball suddenly decided steroids were bad. Worse yet, the owners acted as if these revelations were completely new to them. In reality, for at least nearly 20 years leading up to that point, MLB did not care about steroids. Everyone in the game, from owners down to the players, knew steroids were rampant in the league. MLB didn't bother to test its players; it paid the heaviest hitters handsomely for their hard work, thus emboldening players to use. They purposefully turned their backs as player after player jabbed themselves in the butt to bulk up. These drug-aided supermen then assaulted the record books, consciously knowing they were cheating and breaking the law, not to win more games, but to garner more attention and thus make more money.

That is where baseball stands today. The steroid witch hunt attached to the league's Mitchell Report into steroid usage wasn't about cleaning up the game. The owners' ploy now was to go out of their way to show that baseball was steroid-free simply because it was a good PR move. After Bonds and his home-run chase singlehandedly filled up the Giants' home stadium for the team in the past few seasons, the Giants did an immediate about-face against the slugger in 2008. Not only did the Giants fail to even attempt to res-ign him when his contract expired at the end of 2007, the team stripped AT&T Park of all references to Bonds and his HR titles. What they once hyped as their biggest selling point was now intentionally forgotten. No signs, photos, or anything remains celebrating what is perhaps one of baseball's most cherished records. As for Bonds himself, though he has yet to be convicted of his perjury indictments or officially caught using steroids, he has effectively been blackballed by MLB. Though he wanted to continue his career in 2008 and in 2009, no team offered him a contract.

What's in "baseball's best interest" isn't a clean game, unless a clean game is profitable, first and foremost. And right now, baseball sees profit in running a clean sport. How much of a profit? Ironically, the same day Barry Bonds was indicted by a federal grand jury on four counts of perjury and one count of obstruction of justice relating to his testimony during the fed's BALCO/steroid investigation, commissioner Bud Selig announced that MLB posted record high revenues of over $6 billion for the 2007 season. And as Selig was quoted as saying, "If we just keep doing our work, stay out of controversies, keep the focus on the field, we'll get to numbers someday that will be stunning."[18] Of course, by focusing on the field, where these behemoth players began hitting home runs at a pace never before seen in the history of the sport, baseball created perhaps its biggest controversy since the 1919 World Series.

The question remains, which of these two events was the biggest blight on the game of baseball? The infamous 1919 World Series because eight players profited by accepting bribes to lose a couple of games, or the

20-year-long steroid era, where every owner and numerous players profited billions of dollars by presenting a game to its fans dishonestly?

NASCAR

Is driving an insanely fast car a sport? The men and women competing in NASCAR who have the courage and skill needed to drive them would certainly say yes. Doubt about including a section in this book devoted to NASCAR was dissolved by the realization that the formula: fans + profit to be made = potential for fix.

Like all athletes, drivers need to be physically fit to control cars moving at nearly 200 mph, risking life and limb to be the first to travel a distance of some 500 miles. The main issue that nags about labeling NASCAR a sport is that the equipment seems to matter more than the person behind the wheel. Every sport requires something in order to play it, and though some equipment is specially tailored to fit certain athletes, little of it is mechanized. Because of this, outside of perhaps corking a baseball bat, most of it can't be tampered with to achieve a definitive edge over an opponent. Yet the same doesn't hold true for so-called "stock" cars. A driver with a better set-up car can and often will beat a superior driver simply because it goes faster. The human factor only matters up to a point, otherwise crew chiefs would spend most of their time coddling drivers rather than constantly tinkering with cars. After all, it's about racing *the car*.

It should come as no surprise that with most of the focus on making the machine go faster, car-racing history is filled with stories about teams altering their cars illegally to achieve more speed and advantage. To put it more simply, they cheat as often as they can get away with it. Some cars have been rigged with extra weight that can be dumped once the race has started. Others have been outfitted with illegal ducts hidden behind their body panels for better airflow, and unauthorized devices built into engines to increase horsepower. Car owner Bill Davis was once caught with a driver-operated hydraulic pump used to lower the rear of the car for better aerodynamics. Such deliberate alterations have been going on since NASCAR's inception, and force officials to inspect cars before each race.

Though NASCAR inspectors do their work pretty much out in the open for anyone in the garage area of the track to see, NASCAR rules don't seem to be consistent. Rules appear to change frequently and without much notice. What was legal last month or last week often seems to be judged illegal for the next. Do the Fords seem slower than the Chevys? NASCAR may decide to allow a few extra inches of body length on one or maybe tweak the allowance on a rear spoiler on the other to even out the racetrack for all competitors. That seems to happen even when no one is complaining. The problem is not that NASCAR regulates everything from car inspection to racing protocol but that its regulations appear to be open to interpretation.

Despite a seemingly arbitrary inspection process, cars and their owners get caught violating restrictions redhanded. Prior to NASCAR's Super Bowl, the Daytona 500, five different cars were busted for rules infractions in 2007. This included drivers Matt Kenseth, Kasey Kahne, Scott Riggs, Elliott Sadler, and most interesting of all, Michael Waltrip. What makes Waltrip's case so intriguing is that he wasn't just the team's driver, he was also the race team's owner.

When a NASCAR inspector reached his hand into Waltrip's car's manifold to feel for loose pats, an unknown, illegal substance unlike anything the inspector had ever seen was discovered coating his hand. Nearly five months after this substance was discovered, NASCAR still wasn't sure what it was. Some sources speculated it was an oxygenate that would boost the octane in the fuel; others believed it contained some of the same properties as jet fuel. No one knows for sure. What was known immediately at the time of discovery was that Waltrip had nothing to do with it. Waltrip was quoted as saying prior to the Daytona 500, "This is not the action of an organization, a manufacturer or a sponsor. This was an independent act done without consent or authorization from me or any of my executive management team."[19] NASCAR subsequently suspended Waltrip's crew chief David Hyder and team director Bobby Kennedy indefinitely. Hyder was also fined $100,000 for the infraction and was later fired along with another member of Waltrip's team. Though NASCAR's investigation into the incident revealed nothing more than circumstantial evidence against Hyder, Waltrip would say some five months later, "We've separated ourselves from the people that were responsible."[20]

Everyone but himself, that is. Because even though Waltrip was the racing team's owner and driver, thus connected to the car in question more than anyone else, he denied all allegations leveled against him. For its own reasons, NASCAR believed his denials though many inside the sport remained more than a little skeptical of Waltrip. The only punishment NASCAR levied against Waltrip was to dock him a mere 100 Nextel Cup points which are used to create NASCAR drivers' standings. He, along with the other four drivers whose crew chiefs were suspended for violations prior to the Daytona 500, was allowed to compete in the race (Waltrip finished 30th).

Another tampering scandal broke in 2008, as the Joe Gibbs Racing team was caught attempting to alter the result of chassis dyno tests on the Nationwide Series (not to be confused with the Sprint Cup Series) cars of Tony Stewart and Joey Logano. Apparently someone in the garage—who, exactly, no one seemed to immediately know—placed one-quarter-inch thick magnets on the gas pedal stop to prevent the car from running completely wide open, thus understating the amount of horsepower the cars could generate. NASCAR inspectors found these spacers and that's when the fingers started pointing. Of course, no one in the upper echelon of the Joe Gibbs Racing team ordered such a thing to be done. No, it was clearly the work of some grease monkey who overstepped his bounds. J.D. Gibbs, the team's president and son of Joe Gibbs (former NFL head coach of the Washington Redskins), was quoted as saying, "A couple of guys chose to make a decision there that really impacts all of us. To me, the frustrating part is, why?"[21] Maybe because someone told them to?

Ultimately, NASCAR suspended seven members of the Joe Gibbs Racing team including crew chiefs Jason Ratcliff and Joe Rogers, and both drivers were placed on probation. Ratcliff and Rogers were also fined $50,000 each, and both Stewart and Logano were docked 150 series points. This was rather unprecedented for NASCAR, yet not without merit. Joe Gibbs Racing had won 13 of the 21 races run that season in the Nationwide Series, and if they were cheating in all 13, the entire season was clearly tainted.

One would think if NASCAR really wanted to stop the attempted cheating that was seemingly rampant at each and every race throughout the course of the season, NASCAR wouldn't just suspend the race team's crew chief. They should suspend the team's primary driver along with the crew chief, or better still, suspend the entire team from competing. But this is rarely the case. Why? As Dale Earnhardt, Inc.'s vice president Richie Gilmore was quoted as saying at the time of Waltrip's Daytona 500 incident, "This day and age, with the sponsors and money that are in the sport, you can see why they didn't send [Waltrip] home."[22]

NASCAR, more than any other professional sports league, runs thanks to their sponsors. This corporate sponsorship money fuels the cars more than gasoline. Drivers are affiliated and identified with specific cars, and these cars are painted according to their sponsors' demands. The sponsors use those cars for nothing more than high-speed advertisements, turning your average NASCAR race into a mass-marketing cesspool. No one watching the race in person sees a driver's face, they simply see his car which is covered from bumper to bumper in sponsors' logos. The viewers at home, while able to occasionally see the driver behind the wheel, are subjected to even more obnoxious product placements with advertisements crammed into every available camera shot. After the race, the drivers that are interviewed continue to add to the sponsor's promotion, sounding more like pitchmen than race car drivers. The reason is simple—everyone knows how their bread is buttered.

By suspending an entire race team, NASCAR would effectively be suspending one of their primary sponsors. These individual racing team sponsors are oftentimes official NASCAR sponsors as well, which is a clear conflict of interest. Would the league dare offend one of their biggest supporters? You must remember, though a corporation such as Miller Beer may sponsor a race car, they often aren't directly involved in what's happening in the pits. So truly, they are not responsible for a team's cheating ways. Yet, if NASCAR had an ounce of guts and was willing to suspend an entire team, one such instance may be enough to make every team stand up and pay attention. Having lost the advertising opportunity from that missed race, the angered sponsor might have more influence over its racing team's willingness to amend their ways than NASCAR itself ever could. On top of undercutting the cheating atmosphere in the garage, such a decision by the governing body may do more to legitimize the sport than anything else. Since NASCAR can get away with simply suspending a driver or a crew chief instead of an entire team, the league appears to be more content with its extremely cozy relationships with numerous sponsors rather than showing any sort of integrity to fans.

Maybe it's this sort of behavior on NASCAR's part that's led to the legend of "The Call." Whispered about as a secret, dismissed as salacious rumor, or sometimes outright cited as the gospel, the legend of "The Call" has always lingered in NASCAR's history. As Robert Lipsyte wrote for the *New York Times*, "Old-timers note, cynically yet approvingly, that a car that should win—because a wrong needs to be righted, an old champion needs to be rewarded, the fans need satisfaction—often does, particularly at Daytona, a track owned by NASCAR."[23] "The Call" represents nothing more than NASCAR's way of fixing its own races. The idea behind the legend was that NASCAR, wanting or needing a certain driver (and his sponsor) to win for its own greedy reasons, calls the team in question and lets them know that perhaps they won't be inspected as closely as they should be this week. Or competing drivers are told that maybe this just isn't their race (wink, wink). It's akin to the last-minute instructions jockeys receive prior to a horse race, and if the legends are true, just as corrupt. If a jockey can hold back a horse to intentionally lose a race while avoiding any track inquiries, then it's no stretch of the imagination to believe a NASCAR driver couldn't do the same with a race car.

Back in 1995, Bob Zeller of *The Virginian Pilot* newspaper wrote an article about "The Call." As part of the process he conducted an anonymous survey of 30 "top members of the NASCAR family—drivers, crew chiefs, owners and others" asking just two questions. The first was, "Do you believe that NASCAR secretly singles out teams for favors and tries to tilt the odds in their favor?" According to the article, 14 out of the 30 questioned responded in the affirmative. That means that nearly half of that small (and assumingly random) sample of NASCAR members asked the question believed that their sport actively attempted to alter the outcomes of its own races. Obviously, that could just be a form of sour grapes: people who feel they've been cheated when they haven't or who feel that others are treated differently because they are unfairly deemed to be special. However, the second question asked was, "Has your team ever been secretly singled out by NASCAR to receive exclusive favors or concessions?" Remarkably, two of the 30 people said that they had indeed received secret "help" from NASCAR. Were these two positives just a case of knowingly answering in the affirmative to help keep the legend of "The Call" alive, or was it simply the truth? If it was the latter, then NASCAR has some questions to answer for its fans' sake. No matter what your take on the results of this mini-poll, Zeller quoted one unnamed source as saying, "Has it ever happened to me? No. Have I seen it happen? Yes. I've seen them let a car through (inspection) that was 400 pounds light. I've seen them let a car through with the wrong numbers on the tires. It's The Call."[24]

Perhaps, then, "The Call" is more real than NASCAR would like its fans to believe. Attempts at cheating in races are well-known and often sniffed out, no matter that fines and suspensions constantly loom over the offenders' heads. Like any other sport, NASCAR drivers are as open to blackmail as any other athletes. Meanwhile, the sponsorship money funding NASCAR is perhaps more powerful and overt than in any other sport. Unlike the other four major sports leagues, NASCAR is not a collective of individually owned teams. The league is a family-held business under which multiple teams compete. As such, NASCAR may be more willing to kowtow to the sponsors' demands while craving the TV attention and revenue that's attached to its sport's ratings success. All of this adds up to the fact that NASCAR has the real ability to make "The Call" and, if it were so inclined, intentionally alter the outcome of its races for its own profit.

The question is: has it? Some of NASCAR's most questionable results all took place at the same track and in the same race held in early July.

Perhaps the first notable occurrence of "The Call" took place on July 4, 1984 at the NASCAR-owned Daytona Motor Speedway. That year's Firecracker 400 was an important day for NASCAR. Not only was the race featured on *ABC's Wide World of Sports*, but President Ronald Reagan attended the race, becoming the first sitting president to ever do so. He gave the famous call, "Gentlemen, start your engines," from a phone inside Air Force One. Remarkably, the race that day came down to a shootout between two of the sport's legends, Richard "The King" Petty and Cale Yarborough. Late in the race, a yellow caution flag flew, and Petty out-dueled Yarborough back to the finish line, beating him by mere inches. The race ended under the caution, with Petty winning his 200th and final victory of his career. Oddly enough, both drivers were staunch Republicans, and reportedly, Reagan gave Petty a wink during their congratulatory handshake.

Twenty years later, the Firecracker 400, then dubbed the Pepsi 400, featured the same strange happenings out on the fabled Daytona racetrack. This time the entire nation had something at stake. Pepsi Cola, the obvious sponsor of the race, had a promotion in place that would give everyone in America a free two-liter bottle of their newest offering, Pepsi Edge, should Jeff Gordon win the race. Why Jeff Gordon? Gordon happened to be driving a car specially painted with Pepsi's logo for the race. Guess who won? Gordon won not just the pole position for the race, but led a majority of the laps and took home the checkered flag. He emerged from his Pepsi car to drink a victorious bottle of Pepsi at a racetrack that sells nothing but Pepsi products. America rejoiced in their free bottle of Pepsi Edge, yet within a year, Pepsi pulled the weak-selling product from production. I guess a product-tainted NASCAR victory can only do so much for your soda.

Perhaps the race that has had most NASCAR fans up in arms to this very day was the Pepsi 400 run in 2001. Five months prior to this race, NASCAR's legendary "Intimidator" Dale Earnhardt, Sr. crashed on the final turn of the Daytona 500 and died as a result of his injuries. It was a dark day for NASCAR. Typically seen as the greatest race of its season, the 2001 Daytona 500 was instantly marred by Earnhardt's tragic death. Fans were shocked. NASCAR found itself under scrutiny because the seemingly benign crash that took Earnhardt's life raised numerous safety concerns, both outside and inside the sport. Now, in early July, NASCAR was forced back to the site of the tragedy to race the Pepsi 400 at Daytona.

What occurred that July 7th night was nothing short of amazing. Dale Earnhardt, Jr., who had finished second in the race that claimed his father's life, found himself in seventh place with just six laps remaining as the result of a yellow caution flag. Earnhardt, Jr.'s car had been strong—perhaps too strong—all race long. He passed three or four cars at a time by himself, something rarely ever seen in a restrictor plate race (they are metal plates that restrict airflow into the car's engine, thus equalizing the horsepower and resultant speed of all cars on the track). With six laps to go and six cars ahead of him, the heartwarming story that would go along with an Earnhardt, Jr. victory seemed all but lost. But once again, here came Junior. Within a half -ap after the restart, Junior was in fifth and moved into fourth by the end of lap 155. One lap later, he was in second, up high and behind the race leader Johnny Benson. At that moment, Dave Blanley, who was in a close third place and directly behind Benson, nearly crashed. That ill-timed swerve took a large section of the other cars out of contention. By the end of lap 156—just two laps after the restart of the race—Earnhardt, Jr. was in the lead to stay.

To a certain degree, it is indisputable that Earnhardt, Jr. was allowed to win this race. Michael Waltrip (the same Waltrip who would somehow avoid suspension over the illegal fuel additive in 2007) finished in second place behind Junior. At the time, the two were teammates and had finished first and second in the Daytona 500 just five months earlier. Waltrip was quoted after Earnhardt, Jr.'s win saying, "I didn't even think about it [passing Earnhardt]—I wasn't gonna pass him for nothing—I just wanted to push him home."[25] Elliott Sadler, who finished in third, said, "I was committed to Michael [Waltrip]. I couldn't see the race finishing any other way."[26] Just so it's clear: *neither driver that finished second or third admittedly had any intention of trying to win the race.* They let Junior win.

Johnny Benson, who was in the lead when the green flag restarted the race, questioned Junior's win, if only momentarily. He said, "You don't go by yourself on the outside and make that kind of time up. But it's okay. It was good that Junior won."[27] For NASCAR, Junior's win was more than just good. NASCAR had just signed a $2.8 billion deal with NBC. In an amazingly lucky turn of events, the first race on NBC's NASCAR schedule just happened to be that very Pepsi 400 which featured Junior's heartwarming victory, conquering the track that took his father's life. And prior to the race, NBC's producers admitted to telling drivers to "live it up" in any post-race celebrations, since the prime-time cameras were rolling. NASCAR didn't disappoint NBC. As soon as Junior emerged from his car he was mobbed by hundreds of fellow NASCAR members covered in the colors of every racing team at the track. The race was the highest rated prime-time race in NASCAR's history.

So what made Junior so unbeatable that magical night? As Junior said after the race, "We had a great car—it was all car—100 percent. I just had to hold on."[28] The problem was a restrictor plate race like this controversial Pepsi 400 was meant to keep all cars relatively even. Though each car's setup is obviously different, the restrictor plate shouldn't allow one car to seemingly overpower and dominate the competition. Which was exactly what Junior's number 8 car did that fateful night. If NASCAR made "The Call" that night, perhaps Junior's restrictor plate wasn't the same as everyone else's. Perhaps he didn't even have one. Perhaps the inspectors looked the other way just for this one race. Who's to say? Junior didn't need to know the truth, he simply had to "hold on" and the race would work itself out (much to NBC's delight). Clearly, some of the other drivers were content to let Junior win, but just how many shared that feeling will never be known.

Yet there are other races outside of those held at Daytona that NASCAR historians and fans look at with the same questioning eye. Ricky Craven won an emotional race at his "home" racetrack, the New Hampshire International Speedway, months after being sidelined with a concussion resulting from a crash in another race. Jeff Gordon, then NASCAR's heir apparent, won the first Brickyard 400 in 1994 at the Indianapolis Motor Speedway, having a car that no one else seemed to be able to catch up with thanks to a perhaps lower, and thus more aerodynamic, than allowable body. Then there's 2007 Nextel Cup champion Jimmie Johnson who was sponsored by Lowe's. Johnson had a peculiar affinity for winning at Lowe's Motor Speedway in Charlotte, posting back-to-back-to-back victories in the Coca-Cola 600 in 2003, 2004, and 2005. How strange was it that the driver sponsored by Lowe's, driving a car painted with the Lowe's logo, consistently won at Lowe's racetrack? Were all these results mere coincidence, or was something going on inside NASCAR?

Of course, NASCAR and its defenders refute such claims with the standard "there would be too many people involved to keep this quiet" excuse.

To some degree, they do have a point. NASCAR, unlike any of the other professional sports discussed here, doesn't simply have two teams battling for a win. Each and every week, NASCAR typically has 30 or more cars vying for the top spot in a race. To get that many different drivers and teams to agree to the same outcome, a result that will obviously benefit just one of them, would be quite a process. But just because something is unlikely or difficult doesn't mean it's by any means impossible. NASCAR team owners often own and compete with more than one car in each race. Getting four owners to agree to "The Call" could actually net the instigators anywhere from four to 16 or more cars in a given race. And though independent, all of these team owners still exist under the same unifying flag. They aren't foolish enough to doubt that on certain occasions and in certain races, specific outcomes would and could benefit everyone within the sport. Even if every owner couldn't see eye to eye on a particular outcome, it doesn't mean the others wouldn't be able to make it happen.

Much like the inspection of its cars, officiating in NASCAR is oftentimes a questionable affair. Race officiating in 2008 was overseen at each track by eight individuals including NASCAR president Mike Helton and competition director Robin Pemberton. To whom do either of these people have to answer? No one. They are at the top of the NASCAR food chain. Questions end with these people. When major inconsistencies occur, like when a yellow flag is issued for a mysterious piece of debris, but not when a car (in one case, Clint Bowyer's) flips upside down, who can you turn to for a fair and unbiased ruling? Not these people because it's their judgment that made such determinations in the first place. With NASCAR willing to alter its rules mid-season, it leaves the fans with the impression that rules can be changed to suit the sport's very whim and thus aid the teams in need of help. With so many conflicts of interest within the sport, who's to say that isn't the case?

Certainly not former NASCAR champion Bill Elliott. In his book *Awesome Bill From Dawsonville: My Life in NASCAR*, Elliott wrote, "They [NASCAR] still try to dictate results. Whether it's Petty's Daytona win in 1984 or the questionable yellow flags of the last few years, NASCAR seems to be manufacturing their outcomes a little too much. People in the sport used to laugh at the random yellow flags that would fly during a race due to phantom debris on the track. Most of these yellows were simply intended to tighten up the field for a more exciting finish or to bring the day's 'featured' performer closer to the lead." Elliott clearly stated here that races are manipulated. And he's not the only driver to say that outright.

After losing a race in early 2007 due to what he deemed to be too many questionable caution flags, Tony Stewart dropped a bomb on NASCAR. He said on his own satellite radio program, "It's like playing God. They can almost dictate the race instead of the drivers doing it. It's happened too many times this year. I guess NASCAR thinks 'Hey, wrestling worked, and it was for the most part staged, so I guess it's going to work in racing, too.' I can't understand how long the fans are going to let NASCAR treat them like they're stupid before the fans finally turn on NASCAR. I don't know that they've run a fair race all year."[29] Was that just sour grapes, or was Stewart speaking the outright truth? Stewart, who posted over $6 million in winnings in 2007, added later in the radio program, "To me, it's not all about the money, it's about the integrity of the sport. When I feel our own sanctioning body isn't taking care of that, it's hard to support them and feel proud about being a driver in the Nextel Cup Series."[30]

As for NASCAR, it responded by calling Stewart's rant "very, very disappointing."[31] Yet it did nothing to discipline Stewart since NASCAR has no rule like that in the NFL or NBA that prohibits athletes from criticizing its officials. Amazingly, it's one of the few things over which NASCAR doesn't maintain control.

THE NATIONAL BASKETBALL ASSOCIATION

On the last day of the 2006-2007 NBA season, two woeful teams, the cellar-dwelling Memphis Grizzlies (21–60) and the next-to-last-place Minnesota Timberwolves (32–49), faced off against each other in Minneapolis. Despite the lack of fan interest, the game still had to tip-off. Statistically speaking, the Timberwolves appeared to be the favorites to win that lackluster contest. Not only were they playing the worst team in the NBA in the Grizzlies, the Timberwolves were at home where they had tallied an almost respectable 20–21 record. That wasn't spectacular, but it was much better than the Grizzlies' horrid 8–33 record on the road.

On the surface it appeared as though neither team had anything to play for, but this wasn't exactly true for the Timberwolves. In 2005, the Timberwolves conducted a forgettable trade with the Los Angeles Clippers sending Sam Cassell westward in exchange for Marko Jaric. As part of that deal, however, the Timberwolves were required to send a first-round draft pick to the Clippers, unless that pick happened to be among the draft's top 10. As fate would have it, should they have beaten the Grizzlies that night, the Timberwolves' 33rd win might have cost them one of those coveted top 10 draft picks.

As game time approached, the future of the Minnesota franchise was nearly at stake. The team's premier player, superstar Kevin Garnett, was home nursing a season-ending injury (one that insiders considered rather questionable). Garnett hadn't been overly happy with the direction of the team, and rumors at the time abounded that he wouldn't be leading the Timberwolves on the court the next season. Should the T-wolves topple the hapless Grizzlies that night, the team was also looking to lose its first-round draft pick in the upcoming draft. On top of all that, thanks to some upper management accounting failures, the franchise lacked any salary cap room to sign a significant free agent. Add all this up and it was easy to see that in the off-season the T-wolves could potentially lose their biggest star and have no opportunities to fill the gaping void.

That is, *if* the Timberwolves could beat the Grizzlies. Amazingly, the Grizzlies brought what must be considered their "A" game that night. They beat the Timberwolves 116–94. That loss, capping a season-ending six-game losing streak, locked in a top 10 draft pick for the T-wolves. That was rather fortuitous for them, as Garnett was shipped off to the Boston Celtics in a rare seven-player-for-one trade in the immediate off-season. On the surface, there was nothing overtly suspicious about the T-wolves' loss that night. One bad team lost to another bad team. Around the NBA, there is a name for that sort of "lose, yet win" type of scenario: tanking.

The idea of NBA teams purposely losing or tanking their last few regular season games to improve their draft choices isn't a new one. Up until 1965, the NBA had a system wherein teams were allowed to forfeit their first-round draft choices to select a player from within the team's immediate area.

These were called territorial draft picks. The idea behind it was to keep players with a strong local collegiate following on NBA teams that also played in that locale, thus helping to increase attendance. Once the NBA had established itself, it eliminated those territorial picks, and went with the ever-reliable coin flip method. The two teams that finished in last place in each division were involved in a coin toss to determine which team received the number one overall draft pick. The other, non-playoff teams based their draft position off of their respective records, from worst to first. That was suitable until 1984.

There were five potentially great players available in the 1984 draft: Michael Jordan, Charles Barkley, Hakeem Olajuwon, Sam Bowie, and Sam Perkins, and many teams wanted a piece of that action. By the end of the 1983–1984 season, the focus for some NBA franchises wasn't to see who would win the championship, but rather which team would win the best draft choice by losing the most games. Accusations of game tanking began to fly. These became so harsh, the following season saw the institution of the NBA's draft lottery.

The idea behind the lottery was simple. It was created to prevent game tanking (or by the NBA's reckoning, the appearance of tanking). Each non-playoff-bound team's name was placed in a drawing, which operated something like pulling a name out of a hat. Now all teams were created equal. This raised new complaints among the teams involved in the new lottery system. Some felt the worse a team was, the more it deserved to have a higher draft choice. Thus, within just two years, the NBA altered the lottery so that it merely determined the selection of the top three draft positions with the remainder filled in based on a team's order of finish in the regular season. That way if the worst team in the league was screwed in the lottery, it still would draft no worse than fourth overall. For some, this wasn't fair enough. In 1990, the NBA made the draft lottery look like a state-run lottery by adding the randomness of ping-pong balls. The team with the worst record had the most number of balls (11 out of the 66 total balls), the second worst team had one ball less than that, and so on. This made everyone happy, for about three years.

The Orlando Magic succeeded in securing the highly sought-after number one spot in the 1992 draft, selecting Shaquille O'Neal. Shaq didn't lead the Magic to the playoffs in his rookie season, but they were close enough to receive just one ball out of the 66 in the 1993 draft hopper. As fate, or luck, or something else would have it, that one ball adorned with the Magic's logo was drawn giving the franchise the number one overall pick, yet again. Once again the NBA went to the drawing board to create a new and more weighted lottery system for the 1994 draft. That form of the draft lottery exists today.

The frustrating part of the whole saga is that all of this tinkering and tweaking did nothing to eliminate game tanking in the NBA. If anything, the ping-pong-ball version of the lottery has emboldened the practice. It gives losing teams a good reason to continue to be bad. In fact, it makes them even worse than they should be as the more a team loses, the better chances it has at securing a higher draft choice.

The late season actions of the 2006–2007 Minnesota Timberwolves were not an isolated occurrence. The Timberwolves themselves pulled off perhaps an even more obvious form of these antics at the end of the 2005–2006 season. The ill-fated Cassell-for-Jaric trade with the Clippers took place early that season, by the end of the year the T-wolves were in total tank mode to save that draft pick. They benched their two top players, Kevin Garnett and Ricky Davis, with suspicious injuries late in the season. And in the oddest move seen in recent NBA history, T-wolves head coach Dwane Casey let his center Mark "Mad Dog" Madsen launch seven three-pointers in the season finale against Memphis. He sank none of them. In fact, those seven three-pointers were Madsen's only seven three-point attempts in the 62 games he played that season. Needless to say, the T-wolves lost that game to Memphis 102–92 in overtime. Having dropped seven of their last 10 games that year, the T-wolves retained their top 10 draft-pick.

Fingers could be pointed at several other franchises as well. The 2006–2007 Atlanta Hawks needed a top-three draft choice in order not to lose their first-round pick thanks to an earlier trade with the Phoenix Suns. They just barely finished the season with the fourth worst record in the league, yet still snagged the third overall pick in the draft lottery. The pitiful 2006–2007 version of the Boston Celtics also looked to be tanking games. In one game at the season's end, Boston head coach Doc Rivers kept all five of his starters on the bench as the team blew an 18-point lead over the equally bad Charlotte Bobcats. After the game, Rivers had to answer tanking accusations from the press saying, "I was not tanking games. I was not throwing the game or anything like that."[32]

That raises the very pertinent question: Who, exactly, would call for these games to be tanked? It is not the players. They want to keep their starting jobs rather than be replaced by some hot-shot rookie. Do coaches instruct players to tank games? Not likely. A coach on a bad team is more likely to be a coach looking for a job rather than looking forward to the upcoming draft. Minnesota Timberwolves head coach Randy Wittman was quoted after that surprising loss to the Grizzlies at the end of the 2006–2007 season as saying, "I'm not here thinking about draft picks when you're playing games in the regular season."[33]

If games are purposefully being tanked, the orders to do so must be coming from the very top of the franchise—the owner. If this is the case, then there's no reason to believe that every NBA game couldn't come under the control of the team's ownership or the NBA itself. If owners can dictate how these "meaningless" games end, they can dictate how any game ends.

Of course, no owner would outright admit to that. Near the end of the 2007–2008 season Minnesota Timberwolves owner Glen Taylor, again destined to land a lottery pick as his team posted only 18 wins in 69 games, claimed his team was not tanking games. Taylor said, "the right thing to do is to press these guys to win, win, win, win, win."[34] Taylor elaborated, "We're winning for [the players], but the other thing is I think we're winning for the fans. I think we have to show the fans that, what I call it, there is a plan. That we're going to improve next year. And you can see where we were and this is where we're going and next year we're going to be a better team."[35]

Anyone insinuating that Taylor ordered his team to tank in the past was crazy. As Taylor said, "It was more like KG [Kevin Garnett] tanked it. I think the other guys still wanted to play. But it sure changed the team and didn't make us [as good]."[36] This is in reference to Garnett's injury that held him out of the T-wolves' last five games in 2006–2007. With the media by his side, Taylor turned on his former marquee star Garnett and blamed him for his team's final five losses, despite that fact that with Garnett in the lineup, the T-wolves managed to win just six of their previous 20 games prior to that.

Taylor, as the team owner, didn't make the team bad. No, it was all Garnett's fault, because apparently Garnett wasn't injured, he simply "tanked it." If Taylor is to be believed, he would've rather seen his team win those last five meaningless games while further wrecking his wretched franchise by losing that coveted top-ten draft pick.

Not every franchise and owner wants to win at all costs as Taylor boasted. The Boston Celtics, for one, didn't always possess the championship mindset they were once known for. Celtics former head coach Jim O'Brien quit in the 2003-2004 season after enduring the purposeful dismantling of the Celtics' roster at the hands of team president Danny Ainge. After he had left the team, Ainge was quoted as saying it was just as well, as O'Brien "came in with a design to win every single basketball game."[37] The Celtics were trying to rebuild through the draft, and winning games wasn't going to help that process along.

The purpose behind tanking games for draft picks is the theory that the right draft pick could revitalize a beleaguered franchise. Case in point, the 1996–1997 San Antonio Spurs. Though the Spurs posted 62 wins in 1994–1995 and 59 wins the following year, the Spurs couldn't get over the playoff hump to win a championship. Then came their dreadful 1996–1997 season in which their star David Robinson suffered a serious injury. According to the Spurs' coach at the time, Bob Hill, the team essentially took a dive from that point on, winning only 20 games that season and making them the third worst team in the NBA. Who was waiting at the end of the rainbow? Tim Duncan, far and away the best prospect in the 1997 draft. Aided by the weighted lottery, the Spurs' ball was drawn and they landed Duncan at number one. In Duncan's rookie season, the Spurs again won over 50 games and the following season won their first ever championship. Duncan would lead the Spurs to three more NBA titles and be named Final's MVP for three of those four championships.

Not to be outdone was the 2002–2003 Cleveland Cavaliers. Though they did win two of their last three games of the season (giving them a whopping 17 wins), the Cavs found themselves in a tie for the worst record in the NBA with the Denver Nuggets. Luckily for both teams, there were two prize draft picks on the horizon, LeBron James and

Carmelo Anthony. A coin flip broke the tie, giving the Cavs a few more ping-pong balls in the hopper than the Nuggets. When the Cavs' ball was drawn in the lottery, the resultant draft pick brought LeBron James to Cleveland. In James' rookie season, the Cavs' home attendance rose by nearly 7,000 fans a game, sales of their merchandise skyrocketed, and the value of the franchise jumped over $120 million. In just four seasons, King James would turn the 17-win Cavaliers into a 50-win NBA championship runner-up franchise while James himself would become the NBA's brightest and most marketable star in the process.

The counter-argument could be made that the number one overall draft pick doesn't guarantee a franchise anything. For every David Robinson or Allen Iverson or Elton Brand there's a Pervis Ellison or Michael Olowokandi or Kwame Brown out there. The hit-and-miss ratio of the number one draft choice is about 50-50. What can't be denied is the press and hype that accompanies each number one pick. A number one pick is headline news. What's attached to that player is the promise of an improved future, whether or not he can actually deliver on it. Before he's even suited up for his first practice, the NBA markets him as a star. Even if that player turns out to be a bust, he got to be the center of the NBA universe for a time. His presence draws national media attention, excites the hometown fans, and inevitably boosts ticket sales. The right number one pick can forever alter the course of a team's fortunes, but even the wrong number one pick can still benefit a floundering franchise, if only for a season or two.

That may very well be why there's so much controversy even today surrounding the 1985 NBA draft. The early 1980s were dark times for the NBA. To most outsiders, the league appeared to only consist of the Los Angeles Lakers, Boston Celtics, and maybe to the initiated, the Philadelphia 76ers. The rest of the league was a wasteland and received little to no national media coverage. Enter the NBA's fourth commissioner, David Stern. Stern quickly realized the way to revamp the league was to remake its image. The best way to do that was to focus on the league's stars. In his first draft as commissioner, Stern oversaw the 1984 draft which ushered Michael Jordan, Charles Barkley, and Hakeem Olajuwon into the league. These players were building blocks. They were a way to open up the NBA to cities that had franchises, but treated them as afterthoughts. Yet there was one key city that still seemed unrepresented within the league, a city that not only hosted the NBA's home office but held the biggest television market in the nation. That was New York.

The early 1980s version of the New York Knicks was a miserable lot. Though they posted winning seasons in both 1982–1983 and 1983–1984, their best finish put the Knicks 15 games out of first place. There was a bright spot on the roster in the form of Bernard King. King was the team's scoring leader, twice dropping in over 50 points in a game during the 1983–1984 season while finishing fifth in the league in scoring. In the Knicks' lackluster 1984–1985 season, King again lit up the scoreboard, leading the league with a scoring average of 32.9 points per game. Late in that season, King tore his anterior cruciate ligament (ACL) which many feared would end his career. The Knicks finished that season 24–58, 39 games out of first place and lacking any sort of star power with King sidelined for an unknown amount of time.

There was a silver lining in all of this for the Knicks. Their horrible season granted them a spot in the NBA's first-ever draft lottery, and the jackpot seemed to be the can't-miss prospect Patrick Ewing. In 1985 Ewing seemed to have all the tools necessary to be a force in the NBA. He had the size, the seeming talent, and proved his worth while playing for Georgetown in college, leading the Hoyas to the NCAA championship game three straight years (winning one). Every team coveted him.

The 1985 draft lottery consisted of seven NBA teams: the Atlanta Hawks, Golden State Warriors, Indiana Pacers, Los Angeles Clippers, Sacramento Kings, Seattle Supersonics, and the New York Knicks. Ewing was destined for one of those franchises. From a league standpoint, the best case scenario would've placed Ewing on the Knicks. A number one pick landing smack dab in the nation's biggest city and TV market would be a boon for the NBA. The Knicks lacked a true star with King's career potentially finished, but Ewing would fill those empty shoes and more. His presence in New York could not only help lift the Knicks franchise out of the doldrums, but the entire league as well if the NBA could get their TV network partners to give the team plenty of air time. Considering how big a name Ewing was in basketball circles prior to joining the NBA, it wasn't a hard sell.

The other option for the league sent Ewing to the outer reaches of the NBA. The other six teams vying for Ewing were small-market teams (the Clippers, though based in L.A., are indeed a small-market team compared to the rival Lakers franchise). None were known as basketball powerhouse; in fact, the Sacramento Kings were known as the Kansas City Kings the season before. None had the ability to draw the fans and TV numbers that New York did. Four of the teams played on the West Coast and offered horrible tip-off times for a potential nationwide TV audience. The NBA had just seen three star rookies, Jordan, Barkley, and Olajuwon, move into big markets, Chicago, Philadelphia, and Houston, and create an instant stir within the game. But having Ewing in Sacramento? Or Seattle? He might as well be playing in Alaska.

I believe the league recognized the need to have Ewing playing in New York. The only thing to do was to have them win the draft lottery. The only way to guarantee the Knicks beat those one in seven odds was to rig the results.

If the powers that be within the NBA did indeed fix that first draft lottery for the Knicks, the amazing thing was they were bold enough to do it in front of a live, nationwide TV audience. Broadcast on CBS, this first-ever draft lottery was something of a curiosity. What was to happen was Jack Wagner, a partner in the international accounting firm Ernst & Whinney, would appear on stage in front of Commissioner Stern and representatives from the seven teams involved, and "gingerly," as TV host for the occasion Pat O'Brien stated, place the seven envelopes containing the names of the seven teams in a clear, Plexiglas-like bin. The bin would be spun, mixing the envelopes, and each envelope would then be drawn by Commissioner Stern and placed in order on a board representing each of the seven draft positions. That is exactly what happened, with one glaring exception.

There are several theories on how the NBA could have rigged this lottery. One of my favorites is that the envelope holding the Knicks' logo was frozen and cold to the touch, something unnoticeable on TV or to anyone in attendance, yet easily discernable to whoever was doing the drawing. But if one watches the actual broadcast of the event (and thanks to the internet, anyone can), one will note that the plan didn't need to be so complex. Here's how the lottery occurred and how it was most likely influenced.

When Commissioner Stern introduced the aforementioned Mr. Wagner, he stated "Within the past hour, each of the logos has been placed in an envelope and sealed by Jack Wagner." Stern went on to say that "Mr. Wagner has certified to me that, first, he alone was present in the room when he placed the logos in the envelopes. Second, that he has since contained…maintained continuous and exclusive possession of the envelopes. And third, as of this moment, he does not know which logo is in which envelope."[38] Of course, since Wagner was given all this unmonitored authority, we can only take both him and Commissioner Stern at their word. At this point, Stern told Wagner to place the envelopes into the hopper. But apparently Wagner forgot that the bin was about to be spun and TV commentator O'Brien's earlier statement about the envelopes being placed into the hopper gingerly. Wagner walked to the bin carrying the seven envelopes, but instead of dropping all seven in, he placed them in the hopper one at a time like dealing playing cards. Most likely, he was dealing off the bottom of the deck. The fourth envelope—which would've been fourth no matter if he started at the top or the bottom of the pile of seven envelopes—wasn't just gently tossed inside like the others. Envelope four was slammed against the side of the bin with a force unlike any given to the other six envelopes. There was no reason for such an action. The bin was then spun, mixing the envelopes.

Now Stern got into the act. He walked to the bin, unlocked it, and took a noticeably deep breath. The bin was a crystal-clear, see-thru basketball. Could Stern have taken that deep breath, knowing not just what was on the line, but giving himself an extra moment to locate the one envelope that was damaged by Wagner's intentional slam? Stern reached inside, grabbing three envelopes. It appears from watching the video of the event that this is the only time Stern, grabbed more than one envelope, and, more importantly, looked into the bin as he chose. He flipped that lot of envelopes over and selected the one on the bottom. When he removed it and held it up for all to see, that envelope had a noticeably dog-eared corner. That envelope contained the logo of the team awarded the number one draft pick. No other envelope had such a fold in it. Was it folded by Wagner's unnecessary action, perhaps? Since Wagner was the only one to have control of the envelopes, could he have been in cahoots with the league and made sure Stern picked the right envelope? Was this why envelope number four received such harsh treatment?

The result of the lottery was that the Knicks logo was indeed inside that bent envelope. As Pat O'Brien announced immediately after that revelation, "Basketball is back in New York City."[39] The Knicks were given the number one pick, and in the ensuing draft brought Patrick Ewing to New York. Though he didn't usher the team to the instant success as many expected (in fact, the Knicks went 23–59 in Ewing's rookie season), he did bring an air of credibility and excitement with him to a team in desperate need of it. Ewing would go on to average over 20 points a game for the next 13 years in a Knicks uniform and be inducted into the Hall of Fame.

Commissioner Stern continues to claim that the outcome was just part of the happenstance possible in a lottery. Replying to allegations of manipulation regarding the 1985 lottery results in an *Associated Press* article published prior to the 2009 draft lottery, Stern stated, "I wish I had as much sway as the conspiracists attribute to me. Lotteries have to do with chance and this lottery [1985's] follows that for the most part." Notice the odd addition of "…for the most part" in his comment? What exactly did he mean by that?

Over 20 years after the Ewing incident, perhaps the same sort of chicanery is afoot within the NBA as the draft lottery odds are often defied. In 2007, the Portland Trailblazers won the lottery despite having only a five percent chance of doing so. The Chicago Bulls one-upped them in 2008, winning the number one draft pick with only a 1.7 percent chance. What raises the question of whether today's version of the draft lottery is on the level is that the drawing is made in secret. No one outside of the NBA's closed circle is allowed to watch the balls tumble around in the Plexiglas basketball. Viewers only get to see the results revealed which leaves the whole process open to manipulation.

So much attention and importance is placed on these top draft picks because the NBA, more than any other professional sports league, is star-focused. It markets the best players over and above the teams they play for. Commissioner Stern once called the NBA's mission "the marketing of heroes."[40] To his credit, Stern realized this the day he stepped into the commissioner's role and he's worked that angle ever since. He's built up the league on top of the backs of such talents as Magic Johnson, Larry Bird, Michael Jordan, Charles Barkley, Patrick Ewing, Shaquille O'Neal, Allen Iverson, Dwayne Wade, and LeBron James. There is a downside to that approach. When all the focus is put on star or "heroic" players, what happens when those heroes break the law, or get busted for drugs, or gambling? If too many of them fall, could the whole league collapse along with them? David Stern once said, "We spend most of our time promoting these guys, we're not going to try and bury them."[41]

This was never more the case than it was for Michael Jordan. On October 6, 1993, Michael Jordan, the biggest and brightest star in the entire sporting world, suddenly announced his retirement from the NBA. Having just led his team, the Chicago Bulls, to its third World Championship in as many years, and still reeling from the tragic murder of his father James Jordan in July of that same year, MJ had seemingly had enough.

Almost forgotten in the hubbub surrounding his sudden retirement was the NBA's ongoing investigation into allegations of Michael Jordan's gambling problem. Not surprisingly, just two days after Jordan's farewell press conference, the NBA announced its five-month-long investigation had ended with the league apparently finding nothing of significance regarding Jordan's gambling habits.

The unanswered question still hovering over those remarkably tidy and symbiotic events is did Michael Jordan retire voluntarily, or did commissioner David Stern and the NBA order him to seek counseling for his addiction to gambling? An addiction that was well known both inside and outside the league and one that had to be kept as invisible as possible so as not to tarnish the image of both Michael Jordan and the NBA.

Whichever it was, it was ugly because Michael Jordan wasn't just an NBA superstar. By that point MJ *was* the NBA. It was estimated at one time that 70 percent of all basketball fans considered themselves Chicago Bulls fans, because they were Michael Jordan fans. Jordan was able to almost single-handedly turn the NBA into a commercial powerhouse. Ticket sales increased league-wide (Jordan almost always played to sellouts, both home and away). Merchandise (mainly Bulls jerseys with the number 23 emblazoned on them) flew off shelves. More importantly to the NBA, the money taken in from TV revenues went through the roof. In 1985 (Jordan's rookie year), CBS paid the NBA $188 million for a four-year TV contract. In 1989, NBC was willing to shell out $600 million for that same amount of time thanks mainly to Jordan's draw.

Stories about Jordan's illegal gambling had begun to surface in 1991, and by 1993 when he retired suddenly, they had snowballed to the point that his image had tarnished and threatened to affect his multimillion-dollar revenue production for the league, and all the success that he had brought to the NBA.

At the news conference on October 6, 1993, there were no tears in Michael Jordan's eyes. There was no sadness, no cracking voices. There was merely a statement followed by some quick, easy-to-answer questions. Jordan said, "I just feel that at this particular time in my career, I've reached the pinnacle...that I don't have anything else to prove to myself." Quite hypocritical considering 17 months later he was back playing for the Bulls. I guess even after being named Rookie of the Year, leading the league in scoring for seven years in a row, being named MVP twice, winning the NBA Championship three times, and being hailed as the greatest player to ever play the game, Jordan found something else he needed to prove.

Then came, "The biggest gratification, the biggest positive thing that I can take out of my father not being here with me today is that he saw my last basketball game, and that means a lot." James Jordan's murder in July of 1993 surely weighed heavily on Michael's mind at the time. Although some have speculated that his father's death had something to do with MJ's gambling, that seems improbable. James Jordan wasn't a saint, truth be told. He was found guilty and sentenced to three years in prison (which was suspended) for being a cog in a larger embezzlement scheme in 1985, and at the time of his death, he was the subject of several lawsuits concerning the unpaid bills of his clothing company, JVL Enterprises, Inc.[42] Even though there are some odd facts surrounding his murder, there is no real evidence to support a conspiracy.

Finally Jordan stated, "Now that I'm here, it's time to be a little bit unselfish in terms of spending more time with my family, my wife, my kids, and just get back to a normal life, as close to it as I can." When asked what will he do now, Jordan replied, "In retirement, you do whatever comes to mind. Relax. Enjoy the time you've been deprived of for many years." What came to Michael's mind was playing baseball. Not spending time with the wife and kids, unless of course they were on the bus with him and the rest of the Birmingham Barons while traveling from small town to smaller town across the southern U.S.

This brings up an interesting point. The only reason Jordan was even given an opportunity to play baseball was because Chicago Bulls' owner Jerry Reinsdorf also owned the Chicago White Sox. The Barons were an affiliate of the White Sox, so MJ could easily pass through the filters that would've normally kept him off the team. Reinsdorf stood to lose as much as anyone with MJ's retirement (just compare Bulls tickets sales before and after MJ's days with the team). Yet he was one of the first people Jordan contacted regarding a potential retirement. How did Reinsdorf respond? By paying Jordan $4 million and leaving a contractual window open for him to return[43], even though after being asked would he ever return, Jordan replied, "No. If so, I'd still be playing."

Jordan was a horrible baseball player. In his one full season in Birmingham, he hit .202 even with opposing teams' catchers telling him which pitch was coming next. White Sox general manager Ron Schueler was quoted at the time as saying that Jordan's chance of making the majors was "a million-to-one shot." So was he truly living a childhood dream of his to play baseball, or was it something else? I believe the NBA came to Jordan and laid it out for him. They didn't want to see him go down for gambling, but at the same time, they couldn't seem to control him. So they cut a deal. The NBA asked him to retire and seek some help. If he allowed the media to cool down, the public would forget all about the potential scandal. Jordan could play baseball to keep in shape while remaining somewhat in that coveted media spotlight. Then, when the time was right, Jordan would be allowed to return to the NBA as the mighty king he once was.

He made a very interesting comment during his retirement press conference. When asked, "will you miss the sport?" he replied: "I'm pretty sure I'll miss the sport. To come back is a different thought—I can't answer that. I'm not making this a 'never' issue. I'm saying right now I don't have the mental drive to come out and push myself to play with a certain focus.

Five years down the line, if the urge comes back, if the Bulls will have me, *if David Stern lets me back in the league,* I may come back" [emphasis added]. No reporter there bothered to ask him, why wouldn't the commissioner let you back in, Michael? It's a very interesting choice of words that lends itself to a very different interpretation of the situation.

Even during his second and more formal retirement, Jordan had to again tip his cap to Stern. In thanking a few people that came before him, Jordan said, "And Mr. Stern and what he's done for the league and gave me the opportunity to play the game of basketball." How exactly did Stern give him an opportunity to play basketball? By drafting him? By offering him a contract? By putting him in the starting lineup? No. By, as MJ said at his first retirement press conference, letting him back in the league.

Having seen the financial dip the league took post-Jordan retirement, the league wanted him to return. They needed him to return. There was no replacement for Michael Jordan. Following his two-word press release in the middle of the 1994–1995 season, in which he simply stated, "I'm back," Jordan was. Presumably having put the gambling behind him, Jordan played another three full seasons with the Bulls, winning the championship in all three.

At a certain point in time, Michael Jordan stopped playing by the NBA's rules and began playing by his own. The NBA, not wanting to upset its greatest cash cow, bent as far as it could to accommodate him. Be it with the lack of foul calls, or limited media access, or getting away with a crime, the NBA was always willing to do it for Michael. Before any serious questions were raised or in-depth investigations conducted regarding Jordan's gambling, MJ retired and the NBA closed its books on the matter, never to look back or re-open them, even when Jordan stopped playing for good and stepped into the ownership role he holds today.

Something like Walt Disney, the NBA preferred to promote the fairy tale starring Jordan than reality. Just take a look at Jordan's final game in a Bulls uniform, the 1997–1998 NBA Championship game against the Utah Jazz. With 5.2 seconds left to go and the Bulls in possession of the ball, to whom do you think they'd look? Michael Jordan, of course. But no one on the Jazz could make that determination. So there was MJ, wide open and basically unguarded for that last, game-winning shot. He not only shot, but posed there for the cameras, so that image could be placed on every piece of merchandise the NBA could sell. The NBA allowed the man who made the league rich beyond even its greediest expectations to go out on top, in style, and without a hint of controversy.

During his second, ill-fated comeback as part owner, part player with the Washington Wizards, Jordan's star no longer shone as brightly. Other younger, hipper stars came along who needed to be coddled. Most notable among these new players was Kobe Bryant. Like several other young up-and-coming players, Bryant was deemed "the next Michael Jordan" before ever stepping foot on a NBA court. Kobe had the looks, the marketability, and most importantly, the talent that no one else possessed, to actually live up to those lofty standards. Was it any wonder that the next NBA dynasty team immediately after Jordan's Bulls faded into the past was the Los Angeles Lakers, led by the new Jordan in Bryant and the NBA's other biggest star, Shaquille O'Neal? This fit perfectly in the NBA's marketing scheme. Two of the league's biggest heroes, both of whom took over the marketing reins MJ once held, dominated the league by winning three straight championships in the same style (and with the same coach) as Jordan and the Bulls. What a lucky turn of events for the NBA. As soon as it lost its biggest attraction, a new tag-team partnership emerged to fill the gaping hole.

Then Kobe Bryant ran afoul of the law in 2003. Charged with rape in Colorado during the off-season, Kobe Bryant's star plummeted. Though he was later found innocent of the charges against him, the ensuing melodrama surrounding his court proceedings tore the wheels off the Lakers dynasty. Fans no longer looked at Bryant in the same way, and the league backed off its promotion of the star. He was no longer a safe bet in the league's eyes. New heroes had to be created.

The obvious choice was the once highly sought-after number one draft choice Tim Duncan. His San Antonio Spurs became an on-again-off-again dynasty, winning four NBA titles in nine seasons. Yet for the NBA, Duncan lacked the charisma that both Jordan and Bryant possessed. He was a safe alternative to be sure, but safe to the point of being bland. Duncan was arguably the best player in the NBA, but his lack of panache made him unmarketable in many eyes. He didn't perform wildly acrobatic dunks.

He didn't fake opposing players out of their jocks. He simply played hard and won. Because this wasn't what the NBA could readily market, Duncan couldn't become the face of the NBA.

Luckily for everyone tied to the NBA, yet another "next Michael Jordan" was looming on the horizon. LeBron James, a high school kid who like Bryant skipped college to join ranks of the NBA, was the type of player the league had been salivating for since Bryant's fall from grace. James did all the things Duncan didn't. He was flashy, media-savvy, and despite never having played anyone outside of high school, was made the new face of the NBA. But while James' star immediately shone as the NBA's new "It" kid, his team the Cleveland Cavaliers initially faltered.

While waiting for James to lead the Cavs from the perennial draft-lottery pool, the NBA leaned not on Duncan, but on another newly christened star, Miami Heat's Dwayne Wade. Just three years into his career, Wade was teamed up with Bryant's old partner Shaquille O'Neal. The pair led the Heat to the NBA championship in 2006. While injuries stunted Shaq and Wade's defense of the Heat's title in the following season, James and the forever floundering Cleveland Cavaliers suddenly hit their stride. The Cavs made the instant jump from basement dwellers to NBA finalists; however, James' Cavs couldn't steal the championship from Duncan and the Spurs.

Remarkably, from the 1990-1991 season through the 2008–2009 season the group of Jordan, Duncan, and Bryant was responsible for winning 14 of 19 NBA championships. Of the five NBA Finals not won by any of those three players, Bryant still appeared in two finals (against Detroit in 2003-2004 and Boston in 2007–2008) which resulted in defeat, and meant that 16 of 19 NBA Finals featured either Michael Jordan, Tim Duncan, or Kobe Bryant as the prime attraction. That seems ridiculous, but it is the truth. In those five seasons during which the championship was not won by the NBA's holy trinity, a strong case could be made that NBA stars still featured prominently in the NBA Finals. During the two years between Michael Jordan's first retirement and his return, Hall of Famer Hakeem Olajuwon (assisted one season by fellow Hall of Fame member Clyde Drexler) led the Houston Rockets to a pair of titles. Later, the tandem of Dwayne Wade and Shaquille O'Neal won it all for the Miami Heat. In 2008–2009, the triumvirate of All-Stars in Boston—Kevin Garnett, Ray Allen, and Paul Pierce—brought a championship back to the Celtics. Perhaps it was only in 2003–2004, when the Detroit Pistons won the NBA Championship, that a team in the past 20 years has won a title without featuring a prominent superstar in its lineup.

This points to one of two conclusions. Either NBA basketball isn't a team sport but one easily dominated by a single great player, or something else is occurring within the league. Is it merely a coincidence that the NBA's marketing plan of choice is to promote their heroes above all else, while at the same time these handful of heroes consistently lead their teams to championship after championship? Other modern-day players deemed exceptional—Charles Barkley, Karl Malone, Vince Carter, Allen Iverson, Chris Webber and the previously highlighted Patrick Ewing to name a few—have seen some limited success, but never achieved the pinnacle of winning a championship. At the same time, they were never given the level of promotion that Jordan and Bryant received, or the amount of hype which currently surrounds James.

The question then remains: Does the NBA grant these hero players extra leeway on the court to ensure they reach the levels of success the NBA itself needs to be profitable? As the authors wrote in *Money Players*, "[NBA commissioner] Stern refused to admit it, but the NBA lived year to year, crossing its fingers for the right rating matchups. It seemed the whole world had grown accustomed to the NBA's being able to deliver new episodes of *Star Wars* every season."[44]

It can be amazing how that sort of luck runs the NBA's way. The 2006–2007 NBA Finals saw what appeared to be a solid matchup between Duncan's Spurs and LeBron James' Cavaliers. Yet this star power fizzled. The Spurs swept the Cavs in four games while the Finals garnered some of the worst ratings in recent league history. In fact, the ratings for the 2006–2007 NBA Finals were the lowest since Duncan and the Spurs beat the New Jersey Nets in 2003, which, in turn, had been the lowest the NBA had seen since *1981*. Simply put, while Duncan and the Spurs seemed to be a safe bet for the NBA, they did not draw people to their televisions. On top of that, ratings for the Finals since 2003 have been awful when compared to their heyday during the Jordan era. Kobe Bryant and the Lakers' presence in the 2003–2004

Finals against the Detroit Pistons did cause an uptick in the NBA's numbers, but that was an exception rather than the rule. Despite this steady downturn in ratings, and against any recognizable logic, the 2006–2007 off-season witnessed the league sign its most lucrative contract with the TV networks, bringing in nearly $1 billion a year beginning in 2007–2008.

Prior to the start of the 2007–2008 NBA season, the Timberwolves traded away their marquee player Kevin Garnett to the Boston Celtics for five other players and two draft picks. Despite the lopsidedness of the seven-for-one trade, most NBA pundits felt it was the Timberwolves who were shorted in the deal. Garnett was considered a future Hall of Famer; the seven players the floundering Timberwolves received in return were mere fillers needed to round out a roster. Not to be outdone, midway through the season Kobe Bryant's Los Angeles Lakers acquired Pau Gasol from the Memphis Grizzlies in another shockingly lopsided trade. The Lakers received in Gasol a former rookie of the year and a constant All-Star while the Grizzlies picked up two bench players and a pair of draft picks. As the season wore on, it seemed as if the two franchises, bolstered by their genius trade-making abilities, were destined for greatness. Amazingly for the league, that was exactly what happened.

The NBA was blessed with the dream matchup of the Boston Celtics against the Los Angeles Lakers in the 2007–2008 NBA Finals. Both teams' march to the Finals brought in massive ratings as ESPN's numbers were up some 35 percent and ABC's were up 28 percent according to *Broadcasting & Cable* magazine, which cited Nielsen Media Research. Upon reaching the Conference Finals, the matchups of the Lakers vs. the Spurs and the Celtics against the Pistons kicked ratings up 40 percent over the year before. Then, when both the Lakers and Celtics triumphed, the NBA had its perfect matchup with its two most honored franchises meeting face-to-face. Not only did the league benefit from having both the East and West Coasts covered with each team, they had the two teams with the biggest fan bases in the NBA playing each other. Top that off with the hype of the storied rivalry between these two legendary teams and what resulted? The 2007–2008 Finals saw a ratings boost of nearly 45 percent from just the year before. What better way to make good on that $1 billion-a-year TV revenue contract than by bringing your broadcasting partners the highest ratings in recent memory? Was that luck, coincidence, or something else?

As the NBA likely patted itself on the back for a job well done in 2008, they had to consider a way to keep those ratings climbing. During the 2008–2009 NBA Playoffs, the league looked to be heading toward yet another dream matchup, this time again featuring the Lakers and Kobe Bryant but with the new wrinkle in the Cleveland Cavaliers fronted by LeBron James. Both teams were the number one seed in their respective conferences, with the Cavs having one more regular season win than the Lakers. As the playoffs began, the talk on all of the sports shows was about who was better: Kobe or LeBron? This hype led to another ratings spike for the NBA. The ratings for the playoffs on TNT and ESPN were up 19 percent and 12 percent respectively from the year before. By the time the Conference Finals aired, with both Kobe and LeBron still in the mix, ratings were again up from 2008 for both networks by 30 percent and 32 percent.

Yet something happened on the way to the NBA's latest perfect matchup in the Finals. The Cavaliers lost. LeBron James wound up watching Dwight Howard and the Orlando Magic take his spot against Kobe and the Lakers in the Finals. Without LeBron facing Kobe, ratings for the Finals dipped 10 percent overall from the year before. How'd this happen if the NBA was scripting its own results? Perhaps the Kobe vs. LeBron matchup would've been too obvious (even for the NBA) to allow to happen. Prior to the Magic and Lakers Finals being set, both Vitamin Water and Nike were attempting to cash in by airing commercials featuring the raging NBA debate of who was better: Kobe or LeBron? While the NBA likely would have loved to see LeBron and Kobe square off to settle this question, perhaps too many other questions would have been raised at the same time.

Perhaps there was a good reason why the NBA might have wanted to leave LeBron James out of the Finals at this point. While James' ability on the court cannot be questioned, it is perhaps James' own ego that was getting in the way of his success. He has stated in the past, "I'm just trying to be a global icon." A lofty goal, no doubt, but such a statement never needed to be made by the likes of Michael Jordan or Kobe Bryant. It simply happened for them. James, in stark contrast, seems to be more concerned with hyping himself—even to the point of wearing a T-shirt reading "LBJ MVP"—than anything else. After losing the Conference Finals to the Magic, James walked off the court, refusing to follow the tradition of shaking any of the Magic players' hands after the series concluded. He even ran away from reporters after losing that last game, refusing to answer any of the media's questions. Global icon, huh? The NBA fined James for his actions, but perhaps it explains why James hasn't reached the pinnacle of winning a championship yet. Maybe the NBA needs to teach "the King" some manners before he's given a ring. Of course, with superstar Shaquille O'Neal being added to the Cavaliers roster for the 2009–2010 season—a player whose media drawing power cannot be overlooked—perhaps LeBron's ring is just a year away.

Could the NBA give such star players and their teams an easier passage through the playoffs? Many NBA critics have declared that star players like Jordan and Bryant were given more latitude than should be normally allowed during a game—that extra space was needed to allow them to shine as brightly as they have. If true, such space was granted to them solely by the referees. Either the referees looked the other way, ignoring certain calls against the star player, or they were too quick with the whistle against the star player's opponent. All such options opened the floor up for the star to have his way and aid in his, and by extension, the league's success. The difference between a charging call and a blocking foul in the NBA may be defined in the league's rule book, but it's open to interpretation out on the court at full speed. Most NBA fouls are strictly judgment calls. It's very easy for a referee to overlook a foul and whistle something that didn't really occur because of the pace of the game. If everything is on the level, it's hard to fault the referees for goofs made because of the frenzied pace.

Thanks to the federal case against former NBA referee Tim Donaghy, we now know that not everything was indeed on the level during some NBA games. Through his lawyer Donaghy has leveled accusations, which if they prove to be true, back up this notion 100 percent.

In a letter sent through his lawyer to the court Donaghy claimed, "In 2004, Team 1 was playing a game against Team 2, which was officiated by Referees A, B, and C. Tim [Donaghy] did not officiate that game, but spoke to Referee B by telephone, who confirmed that Referee A had spoken with Team 1's general manager that day. Referee B told Tim that Referee A planned to favor Team 1 at that night's game. Indeed, the referees called 25 personal fouls on Team 2, and far fewer on Team 1." Another nugget provided by Donaghy stated, "Tim explained that league officials would tell referees that they should withhold calling technical fouls on certain star players because doing so hurt ticket sales and television ratings. As an example, Tim explained how there were times when a referee supervisor would tell referees that NBA Executive X did not want them to call technical fouls on star players or remove them from the game. In January 2000, Referee D went against these instructions and ejected a star player in the first quarter of the game. Referee D later was reprimanded privately by the league for that ejection."

Apparently, during the investigation Donaghy spilled the beans on every dirty thing the NBA does. Donaghy wasn't making these accusations as a form of revenge against the league. The league didn't drop him into the FBI's lap; the NBA allowed him to ref games and would have continued to allow his career to flourish had the feds not intervened and arrested him. He was most likely telling the truth, hoping to save himself some jail time, which is not an unreasonable thing given the circumstances. Donaghy explained the cozy relationship between referees, teams, players, and league executives. He also explained the subtle ways the league had referees manipulate the outcomes of games.

Former NBA referee Tim Donaghy told federal investigators that the NBA intentionally alters the outcomes of their own games for ratings and money. So, why didn't the feds investigate the NBA for its actions? *Because it is not against the law.* The NBA and every other league for that matter can legally alter the outcomes of their games.

Donaghy pointed to two prime examples: the first round playoff matchup between the Houston Rockets and Dallas Mavericks in 2005 and the Conference Finals between the Los Angeles Lakers and Sacramento Kings in 2002.

In the case of the Rockets-Mavericks matchup, Donaghy said, "Team 3 lost the first two games in the series and Team 3's owner complained to

NBA officials. Team 3's owner alleged that referees were letting a Team 4 player get away with illegal screens. NBA Executive Y told Referee Supervisor Z that the referees for that game were to enforce the screening rules strictly against that Team 4 player. Referee Supervisor Z informed the referees about his instructions. As an alternate referee for that game, Tim also received these instructions. The referees followed the league's instructions and Team 3 came back from behind to win the series. The NBA benefited from this because it prolonged the series, resulting in more tickets sold and more games televised."

Jeff Van Gundy was the Rockets' coach in that series, and according to Donaghy, Van Gundy was fined $100,000 after the series ended for "not disclosing the name of the official who had informed him [Van Gundy] of the behind-the-scenes instructions." Apparently the NBA was concerned that there was a leak within the league and wanted to keep such damaging information from becoming public. Of course, when confronted with this tidbit while working as a member of ABC's broadcasting team for the 2007–2008 NBA Finals, Van Gundy backed away from what he had said regarding the officiating for that series. A wise move for someone wanting to remain employed within the NBA.

As for the 2002 Lakers-Kings series, Donaghy stated that the league wanted the matchup to reach a pivotal Game 7 instead of ending in Game 6. So what happened? The frustrated Kings watched as the Lakers were awarded 27 free throw attempts in the fourth quarter alone while the Kings attempted only nine in that same time span. This game has been called by many longtime NBA reporters as the worst officiated game in NBA history. Even the announcers for NBC calling the game were shocked by the seemingly blatant actions of the referees on the court. The Kings saw their best defensive option against the Lakers' Shaquille O'Neal, Scot Pollard, foul out in just 10 minutes of play. The Kings' other center, Vlade Divac, also fouled out in the fourth quarter on ticky-tack calls. With both of the Kings' centers out of the game, O'Neal was able to destroy the Kings under the basket. Even so, with 12 seconds left in the game, the Kings were down by just one point. As the Lakers attempted to inbound the ball, Kobe Bryant clearly elbowed the Kings' Mike Bibby in the face while trying to get open. Yet somehow it was Bibby who was called with the foul. Bryant sank his free throws and the Lakers won Game 6 by a final score of 106–102. The Lakers then won Game 7 over the Kings and ultimately the NBA Championship that season.

The more one digs through the NBA's recent past, the more such shenanigans seem to come to light. A prime example may just be the 2001 NBA Eastern Conference Finals between the Milwaukee Bucks and the Philadelphia 76ers. Both teams had finished first in their respective division. During the course of their seven-game series, all of the calls went the 76ers' way. The Bucks were called for 43 more fouls than the 76ers while also being called for 11 technical fouls compared to two for the 76ers. The Bucks also were tagged with four flagrant fouls (none for the 76ers), one of which suspended Bucks center Scott Williams for Game Seven. Here's the strange part: at that time in NBA history, there was a point system amassed by the league for counting intentional and flagrant fouls. When a player's tally reached 12 points, he was automatically suspended for a game. In Game Six, Williams accrued his 11th point. The NBA reviewed Williams' flagrant foul and decided it wasn't a one-point flagrant foul, but a two-point flagrant thus giving Williams 12 points and instantly suspending him for Game Seven.

Rumors abounded that should the Bucks complain to the media regarding the situation, the NBA threatened to penalize the Bucks their first-round draft pick in the upcoming draft. This was after the Bucks franchise as well as both Bucks head coach George Karl and guard Ray Allen had already been fined a grand total of $85,000 for saying that the NBA would rather see the 76ers in the Finals against the Lakers rather than the Bucks. Allen was quoted as saying, "I think there's no question. The league, as a marketing machine, the bottom line is about making money. It behooves everybody for the league to make more money, and the league knows that Philadelphia is going to make more money with L.A. than we would with L.A." Needless to say, the 76ers won Game Seven by the score of 108–91.

While Donaghy didn't point out the 76ers-Bucks series or any of the other NBA playoff series that seemed to always have the ball bounce the NBA's way, what was the case for Donaghy doesn't necessarily translate into an accusation against the entire league. At the same time, it proves the obvious—referees can indeed control the outcome of games. In fact, Donaghy may not be the only referee the FBI was after. Reports from ESPN claim that federal investigators were questioning former NBA referees about longtime referee Dick Bavetta. Bavetta has been with the NBA since 1975 and was one of the referees on the court during that pivotal Game Six in 2002 between the Kings and Lakers. While asking about certain games Bavetta officiated, what the feds were after wasn't completely known. What seems to be certain was that while commissioner David Stern denies any and all allegations made by Donaghy, the feds took a keen interest in what he had to say.

Hypothetically, if the NBA was pre-armed with such damning knowledge of their referees' gambling indiscretions, instead of firing all of their referees—as their collective bargaining agreement calls for—it could easily have used that information against them. Perhaps it wouldn't even need to reach those depths for such a thing to transpire. The league's referees have always worked hand-in-hand with their employers, including subjecting themselves to both self- and league-imposed reviews and rankings. The NBA chooses and pays only their best referees to oversee its most important games of the year, the playoffs, based on those reports. Tim Donaghy was once deemed one of the NBA's best and was assigned such playoff work. Donaghy claimed that even the league's review and ranking system was manipulated. He stated that the league-mandated observers who attended games to monitor referees' calls were not as anonymous as they were supposed to be. In fact, referees were aware of the observers and maintained good relations with them to receive positive reports. It is likely that the NBA's best were really those most willing to bend to the league's will. Couldn't that make bonus pay for playoff work bribe money? If everyone involved, including referees, stand to prosper, then why does "the call" from the higher-ups even need to be made?

But to quell all such rumors and accusations, in October 2008, the NBA released the "Report to the Board of Governors of the National Basketball Association." Known as the Pedowitz Report, the league's "independent investigation" into the Donaghy mess was led by lawyer Lawrence B.

Pedowitz. In typical league-mandated investigative fashion, Pedowitz's report found Donaghy acted alone and that all other officials in the NBA were doing exactly as they were supposed to according to NBA rules (never mind the facts about all those referees gambling). While Pedowitz and his team had unfettered access to league documents and employees, they had none of the power that the FBI had over Donaghy. None of the 50+ NBA officials they interviewed were under oath. Supposedly, any ref found lying to Pedowitz and his crew could have instantly lost employment with the NBA, yet how could liars be ferreted out in such an investigation? What incentive did any of the referees have to reveal truth in the event they did know of conspiracies to fix within the NBA? Every referee's livelihood and credibility would have been destroyed with such a revelation. As interconnected as Pedowitz's report claims the NBA's brotherhood of referees is, it wouldn't be such a stretch of the imagination to believe they could have communicated with each other before, during, and after this investigation.

What's even worse, Pedowitz's main focus wasn't proving/disproving Donaghy's accusations. The report mainly existed as a "compliance review." While they did attack, and in their opinion refute Donaghy's accusations, the main purpose of the report was to belay future problems of the same kind. Team Pedowitz boasts how the NBA made most of their resultant suggestions part of the league's daily operations, but so what? Many of their recommendations merely tweaked and clarified rules the league already had. The report also suggested that the league, its officials, and each team communicate more effectively so that incidents could be quelled before they escalated. Again, so what? The league supposedly had observers watching referees, the referees watching themselves, the home office reviewing game video, and its security division watching over everyone. And still Tim Donaghy did what he did without getting caught by any of them. As transparent as this all seems to me, most everyone goes along with the NBA's way of doing business without questioning it. Sports reporters should be hammering the NBA on a daily basis in an attempt to expose league manipulations. A prime example of reporters overlooking an owner's shenanigans came in the middle of the NBA's 2008–2009 season, when the Portland Trailblazers sent out a league-wide email signed by its president Larry Miller that warned the rest of the league not to sign their player Darius Miles off of waivers. Why? If Miles played in another two games, the team would have to pay him $18 million over the next two seasons and it would count against the Trailblazers' salary cap. While everyone within the NBA acted outraged, Miller defended his actions and unsurprisingly, the NBA officially said it would do nothing to punish the franchise. One would think the Trailblazers' rivals would do the exact opposite of Miller's request and pick Miles up, simply to put the screws to the franchise. While league officials and lawyers began to get involved in the ongoing affair, no other team picked up Miles. Is that common practice within the NBA? It reeks of the collusion charges that were correctly filed against MLB in the mid-1980s, yet within the sports reporting world, barely a word was written on this matter.

Reporters could also be hounding Tim Donaghy in prison to get more of his story. They should be calling for Commissioner Stern to step down and every owner to come clean about how the NBA does business with the TV networks. They should be digging for the truth. Instead, sports leader ESPN would rather celebrate the Lakers' latest championship (and the revenues the network reaped with the resurgence in ratings) instead of stepping back and questioning how the Lakers managed to get there in the first place.

THE NATIONAL HOCKEY LEAGUE

The National Hockey League gets little of the respect it deserves in the sporting world. Founded in 1917, the league is the second oldest in professional sports, predating both the NFL and NBA. Its championship trophy, the Stanley Cup, has been fought over even longer, dating back to 1893, 10 years before the first World Series. The NHL's fabled "Original Six" teams—the Montreal Canadiens, Toronto Maple Leafs, Chicago Blackhawks, Boston Bruins, New York Rangers, and Detroit Red Wings— while not truly being the first six teams in the NHL, all can trace their origins to the 1920s or before. Despite all of that history, many Americans just can't get into the sport of hockey. Few books are written about the subject, its playoff schedule receives scant television airtime, and the league itself gets minuscule media attention. As a result, many people no longer even consider the NHL to be a major sports league. On August 9, 1988, the NHL made headlines across both the United States and Canada. The NHL's greatest player, Wayne Gretzky, who at the age of 27 had just led his team, the Edmonton Oilers, to their fourth Stanley Cup championship in five seasons, was traded to the Los Angeles Kings. This was not just a monumental trade, it was a true piece of sports history.

Despite playing in the remote outpost of Edmonton, Alberta, Canada, Gretzky was the most recognizable face in the NHL. His star power and talent seemed unmatched. He was breaking long-standing scoring records with each game and season he played. As flashy as he was on the ice, Gretzky was just the opposite off it. He appeared humble, reserved, and possessed a solid respect for those who came before him in the NHL. That is why he was labeled "The Great One."

People who didn't follow hockey knew Wayne Gretzky's name. His number 99 Edmonton Oilers jersey was available nationwide in the United States at a time when hockey jerseys weren't normally found in retail stores. There was a Wayne Gretzky hockey doll, something of a cross between a Barbie doll and an old-school G.I. Joe action figure. In 1983, Canada issued a Wayne Gretzky dollar coin which was actual legal tender at the time. He was the perfect superstar; easy to hype and readily exploited. With him in their control, the NHL possessed its greatest marketing weapon in years, which is exactly why the league needed to get him out of Edmonton.

More than 20 years later, questions remain surrounding the trade. For his own part, Gretzky maintains that he had nothing to do with the trade. Despite the fact that he had just married Janet Jones, then a rising Hollywood actress just a month before, Gretzky claimed to have not wanted to leave Edmonton. Born and raised in Canada, Gretzky wanted to finish his career right where he started it. If we're to believe Gretzky's version, the Oilers ignored their star's wishes and sent him packing to sunny California.

The Edmonton Oilers' owner Peter Pocklington told a different tale. He claimed that he often received trade offers for Gretzky but always rejected them, knowing full well who Gretzky was and what he meant to the franchise. It was Pocklington's contention that Gretzky approached him with the L.A. trade offer. Assuming Gretzky's days in Edmonton were numbered due to the automatic free agency clause in every NHL player's contract (that wasn't due to kick in for four more years, when Gretzky was 31 years old), Pocklington bent to his star's wishes to ensure the team got something out of Gretzky's inevitable departure. As he told Canada's CBC television, "My first love is to the team, not Wayne Gretzky."[45] Pocklington claimed that some 20 minutes prior to the press conference announcing the deal, he pulled Gretzky aside, giving him a final opportunity to back out of it before it was too late. But Gretzky was determined to go to L.A. Rumors abounded that Pocklington was cash-strapped at the time from other bad financial decisions (in fact, he would sell the Oilers in 1998, file bankruptcy in 2008, and be arrested by the FBI for bankruptcy fraud in 2009) and needed to deal Gretzky not for the three players or three first-round draft picks that were included, but for the $15 million in cash attached to the transaction.

Both sides sound as if they were attempting a certain amount of damage control regarding the situation. Gretzky didn't want to soil his squeaky-clean reputation and be made the heavy, demanding an exit out of Canada for the bright lights of Hollywood that came attached to his new starlet wife. Pocklington couldn't afford to infuriate his fan base and admit to shipping off not just the Oilers' top player, but perhaps the greatest player the game had ever seen, for a few extra bucks. Not to the likes of the Winnipeg Jets (another Canadian team seeking Gretzky at the time), but to an American team, no less. Each camp had much riding on the deal, as the trade angered many Canadian citizens. Their national game had just lost its greatest home-grown hero. It went so far as New Democratic Party House Leader Nelson Riis attempting to force the Canadian government to step in and stop the trade.

Canada's loss was clearly the NHL's gain. It was perhaps the most significant event to occur in NHL history for 20 years. Arguably, Gretzky's trade was more important to the NHL than the 2004–2005 owners' lockout that saw the cancellation of the awarding of the Stanley Cup for the first time in over 100 years. In fact, the modern-day history of the NHL can almost be written as the pre- and post-Gretzky trade era as the deal that snatched Gretzky from his homeland and shipped him to the second biggest market in the U.S. may have been brokered in part by the league itself in an attempt to milk the Great One for all he was worth.

Some of the statements made during the announcement of Gretzky's trade to L.A. seem to bear that out. Many of the quotes are oddly reminiscent of those spoken during Michael Jordan's original retirement press conference. Gretzky wept openly during the ceremony, and between tears, managed to utter, "For the benefit of Wayne Gretzky, my new wife and our expected child in the new year, I thought it was beneficial to all involved if they let me play with the Kings."[46] Who was the "they" Gretzky spoke of? Were "they" the Oilers organization? Who, if we're to believe Pocklington, didn't want to trade away his superstar? Or was the "they" in question actually the NHL itself? The Oilers' general manager and head coach Glen Sather wept at the press conference, too, adding, "I don't want to try and philosophize on what happened. We tried to do what was good for Wayne, the Oilers and the NHL. We all would like to be proud of what we do for a living...I know we'll adjust."[47] What an odd comment. What did it matter if the deal was "good" for the NHL? No other trade in any other league is made for the good of the league, but rather for the benefit of the franchises involved. Of what, exactly, wasn't Sather "proud"? Were his tears an admission of guilt, signifying that he had little control over the trade? Was an unseen hand behind the scenes orchestrating the events of that day?

The truth of the situation was Gretzky in Edmonton did next to nothing for the NHL. Edmonton might as well have been Siberia as far as the U.S. media was concerned. Gretzky was the sort of once-in-a-lifetime talent on which the league desperately needed to capitalize. By the time of Gretzky's trade to L.A., the league knew it couldn't lose the opportunity. To have him go from Edmonton to Winnipeg or Detroit (which allegedly also made an offer for Gretzky) would not have succeeded in opening up the NHL to new fans. Even landing in New York City wouldn't have converted many new fans to the game as New England was already one of the few hockey hot spots in the U.S.

Los Angeles was different. In 1988, the NHL didn't exist south of St. Louis with the sole exception of Los Angeles. If Gretzky could succeed there, and by all practical appearances the Great One had the talent to succeed no matter where he played, the NHL could open itself up in the "Sun Belt." There were millions of potential fans residing in the southern half of the United States that up until then seemed uninterested in hockey and were largely ignored by the league.

If the league was thinking that way, then it found three willing participants to make the deal work for not just the principals involved, but for everyone in the NHL. Pocklington was reportedly in need of cash, and he got it with a quick influx of $15 million in the deal. The Oilers would win another Stanley Cup just two years after Gretzky's departure. Los Angeles Kings owner Bruce McNall, a coin dealer turned millionaire (and later, jailbird), wanted a big-name star to help bolster the team's sagging attendance. With Gretzky on the roster, McNall ushered in a highly profitable hockey renaissance in Los Angeles as ticket and jersey sales shot through the roof. The newly married Gretzky wanted to be with his bride, the city of Edmonton be damned. It also couldn't have bothered the Great One that the deal included a 10 percent share in the ownership of the Kings (and if that wasn't allowed by NHL by-laws, Gretzky was to receive a $5 million bonus as well as a percentage of the Kings' gate receipts). Plus, the L.A. star factory began to market Gretzky in much the same fashion as Michael Jordan, including creating a Saturday morning cartoon called *The Pro Stars* which featured Gretzky, Jordan, and Bo Jackson as superheroes. So despite all of the public finger-pointing and the tears shed, financially everyone made out in spades on the deal.

Gretzky's personal success aside, his time in Los Angeles did exactly what the NHL had presumably hoped for: it opened up the southern half of the United States for hockey. Not since baseball's Brooklyn Dodgers and New York Giants moved westward, to Los Angeles and San Francisco, had a league forced the relocation of its teams to open up new markets as much as the NHL. Canada saw the loss of two teams, the Winnipeg Jets and the Quebec Nordiques, which left the Great White North for greener pastures in Phoenix (in 1996) and Colorado (in 1995, never mind the doomed Colorado Rockies NHL franchise of the '70s) respectively. One would think a move in the opposite direction, such as the Atlanta Flames' relocation to Calgary in 1980, would make more sense: Go where the hockey fans are. Apparently such thoughts are foolish as America's two biggest hockey hot spots, Minnesota and New England, also saw teams abandon their hardcore fans for unusual choices. The Minnesota North Stars moved to Dallas in 1993 and the Hartford Whalers became the (Raleigh, North) Carolina Hurricanes in 1997. Absurd on the surface, these franchise moves strategically dotted the southern U.S. with hockey teams.

The NHL has done more than just relocate teams to warmer climates. The league has also expanded to welcome in new franchises, a majority of which reside south of the Mason-Dixon line. One of the first was the San Jose Sharks, the entry of which in 1991 was a direct result of Gretzky's monstrous success in Los Angeles. He had officially made NHL hockey a hot commodity in southern California and the NHL was quick to reap the rewards of a second So-Cal franchise (the memory of the ill-fated California Golden Seals long forgotten). San Jose's amazing and instantaneous popularity paved the way for yet a third NHL team in California as the Mighty Ducks of Anaheim hit the ice in 1993. Originally owned by the Disney Corporation, the Ducks (as they are now more simply known) were perhaps the first team in professional sports history to exist as part of a larger marketing ploy. Their deplorable name was the result of the success of the Walt Disney movie *The Mighty Ducks* which revolved around a pee-wee hockey team. The original film was released in 1992, a year before the NHL team first skated, but the real Mighty Ducks were used to promote the film's two sequels more than they were NHL hockey. The franchise managed to blur the line between sports, entertainment, and advertising more than most thought possible.

The NHL would continue to expand with Tampa Bay, Atlanta, Nashville, Columbus (OH), and Florida (Miami) joining the league. Later the NHL would wisely return its sport to the cities of Minnesota and Ottawa, Canada as well. All of this expansion came on the heels of Gretzky's arrival in the United States. Within 20 years the NHL went from consisting of 21 teams—seven of which (or 33 percent) called Canada home—to 30 teams, of which only six (or 20 percent) played in Canada. Meanwhile, a full third of the current NHL franchises (a total of 10)—Los

Angeles, San Jose, Anaheim, Nashville, Tampa Bay, Carolina (Raleigh), Dallas, Florida (Miami), Phoenix, and Atlanta—play in the southern half of the United States. This is a complete shift in the NHL's fan base. It's as if MLB suddenly abandoned its fans in the United States in favor of adding more Canadian teams while at the same time ignoring the recent failure of the Montreal Expos. It doesn't quite make sense.

As amazing as the NHL's sudden shift southward was, what perhaps overshadows it was the level of overnight success many of these new teams enjoyed. Success was almost immediate for three of the four relocated NHL franchises, none of which ever approached those same levels of achievement in their original cities. The same year the Nordiques became the Avalanche, instead of being a disorganized and discombobulated team, they skated right out and won the Stanley Cup, a feat they would repeat a few years later. Minnesota's long-established North Stars dropped the location from their name when they moved to Dallas, and five years later they were hoisting the Stanley Cup, thanks to Brett Hull's controversial "kicked" game-winning goal. The long-suffering Whalers moved 1,000 miles down the Eastern seaboard to find a home in North Carolina and a Stanley Cup waiting for them just nine years later. Only Phoenix, oddly enough coached and partially owned by Gretzky himself, have yet to see the level of success these other relocated franchises have enjoyed.

As for the new expansion franchises, members of their ranks have also quickly achieved the ultimate goal of winning the championship. In 2003-2004, the Tampa Bay Lightning victoriously hoisted Lord Stanley's Cup. Three years later, in 2006–2007, the Anaheim Ducks dropped their worn-out advertising "Mighty" motto and consequently won the championship for their new owners, topping fellow expansion team the Ottawa Senators for the crown. Another near-champion expansion team was the Florida Panthers who lost the Stanley Cup to the freshly relocated Colorado Avalanche in 1995–1996. Meanwhile both the San Jose Sharks and Atlanta Thrashers have won their respective divisions in the recent past. It seems that the equation for winning in the NHL is as simple as new franchise/city = success.

While all these newfangled NHL franchises have seen recent triumph, what has happened to the "Original Six"? Outside of Detroit, which has been dubbed "Hockey Town, USA", none of the stalwarts of the league have won a championship since the New York Rangers grabbed the Stanley Cup in 1993–1994 on boast of Mark Messier's famous guarantee. Boston, Chicago, and Toronto have fallen off the NHL's radar (the last Stanley Cup win for any of these franchises came in 1971–1972), yet they still have die-hard fans that show up to games regardless of their standings. Other long established teams like Philadelphia, Buffalo, and the New York Islanders also haven't seen a championship run in decades. Even the Montreal Canadiens, once considered the New York Yankees of the NHL thanks to their ability to consistently win championships, haven't seen such success since their last Stanley Cup win in 1992–1993. Success hasn't been able to land on these long-standing franchises no matter how much effort they put forth.

Could the recent success of these new southern U.S. teams be orchestrated? If the NHL set out to revamp itself through this new southern fan base, could the success of all these expansion and relocated teams just be a pure coincidence? Could the NHL have engineered such success among these new teams in an attempt to attract more fans from these southern states to bolster its profitability? The numbers are interesting. Between 1995–1996 and 2007–2008, six of the 12 Stanley Cup champions have been expansion/relocated teams. Considering the fact that the NHL is fighting for its own survival, how better to attract new fans than to introduce them to a championship team right from the start? Would a league desperate for attention consider or implement such a plan to save itself? Before one dismisses this possibility, an examination of the 2008–2009 Stanley Cup playoffs is in order.

As the 2008–2009 NHL season wound down, the league was facing a dilemma. Its TV contract with NBC was coming to an end. While the NHL would still have its partnership with the cable network Versus through 2011, NBC was the only major U.S. television network willing to work with the beleaguered league. Yet, the brief history between NBC and the NHL was already a bit peculiar. The two entities had originally hooked up after the league returned from its year-long lockout, when NBC agreed to air a limited number of NHL games. The deal struck was unlike any other between a sports league and a TV network. Instead of paying the NHL a certain amount of money up front as the other networks do with the NFL and NBA, NBC agreed to a deal in which both partners would equally split the income from the TV revenue once NBC recouped its operating costs. This meant that instead of NBC supplying a pile of money for the league to work with when each season began, the NHL had to scrape by with what earnings it could gather from NBC's sale of advertising during its games. If NBC didn't make a nickel televising the NHL's games, neither did the league.

As the 2008–2009 NHL playoffs began, the league needed solid ratings to make a profit, and to renew its unusual deal with NBC. In order to achieve that, the league would need great matchups to hype, plus excitement and drama to draw in more fans than the usual hardcore hockey-heads. Much like the NBA, the NHL had franchises that simply were not TV-worthy. No amount of self-created hype was going to make the likes of the Columbus Blue Jackets, St. Louis Blues, Carolina Hurricanes, or that season's controversy-plagued Montreal Canadiens interesting to fans.

There were bright spots among the playoff-caliber teams. The top two were clearly the Pittsburgh Penguins, led by "the next Wayne Gretzky" Sidney Crosby, and the Washington Capitals, led by another "the next Wayne Gretzky" in Alexandre Ovechkin. The league would've sold its soul to see these two go head-to-head in a battle for Lord Stanley's Cup. Unfortunately, Pittsburgh and Washington play in the same conference and could not meet up in the Stanley Cup Finals. Yet, as fate would have it, the two clubs still managed to face off earlier in the playoff schedule.

The results were more spectacular than the league could have wished. Five of the first six games were won by just one goal. Both Crosby and Ovechkin relished their moments in the spotlight as they splashed their brilliance from one end of the ice to the other. The show these two put on momentarily stole the thunder away from the NBA playoffs and the concurrent debate over whether Kobe or LeBron was the greater star. The talk now turned to who was better: Crosby or Ovechkin? Hockey was suddenly news again. Ratings both locally in Pittsburgh and Washington reached record highs while Versus also saw new viewership peaks unlike any they had previously witnessed. The back-and-forth series reached a decisive Game Seven which Pittsburgh dominated. The Penguins then trounced the Carolina Hurricanes in the Conference Finals, sweeping the series 4–0, and advancing to the Stanley Cup Finals.

From the NHL's perspective, there was only one magical ratings hope for the ensuing matchup: the Detroit Red Wings. Not only had Hockey Town's finest become the league's gold standard franchise, they featured a roster stacked top to bottom with stars that had posted the third best record in the league in 2008–2009. Perhaps more importantly, the Red Wings were the reigning Stanley Cup Champions, an honor they earned by defeating the Pittsburgh Penguins the year before. Could anyone say "rematch"? The only team standing in the Red Wings' way was the upstart Chicago Blackhawks. The Blackhawks returned from obscurity in 2008–2009 on the play of a heap of young talent, but it just wasn't their time. Detroit polished them off four games to one in the Conference Finals, and created the coveted Stanley Cup Finals rematch.

Could the NHL have asked for anything more? Out of the 64 possibilities of potential Stanley Cup Finals matchups, perhaps the one the NHL would have hand selected was about to face off. And it was a rematch, no less. Yet the coincidences didn't end there. In fact, they were just beginning.

The Red Wings won the first two games 3–1 in Detroit. Interestingly, NBC determined when both games were to be played. Due to scheduling issues, the start of the NBA Finals, and with hopes of increasing its audience, NBC forced the NHL to hold Games One and Two on successive days—Saturday and Sunday—something the NHL would not normally do. To placate its primary TV partner, the NHL kowtowed to NBC's demands. At the conclusion of Game Two, however, the NHL took an action that caused eyebrows to rise.

Down by a score of 3–1 with under a minute remaining, the Penguins Evgeni Malkin—the team's number-two star behind Sidney Crosby—started a fight with the Red Wings' Henrik Zetterberg. As a result of the shoving match, Malkin was charged with penalties for fighting and for instigating a fight, as well as a 10-minute misconduct penalty. It didn't really matter at that point; the game was all but over. However, the NHL has a standing rule regarding any player instigating a fight in the final five minutes of a game. Rule 47.22 reads: "A player who is deemed to be the instigator of an altercation in the final five minutes or at any time in overtime shall be suspended for one game, pending a review of the incident. The director of hockey operations will review every such incident and may rescind the suspension based on a number of criteria. The criteria for the review shall include, but not be limited to, the score, previous incidents, etc…." Malkin was facing a Game Three suspension.

Now Malkin was no goon to be sure, but he clearly started the fight. Despite this, NHL executive vice-president and director of hockey operations Colin Campbell quickly reviewed the incident and determined no suspension was necessary. He said, "None of the criteria in this rule applied in this situation. Suspensions are applied under this rule when a team attempts to send a message in the last five minutes by having a player instigate a fight. A suspension could also be applied when a player seeks retribution for a prior incident. Neither was the case here and therefore the one-game suspension is rescinded." How Campbell could clearly tell that Malkin was not attempting to send a message or fire up his teammates, only he can say for certain. The Penguins were on the very cusp of being down two games to none in the Stanley Cup Finals at the very moment Malkin decided to have at it with Zetterberg. Perhaps the criterion that actually guided Campbell's decision was one that is not in the rulebook but implicitly understood: Franchise stars don't get suspended during the Stanley Cup finals. To some, Campbell's snap decision looked a lot like the NBA's tendency to protect star players. Malkin was a prime attraction for the league, a rising star in his own right, and without him the competition between the two teams would have swung even more in the Red Wings' favor. Maybe the NHL didn't want to see its dream finals matchup end prematurely. Malkin did skate in Game Three in Pittsburgh, tallying three assists in the Penguins 4–2 victory. Had he not been on the ice that night, might the entire series have swung the Red Wings' way with an insurmountable 3–0 series advantage?

With Malkin spared from a one-game suspension and Game Three in their back pocket, the Penguins skated to another 4–2 victory in Game Four. It was after this game with the series tied 2–2 that the Canadian newspaper *The Globe and Mail* reported that the NHL and NBC had agreed to a two-year extension on their TV deal. Odd timing to be sure, but the deal at this juncture made sense. The Crosby-Ovechkin duel proved hockey could still make headlines, and with the way the current Stanley Cup Finals' ratings were tracking, everything was up from the year before. In fact, Game Three was the most watched telecast in Versus' history, and that was immediately eclipsed by Game Four. These ratings were a 42 percent increase the 2007–2008 Finals which featured the same two teams. Without a doubt, the Stanley Cup Finals ratings had been improving with each season since the lockout cancelled it. The numbers weren't what NBC got in partnership with the NBA, but they were promising. The NHL and NBC had great success with the Winter Classic outdoor game played for two seasons on New Year's Day, and will team up for the 2010 Winter Olympics, which will feature ice hockey stocked with NHL All-Stars as a prime attraction. Even though the NHL didn't profit greatly by keeping its unusual revenue-sharing deal with NBC, it was keeping the league in the limelight. What more could the NHL want at that point? Officially, this deal was not announced until mid-July, some six weeks later, but everything *The Globe and Mail* reported in its piece on the agreement was accurate.

If one assumes *The Globe and Mail* was correct in its piece and the NHL and NBC struck their renewal deal at that juncture, then what happened next continued the string of oddities surrounding the 2008–2009 Stanley Cup Finals. Back in Detroit, the Red Wings pounded the Penguins in Game Five, winning 5-0. Nonetheless, it was the highest-rated program on television that night, giving the NHL and NBC a clear victory as well. Game Six was back in Pittsburgh. Just the year before, it was on the Penguins' home ice in Game Six when the Red Wings beat the Penguins to hoist the Cup as champions. Despite being on the verge of winning a championship yet again in Pittsburgh, the Red Wings came out in Game Six and took just three shots in the first period. They followed that up with only nine more in the second. While the Red Wings fired 14 shots on goal in the final period, they couldn't overcome a two-goal deficit and lost 2–1. The stage was set for a Game Seven.

Could the NHL have manufactured that result? Considering everything that preceded Game Seven, it might not be as farfetched as it appeared. With NBC and the NHL splitting the television profits, a Game

Seven was in everyone's best interest. Ratings were rising with each game played, and profits were increasing. The Red Wings franchise, if convinced to drop Game Six, stood to gain as well. Game Seven would be played in Detroit, and promised more ticket, T-shirt, hot dog and beer sales across the board. Whether the Red Wings actually won on their home ice would matter little to ownership; fans weren't going to walk away from their beloved team at that point. The team was a dynasty, having won four championships in 12 years. Season ticket sales and interest in the Red Wings wouldn't drop in 2009–2010 if they failed to win the Stanley Cup. Game Seven would be profitable—very profitable—to those running the organization regardless of the ultimate outcome.

The hype for a Game Seven was enormous, the largest marketing push the NHL had attempted in some time. The Finals schedule aided in attracting viewers as Game Seven occurred on a Friday night and was not competing with NBA playoff games. Once the puck dropped, the NHL's and NBC's job was complete. They just needed to sit back and see what amount of success they would reap.

Meanwhile, one would think the Red Wings, having ripped the Penguins 5–0 the last time they faced off in Detroit and coming off a lackluster performance in Game Six, would once again come out firing considering hockey's grandest prize was on the line. They did outshoot Pittsburgh 25–18 and held the Penguins to just one shot on goal in the third period, yet the Red Wings fell 2–1. Perhaps the Penguins just played a perfect game that night. Even if that was the case, it is interesting to note that throughout the entire 2008–2009 season including the playoffs prior to that Game Seven, the Red Wings were held to less than two goals at home just twice, in a 3–1 loss to Montreal and a 2-0 shutout versus the Islanders (both games were regular season contests). The Red Wings normally scored goals in bunches in Detroit, like they had in Game Five, yet here with the Cup awaiting the victor they could only tally a single point.

While the Penguins won the Stanley Cup in a game for the ages, what happened off the ice was more impressive to the NHL and its broadcast partner NBC. Game Seven of the 2008–2009 Stanley Cup Finals was the most-watched NHL game in *36 years* (since Game Six of the 1973 Stanley

Cup Finals between the Montreal Canadiens and Chicago Blackhawks). It averaged over eight million viewers and held a 4.3 ratings share, the highest since the pre-lockout Game Seven of the Finals between New Jersey and Anaheim in 2003.

With the renewal of the TV deal with NBC, officially announced in July 2009, the NHL is seeing the beginning perhaps of its own resurgence. The 2009 Winter Classic, played between the Detroit Red Wings and Chicago Blackhawks in Wrigley Field, was the most-watched regular-season game in the NHL in 34 years. NBC Sports won an Emmy award for the Winter Classic, not for its coverage of the game, but for its promotion of it. At that point the NHL and NBC appeared more than happy with the results of their partnership. NHL commissioner Gary Bettman stated, "We're delighted with the coverage NBC has given us, and we know that NBC is happy to have us in their stable of sports properties." NBC Sports president Ken Schanzer seconded the motion, adding "We're thrilled to be able to continue our relationship with the NHL and build on the positive momentum on and off the ice. Together, we have attained viewership milestones not seen in more than three decades."

Have the happy partners achieved these heights just through hard work, strong marketing, and a renewed focus on young talent? Or, coupled with an eager broadcast partner, has the league willingly emboldened itself to manipulating games in order to garner higher ratings, more attention, and ultimately more profit? How cutthroat might a struggling league be to ensure its own success?

THE NATIONAL FOOTBALL LEAGUE

According to a 2008 Harris poll, today 30 percent of sports fans call the NFL their favorite sports league. Second closest was MLB at 15 percent. Amazingly in 1985, this same poll found the NFL's and MLB's popularity to be virtually equal with percentages of 24 percent and 23 percent respectively. In 2006, some 222 million people tuned in to an NFL game. That's nearly three out of every four people living in the U.S. Also in 2006, the NFL playoffs (not the Super Bowl, mind you) doubled the ratings of the World Series and tripled that of the NBA Finals. More women tuned in to the Super Bowl than to watch the Academy Awards. Simply put, in terms of popularity, ratings, and money, the NFL currently stands as the undisputed king of professional sports.

Perhaps what made the game such a fan favorite was the uniqueness of its schedule. Only the NFL plays one game a week, which more often than not can always be found on the same day of the week. This allows even the most casual of fan the ability to watch every game his favorite team plays without much effort or time spent away from other endeavors. The quirk of the NFL schedule that led to the league's dominance over its rivals was a double-edged sword. With each team only playing eight home games a season (or 10 if you want to include preseason games), there is no chance for any NFL team to recoup its operating costs through ticket sales alone. While even the worst of MLB teams can draw over a million fans over the course of a 162-game season, selling out all eight home games can only do so much for a NFL team's bottom line. This is why the NFL is so dependent on the revenue from its television contracts. That money literally keeps the NFL operational.

Even by the 1970s, the NFL required the money from the TV networks to pay its players competitive salaries. Without the millions and now billions of dollars the networks pay to the NFL, the league wouldn't have the caliber of athletes it possesses. It is very likely the NFL would have remained a much smaller league with a few strong teams, or at the very least, ranked behind both baseball and basketball in fan popularity because the level of competition would have suffered greatly. Athletes go where the money is. Few would be willing to put their physical well-being on the line in a violent game like football if there were no rewards. Yet, thanks to TV's participation, the NFL currently thrives unlike any other sport.

In a sense, the NFL made a deal with the devil to secure such great success. The league is now completely committed to its television partners. Its need for the networks' money forced the NFL to cater to its television audience and not the fans in the stadium seats. Ratings mean more to the league than ticket sales. Thus luring fans to their TV sets became the NFL's number one priority, and it remains so today. This shift in focus completely changed the game of football and the way the NFL operated and marketed itself.

One of the first and longest-lasting ideas the NFL implemented was parity. Originally dubbed "Pete's parity" after former NFL commissioner Pete Rozelle who christened the plan, parity is the attempt to balance every team in the league by giving struggling teams a better opportunity to improve from year to year while at the same time making it more difficult for the best teams to repeat their past success. With the creation of rules like allowing the worst teams to have the following year's top draft choices as well as the first crack at any players available on the waiver wire, tweaking the schedule based on each team's record the season before, and the addition of the salary cap, the league believed it could ensure that no team dominated its rivals for too long. The owners accepted those alterations for one specific and important reason: television.

Parity was a concerted attempt to equal every franchise only because such actions would keep more teams in the playoff hunt deeper into the season. Those changes were instituted to maximize viewer interest throughout the course of the entire 16-game season much to the joy of the networks that paid the NFL those billions of dollars. Parity gave fans hope that their team would have a shot of making the playoffs and perhaps enjoying a Super Bowl run even if that team was hovering around the .500 mark late into the season. Dennis Lewin, the NFL's senior vice president for broadcasting, said in 2002, "Clearly, parity is good. More teams, more cities, more interest later in the season. People care about the division races, and with more teams with a shot to get into playoffs, it speaks well for parity."[48]

Though on the surface the idea behind parity seems rather sound and keeps the league fair for every owner, it actually reeks of collusion. Somehow the 32 different NFL owners agreed that making everyone equally balanced was more beneficial to each individual owner than was having an open, free-market-league. In fact, the owners all voted upon the rules that now force their own hands and make parity a reality. The NFL has always engaged in revenue sharing from the highly valued TV contracts down to sharing the money earned from souvenir sales. But parity would have us believe that the NFL is some form of utopian collective where all 32 owners are working more for the collective good than they are for self-prosperity.

Maybe they are, which, if true, actually makes the league more open for the sort of tampering many believe to be occurring behind closed doors.

What the fan has to look at is does parity actually work as the league intended? On the surface, it appears as though it does. Teams often bounce from worst to first in a single season. Each division seems to undergo radical changes from year to year, but part of that has to do with the current alignment of teams. With only four teams in each division within the league, dramatic turnarounds really aren't that impressive. A difference of two wins in a season can turn a last place 7–9 team into a 9–7 divisional champion. Considering that in 2006, one in every four NFL games ended with a margin of victory that was three points or less, winning two more games could mean just scoring six more points in the course of a season. Potentially, a few extra field goals could turn a bunch of also-rans into playoff contenders, which shows how delicate it is for a team to make the playoffs in the NFL. In fact, from 2003 through 2008, 27 of the NFL's 32 teams have reached the playoffs.

Parity is supposed to mean more than just giving any team a shot at a playoff birth. Parity is meant to propel unlikely teams to championships. Again, the NFL appears to do just that. Out of the 43 Super Bowls played, 17 different franchises (out of a current total of 32 teams—that's 53 percent) have been crowned champions. Another 10 teams have played in the Super Bowl but failed to win. Only five of the NFL's 2009 teams—the Cleveland Browns, Jacksonville Jaguars, Houston Texans, Detroit Lions and New Orleans Saints—have yet to make a Super Bowl appearance (however, both Cleveland's and Houston's current franchises are less than 10 years old). When compared to Major League Baseball, a league that has nearly ripped itself apart in a prolonged fight to keep such league-sanctioned parity from being born, the NFL's record isn't all that impressive. During this same Super Bowl era, MLB has seen 19 different franchises (out of 30 teams—that's 63 percent) win the World Series while seven other teams reached that peak but failed to capture the title in the past 43 years. Only four MLB teams—the Chicago Cubs, Washington Senators, Seattle Mariners, and Texas Rangers—have yet to take the field in a World Series in that same time span.

Parity was also supposed to crush any sort of dynasty before it got a foothold within the league. Yet in this mandate, parity has completely failed. The Pittsburgh Steelers of the 1970s, the San Francisco 49ers of the 1980s, the Dallas Cowboys of the 1990s, and the New England Patriots of the 2000s have all been labeled as dynasty teams by league pundits. Other teams, such as the 1980s Oakland Raiders, the 1990s Buffalo Bills, and the 2000s Philadelphia Eagles could also be labeled as dynasty teams. Though these teams failed to win Super Bowl after Super Bowl, each had great success over a four- to six-year period of time, much like their dynasty counterparts. Parity was supposed to combat this by bolstering the cellar-dwellers into legitimate rivals. Yet during these dynasty years, teams such as the Cincinnati Bengals, New Orleans Saints, and Phoenix Cardinals consistently remained laughable as league doormats. Just as the system didn't work to suppress the dynasty teams, it failed to assist the perennial losers.

So, maybe the NFL's version of parity works, and then again, maybe it doesn't. Perhaps it doesn't really matter. In 2002, Sean McManus, the president of CBS Sports, said, "Parity is great, but close games are as important."[49] Adding to that sentiment was Ed Goren, the president of Fox Sports, who also in 2002 stated, "I appreciate parity, yet for everyone who's a fan of parity, I'm a fan of having super matchups."[50] Apparently two of the NFL's biggest partners don't care one way or the other if parity is actually successful in its goals; they simply care about the ultimate results, keeping fans interested, because that's what most affects the bottom line.

In looking at it, the NFL may share a very similar sentiment. Maybe the league doesn't care if the rules meant to create parity actually do the job. What the league may prefer is the *illusion* of parity. If you claim to have a system in place that can take a pathetic team and turn it Cinderella-like into a champion in a year's time, it gives the league the ability to do whatever it pleases at any given opportunity and simply chalk up unbelievable outcome to parity. It is a perfect cloak, allowing the NFL to wash its hands of any notion that outcomes might be predetermined. That, perhaps, is the greatest genius behind parity.

To witness parity in action, one needs look no further than the amazing success of the NFL's two expansion teams that joined the league in 1995. When the NFL decided the time was right to expand its size, there were five cities considered to be the best candidates for expansion: Charlotte, St. Louis, Baltimore, Memphis, and Jacksonville. Of course, no one seemed to remember that both St. Louis and Baltimore previously had teams that ditched those cities for greener pastures elsewhere. Apparently, with that forgotten, those two cities had what it took to host NFL franchises—an ownership group with lots of cash to spend. Although it only took a $16 million "expansion fee" for Seattle and Tampa Bay to join the league in 1976, in 1995 that fee shot up to a whopping $140 million. Why so much? According to NFL commissioner Paul Tagliabue, "The $140 million was a result of a very thorough and exhaustive analysis that looked at communities, other sports fees, and the value of NFL teams in recent years. We've worked very hard to come up with a fair price and fair terms. We think this is."[51] What Tagliabue failed to mention was that if a team tacked on to that initial $140 million the interest charged for spreading that payment over a three-year time frame (only 50 percent of the money was required up front), and added on the fact that no new team would receive a full share of the NFL's coveted TV revenues for its first three years in the league, that expansion fee climbed to $190–$200 million.

The two cities that were awarded the new franchises were Charlotte and Jacksonville (despite losing at the time, the other three cities being considered, St. Louis, Baltimore, and Memphis, all had NFL teams by 1997, because other franchises relocated). One would think that both the Carolina Panthers and Jacksonville Jaguars would face some tough times right out of the gate as new NFL teams, parity or not. Though given an initial high draft pick, the majority of both teams were really comprised of the dreck the other teams had cast off and left available in the expansion draft. Stocked with coaching staffs unfamiliar with their personnel and players not used to playing together, each team looked weak. In that initial season they were, as the Panthers posted a 7–9 record while the Jaguars went 4–12. On the other hand, both franchises did manage to break the record for most games won by an expansion team set by the Cincinnati Bengals in 1968 with three.

The following season, 1996, didn't seem to hold much promise for either team as neither was predicted by the major football pundits to be serious contenders. The magic of parity, however, seemed to be on both franchises' side. Having added a few new faces, the Panthers rode a mid-season seven-game winning streak to a remarkable 12–4 season, finishing atop the NFC West and ranking as the number two overall seed in the NFC playoffs. Their expansion counterparts, the Jaguars, managed to put together a five-game winningstreak themselves to finish the season at 9–7, good enough for the fifth seed in the AFC playoffs. Both the Panthers and Jaguars clawed their way through the playoffs, each reaching their respective conference's championship game. The Super Bowl was not in the cards for either team though, as the Panthers lost to the Green Bay Packers 30–13, and the Jaguars lost to the New England Patriots 20–6.

The miracle of parity had launched each expansion franchise to within a game of reaching every team's ultimate goal, the Super Bowl. Somehow these two teams that had existed for barely two full seasons had achieved a level of success that the previous two expansion teams, the Tampa Bay Buccaneers and Seattle Seahawks, had accomplished only once each in 20 years of playing. Even longer-established franchises like the St. Louis/Arizona Cardinals and the New Orleans Saints had never gone that deep into the playoffs, while other aged franchises like the Baltimore/Indianapolis Colts, Minnesota Vikings, New York Jets, and Philadelphia Eagles hadn't seen such playoff success in well over a decade. That success can be credited to one of two causes. Either parity created an opportunity that both the Panthers and Jaguars were able to exploit faster and with more ease than most of their older, more established rivals, or the NFL openly paved the way for both teams to succeed beyond their actual means.

Surely, the NFL didn't want to expand to add these two new franchises and then watch them fail miserably. The NFL had never completely lost a franchise since World War II, and while neither of those teams was in danger in their early existence, the NFL was undoubtedly unwilling to take any chances. Jacksonville was a small-market team (the city did not rank in the top 50 in TV markets) and perhaps the riskiest choice of the five cities the NFL was considering prior to its selection. Carolina was less of a gamble, and in fact, it was the first city chosen of the five competitors. No matter how quickly fans lined up for tickets and T-shirts, only real, on-the-field success would truly engage fans beyond the initial honeymoon period new teams often enjoy. How many fans would be willing to gut it out and root for a team lacking any sort of history that posts losing season after losing season? Yet immediate success, like reaching the conference championship game, would easily move fans to their hometown team's side of the fence for good. Having already begun payment on the $140 million entry fee, could the NFL have somehow guaranteed each team's ownership instant success as an insurance policy on their investment?

For the rest of the league, the sort of immediate and good fortune both Carolina and Jacksonville enjoyed would make expansion look nice and easy (and profitable) to any future cities/owners thinking of joining the NFL. All the NFL would have to do is point to the 1996 season and the results both the Panthers and Jaguars enjoyed to lure a fresh catch to the league. Soon afterwards, the NFL snagged two more fish with such bait, the Houston Texans and the "new" Cleveland Browns. Not surprisingly, both the Texans' and Browns' initial success resembled the mediocrity the Buccaneers and Seahawks suffered through rather than the meteoric rise both the Panthers and Jaguars enjoyed just a few seasons earlier. How long will parity take to lift these two new franchises out of the NFL's basement?

Another perennial NFL cellar-dweller, the New Orleans Saints, saw the fickle finger of parity point in its direction in 2006. Historically speaking, the Saints are one of the worst franchises in the NFL. In its 40-year history prior to 2006, it had posted a winning record against only one team, the Tampa Bay Buccaneers. The Saints managed to reach the playoffs on just six occasions and had won a grand total of two playoff games. The team had never played in a Super Bowl.

When the Gulf Coast of the United States was battered by Hurricane Katrina in 2005, the city of New Orleans was swamped. The Superdome located in downtown New Orleans was the home of the Saints, but due to the damage caused by the disaster, the stadium was unusable for the Saints 2005 season. The Saints became a team without a home, playing their home games in New York City (against the Giants), in Baton Rouge (at

LSU's Tiger Stadium), and in San Antonio (at the Alamodome). Needless to say, that sort of upheaval wrecked the spirits of the players and coaches. Consequently, the Saints posted a miserable 3–13 record. Not that the Saints were considered contenders prior to the start of the 2005 season having come off back-to-back 8–8 seasons, but no one could fault the team for the horrific season it endured.

By the end of the following season, the Saints would rebound and post a 10–6 record, coming within a game of reaching their first-ever Super Bowl appearance. How was that possible? The NFL would claim parity. The Saints had more than just parity on their side in achieving that; they had a helluva lot of help.

Let's first take a gander at the rebuilding of the Superdome itself. The hurricane did a lot of damage with the high winds ripping open sections of the roof, allowing rainwater to pour in, and mold and mildew grew unchecked. Those given refuge in the Superdome did a terrific amount of damage as well: the skyboxes were looted of all video and audio equipment, plateglass windows were shattered throughout the stadium, chemical fire extinguishers were emptied on valuables that couldn't be looted, and despite a stadium full of restrooms, areas of the Superdome (including skyboxes) were used as toilets. In fact, the amount of human waste was so overwhelming, repair personnel had to don full biochemical suits with respirators in order to clean up the filth.[52]

It cost $180–$190 million to renovate the Superdome. Who footed the bill? The state of Louisiana forked out a little over $50 million while the Federal Emergency Management Agency (FEMA) willingly spent over $100 million on the renovation. As for the NFL, who would later take all the credit for the Superdome and how it created "the rebirth of New Orleans," it paid a whopping $8 million or five percent of the total renovation costs (some reports would claim the NFL spent $20 million or 11 percent of the total costs). Of course, who reaped the immediate benefits of the restored Superdome? The Saints, not the people of New Orleans as the NFL preferred it to be touted.

With the often reviled owner of the Saints, Tom Benson, not having to worry about where his team was to play its games in 2006 (or having to fork out any cash to repair the stadium), he could focus his energies on rebuilding his team. Between the 2005 and 2006 seasons, the Saints would drop *over half* of its 2005 roster, some 34 players of its active 53-man roster, in favor of free agents and rookies. The most notable of these new additions was rookie running back, number two overall draft pick, Reggie Bush. Many football pundits felt Bush was a "once in a lifetime" player and a sure number one pick. Amazingly, the team with the number one choice, the Houston Texans, passed on Bush, who fell into the Saints' lap. The Saints other big off-season acquisition was quarterback Drew Brees. Brees was thought to be damaged goods and in need of shoulder surgery which carried the potential of ending his career. Thirty-two other players along with Bush and Brees joined first-year, first-time head coach Sean Payton and an entirely new coaching staff as members of the 2006 New Orleans Saints.

With the stadium and team rebuilt, the "new" Saints were hailed by the NFL as the saviors of the city of New Orleans regardless of the fact they had yet to play a game in New Orleans. Considering the overhauled coaching staff and roster, they weren't expected by many experts to be all that impressive. Thankfully for the Saints, the NFL, and the city of New Orleans, there was the miracle of parity.

The Saints began their 2006 season with road wins over both the Cleveland Browns and the Green Bay Packers. That was mere prelude for what was to transpire on September 25, 2006. On *Monday Night Football*, the Saints were set to play their first home game in the renovated Superdome. Somehow, the entire nation was force fed the notion that this one football game signified the rebirth of the city of New Orleans. For the NFL, the occasion gave the league the chance to pat itself on the back while trumpeting its importance to both the people of the city and the entire nation, well above and beyond its actual level of influence and contribution. To watch this love fest nationally televised on ESPN required an iron stomach. Broadcasters Mike Tirico, Joe Theismann, and Tony Kornheiser behaved as shills for both the league, perpetuating the lie that the NFL alone could revitalize the hurricane ravaged city, and for the Saints, as if a team known for having fans that wear paper bags over their heads in shame (when they decided to show up) could actually reunite a city divided by racism, wealth, and water.

The game itself played that Monday night against the Atlanta Falcons was magical to say the least. All the breaks went the Saints' way. The Falcons' first possession resulted in a blocked punt the Saints recovered for a touchdown. Later in the first quarter, a wide-open Alge Crumpler dropped a sure Falcons touchdown pass. This was quickly followed up by a short 25-yard field goal attempt by former Saints kicker Morten Anderson which, like that first punt, was also blocked. The referees got into the act as well, picking up a flag thrown for pass interference that would've extended a Falcons drive in the third quarter. By the end of the night, the Saints had held the Falcons to just 117 yards rushing just a week after that same Falcons team posted a franchise record 306 yards rushing against the Buccaneers. Falcons quarterback Michael Vick completed just 12 of 31 passes for 137 yards. A Saints team comprised primarily of non-New Orleans players and coaches who didn't suffer through the immediate aftermath of Hurricane Katrina won the game 23–3 thanks to the overwhelming emotion of the night.

Could this game have gone any other way? The telecast was marketed as the Saints' triumphant return home. Former President George Bush was on hand for the pregame coin toss. U2 and Green Day performed their newly-written song, "The Saints are Coming," prior to kickoff. Every portion of the broadcast, which included visits to the booth from famous New Orleans residents, was Saints this and Saints that. What would all this have added up to had the Saints *lost*? Luckily, a Saints victory never seemed in doubt as they took command of the game from the blocked punt onwards. As ESPN.com wrote the next day, "This one couldn't have been scripted any better for a team that spent all of last season on the road, and it couldn't have come at a better time for a city that is still struggling to overcome the devastation of Hurricane Katrina."[53] How often can someone write a comment about the NFL saying "it couldn't have been scripted any better" without thinking the outcome *was* in fact scripted? Even the losing head coach, Jim Mora of the Falcons, whose father had been the head coach of the Saints years past said, "As tough as it is to lose a game, I'd be lying if I said there isn't a little, little, little piece of me that didn't appreciate what this game meant to the city. It meant a lot."[54]

This game and subsequent victory propelled the Saints into the national media spotlight. It also helped drive them to a 10–6 record, a divisional championship, and their first playoff game since 2000. Suddenly, the Saints were, as NBC put it in a promo for a *Sunday Night Football* broadcast, "the team America is rooting for." How exactly did that come about outside of some brainwashing marketing campaign put on by the NFL? Did it help that the credit card corporation Visa used the Saints in their national advertising campaign during the 2006 NFL season (and again in 2007) while promoting their affiliation with the league? Or was that just a coincidence? Whatever it was, it seemed to be more than just bandwagon fandom at work. In a poll posted on ESPN.com on January 20, 2007, approximately 70 percent of the 360,000+ respondents said they would like to see the Saints in the Super Bowl. But the Saints still had some games to win to reach that pinnacle.

The Saints first playoff game, after a wildcard weekend bye, was conveniently a home game against the 10–6 Philadelphia Eagles. The Eagles kept the playoff game against the Saints close throughout, but ultimately lost 27–24. The game spawned some controversy. Gambling Eagles fans may have not wanted to see their team lose, but they had to be happy that their boys covered the five-and-a-half-point spread, losing by only three. Of course, that's where the controversy comes into play. Late in the fourth quarter as the Saints were marching toward another touchdown (which would've covered the spread), Reggie Bush dropped a routine pitch and watched the ball roll on the turf instead of chasing after it as several Eagles did, pouncing on the loose ball. Then Eagles head coach Andy Reid completely mismanaged the clock and the Eagles timeouts, negating any chance his team had at kicking a game-tying field goal, much less winning the game outright.

The Saints bandwagon rolled on for yet another week, marching into Chicago to face the 13–3 Bears for the NFC Championship. In the cold Chicago winter, the wheels fell completely off the Saints bandwagon one game shy of the Super Bowl. The Bears won decidedly 39–14. Perhaps the Bears, armed with a stellar defense and home field advantage, simply outplayed the Saints, or perhaps it was because the Saints finally faced a team that wasn't laying down for them. The question left lingering was if the league orchestrated the Saints season-long run, why not give them the Super Bowl as well? By this point both the Saints organization and the NFL had gotten all they could have asked for out of a miracle season. The Saints franchise was revitalized and had the bonus of a home playoff game (generating extra team revenue) tossed in as well. Maybe the league felt bumping up the Super Bowl ratings at that point was a touch more important than worrying about a bunch of "conspiracy freaks" complaining about the Super Bowl being rigged again.

When the Saints returned to the field in 2007, they were touted as true NFL contenders. Picked by many to win not just their division, but reach the Super Bowl, an interesting thing happened along the way: parity. The same bug that supposedly generated the Saints' amazing success the year before caused their utter collapse. Consisting primarily of the same roster and coaching staff as the year before, the stability that was supposed to propel the Saints to greater heights dragged the team to a dismal 7–9 record, keeping them from the playoffs. In 2008, the Saints possessed the NFL's best offense, yet they managed just one more win than they did the year before. Their 8–8 record placed them dead last in the NFC's South Division and kept them home watching the playoffs on TV. So what actually lifted the Saints to the heights they reached in 2006? Was it luck, parity, or something else?

An obvious question to ask is how could the league convince one team to lie down for another? What benefit would there be for everyone involved if one team succeeded while others purposefully failed? Since the NFL is such a revenue-sharing league, every team profits from sales and ratings increases. So, when a story like the 2006 Saints' breaks upon the national scene, every team realizes benefit from the increased ratings, merchandise sales, and overall attention that one team receives. Perhaps no better example of that can be found than the New England Patriots' 16–0 season in 2007.

Though the 2000s version of the New England Patriots rates as a NFL dynasty thanks to their three recent Super Bowl victories, no one in football saw what the team had in store for the league in 2007. The Patriots did something that had not been accomplished since the NFL began its

16-game schedule in 1978—they won every game they played. To point at the Patriots' perfect season and say something fishy may have been occurring behind the scenes seems ridiculous. Looking at the numbers and what the Patriots run did for the NFL, it is easy to see why the league and its broadcast partners may not have wanted to see that streak end. In week nine of the 2007 season, the Patriots matched up against the also undefeated Indianapolis Colts. That highly touted game resulted in not just a Patriots victory, but more importantly for the NFL, the highest rated regular season NFL game since 1987. Three weeks later, when the Patriots took on the Philadelphia Eagles on NBC's *Sunday Night Football*, the game gave NBC its highest ratings ever for a Sunday night game, beating the previous figure by over 40 percent. The following week as the Patriots' march to perfection reached the Baltimore Ravens and ESPN's *Monday Night Football*, the game resulted in the biggest audience in cable television history, drawing in some 12.5 million viewers. As CBS Sports president Sean McManus said, "The Patriots have been a great story for us. They're the driving force behind our ratings."[55]

That's just the tip of the iceberg. The Patriots bandwagon was fully operational in 2007. Merchandise sales had more than doubled from the year before which translated into profit for every team in the NFL. Since the Patriots continued to draw in viewers in record numbers, suddenly the asking prices for TV commercial spots escalated dramatically. According to an article on Bloomberg.com, CBS's asking price for a commercial during the Pats-Colts game in week nine was $700,000 for a 30-second spot. Compare that to the $400,000 per commercial asked for on TV's top-rated show, *Grey's Anatomy*, and it's easy to see how everyone involved was profiting. The NFL Network, by a supposed quirk of fate, was the beneficiary of the Patriots' last regular season game in week 17 against the New York Giants, which was hyped as the Patriots' chance as being undefeated *prior* to them actually beating the 1–14 Dolphins in week 16. For that final game on which the perfect season hung in the balance, the NFL Network more than doubled its asking price for commercial spots. The league then took everything a step further. It so wanted to use the Patriots' run at perfection to its utmost, the NFL did the unthinkable. The league broadcast the Patriots' final regular-season game on three different networks simultaneously—CBS, NBC, and its own NFL Network. This was the first time an NFL game was broadcast on more than one TV network since Super Bowl I was shown on both CBS and NBC. As NFL spokesman Brian McCarthy was quoted as saying, "There's increased interest throughout the country. The scriptwriters on strike [the Writers Guild of America was on strike at this time] couldn't have come up with a better storyline."[56] Yes, once again someone within the NFL did in fact say, we've couldn't have scripted this any better.

What's perhaps the most amazing aspect of the Patriots' undefeated season is that the four record-setting ratings games—vs. the Colts, the Eagles, the Ravens, and the Giants—all were won by the Patriots in come-from-behind fashion. In fact, the Patriots managed just a three-point win against each the Eagles, Ravens, and Giants while eking out a four-point victory against the Colts. That wouldn't seem odd except for the fact that the Patriots won their 12 other games by a grand total of 435 to 167 points. The closest of these games was a 20–10 victory over the New York Jets that was played in a combination snow- and windstorm that rocked the East Coast late in December and hindered play on the field. Two of the teams the Patriots struggled to beat, the Eagles who posted an 8–8 record and the Ravens who went 5–11 and fired their head coach, failed to make the playoffs. So were the four games made a touch more dramatic to hold the viewers' attention throughout and maybe make some of those sponsors that shelled out all that extra cash for an advertising spot a little less apprehensive?

None of those four games were without controversy, especially the Patriots' last-minute win over the Baltimore Ravens. The Ravens held a 24–20 lead as the Patriots took possession of the ball for what would be a do-or-die last drive. The Ravens defense didn't know what they would be up against in those final minutes. Some 70 yards later, and after the Patriots converted two separate fourth-down situations (one of which came on a highly questionable defensive holding penalty), Tom Brady's eight-yard touchdown pass put the Patriots in the lead for good 27–24 with just 44 seconds left in the game. Though it was the Patriots that won the game, several members of the Ravens pointed their fingers at the referees, crediting them more than anyone for the

Patriots' victory. The complaints over the officiating in the last moments of the game were so overwhelming, the NFL's senior vice president of officiating Mike Pereira had to later make a pronouncement that all of the calls made in the game were indeed correct. Correct, that is, if you were rooting for the Patriots. As for the Ravens, Baltimore cornerback Chris McAlister summed it up best when he said, "It's hard to go out there and play the Patriots and the refs at the same time. They put the crown on top of them, they want them to win. They won."[57]

As if that weren't enough, late in the 2007 season it was revealed that CBS, the network that broadcasts the AFC's games of which the Patriots are members, had made a deal with Patriots owner Bob Kraft to open up a CBS-themed restaurant in the Patriots' home, Gillette Stadium. The restaurant, named "CBS Scene," was a joint venture with the team. CBS Sports president Sean McManus said, "It's not a business we've been in before, but we thought it was a no-brainer to further associate ourselves with NFL football and the Patriots."[58] Of course, this deal begins and ends with the restaurant, right? Even though McManus also said, "It's hard to overestimate the value of NFL programming, especially when you're having the kind of season that we're having with the Patriots. That obviously translates into significant revenue."[59] It's just a coincidence that since 2005, Patriots owner Robert Kraft has been on the board of directors for the media giant Viacom, the company that up until Kraft joined was partnered with/owned CBS. So, it's safe to assume that the Kraft/Viacom/CBS connection was simply circumstantial. Right? We're supposed to believe that all this revenue generated by the Patriots and such direct deals with CBS in no way, shape, or form could influence the outcome of any game involving their money-making machine. That's where the line is drawn in these business deals, right on the sidelines. Nothing crosses over onto the field of play. It's blasphemy to even think such thoughts.

The Patriots' perfect run lasted all the way to the Super Bowl. Out of all the major sports leagues only the NFL has a single game championship to determine its ultimate winner. No other league possesses such a simple setup to culminate its season. That is why Super Bowl Sunday has turned into such an event. The day has become a new national holiday celebrated among friends and families with parties raging from coast to coast. In many circles, the activities surrounding the game—the pregame concerts, the halftime show, and the commercials—overshadow the game itself. Many who tune in to watch the game do so not caring about the outcome, unless some sort of office betting pool hangs in the balance. This has made the Super Bowl consistently one of the most-watched televised events every year. Out of the top 10 most-watched prime-time telecasts in the United States since 2000, the Super Bowl holds all 10 slots, and by a significant margin. Number 10 is Super Bowl XXXV with some 84 million viewers compared to the number 12 telecast, the final episode of *Friends*, with 52 million viewers. Number 11 is the 2007 NFC Championship Game between the Green Bay Packers and New York Giants that garnered some 54 million viewers. The Super Bowl also holds 17 of the top 30 slots as the most-watched television programs *ever aired*.

This is why most would slough off any notion that the NFL actually cares which two teams meet up in the Super Bowl. If the ratings are always through the roof, if a 30-second commercial is selling for over $2.5 million (and for Super Bowl XLII, the 58 commercial "units" for the game were 90 percent sold out by November 1st, some three months prior to kickoff), and if the day is nearly a national holiday and seen by people worldwide, does it really matter who's playing? On the surface, that would seem very true; however, two teams do ultimately have to take the field. Not only that, but one of them has to win.

If the NFL has the ability to sculpt a season in a certain team's favor thanks to the parity scheme, similar manipulations within playoff schedules leading to the Super Bowl would be possible. Late in a season, when wild-card weekend kicks off, the NFL knows well which teams and players will star in their storylines, and generate the most money. With the assistance of their contacts in Las Vegas and the gambling world, they know which teams the public favors over their opponents. All that information can be quite advantageous. If something wasn't arranged prior to the start of the season, by the time the playoffs arrive it would take just two or three properly arranged games to propel any playoff team into the Super Bowl. An unlikely underdog, a league powerhouse, whatever the league might feel is the team du jour could easily have their way paved to a championship.

If the NFL truly wants to appear magnanimous in sharing every aspect of the league among its owners, then why wouldn't it also be willing to share Super Bowl rings in a similar fashion? Does that mean it happens every year and every team is given its time in the spotlight? No, but parity enables the possibility of it. Constant upheaval wouldn't benefit the league as suspicion could be aroused if a different team won every season. Random outcomes allow teams to repeat occasionally, so accommodating dynasties is necessary for the illusion to seem real.

A brief look back at the past 14 Super Bowls might clear this idea up as it reveals some very odd occurrences that sometimes hint at, and other times reek of, league-sponsored chicanery and subterfuge.

Super Bowl XXX – Pittsburgh Steelers vs. Dallas Cowboys – January 28, 1996. Having defeated the Green Bay Packers in the NFC Championship game, the Cowboys were playing in their third Super Bowl in four years, officially making them a dynasty. The Steelers, the number-two seeded team in the AFC, were captained by quarterback Neil O'Donnell who had (still to this day) the lowest interception per pass attempt ratio of any quarterback in NFL history. On the surface, the game harkened back to both teams' 1970s glory days in which these teams twice matched up in what are remembered as two of the greatest Super Bowls ever played. Fans nationwide were hoping this game would be on par with those previous Steelers-Cowboys Super Bowls; hence the game garnered the third most viewers in American television history, averaging over 94 million people for the course of the game.

The game itself didn't disappoint, unless you were a Steelers fan and believed in the accuracy of O'Donnell. The Cowboys jumped out to a 13–0 lead, thanks in part to O'Donnell's shaky passing; he was constantly heaving passes high or behind his receivers, and a botched shotgun snap sailed over O'Donnell's head resulting in a drive-killing sack. The Steelers managed to claw their way back into the game, however, cutting the Cowboys' lead to 13–7 at halftime.

Then O'Donnell came completely apart, and that was something he could not afford to have happen. Title aside, O'Donnell was set to become a free agent at season's end, and a great performance in the Super Bowl would only up his asking price. This was not to be. The man who almost never threw interceptions gift-wrapped not one but two to the Cowboys' DB Larry Brown and added a third to Cowboys safety Brock Marion. Both of Brown's interceptions looked like he, not a Steelers receiver, was O'Donnell's intended target. It was the second interception by Brown that was the game-killer, coming with less than five minutes remaining in the fourth quarter and the Cowboys' lead cut down to 20–17. The Steelers, despite holding the NFL's all-time leading rusher Emmitt Smith to just 49 yards for the game while outgaining the Cowboys 201 yards to a mere 61 yards in the second half, couldn't overcome O'Donnell's penchant for throwing the ball directly to Brown. For his two interceptions, Brown was named the game's MVP, the first and only defensive back ever to receive the honor. As Steelers running back Eric Pegram was quoted as saying after the game, "All Brown did was stand out there. No MVP award should have been given. It's the first MVP award where the guy didn't earn the thing."[60]

In the ensuing off-season, both O'Donnell and Brown left their respective teams via free agency. Despite playing a horrific Super Bowl, O'Donnell found that the New York Jets were willing to invest $25 million for a quarterback who "choked" on the biggest stage there is in professional football. O'Donnell would play in only 21 games for the Jets over two mediocre seasons before he was sent packing to the Bengals, and a year later to the Titans. Brown would also sign a multimillion-dollar contract in the neighborhood of $12–$15 million with the Oakland Raiders right after his Super Bowl MVP performance. Brown, too, would be a major disappointment for his new team, intercepting fewer passes (one) in the three seasons he spent with the Raiders than he did in Super Bowl XXX alone. In fact, Brown would only play in 16 games in those three seasons with the Raiders. Were these two paid off via free agency for services rendered in the Super Bowl? Certainly, their high (or low) career watermarks took place in Super Bowl XXX.

Super Bowl XXXI – Green Bay Packers vs. New England Patriots – January 26, 1997. While being one of, if not the, most dominant teams in the NFL during the regular season, the Packers caught a bit of a break in the playoffs. The Packers avoided meeting their archrivals the Dallas Cowboys in the playoffs thanks to the surprising success of the expansion Carolina Panthers who eliminated the Cowboys 26–17 the week before. The Packers subsequently dismantled the Panthers in the NFC Championship game 30–13 for a Super Bowl berth. Even though fate seemed to be on the Packers' side, the team somehow earned itself a new nickname as the season wore on, courtesy of the NFL's marketing department. The Packers were inexplicably dubbed "America's Team." Which is very strange, considering that nickname had long been (and still is) attributed to the Dallas Cowboys, who were at that time the reigning NFL champions.

Meanwhile, the New England Patriots also had their paths cleared for them to play in the Super Bowl. The team tied with the Packers for the best record in the league that season, the 13–3 Denver Broncos, met their match at the hands of the expansion Jacksonville Jaguars who topped the Broncos 30–27 in the playoffs. The Jaguars' win was convenient enough for the Patriots who swept them aside 20–6 a week later in the AFC Championship game to reach Super Bowl XXXI.

While the Packers seemed destined for greatness, as time would reveal, their Super Bowl opponents were destined to unravel. The Patriots were coached by the legendary Bill Parcells, who had led the New York Giants to two previous Super Bowl victories. Parcells, however, wasn't seeing eye-to-eye with the Patriots' new owner, Robert Kraft. Their relationship was so tumultuous that Parcells was actively seeking employment with other teams, specifically the New York Jets, *during the very week leading up to the Super Bowl*. According to the book *Patriot Reign*, author William Morrow revealed that telephone records from the New Orleans Marriott where the Patriots stayed prior to the Super Bowl showed numerous calls between Parcells and the Jets organization. Clearly, Parcells wasn't focusing on the task at hand. Morrow quoted the (then) Patriots assistant coach Bill Belichick as saying, "Yeah, I'd say it was a little bit of a distraction all the way around. I can tell you first-hand, there was a lot of stuff going on prior to the game. I mean, him [Parcells] talking to other teams. He was trying to make up his mind about what he was going to do. Which, honestly, I felt [was] totally inappropriate. How many chances do you get to play for the Super Bowl? Tell them to get back to you in a couple of days. I'm not saying it was disrespectful to me, but it was in terms of the overall commitment to the team."[61]

With their head coach not paying attention to the upcoming game, was the ultimate result, a 35--21 Packers victory, really surprising? Especially when one examines how the game transpired. Parcells, highly respected and regarded for his coaching genius, repeatedly kicked the ball to Green Bay Packers return specialist Desmond Howard who had led the NFL in punt return yardage that season. Howard responded by posting a still-standing Super Bowl record of 244 total return yards, including a 99-yard kickoff return for a touchdown late in the third quarter. That TD return was both a rally and game-killer for the Patriots who could never recover from it. After the final gun sounded, Howard was named the game's MVP, the only return specialist to ever receive the award.

Once again in the succeeding off-season, much like O'Donnell and Brown, two of the biggest names in the Super Bowl signed multimillion-dollar deals with other teams. Five days after losing the Super Bowl, Parcells quit the Patriots and signed a $14 million deal with the Jets. Parcells would never reach the Super Bowl again. Howard jumped ship after the Super Bowl to sign a $6 million deal with the Oakland Raiders. Three years later, Howard would be back with the Packers for half a season, but never achieved the level of success he did playing on "America's Team" in 1996.

Perhaps the most interesting story was the one that spans both that Super Bowl and the one played the following year. Prior to the start of the Packers' 1996 season, their MVP quarterback Brett Favre publicly admitted to having an addiction to the painkiller Vicodin. Favre's father would also claim his son was battling an alcohol addiction at the time. The revelation of Favre's drinking was somewhat less shocking as Favre had shown up drunk at a few practices while a member of the Atlanta Falcons, actions that created his nickname, "Barfly." Favre's Vicodin addiction was so bad that he pressured both his girlfriend (and future wife) Deanna as well as his brother Scott into obtaining the pills for him when he ran out. Favre also admitted to taking them by the handful, getting so sick on them at some times that he'd vomit out the pills, wash them off, and then take the same pills again. Due to this addiction, Favre entered rehab. The NFL did nothing to punish him—no suspension or fine. Most likely it was because Favre did this of his own accord, but perhaps it was because the NFL wanted to keep an ace up its sleeve.

As part of his recovery, Favre was supposed to stop taking Vicodin and quit drinking alcohol. During the week leading up to the Super Bowl, however, Favre was seen drinking in and around New Orleans. The NFL willingly covered up for the two-time MVP, saying Favre was cleared to drink. Yet Favre himself revealed in his book *Favre: For the Record* that the NFL had in fact not done this (in fact, Favre reportedly didn't stop drinking until his wife issued him an ultimatum sometime in 1999). Then, just prior to Super Bowl XXXI's kickoff, Favre was reportedly seen having dry heaves. The cover story was that Favre had the flu, yet considering his tales of addiction and the fact that he was drinking in the week leading up to the game, his flu very well may have been more of a hangover or something worse. The NFL, of course, did nothing publicly to punish the star.

Super Bowl XXXII – Green Bay Packers vs. Denver Broncos – January 25, 1998. Brett Favre's punishment for his past transgressions may have been losing Super Bowl XXXII to the Broncos. If Favre wasn't sticking to his recovery plan, he was open to punishment in the NFL's substance abuse program. After that season, Favre was named MVP for an unprecedented third time, and what were the chances that the NFL would suspend such a player for that sort of failing? Instead of a public humiliation followed by more rehab, perhaps Favre was ordered to take a dive in the Super Bowl. Though his stat line in the game was an impressive 25 for 42 passing for 256 yards and three touchdowns, Favre had two costly turnovers, an interception and a fumble, that occurred on back-to-back possessions early in the game. Both turnovers led directly to Broncos scores, giving them a 17–7 lead that the Packers never overcame.

Maybe that was not just Brett Favre's fault. Head coach Mike Holmgren should take a great deal of blame as well. In fact, the Packers' former general manager Ron Wolf seems to completely blame Holmgren for the loss. He said in 2007, "Certain calls were to be made that weren't made. Mike Holmgren refused those calls. There would have been an adjustment on the blocking scheme and it would have been over."[62] "Adjustment on the blocking scheme" refers to the fact that the Packers did not make any on-the-fly changes in an attempt to stop the Broncos' constant blitzing that resulted in Favre's two turnovers. Not only did the Packers offense not make any needed adjustments, according to Packers safety LeRoy Butler, the defense didn't attempt to switch things up either. Butler said, "At halftime, we made no adjustments. We just sat there and drank Kool-Aid, and they bitched at us for a while."[63] What was perhaps even more revealing was that Holmgren later admitted that he let the other team win.

The Denver Broncos were the NFL's team of choice to hype that season, even though the defending champion Packers once again posted the best record in the NFL (tied with both the San Francisco 49ers and Kansas City Chiefs at 13-3). Denver was led by the aging quarterback John Elway, who had been elevated to legend status despite having lost three previous Super Bowls including two of the biggest blowouts ever, 42–10 to the Washington Redskins and 55–10 to the San Francisco 49ers. Gamblers had the Packers as huge favorites that day, posting an 11½ point spread in favor of Green Bay. The question on every NFL commentator's lips was, could John Elway finally win the big one? The answer to the question came from Packers head coach Mike Holmgren, who effectively said "Yes."

The game stood tied at 24–24 with about three minutes to play in the game. The Broncos had the ball on the Packers' 49-yard line, courtesy of a poor Packers punt. On first down, the Broncos ran the ball for only two yards, but a face-masking penalty conveniently moved the Broncos ahead another 15 yards to the Packers' 32-yard line. The Broncos continued to advance the ball, eventually settling down at the Packers' one-yard line with just 1:47 left in the game. That was when everything got interesting.

With the clock stopped and the ball sitting second-and-goal from the one, the Packers still had two timeouts remaining. If they could keep the Broncos out of the end zone on the next two plays and call immediate timeouts, and then should the Broncos actually convert a go-ahead field goal, the Packers would still have been able to get the ball back with time left on the clock for a final drive to attempt to tie the score or win the game outright. That would've been any coach's strategy of choice, yet as Holmgren later admitted *he didn't know what down it was*. Holmgren thought it was first down on the one—not second down—thus, the two remaining timeouts would not have been enough to stop the clock during a three-down goal-line stand. Despite Holmgren getting all the resultant blame for this, in truth, none of his assistant coaches or any members of the Packers defense out on the field apparently knew any better, otherwise someone would've pointed out the error to their head coach before it was too late. Instead, being ignorant of the true nature of the team's situation, Holmgren told his defense to *lie down and let the Broncos score*. Never mind the possibility of a fumble or a blocked kick. No, the best option for Holmgren and the Packers was to go ahead and let the Broncos take the lead with a touchdown, and hope that in the 1:45 remaining, the team could march its way to a touchdown, not to win the game, but simply re-tie the score and hope for better results in overtime. That begs the question: what play, exactly, could be called in from the sidelines to order the defense to let the other team score? And why, upon hearing such a call, did no member of the Packers defense protest or inform their coach of the error he was making? Are players really that robotic? If so, every NFL game is vulnerable to excessive coach control.

This "concession touchdown" as it's now known clearly cost the Packers the Super Bowl. As Holmgren said later in 2006, "I've never done it since, but I would do it again. The choice I had at the time was to let the clock go down and lose the game on a field goal with no time on the clock, or allow them to score and maybe we could score with more time on the clock. I looked at it and said, 'This is our best chance in my opinion.' I suppose we could have blocked the conversion or the field goal, but I just made a choice at the time. I think in the same circumstance I would do the same thing again. At that point it was all about the clock."[64] Or maybe simply knowing what down it was. How the head coach of a professional football team in the Super Bowl didn't know what down it was in the final two minutes of the game is unbelievable.

Holmgren's dementia aside, the Packers still had a shot at tying the game. With the ball on the Broncos' 31-yard line for a fourth-and-six play with 32 seconds remaining, the Packers had some time to think about the last play thanks to a pair of injuries that occurred on third down. What did Holmgren decide to call on this make-or-break play? As former Packers tight end Mark Chmura said, "The last call of the game was maybe the dumbest ever. You should have seen the look in the huddle when Two Jet Winston comes in. We had never run this play all year long. We maybe practiced it three times in training camp and this is the best you can give us? A player knows when his number is called. Two Jet Winston is no one's number called."[65] Needless to say, the play didn't succeed. The Broncos blitzed yet again, forcing Favre to lob up a pass that was knocked down by linebacker John Mobley. Game over.

As for the Broncos, their head coach was a little surprised by the Packers' actions. In referring to the concession touchdown that gave the Broncos the 31–24 victory, Broncos head coach Mike Shanahan said, "I thought it was just really good blocking by us, but then I saw the highlight and realized what really happened. There are a lot of ways to look at that situation. But I'm not one to second-guess."[66] NFL commissioner Paul Tagliabue was 100 percent behind Holmgren, saying, "I don't have any question whatsoever with what Mike Holmgren did."[67] Apparently, the NFL was rooting for the Broncos that day, too.

Super Bowl XXXIII – Denver Broncos vs. Atlanta Falcons – January 31, 1999. It does not seem as though the Falcons were the NFL's team of choice for that Super Bowl. While tied with the Broncos for the second-best record in the NFL at 14–2, the 15–1 Minnesota Vikings seemed to be the team to beat. However in the NFC Championship game, the league's leading scorer, Vikings 16-year veteran kicker Gary Anderson, who had remarkably made all 35 of his field goal attempts as well as all 59 of his extra point attempts during the regular season (the only kicker in NFL history to make 100 percent of his kicks during a season), missed a 38-yard field goal attempt late in the fourth quarter which would have sealed the game for the Vikings. Instead, the Falcons rallied and tied the game, eventually winning it in overtime on a 38-yard field goal by Morten Anderson.

One would think such an amazing turn of fortune would have made the Falcons not look such a gift horse in the mouth. That every player on the Falcons would use the opportunity to focus on winning the biggest game of their careers, and not be distracted by any outside influences. As the Super Bowl approached, however, the Falcons players could not avoid the nightlife in its host city of Miami. The night before Super Bowl XXXIII, the Falcons Pro-Bowl safety Eugene Robinson was arrested for soliciting an undercover police officer for sex. Robinson, who had joined the Falcons that season after spending the previous two as a member of the Green Bay Packers for their Super Bowl runs, had just been awarded the Bart Starr Award for "leadership in the home, on the field, and in the community" less than 24 hours prior to his arrest. Robinson was married with two children at the time. He would later return the award.

Though all attention was immediately focused on Robinson, apparently he wasn't the only Falcons player more interested in scoring with prostitutes than out on the field. Another Falcons starter was quoted in the *New York Times* saying, "Guys had been going there [a seedy section of Miami] all week. It's just that Eugene was the only one who got caught."[68] That wasn't the first, or last time, a player was caught partying too much prior to playing in a Super Bowl. Most notably was Cincinnati Bengals fullback Stanley Wilson. After missing a team meeting just prior to the Bengals facing the San Francisco 49ers in Super Bowl XXIII, Wilson was found in his hotel room suffering from the effects of a cocaine overdose. Wilson didn't play in the game, and the Bengals lost to the 49ers 20–16.

Though not publicly acknowledged prior to the Super Bowl, after they were thrashed by the Broncos 34–19 several Falcons players admitted that Robinson's arrest was a major distraction. Robinson, who maintained his innocence in the matter (though later would agree to enter a diversion program stemming from the misdemeanor charge), claimed the arrest and ensuing lack of sleep had no effect on his play in the game, despite the fact that Robinson was burned by Broncos wide receiver Rod Smith on an 80-yard touchdown pass in the second quarter. To quote Robinson after the game, "I was extremely focused on the game today. It didn't affect my play because it was pretty much therapeutic."[69]

Though no player outright fingered Robinson's arrest or any of the team's other Super Bowl week distractions for the loss, the normally sharp

Falcons played horribly. Falcons quarterback Chris Chandler threw three interceptions, kicker Morten Anderson missed a 26-yard field goal, and running back Jamal Anderson fumbled late in the fourth quarter. The Falcons were inside the Broncos 30-yard line seven times, but managed to get just two field goals and a late fourth-quarter touchdown out of such excellent opportunities throughout the game.

Meanwhile, future Hall of Fame quarterbacking legend John Elway led his Broncos to a second straight Super Bowl victory despite injuries to key players Terrell Davis and Shannon Sharpe. They easily covered the seven-and-a-half-point spread set in Las Vegas, and short of the 94-yard kickoff return for a touchdown by the Falcons' Tim Dwight, the Broncos seemed in control of the game from beginning to end. Named the Super Bowl's MVP, Elway promptly retired from the game.

Super Bowl XXXIV – St. Louis Rams vs. Tennessee Titans – January 30, 2000. While that game is remembered mainly for the Titans coming up one yard short on the last play of the game, what should not be forgotten is the path both teams took to get to that point.

The Titans' path began in a most memorable wild-card game against the Buffalo Bills. That game has been set forever in NFL lore thanks to the play now known as "The Music City Miracle." With Buffalo in the lead 16–15 after a field goal, the Titans were set to receive the ensuing kickoff with just 16 seconds left to play in the game. To say it looked bleak for the Titans is an understatement. The kickoff went to Lorenzo Neal who handed the ball off to Titans tight end Frank Wycheck. Wycheck turned and fired the ball across the field to wide receiver Kevin Dyson. The wacky play caught the Bills completely off guard and Dyson ran 75 yards untouched for the game-winning touchdown. The designed play was known within the Titans team as the "home run throwback" and worked to perfection that day, or so it seemed.

Prior to the start of that 1999 season, the NFL reinstated the instant replay rule. That allowed coaches two challenges per game on questionable calls, or as in that instance, when less than two minutes remained in the game, the officials could call for a second look at a questionable play. Little did the NFL know how much of a factor the instant replay rule would be during its first reinstated year in the playoffs.

Due to the unusual nature of the "home run throwback" play and what its result meant to the game at hand, officials felt the play had to be reviewed to ensure that Wycheck's across-the-field toss was indeed backwards and not forwards, thus legal as a lateral. Despite numerous replays and angles, it could not be determined conclusively that Wycheck's throw was a forward pass, thus the play was allowed to stand as called (which is the open flaw within the instant replay rule that the NFL is free to exploit—the definition of "conclusive" evidence within a replay). The Titans won the game 22–16 to advance deeper into the playoffs. As Titans head coach Jeff Fisher said after the game, "It wasn't really in the hands of the officials, it was in the hands of someone higher up."[70]

What many forget about in that same game were the Bills' pregame actions. Doug Flutie had been the Bills' starting quarterback for 15 of their 16 games that year, leading the Bills to a 10–5 record when he was at the helm. Yet head coach Wade Phillips unexpectedly benched Flutie against the Titans in favor of back–up quarterback Rob Johnson. Johnson had attempted all of 34 passes up to that point in the season, most which came in the Bills' season finale against the Colts. Though Johnson performed impressively as the starter in that meaningless last game of the regular season, no one expected Johnson to start over Flutie in the playoff game against the Titans. How wrong everyone was. Though Johnson led the Bills to within 16 seconds of victory against the Titans that day, Coach Phillips' decision was highly controversial. What better way is there to screw up an offense than to substitute your starting quarterback prior to the biggest game of the season? Could Phillips' decision point to an obvious attempt to give the Titans the game? Was longtime quarterback Flutie, who as a player in the Canadian Football League won numerous championships, unwilling to intentionally lose to the Titans? Was that why Johnson got the unexpected nod as the starter? And when Johnson performed over and above all expectations, was the controversial "Music City Miracle" the league's only way to give the Titans the win? As Bills linebacker Gabe Northern claimed after the game, "The whole game, they [the referees] gave them calls. I don't know, maybe I am not supposed to speak on it, but the whole game we came out and we played hard and we fought and we earned a victory. But through different ways, it was taken away from us."[71]

The Titans would forge ahead and squeeze by the Indianapolis Colts 19–16 in the divisional round of the playoffs. Of course, instant replay yet again helped the Titans in securing the win. With the Titans winning 16–9 in the fourth quarter, Colts return man Terrence Wilkins took a punt 87 yards down to the Titans' 3-yard line. However, the Titans challenged the play and it was ruled (suspiciously) that Wilkins had stepped out of bounds way back at the Colts' 34-yard line. The call completely changed the dynamics of the game coming as it did in the fourth quarter. The Titans would hold on to win the game and meet the Jacksonville Jaguars in the AFC Championship game. The Jaguars, having been the AFC's number one seed after posting a 14–2 record, demolished the Miami Dolphins the week before by the score of 62–7. Meeting in the championship game, the Jaguars turned into pussycats, losing 33–14 at home against the Titans.

For the Super Bowl, the Titans were set to face the St. Louis Rams, better known that year as "the Greatest Show on Turf" due to their high scoring offense. And though the Rams showed off that scoring power by beating the Minnesota Vikings 49–37 in the divisional playoffs, they ran into some problems against a stoic Tampa Bay Buccaneers defense in the NFC Championship game. Luckily for the Rams, instant replay was on their side as well.

With the Rams winning 11–6 with just under a minute left in the game, the Buccaneers had the ball on the Rams' 35-yard line. On second down, with 23 yards to go for a first down, Buccaneers quarterback Shaun King threw a low pass to wide receiver Bert Emanuel. Emanuel dove to catch the ball, and immediately thereafter, the Buccaneers called timeout to stop the clock with an apparent 3-and-10 situation on the Rams' 22. Yet during that timeout, the referees suddenly decided that they needed to review Emanuel's catch to make sure he caught the ball. According to the NFL's rule, if the ball touches the ground during the act of making the catch, the pass is incomplete. In watching the replay, despite Emanuel wrapping the ball up while making the catch, the referee ruled that the ball touched the ground. No catch. The reversal not only incensed the Buccaneers who were still assessed a timeout, but even the booth announcers could not believe that the referees didn't rule the pass a catch. The Buccaneers were faced with a 3-and-23 situation back on the Rams' 35-yard line, not the more convertible 3-and-10 situation from the 22. The wind sucked from their sails, Bucs could go no further. The Rams won the game 11–6 to advance to the Super Bowl against the Titans. As if it mattered to the Buccaneers, after the season ended the NFL's competition committee decided to alter the rule regarding the ball's ability to touch the ground, making what Emanuel did against the Rams officially a completed pass starting in the 2000 season (henceforth known as the "Bert Emanuel Rule").

What makes this Super Bowl odd was that both the Rams and Titans were teams that willingly moved out of their original home cities to places the NFL deemed best for expansion just a few years earlier. Owned by Georgia Fontiere, the wife of the now deceased (under suspicious circumstances) Carroll Rosenbloom (he of the $1 million bet in the 1958 championship game), the Rams moved to St. Louis from Los Angeles in 1995. As for the Titans, they left Houston to become the (Memphis) Tennessee Oilers in 1997. In 1999, the season they reached the Super Bowl, they were rechristened the Titans while the Oilers name was officially retired. Was it merely a coincidence that these two freshly relocated teams found themselves in the Super Bowl? Or were both these teams rewarded for sacrificing themselves for the betterment of the league?

Super Bowl XXXV – Baltimore Ravens vs. New York Giants – January 28, 2001. Though deemed an expansion team, the Baltimore Ravens were in fact none other than the Cleveland Browns. Having left Cleveland amidst much controversy in 1996, the Browns/Ravens, like the Rams and Titans, just so happened to leave their original city for one of the five cities the NFL had pre-christened for expansion. Longtime Browns owner Art Modell took a thrashing from the city of Cleveland and Browns fans for his decision to pull the team out of the city. The NFL, as it is always apt to do, comforted and applauded the old man for making such a sound decision. Coincidentally enough, just a year after the other two relocated teams had reached the Super Bowl, the Ravens, following an 8–8 season in 1999, turned up the heat and became the 12–4 Ravens of 2000.

While the Ravens possessed one of the most dominant defenses in NFL history which allowed just 165 total points during the regular season, their offense was miserable. Starting two different quarterbacks during the season (the amazing duo of Tony Banks and Trent Dilfer), the Ravens constantly struggled to score. At one point in 2000, the Ravens played five consecutive games without scoring a touchdown on offense. Amazingly, they won two of those games. Still, the Ravens' selling point was their dominating defense which allowed a grand total of 16 points in their three-game playoff march leading up to Super Bowl XXXV.

On the flip side of the Ravens was the New York Giants. Led by the running back combo of Tiki Barber and Ron Dayne, the Giants had also marched to an impressive 12-4 record in 2000. In the playoffs, the Giants beat the Eagles 20-10 then ran over the Vikings 41-0 in the NFC Championship game. Yet commanding the Giants offense was quarterback Kerry Collins who had his best success leading the Carolina Panthers to the NFC Championship game four years earlier. Since then, Collins had gone through a serious drinking problem which led to questions surrounding his character. That often led to conflicts with his teammates, and Collins went from the Panthers to the New Orleans Saints before landing his position leading the Giants to the Super Bowl.

Despite the Ravens record-setting defense, the Las Vegas line on the game favored the Ravens by just three points. By halftime, that didn't seem too far out of line as the Ravens led by a mere 10-0 score. Then, much like Neil O'Donnell, Kerry Collins would completely fall apart. The relentless Ravens defense would cause Collins to throw four interceptions, one of which was returned for a touchdown. Sacked four times, Collins completed just 15 of 39 passes for 112 yards. As a team, the Giants gained a total of just 152 yards for the entire game, and did not score an offensive touchdown.

Though Collins and the Giants offense may have just simply been outmatched by the Ravens' smothering defense, what can't be overlooked is Modell's longtime membership in the NFL's owner club. Having owned the Browns/Ravens since 1961, Modell was involved in the evolution of the NFL from a second-rate, 14-team league into the 32-team, TV ratings behemoth it had become. At the ripe old age of 75 when Super Bowl XXXV was played, it seemed unlikely that Modell had many more seasons in him, especially the type that could end in a championship like the 2000 season.

Having ripped his team from its beloved home for the greener pastures of Baltimore, a city that the league fully endorsed, Modell had given his league good service. Could the victory in Super Bowl XXXV been the NFL's way of giving Modell a version of a gold retirement watch, rewarding him for a long and successful career?

Super Bowl XXXVI – St. Louis Rams vs. New England Patriots – February 3, 2002. When the terrorist attacks of September 11, 2001 occurred, the NFL did something unprecedented in its 80+-year history—it postponed its games. Its week two schedule was pushed back a week in the resulting aftermath, creating a season that was in essence 18 weeks long. When the season resumed, the New England Patriots were dealt a crushing blow in their second game. Starting quarterback Drew Bledsoe, who had been with the team since his rookie year and had led them to a Super Bowl in 1996, was hit while running out of bounds in a game against the New York Jets. Bledsoe was severely injured on the play, losing some two liters of blood due to internal injuries. The Patriots suddenly found themselves without the quarterback they had just signed to a record $103 million contract.

In stepped Tom Brady, a second-year quarterback who had attempted all of three passes in the NFL at that point, but who suddenly sparked the 0–2 Patriots. By season's end, Brady—not Bledsoe, who was physically able to return after just two missed games—rallied the Patriots to victories in 11 of their last 14 contests, making the Patriots the number two seed in the AFC with an 11–5 record.

Brady's first playoff appearance was in the divisional playoff game that matched the 10–6 Oakland Raiders against the Patriots. Played in a heavy snowstorm, the severe weather conditions kept scoring to a minimum, and found the Patriots down 13–3 entering the fourth quarter. As the snow piled up on the ever-worsening field, Brady completed nine straight passes for 61 yards, and then capped the 67-yard drive by himself with a six-yard touchdown run. The score was now cut to a three-point Oakland lead. The two teams battled back and forth until, with less than two minutes remaining, the Patriots found themselves with the ball for a do-or-die final drive. With the ball on the Raiders' 48-yard line, Brady dropped back to pass, but Raiders cornerback Charles Woodson blitzed and hit Brady, forcing a fumble which the Raiders recovered. Basically, the game was over. The Raiders had won, almost. The NFL's instant replay rule once again reared its ugly head to alter an outcome.

A rule initiated in 1999 stated that when a "player is holding the ball to pass it forward, any intentional forward movement of his arm starts a forward pass, even if the player loses possession of the ball as he is attempting to tuck it back toward his body." It was known as the "Tuck Rule." The rule says nothing about a ball moving forward as the player is hit by another, as Brady was by Woodson which seemed to be the true cause of the ball's forward momentum. Spurred on by the call from the replay official seated high above the field and out of the elements, head referee Walt Coleman reviewed the play. Despite the fact that it appeared Brady fumbled the ball—in fact, it is nearly impossible not to witness the play and call it anything *but* a fumble—as it was initially ruled on the field, the play was overturned and ruled an incomplete forward pass. The Patriots kept possession of the ball, and a few plays later Adam Vinatieri kicked an impossible 45-yard field goal in the snow to tie the game with just 27 seconds remaining. In overtime, the Patriots won the coin toss, marched down the field in 15 plays, and Vinatieri struck again, kicking a 23-yard field goal to forever cement the "Tuck Rule" game in NFL history.

After the game, referee Coleman defended his overturning of the play stating, "When I got over to the replay monitor and looked it was obvious that his arm was coming forward, he was trying to tuck the ball and they just knocked it out of his hand. His hand was coming forward, which makes it an incomplete pass."[72] That minute detail didn't get past Coleman. For him, Brady's arm movement meant nothing but an intention to tuck the ball away. This ever-so-slight forward motion, only clearly visible in a slow-motion replay, was enough for Coleman to overrule the call on the field and ultimately change the course of the game. No one else, at least on the Raiders' side, saw it the same way. Raiders head coach Jon Gruden said, "I don't understand how that play is looked at, but I thought it was a fumble."[73] As for Woodson, who caused the non-fumble, he put it more bluntly adding, "I thought it was bullshit.

It never should have been overturned."[74] Regardless of varying opinions, the Patriots marched onward.

What is often forgotten is the fact that this game didn't put the Patriots in the Super Bowl. A week later, the Patriots had to square off against the number-one-ranked 13–3 Pittsburgh Steelers in Pittsburgh. With the Patriots leading 7–3 in the second quarter, Brady sprained his ankle and was knocked out for the reminder of the game. In came the forgotten $103 million man, Drew Bledsoe. Bledsoe performed well if not unremarkably for the remainder of the game, but it was the poor play of Steelers quarterback Kordell Stewart that made the difference. Stewart fumbled a snap early in the second half, and then threw two fourth-quarter interceptions that sealed the deal for the Patriots 24–17. The nondescript and often-overlooked Patriots were now Super Bowl-bound.

Their opponents were to be the unstoppable St. Louis Rams. The Rams held a 14–2 record bolstered by their number-one-ranked offense which gave them the best scoring differential in the leaue, winning by an average of 14.4 points per game. Led by MVP quarterback Kurt Warner and the NFL Offensive Player of the Year running back Marshall Faulk, the Rams tore through the Packers 45–17 in the division playoff round, then wore out the Eagles in the NFC Championship game 29–24. The Rams seemed poised to win their second Super Bowl in three years. They possessed the best passing offense in 2001 accompanied by the fifth best rushing offense. Meanwhile, though the Patriots were ranked as the sixth best defense in the NFL for points allowed, yardage-wise their rushing defense ranked 19th while their passing defense ranked a miserable 24th. Those were the weaknesses the high-powered Rams offense was poised to exploit.

The Las Vegas linesmakers made the Rams 14-point favorites over the Patriots. Considering the fact that the Rams outgained the Patriots 427–267 in total yards in the Super Bowl, it is easy to see why they were such heavy favorites. Yet three turnovers by the Rams eventually cost them the game. With the Rams leading 3-0 in the second quarter, league MVP Kurt Warner threw a pass that was intercepted by the Patriots' Ty Law who returned it for a touchdown. After a fumble that led to another Patriots touchdown, the Rams found themselves down 14–3 at halftime. Late in the third quarter and still down by that score, Rams Pro-Bowl wide receiver Torry Holt would "slip" on the Superdome AstroTurf which caused Warner's second interception of the day. That would lead to a Patriots field goal, making it a 17–3 deficit for the Rams. Then, with just under 10 minutes left in the game, the Rams seemed to get serious. Their offense began to click, and with just 1:30 left in the game, the Rams tied the score 17–17. With no time outs, the Patriots offense led by Brady would march 53 yards in nine plays to set up a game-winning field goal attempt. Vinatieri nailed the 48-yard field goal to give the Patriots their first-ever Super Bowl championship. Somehow Tom Brady would be named the game's MVP, despite a stat line that read 16 for 27 passing for 145 yards and a touchdown.

The game was perhaps the biggest upset in Super Bowl history since Joe Namath and the Jets downed the favored Baltimore Colts in Super Bowl III. Even though they coughed the ball up three times while not forcing a Patriots turnover, the Rams were not outplayed. They led in total yards, time of possession, first downs, and third down conversions. Everything seemed to point in their favor except the final score. Yet this victory launched the resultant Patriots dynasty. Suddenly, the Patriots were a classy organization, Tom Brady was a hero, and head coach Bill Belichick was a genius (even though after winning the Super Bowl his career regular season win-loss record was a below-average 52–60).

What was perhaps more bizarre was the fact that a team named the Patriots won the Super Bowl immediately after the 9/11 attacks. This little coincidence should not be ignored. Even though not 10 years have passed since that tragic day in American history, people forget the feeling and the sentiment within the nation in the days and weeks following 9/11. For the first time in a long time, the citizens of this country felt united as one, as Americans. As such, we tend to trumpet our standing by labeling ourselves as patriots and by acting patriotic. Somehow, out of the potential 31 NFL teams that would come swirling out of this renewed nationwide maelstrom of patriotism, the New England Patriots rose up to become league champions. The NFL would want us to believe that was just happenstance.

Always wanting to further embed itself within the national consciousness, the NFL could have very easily sculpted the Patriots into the team they became in 2001. The year prior to their Super Bowl run, the Patriots posted a 5–11 record. Their starting quarterback nearly died on the sidelines during the second game of the season, and the team began 0–2. Eight weeks later, the Patriots were just 5–5. Then, led by a no-name quarterback drafted the year before in the sixth round, that same team was propelled into the national spotlight that took them all the way to the Super Bowl championship. Was that simply parity at work yet again, or was the NFL, like so many other charlatans at the time, attempting to capitalize on the nation's unfettered patriotic sentiment?

Super Bowl XXXVII – Oakland Raiders vs. Tampa Bay Buccaneers – January 26, 2003. A year removed from the "Tuck Rule" game saw the reversal of fortunes for both franchises involved. The Patriots dropped to a 9–7 record which kept them out of the playoffs and unable to defend their championship status. The Oakland Raiders' high-powered offense allowed them to walk over their competition straight into the Super Bowl. They beat the New York Jets 30–10 in the divisional round, and then dropped the hammer on the Tennessee Titans in the AFC Championship game, winning 41–24.

However, Jon Gruden, who had been the Raiders' head coach in that "Tuck Rule" game, now lorded over the bench of the NFC Champions, the Tampa Bay Buccaneers. In an odd and highly publicized move, the Raiders traded their head coach to the Buccaneers during the off-season, receiving $8 million and some high draft picks in exchange for Gruden's services. Gruden consequently led the Buccaneers to a 12–4 record that season, predicated on their strong defense which held the San Francisco 49ers to just six points in a 31–6 victory in the divisional playoffs, and did likewise to the Philadelphia Eagles in the NFC Championship game, winning 27–10.

The Super Bowl then became a much-hyped matchup of Gruden's former team against his current squad. The question that dominated the media's talk surrounding the game was "Which team fared better in the Gruden trade?" Oddsmakers seemed to favor the Raiders, making them four-point favorites in what was dubbed "The Pirate Bowl." Did the oddsmakers (or anyone else) know that behind the scenes, the wheels were falling off the Raiders bandwagon?

The story that emerged chronicled the strange disappearance of the Raiders' All-Pro center Barrett Robbins. Robbins vanished from the Raiders team the Friday night before the Super Bowl. He did not return until late Saturday night, missing the team's final day of preparation for the game. Some reports, including unnamed sources on the Raiders, claimed that Robbins hopped over the border to Mexico (the Super Bowl was in San Diego that year), spent the night drinking heavily in Tijuana, and wound up with alcohol poisoning. Other reports stated that Robbins was either suffering from depression or bipolar disorder (or both), and had been off his medication for some time which led to his walking away from the team. When he did return to the team's hotel, he was reportedly incoherent and did not know where he was. Robbins would be suspended from the team, not play in the Super Bowl, and spend 30 days in a treatment facility for a mental disorder and alcohol abuse.

Robbins' disappearance was not just an emotional blow to the team; it affected the makeup of their high-powered offense. As center, Robbins was solely responsible for the line's blocking assignments, something that could have major implications in facing the Buccaneers' punishing defense. Instead of being able to rely on their All-Pro, the Raiders had to make the immediate adjustment to his backup, Adam Treu. Though thrust into the spotlight on short notice, Treu seemed to perform well in the Super Bowl, but the absence of Robbins' experience at the position was a big loss. Some would say that the Robbins episode, which was on par with Eugene Robinson's arrest the night before Super Bowl XXXIII, was enough of a distraction to seriously affect the Raiders, but there was more. Raiders linebacker Bill Romanowski wrote, "Instead of going out 45 minutes before the game, as we always did, the NFL sent us out 90 minutes in advance, because it tells you what to do on Super Bowl Sunday. But before we went out, coaches gave us explicit instructions: keep it toned down."[75] The command was meant to conserve the players' energy prior to game time, yet as Romanowski pointed out, it actually had a negative effect. "I remember standing in the tunnel, about to charge on to the field, and linebacker Eric Barton asked Coach Giemont, 'Can we get fired up now?' At that point, it was too late."[76] Romanowski was right; the Buccaneers steamrolled over the Raiders 48–21 to become world champions.

While it's easy to blame Robbins' disappearance from the team or the Raiders' low-key attitude for their defeat, truth be told, they lost because their former coach held all the cards regarding the Raiders offense. That's not understatement. When Jon Gruden was the Raiders' head coach, he had devised the Raiders' offense—the exact same offense that the Raiders attempted to use in the Super Bowl. Gruden didn't just have the Raiders playbook, he *was* their playbook. In the Bucs' practices leading up to the Super Bowl, Gruden played the role of Raiders quarterback Rich Gannon, barking out Gannon's signal-calling cadence and even throwing the ball like Gannon to prepare his team. To prep his team further, Gruden instructed his players on the audibles Gannon and the Raiders used during his time there. Supposedly Gruden didn't know it beforehand, but in fact the Raiders were still using those same audibles and would do so in the Super Bowl. As a result, the Buccaneers defense literally *knew the play the Raiders were going to run before the ball was snapped.* For some unknown reason, no one within the Raiders organization thought twice about the fact that the coach they were about to play against in the Super Bowl knew all their offensive calls. How could the Raiders coaching staff be so dumb?

Even if the Raiders coaching staff suffered from a hubris that made them feel superior to Gruden's ability, Raiders quarterback Rich Gannon should've known better. Gannon had remained in constant contact with Gruden since Gruden left the Raiders organization. In fact, the two spoke regularly, including the week leading up to the Super Bowl. Author Mike Freeman wrote, "Tampa Bay defensive players believe Gruden used the friendship to his advantage while preparing for the championship, somehow drilling inside Gannon's head, as he once did when both were with the Raiders, and picking up small, inside details about the Raiders offense, doing so without Gannon ever being aware he was being mentally pickpocketed."[77] Could Gannon, the league's MVP at the time, been that gullible, or were the pair acting in cahoots? Gannon's performance in the Super Bowl indicated that Tampa Bay knew what was coming all day long. Gannon threw a Super Bowl record five interceptions, three of which were returned for touchdowns. Gannon was sacked five times, and though the game was tied 3–3 at the end of the first quarter, the Raiders only attempted to run the ball *nine times* in the course of the entire game. The ball was constantly in Gannon's hand; only he was able to call audibles, and the Buccaneers defense knew all of them. How could the Raiders win under those circumstances?

Super Bowl XXXVIII – New England Patriots vs. Carolina Panthers – February 1, 2004 & Super Bowl XXXIX – New England Patriots vs. Philadelphia Eagles – February 6, 2005. These two Super Bowls are lumped together because when they were played, nothing appeared out of the ordinary about either game. The Patriots won both which cemented their dynasty standing. Nevertheless, there are a few oddities that need to be discussed regarding these two games.

The first, in which the Patriots beat the Carolina Panthers in a hard-fought and exciting contest 32–29, managed to cap a true Cinderella season for the Panthers. Since their exit in the NFC Championship against the Green Bay Packers in 1996, the Panthers had endured six straight losing seasons, including a horrific 1–15 year in 2001. In 2003, the Panthers put together an 11–5 season to win the NFC South. They dropped the Dallas Cowboys in the wild card round 29–10, then squeaked by the St. Louis Rams 29–23 in a double overtime thriller, and finally toppled the Philadelphia Eagles 14–3 in the NFC Championship game to reach the Super Bowl.

These "Cardiac Cats" took a while to heat up in the Super Bowl as the game was nearly 27 minutes old before the first points were scored. By the fourth quarter, both teams were on a tear combining to light up the scoreboard for 37 fourth-quarter points. It's the final three points that raises most eyebrows. As the Panthers had tied it up 29–29 with just 1:08 remaining in the game, the Patriots awaited the kickoff to start their final drive. The Panthers' 11-year veteran kicker, John Kasay, did the unthinkable; he shanked the kick, sending the ball out of bounds. That penalized the Panthers and gave the Patriots the ball on their own 40-yard line, which was tremendous field position to begin a final drive. Six plays later, Patriots quarterback Tom Brady marched his team down to the Panthers' 24-yard line. The hero from the Patriots "Tuck Rule" game as well as Super Bowl XXXVI, kicker Adam Vinatieri, kicked a 41-yard field goal with no time remaining to give the Patriots the second Super Bowl title in three years.

It would be discovered shortly after the game that several members of the Panthers (as detailed earlier in this book) were using illegally prescribed steroids in the months and weeks leading up to the game. Could the NFL have known such information prior to the game, and used it as leverage against the players to ensure the Patriots' victory?

The following season, the Philadelphia Eagles finally got their shot at Super Bowl glory. The Eagles had played the "always the bridesmaid, never the bride" role for three straight seasons, dropping the NFC Championship game to the future Super Bowl champs the Rams in '01, the future Super Bowl champs the Buccaneers in '02, and the Panthers in '03. Finally, in 2004, the Eagles had their moment by beating the Atlanta Falcons 27–10 in the NFC Championship game. Now they just had to beat the New England Patriots.

Super Bowl XXXIX was a tightly played contest, with both teams tied 14–14 heading into the fourth quarter. Once again, the end of the game was the undoing for the Patriots' Super Bowl opponents. Earlier in the game, Eagles quarterback Donovan McNabb was twice intercepted deep in Patriots territory. With the Eagles down 24–14 and having forced the Patriots to punt, the Eagles had just 5:40 left to make something happen. For some still-unexplained reason, McNabb and the Eagles appeared oblivious to the urgency of the situation. Neither McNabb nor head coach Andy Reid put the Eagles offense into a hurry-up or no-huddle mode to conserve time. Instead, McNabb methodically strolled them down the field, covering 79 yard in 13 plays to score a touchdown, but chewing up nearly four minutes of the clock. The only explanation for why came a few days later when Eagles center Hank Fraley claimed that McNabb was nearly unable to call the plays. Fraley revealed in an interview, "He [McNabb] fought to the end. He gave it his all. He could hardly call the plays. That's how exhausted he was trying to give it his all. He exhausted everything he had. He didn't get a play call in one time. He mumbled, and Freddie Mitchell yelled out the play we were trying to bring in. He was puking at the same time, trying to hold it in."[78] The Eagles regained possession of the ball on their four-yard line with just 46 seconds left to play, then McNabb's third-down pass was intercepted, and the game was over. Afterwards, McNabb didn't appear sick, and upon hearing his teammate's comments regarding his on-the-field condition, McNabb denied that it happened.

The Patriots were then officially a dynasty, having won a third Super Bowl in just four years. Their path to Super Bowl victories twice crossed the path of the Indianapolis Colts led by quarterback Peyton Manning. Manning, who had led the NFL in passing yards in 2003, and then set the NFL record for most touchdown passes in a season in 2004 with 49 TDs, couldn't seem to figure out the Patriots defense. In the matchup against the Patriots in the 2003 AFC Championship game, Manning tossed up four interceptions (three to the Patriots' Ty Law alone) despite only throwing 10 in the course of the entire season. After that 24–14 loss, several members of the Colts would openly complain about the officiating in the game, citing the numerous times the referees failed to call pass interference or defensive holding against the Patriots while covering the Colts' wide receivers. In the ensuing off-season, the NFL would make it known that the league explicitly told its referees to strictly enforce the rules henceforth (as apparently not *all* of the NFL's rules need to be enforced *all* the time). When the two teams met up again the following year in the divisional playoffs, Manning fared little better. Though the NFL's MVP Manning would only throw one interception in that snow-ridden game, the Colts, who averaged scoring nearly 35 points a game that season, could only muster 3 points in a 14–3 loss. The Patriots seemed to have all the answers when it came to facing off against one of the NFL's best quarterbacks.

Maybe, just maybe, the Patriots had been cheating. In the first week of the 2007 season, the Patriots were caught videotaping the New York Jets' coaching signals. In the ensuing maelstrom, which the Patriots and their head coach Bill Belichick claimed was a one-time, first-time offense, Belichick was fined a league-record $500,000 for a coach, the organization was fined another $250,000, and the Patriots had a first-round draft pick stripped away due to the infraction. It was a pretty stiff penalty for a first-time offense, and seemed atypical of a league that doesn't suspend its players for breaking the law or even the league's own substance abuse policy. In this case, the NFL came down swift and hard on the Patriots. Why? In the previous season, three teams—the Packers, Lions, and Bills—had all complained to the league that the Patriots were *using the video recording tactic against them*. So prior to week one of the 2007 season, the NFL sent out a league-wide memo reminding each team that video recording was strictly against league rules. Somehow coaching genius Belichick didn't get the message. Of course at season's end, despite the $500,000 fine and subsequent controversy, Belichick was named the NFL's Coach of the Year for 2007.

That was possibly just a fraction of the Patriots' cheating empire. In a *New York Times* article written in May 2008, it was reported, "Every Monday during the football season, the league says it fields complaints from and about many teams. If a persistent problem is identified, the league's eight-member competition committee suggests changes to rules. In discussions of changes since 2000, one team, the New England Patriots, has surfaced more than any other, according to a longtime NFL team executive with direct knowledge of the meetings. The committee heard accusations that the Patriots had taped opposing coaches' signals, placed microphones on defensive players to steal quarterbacks' audible signals, and manipulated clocks and coach-to-quarterback radio systems."[79] Was the NFL dealing with one of its teams, or a subsection of the CIA? If the Patriots were consistently being accused of that behavior while winning Super Bowl after Super Bowl, why didn't the league take action sooner? The answer is simple. The charges were pure poppycock; an NFL team couldn't have been cheating. In that same *New York Times* article, officials within the NFL were quoted as saying that the only time charges of this nature against the Patriots (or any other team for that matter) could be substantiated was on the sole occasion in that 2007 game against the Jets which led to the subsequent sanctions against the Patriots.

When those charges against Belichick and the Patriots became public knowledge, it caused some members of the Eagles to wonder "what if" in regards to the Super Bowl they lost to the Patriots. In recalling the game, it appeared that the Patriots had the uncanny ability to run a screen pass every time the Eagles blitzed. What a coincidence. Many Eagles would laugh off or ignore the story, but other members of that Super Bowl team weren't so quiet. Eagles cornerback Sheldon Brown said, "Do I think about it? Mmm hmmm. It's crazy. I just don't know how far back it goes. Something's not right about that."[80] He added, "It was like, 'Man, I never saw that many screens.'"[81] Eagles safety Brian Dawkins chimed in saying, "Now there's always going to be questions about the situation. Was it great adjustments at halftime or what?"[82] Recall that the Buccaneers' ability to dismantle the Raiders offense in Super Bowl XXXVII was due largely to the Bucs' foreknowledge of the Raiders' calls. Armed with similar knowledge could very well have been all the edge the Patriots needed to beat both the Panthers and Eagles (and any one else in their path) in the Super Bowl.

All of this may be why a Pennsylvania senator thrust himself into the situation. Senator Arlen Specter (perhaps best known as the mastermind behind the "magic bullet theory" in the JFK assassination) twice attempted to contact NFL commissioner Roger Goodell regarding the situation, first in November of 2007, then after not getting any response, again about a month later. Specter wanted to know if any of the information the NFL gathered in its investigation related to the Patriots' victory over the Eagles in the Super Bowl. (Specter has long been known to be an ardent Eagles fan.) Specter was serious when he was quoted as saying two days before Super Bowl XLII, "That [the NFL's destruction of the Patriots video tapes] requires an explanation. The NFL has a very preferred status in our country with their antitrust exemption. The American people are entitled to be sure about the integrity of the game. It's analogous to the CIA destruction of tapes, or any time you have records destroyed."[83] Of course, in a response to the questions Senator Specter raised, Commissioner Goodell, the Patriots, and Coach Belichick all stuck to the original story.

Perhaps the true story was never told. The New York Jets' head coach Eric Mangini, who ratted out his rival Belichick regarding the taping, used to work for Belichick and the Patriots as did a handful of the Jets' other assistant coaches who joined the Jets as part of Mangini's staff at the start of the 2007 season. Maybe that's why they were so fast to tattle on Belichick, because they knew from experience what he and the Patriots were up to. It was rumored that one of the Jets' coaches actually waved to the camera that was recording his coaching signals. As the story progressed, rumors abounded that the

Patriots had videotaped the St. Louis Rams at their final "walk-through" practice prior to Super Bowl XXXVI. The NFL begrudgingly admitted to knowing and hearing such allegations *months* prior to their public outing in 2008, but claimed there was no truth to such rumors.

Another former member of the Patriots organization, Matt Walsh, had first-hand knowledge of Belichick's methods. Walsh was a video assistant with the Patriots during part of his seven years with the team, including during the Patriots' Super Bowl victory over the Rams. Speaking to the *New York Times* and ESPN early in 2008, Walsh claimed no one from the NFL ever contacted him regarding the investigation into the Patriots. He hinted that he knew more about the situation than perhaps anyone. Walsh even indicated that he possessed pertinent evidence in the matter, yet he was bound by a non-disclosure agreement he signed with the team.

That's where things became rather interesting. Commissioner Goodell told the press that he wanted to get to the bottom of it, yet the NFL's lawyers were holding up the process. However, that wasn't the case according to Patriots owner Robert Kraft. Kraft claimed that Walsh never signed any sort of confidentiality clause with the Patriots. The whole situation seemed to be getting under Kraft's skin as he stated in early 2008, "I told you, a newspaper made a damaging allegation about the so-called Matt Walsh affair. I believe it's something that never happened. If so, why wouldn't—two months later—anything come out? But we live in a society where people can make any kind of allegation. It has to be substantiated."[84] In the end, much of what Walsh claimed was substantiated.

Eventually, Walsh took his videotapes to New York and met with Commissioner Goodell. What Belichick originally claimed to be a one-time offense turned out to be standard operating procedure for the Patriots. Belichick and his staff had been illegally videotaping their oppositions' coaching signals and using that knowledge to their advantage dating back to Belichick's start as the Patriots' head coach. Instead of owning up to that fact, Belichick went on the *CBS Evening News* (note again that the Patriots affiliated themselves with CBS) and ripped Matt Walsh's credibility. How he could get away with it when Walsh had the evidence to back up his claim goes to show you the depth of collusion extant in professional sports in this nation. Belichick's credibility didn't suffer despite being caught cheating red-handed. Belichick did admit that he "made a mistake" and was "wrong" to use those methods. Belichick's public apology and Walsh's meeting with Goodell ended the "Spygate" controversy to the NFL's satisfaction. Commissioner Goodell let Belichick and the Patriots off without adding to the original fines levied at the beginning of the 2007 season.

Most importantly to the league, the Patriots' back-to-back Super Bowl victories forever remain legitimate.

Super Bowl XL – Pittsburgh Steelers vs. Seattle Seahawks – February 5, 2006. Maybe the Steelers were supposed to be in the Super Bowl, and then again, maybe they weren't. The AFC's number six seed in the playoffs beat the Cincinnati Bengals in the Wild Card game 31–17, thanks in large part to the injury sustained by Bengals star quarterback Carson Palmer during the Bengals' opening drive of the game. In the next game, in the divisional round against the number one seed Indianapolis Colts, it didn't appear to be in the Steelers' cards to advance any further.

Though the Steelers jumped out to a dominating 21–3 lead, the Colts cut that down to 21–10 and had the ball in their possession with just over six minutes left in the game. Then, Colts quarterback Peyton Manning threw a pass that was intercepted by the Steelers' safety Troy Polamalu. The Colts challenged the interception call. The replay showed that Polamalu cleanly intercepted the pass, but the referee overturned the call, giving the ball back to the Colts. (After the game, the NFL would admit that overturning this call was incorrect.) With the gift repossession, Manning continued to lead the Colts downfield, scoring a touchdown and subsequent two-point conversion to make the score 21–18. Still, all seemed lost for the Colts as the Steelers had the ball on the Colts' two-yard line with just 1:20 left to play in the game. On first down, however, Steelers running back Jerome Bettis fumbled. The ball was picked up by Colts DB Nick Harper who appeared to be free to run the ball 98 yards in the opposite direction for a go-ahead touchdown. Steelers quarterback Ben Roethlisberger somehow made a game-saving tackle, stopping Harper on the Colts' 42-yard line. Given another chance, Manning again moved the Colts into scoring position, and with 17 seconds left, seemed poised to tie the game with a 46-yard field goal attempt. Colts kicker Mike Vanderjagt, who had a public feud going with Manning because Manning had called Vanderjagt "an idiot kicker," horribly missed the field goal attempt. Some believed that Vanderjagt's kick was so far off that he'd missed it intentionally to spite Manning who had a reputation for not being able to win the big game. Regardless of how/why the kick was missed, Vanderjagt never played for the Colts again. He would play a little over half of the following season with the Dallas Cowboys before his career came to an abrupt end.

By the time the Steelers reached the Super Bowl, they were the NFL's lead story. They became the first number six seeded team to reach the Super Bowl, and the only number six seed team to beat the number one, two, and three playoff seeds along the way. Bettis, a sure Hall of Famer who had nearly become the goat by fumbling the ball so late in the Colts game, now was seen as a conquering hero as he returned to his home city of Detroit for the Super Bowl. The Steelers head coach, 14-year veteran and longtime fan favorite Bill Cowher, seemed ready to retire but needed to win a Super Bowl to cement his legacy with the Steelers and the NFL. Cowher had been the losing coach in Super Bowl XXX, when nearly interception-free quarterback Neil O'Donnell tossed three ill-advised passes that cost the Steelers the championship. As if that weren't enough for any coach, Cowher also led the Steelers to losses in the AFC Championship game in 1997 against the Broncos, and in 2001 and again in 2004 to the Patriots. In all of those seasons, the AFC team went on to win the Super Bowl. Cowher and the Steelers were due some payback.

If one were to look strictly at the stats put up by Steelers second-year quarterback Ben Roethlisberger in Super Bowl XL, there would be little question that the Steelers lost the game. Roethlisberger was 9 for 21 passing for 123 yards along with two interceptions. His quarterback rating (if one believes in such contrived stats) was a Super Bowl record low 22.6. But the Steelers didn't need to rely solely on Roethlisberger to win the game; they had the referees' help.

Though the Seattle Seahawks didn't help themselves as their receivers dropped numerous passes, quarterback Matt Hasselbeck threw a critical interception in the fourth quarter, and head coach Mike Holmgren (once again) showed poor clock management late in the game. The Seahawks' biggest competition seemed to come from the referees who doled out seven penalties against the Seahawks for 70 yards. It wasn't just the yardage lost that killed the Seahawks; it was the situations under which the penalties occurred that proved costly. Early in the game, the Seahawks had a touchdown nullified on a ticky-tack offensive pass interference call. The Seahawks had to settle for a field goal and a 3–0 lead. Then in the fourth quarter, down just 14–10, two penalties eliminated any hope of a Seahawks victory. An 18-yard completion by Hasselbeck was erased with a phantom holding call which took the Seahawks out of a first-and-goal situation on the Steelers' one-yard line. Had that call not been made (in reviewing the instant replay, the holding penalty was impossible to see), the situation likely would have resulted in an easy touchdown, making the game 17–14 in the Seahawks' favor. Following the holding call, Hasselbeck threw an interception to Steelers DB Ike Taylor. During Taylor's interception return, Hasselbeck was flagged for an illegal block (again, replays showed no infraction), tacking 15 yards onto the end of the play. Four plays later, the Steelers scored a touchdown, making the final score 21–10.

On the day after the game, Seahawks head coach Mike Holmgren stated, "Penalties, as much as anything, were the story of the game, and that's unfortunate."[85] At a rally held for the defeated Seahawks in Seattle later that day, Holmgren added fuel to the growing fire by telling the crowd, "We knew it was going to be tough going up against the Pittsburgh Steelers. I didn't know we were going to have to play the guys in the striped shirts as well."[86] This sent the NFL into immediate damage control. In a statement, NFL spokesman Greg Aiello stated, "The game was properly officiated, including, as in most NFL games, some tight plays that produced disagreement about the calls made by the officials."[87] Another unnamed league official chimed in, adding, "I'm guessing that part of it was Mike playing to the crowd a little, giving [the fans] what they wanted to hear, but I'm not sure that's an excuse for what he said. We'll definitely look into it."[88]

The reason the NFL would "look into it" was because Holmgren very well should have been fined for his comments. There is no freedom of speech in the NFL, unless you're willing to cough up some money to pay any league-mandated fines for questioning the officiating in NFL games. Holmgren, as the former head of the league's competition committee, had to be aware of what he was saying and the potential for a financial penalty as a result, but he still felt compelled to say what he said. Was he fined, as nearly every other coach and player is for such remarks? No. Why? According to an Associated Press article posted on FOX Sports. com, "Commissioner Paul Tagliabue said Wednesday that he had a letter from his staff sitting on his desk informing Holmgren that he was being fined. But, remembering Holmgren's contributions to the league during his 14 seasons in Green Bay and Seattle—and how much Holmgren helped Tagliabue do his job—the commissioner never mailed it. 'So I adhered to a rule that I learned long ago that the first draft of a letter is better put in the trash can,' the commissioner said. 'The issue is resolved.'"[89] Was this the final payback for Holmgren's "concession touchdown" against the Broncos way back in Super Bowl XXXII? Clearly, the NFL and its commissioner let Holmgren get away with this one.

Super Bowl XLI – Chicago Bears vs. Indianapolis Colts – February 4, 2007. There is little doubt that Indianapolis Colts quarterback Peyton Manning was the NFL's prime poster boy. Manning was clean-cut, good-natured, and a damn fine quarterback. He endorsed numerous NFL-related products and was even the host for an episode of *Saturday Night Live*. What the Colts seemed to need more that year than Manning's passing ability was a defense that was able to stop the run if they planned to go anywhere in the playoffs. Their defense was ranked 23rd in points allowed, and a league worst 32nd in yardage given up against the run. In fact, the Colts' rushing defense gave up nearly 450 yards more than any other 2006 team in the NFL, with the opposition averaging 173 yards rushing per game. These stats considered, all did not bode well for the Colts in their first playoff game. The Colts had to face the NFL's number two running back, Kansas City's Larry Johnson, who had rushed for nearly 1,800 yards on the season and averaged over 110 yards a game. This seemed like more than the Colts defense could handle. That much-maligned group, however, came up huge, stuffing Johnson for just 32 yards on 13 carries. Thanks to that performance, the Colts beat the Chiefs 23–8.

The second challenge for the Colts' rushing defense came against the Baltimore Ravens and their running back Jamal Lewis who had rushed for over 1,100 yards on the season. Once again, the Colts were able to stop the run, holding Lewis to just 53 yards on the ground. Though held to just five field goals, the Colts were able to "out-defense" one of the league's best in the Ravens' defense, winning 15–8.

Then it was time for Manning to show that he was indeed capable of winning the big game. In the AFC Championship game, the Colts once again battled the New England Patriots. It looked bleak for the Colts, as the Patriots jumped out to a 21–6 halftime lead, but in the second half, Manning took over the game. In a shootout, Manning topped Brady 38–34. Having finally vanquished the Patriots in a playoff setting, Manning was heading to the Super Bowl.

In the Super Bowl, the Colts were matched up against the Chicago Bears whose rough, ready, and opportunistic defense regularly dominated their opponents. The Bears were in the midst of a dream season, reaching their first Super Bowl in over 20 years thanks to their win over media darlings the New Orleans Saints in the NFC Championship game. Though on the surface a Colts-Bears Super Bowl looked to have little nationwide interest, in fact, Super Bowl XLI wound up being the fourth most-watched televised event in American history. The NFL's hype machine was able to make the most out of the battle between the high-octane Colts offense, led by Manning, facing off against the Bears' stingy defense, led by another national media sensation, linebacker Brian Urlacher. The Bears' other national star was the surprising rookie return-man Devin Hester, who had made a name for himself by returning six kicks for touchdowns that year, including a 108-yard return of a missed field goal.

Hester would not disappoint in the Super Bowl, returning the opening kickoff 92 yards for a touchdown. Though the Bears led 14–6 at the end of the first quarter, this game belonged to Peyton Manning. By halftime, Manning guided the Colts to a 16–14 lead which the Bears never overcame. Instead of the game coming down to a battle between the Colts' offense and the Bears' defense, the actual contest relied on the matchup between the Bears' offense and the Colts' defense. The Colts' defense, which had only begun to show any signs of life in the postseason, once again stood up to their opponents' best. They held the Bears to just three points in the final three quarters and wisely kept the ball out of return-man Hester's hands at all costs. Most importantly, the Colts' defense intercepted Bears quarterback Rex Grossman twice in the fourth quarter, one of which went 56 yards for a touchdown, snuffing out all hopes of a Bears comeback. Manning, the most publicized face in the NFL, had overcome his demons and won the biggest game there is by a final score of 29–17.

Was this Super Bowl run just the Colts' ability to finally get over that perceived hump, or was it a little NFL-inspired payback for Manning's and the Colts' willingness to take a fall for both the Patriots' and Steelers' previous benefits? No one ever doubted Manning's abilities as a quarterback as he seemed to set a new personal best or NFL record with each passing season. Why couldn't Manning seem to win the big game prior to the Colts' run in 2006? Was it just bad luck? Did the Patriots, who eliminated the Colts in 2003 and 2004, simply know how to best beat him, thanks to cheating via videotape? Was Manning, as the anointed representative for anything NFL, told to lie down at certain times with the knowledge that one day he would get his reward as he did in Super Bowl XLI?

Super Bowl XLII – New England Patriots vs. New York Giants – February 3, 2008. While no one was surprised by the fact that Peyton Manning won a Super Bowl once he reached that level of play, what was truly shocking was that the following year Manning's younger brother Eli matched his older brother's accomplishment. Though a number one overall draft pick like Peyton, Eli was always looked at as the other Manning. Never one to set records or win big games, Eli was a huge question mark on the Giants' roster as the 2007 season began, and the rest of the New York Giants didn't get much credit either. Most pundits considered them mediocre at best; some called them hopeless, and having started the season 0–2, the Giants didn't appear able to change those opinions. Midway through their third game of the season, the Giants suddenly came alive, sparked by a second-half comeback win over the rival Washington Redskins 24–17. By the end of the season their record stood at 10–6, good enough for a wild-card berth as the number five seed in the NFC.

Though they won all 10 road games they played in 2007, including road victories in the playoffs against the number one seeded Dallas Cowboys and the number two seeded Green Bay Packers, their final road game in Super Bowl XLII seemed like the greatest uphill battle they would have to face. Once again, the dynasty New England Patriots marched their way to the Super Bowl, making it their fourth appearance in seven years. This time, the Patriots stepped onto the field in the grandest fashion possible, having won all 18 games they played that season. Thanks to that impressive run, the Patriots were 12-point favorites over the Giants. In the face of such overwhelming odds, Eli Manning performed the greatest Joe Namath impersonation to date, as he and the Giants upset the Patriots 17–14 to win Super Bowl XLII. Though Patriots quarterback Tom Brady didn't exactly resemble Earl Morrall in the game (Brady didn't throw a single interception), the Patriots' offense underperformed much like the Baltimore Colts did in Super Bowl III.

After all, this was a Patriots offense known for stomping their opponents. Posting an average margin of victory of 19.7 points while setting a NFL record for points scored in a season with 589, the Patriots' offense was virtually unstoppable all year long. Tom Brady set the single-season touchdown record for a quarterback by lofting 50 TD passes in 2007. His primary target for those touchdowns was Randy Moss, who also set a single-season TD record for wide receivers by hauling in 23 TD receptions. Brady and Moss set those records primarily because the Patriots never let up on their opponents. Even when leading big late in the fourth quarter of games, Belichick would keep his starting offense on the field and run up the score, often going for it on fourth down when a field goal could have easily been attempted. Even though they scored 38 points against this same Giants defense in the final game of the regular season, the Patriots could only muster up 14 points in the Super Bowl, the lowest total they posted in any game all season. Can that all be credited to the swarming Giants defense, or were they patsies, like their Super Bowl III Colts brethren, lying down?

The Patriots' offense on display in the Super Bowl looked nothing like the team seen during the regular season. Their strong offensive line could not contain the four-man front of the Giants. Running the ball seemed fruitless as the Patriots gained only 45 yards on the ground. The Patriots were primarily a passing team all season long, so losing this portion of their game shouldn't have affected them, yet Tom Brady was ineffective. Oftentimes rushed and hit as he released the ball, Brady was inaccurate all game long. Though he completed 60 percent of his passes (going 29 for 48), it was actually subpar to his regular season average of 70 percent. He was sacked five times and fumbled away the ball with under two minutes remaining in the second quarter in Giants territory.

It wasn't just Brady that was questionable that day. The offensive play calling was very conservative compared to what they'd done all season long. The Patriots did not appear to be going for the throat at any point. Adjustments were not made to slow down the Giants' rush. Head coach Belichick made a questionable decision by not attempting a 48-yard field goal midway through the third quarter with the score just 7–3 in their favor, but rather chose to go for it on 4th-and-13. The resultant play had Brady launch a 31-yard bomb into the end zone, but his pass was thrown well out of bounds. The only other time the Patriots would choose not to punt on fourth down came in the final 10 seconds of the game when losing 17–14.

The Giants' upset of the mighty Patriots was the NFL's story of the year. Nothing sells like an underdog's victory. The Patriots engineered a big upset themselves just a few years prior when they beat the "Greatest Show on Turf" Rams. The Jets had perhaps the greatest upset of all time, when they toppled the juggernaut Colts in Super Bowl III. The Patriots' run at perfection made the 2007 NFL season a ratings sensation. Super Bowl XLII was the highest-rated Super Bowl of all time, becoming the second most-watched television program in U.S. history averaging some 97.5 million viewers during its broadcast. It was said that over 148 million people watched at least a portion of the game, meaning approximately half of the population of the U.S. tuned in at one point or another. As the game grew closer and closer to its dramatic end, the ratings rose along with the on-the-field tension, gaining a maximum of 105 million viewers in the final 30 minutes of the broadcast.

For all the Patriots did for the league in 2007, why did they have to lose Super Bowl XLII? The underdog/upset story aside, the Patriots organization had some heat applied to it in the two weeks leading up to the Super Bowl.

Though it seemed as though the NFL had managed to wash away all "Spygate" residue, somehow the story returned. The NFL and commissioner Roger Goodell had dodged many questions regarding that wound all season, yet when Senator Arlen Specter and former Patriots video assistant Matt Walsh picked at the scab in the media prior to the game, the Patriots suddenly were reinfected. Looking beat before they stepped on the field for the opening kickoff, the Patriots' perfect season died with just 35 seconds left in the game. The controversy surrounding "Spygate" shouldn't have factored into the game at all, and while no one on the Patriots cited it as a cause for their loss, it seemed odd that this issue reared its ugly head at such an inopportune time for both the Patriots and the NFL—unless the NFL wanted it to.

The NFL is nothing if not controlling, especially when it comes to the media. It squashed the TV show *Playmakers* because of its negative portrayal of football players; it clamped down on churches (of all places) that attempted to show games on TV screens bigger than 55 inches, and it even managed to control the usage of the name "Super Bowl" in unlicensed promotions. Commissioner Pete Rozelle realized early on that public relations was the key to marketing the NFL, and the league has never hesitated to use the media to its best advantage. So why did this story that was originally nothing more than a week-one nuisance become a lead story the week of the Super Bowl? Perhaps it was all part of the smoke and mirrors show the NFL runs with startling regularity. A distraction purposefully created to take some of the heat off the players in a game they were meant to lose. If the Patriots had won, would the question have been, "Well, were they cheating or not?" By losing the story could fade from fans' memories. While Commissioner Goodell claimed to have "good reason" to destroy the evidence in the "Spygate" case against the Patriots while "reserving the right to revisit" the situation should some new information come to light, what should be questioned more was how the Patriots seemed to get such preferred status within the NFL in the first place.

It all rests on the shoulders of Patriots owner Robert Kraft. Since buying the Patriots in 1994, Kraft had muscled his way into becoming the most influential owner in the NFL. He was the chairman of the NFL's financial committee, and sat on the league's audit, investment, broadcasting, business ventures, and expansion committees, as well as the special committee on league economics, and the Los Angeles Stadium working group. What's more, Kraft was very involved in securing the NFL's prized contracts with the major television networks which gives the NFL the bulk of its money every season. Kraft also brokered a deal in 2001 with his friend Paul Fireman valued at some $250 million for Fireman's company Reebok to provide uniforms for every team in the NFL for the next 10 years. Kraft was also instrumental in bringing the Texans to Houston as an expansion team, basically telling Texans owner Bob McNair that his investment in the NFL wouldn't just give him the team, but would guarantee Houston the rights to the Super Bowl in 2004. Kraft was correct in making that promise. As fate would have it, Kraft's Patriots won that same Super Bowl played in Houston.

Does such standing within the league mean Kraft's team gets some preferential treatment? It's known that Kraft, thanks to his role on the league's finance committee, authorized a league program that allowed teams in the NFL's six largest media markets $150 million each in low-interest loans to build new stadiums (every other team was allowed up to $100 million). Unsurprisingly, Kraft's own Patriots were one of those six elite teams to which the $150 million was available. He immediately seized the opportunity for the loan, and then leveraged another $70 million out of Massachusetts' infrastructure (under the threat of moving the team to Connecticut where he already had a deal in place, but later rebuked) to build his Patriots a $325 million stadium to which he already owned the valuable parking lots. From that loan came the Patriots' dynasty.

In 1998, the New England Patriots were valued at $252 million by *Forbes* magazine. Ten years later, the same source claims the Patriots are worth $1.2 billion. Meanwhile, Kraft's work for the NFL reaches around the world. Kraft met and gave Russian president Vladimir Putin one of his Super Bowl rings (or Putin simply took it in a misunderstanding, depending on which version of the story is read). He took the Vince Lombardi trophy from the Patriots' third Super Bowl victory with him to Israel for a meeting with Prime Minister Ariel Sharon. It was there in Israel where Kraft has spent some $500,000 to dedicate the Kraft Family Stadium—the only stadium in Israel dedicated to American football.

Kraft also helped build what's known as "American Football in Israel," a flag football league with some 900 active players.

All of this stems from a man who hasn't been an owner in the league for more than 15 years. Was the Patriots' success just a coincidence and a prime example of parity at work? Was Kraft simply a great owner, who realized from the start what it takes to run a successful NFL franchise and create a winning formula? Was he just lucky to fall into players in the draft like Tom Brady or pick up forgotten veterans like Corey Dillon, Junior Seau, and Randy Moss while casting off such stars as Ty Law and Lawyer Milloy at the right times? Did Kraft's hard work behind the scenes within the NFL earn his team its on-the-field success? The more Kraft immersed himself within the ranks of other NFL owners, the more the Patriots succeeded as a team. That cannot be questioned. What can be is how such success was possible.

Super Bowl XLIII – Pittsburgh Steelers vs. Arizona Cardinals – February 1, 2009 With less than four days before the kickoff of Super Bowl XLIII, in an ESPN.com poll in which the question asked was "Which team will win Super Bowl XLIII?" and over 370,000 votes had been cast, the results had the Arizona Cardinals leading the Pittsburgh Steelers by a count of 51 percent to 49 percent. On the morning of the Super Bowl, the website VegasInsider.com, which tracks the betting tendencies at most of the major Las Vegas casinos and internet sports books, reported that 88 percent of the people betting the "money line" on the game (that is, picking a winner without using the point spread) were putting their money down on the Cardinals to win.

How could that be? How could rational and knowledgeable people believe that the Arizona Cardinals stood a chance of winning that game, especially if they stopped to consider the relevant statistics?

The Steelers posted a 12–4 record, had the number one defense in the NFL, and scored 124 more points than they had allowed. As for the Cardinals, they won their division with a paltry 9–7 record with a scoring differential of just one point. The only reason the Cardinals even made the post-season was due to the ineptitude of their division rivals. The other three teams vying for NFC West title posted a combined record of 13–35.

The Cardinals were 6–2 at home, 3–5 on the road, and 7–5 within the NFC conference, yet six of those seven wins came against their division rivals, making them just 1–5 against the rest of the NFC. Even so, it wasn't until week 13 that the Cardinals actually clinched a playoff berth. In the last six weeks of the regular season, they won just two games, not coincidentally against divisional rivals St. Louis and Seattle. The other four games in which they played at the season's end—three against teams that also made the playoffs, the New York Giants, Eagles and Vikings, and one team that very well could have been in the playoffs, the Patriots—the Cardinals lost by a combined score of 167–70.

Defense was not the Cardinals' strong suit. They ranked 16th in the NFL in rushing yards allowed, and were only +9 in turnovers. Yet much like the Colts' defense in their march to Super Bowl XLI, the Cardinals' defense appeared to play inspired football. In the first round of the playoffs the Cardinals matched up against the Atlanta Falcons, led by rookie quarterback Matt Ryan and the NFL's second best rushing attack which averaged nearly 153 yards a game. In that wild-card matchup, the Cardinals' defense forced Ryan to turn the ball over three times (2 INTs, 1 fumble) and held the Falcons' leading running back Michael Turner to just 42 rushing yards. Even so, the Cardinals squeaked out a 30–24 win.

In round two of the playoffs, the Cardinals traveled to face the Carolina Panthers. While quarterbacked by Jake Delhomme, who just a few years back led this team to Super Bowl XXXVIIII, the Panthers' main offensive weapon was the running back tandem of DeAngelo Williams and Jonathan Stewart. The pair combined for over 2,300 rushing yards, making the Panthers the NFL's third best rushing attack. Despite the Panthers jumping out to a quick 7–0 lead, the Cardinals ultimately crushed the Panthers 33–13. How? Williams and Stewart were held to a combined 75-yard rushing on 15 attempts. Why so few rushing attempts? The answer is simple—Jake Delhomme's sudden ineptitude. Delhomme fumbled once and threw five interceptions in just 34 passing attempts. During the regular season in which he attempted 414 passes, Delhomme was intercepted just 12 times.

From there, the Cardinals playing in the Super Bowl was rather a given. They were suddenly deemed a team of destiny. Against the Eagles in the NFC Championship game, the Cardinals were outgained 454–369 yards. Yet they won 32–25 thanks to yet another three turnovers, two by quarterback Donovan McNabb. That made for 12 turnovers in three playoff games that went in the Cardinals' favor.

There was nothing strange going on in the NFL. Games were not fixed. Teams were not rewarded. Never mind that the Cardinals, one of the league's oldest franchises—in fact, one of the few founding franchises still playing in the NFL—had not won a championship in 61 years (which is the second longest drought currently in sports behind the Chicago Cubs). The last time they won, 1947, they were the Chicago Cardinals and played in Comiskey Park. The team had not played for a championship since 1948.

The Bidwill family purchased the team in 1933 and still owns the franchise today. Bill Bidwill, the Cardinals' current owner and son of Charles Bidwill, Sr. who purchased the team in the '30s for $50,000, was 77 years old, which made him the oldest active owner in the NFL. As a franchise, the Cardinals were ranked as the 25th overall most valuable team in the NFL at the start of the 2008 season, one spot below the winless Detroit Lions.

The main reason the Cardinals were not last on that *Forbes* list was because they helped con the state of Arizona into building them (and Arizona University) a new $450 million domed stadium which opened in 2006. The vote on funding the stadium passed with just 51.89 percent of the vote—a mere 33,000-vote victory. Upon agreeing to build the new stadium, the NFL rewarded the city of Phoenix Super Bowl XLII, which was played there in 2008. Remarkably, the team that called that new stadium home was now playing in the Super Bowl themselves. An unlikely coincidence, considering the Cardinals had only reached the playoffs on four occasions since the NFL's merger with the AFL, the last time coming in 1998.

The team that by all accounts was favored won the Super Bowl, despite the numbers posted on the ESPN poll, and all those who dropped millions on the money line. The Pittsburgh Steelers won 27–23, scoring the winning touchdown with just 35 seconds left to play. Of course, as seems to be recent tradition, the game did not go without controversy. Never mind the disparity in penalties (of the 18 called—the most in Super Bowl history—11 went against the Cardinals), or the oddity of those calls which included a rarely called "running into the holder" penalty, and a highly questionable "roughing the passer" call, both of which were blown against the Cardinals. There was even a questionable non-call made. After he caught the go-ahead (and ultimately game-winning) touchdown pass, Santonio Holmes should have been penalized 15 yards for using the football as a prop during his end-zone celebration. That was exactly the sort of behavior the NFL had made a point to crack down on during the regular season. Yet no flag was thrown because, according to the NFL, the referees on the field were too busy setting up for the point after attempt, and none of the seven officials on the field saw it. That penalty would have given the Cardinals a much better field position to start their final drive of the game. That, however, didn't happen. Long after the Super Bowl had ended and the Steelers were crowned champions, Holmes was issued a $10,000 fine for his on-the-field antics.

Even with these oddities, the strangest officiating move came with just five seconds left in the game. While poor officiating seemed to have become an NFL standard, the fact that Kurt Warner's final play fumble was not reviewed to determine whether it was truly a fumble or simply an incomplete forward pass (much like Tom Brady and the "Tuck Rule" game) will leave this Super Bowl with an eternal "what if?" ending. The NFL claimed, well after the game ended, that officials did take a look at the play, but didn't bother to follow their usual protocol to let fans know the play was either under review or actually reviewed. That bizarre action even caught NBC broadcaster Al Michaels by surprise as he assumed the play would be reviewed as well. It never was, at least officially. Maybe that's what the NFL wants—controversy to keep fans talking about the game and the play long after the fact. Whether it points to something under the table occurring within the league is inconsequential to the powers that be. It's the ratings, which as usual placed that Super Bowl in television's all-time top 10, that really matter.

Taken individually, all of the results of these past few Super Bowl games may amount to nothing sinister. Neil O'Donnell may have just played the worst game of his life that fateful day. Eugene Robinson may have just had weakness of the libido the night before the Super Bowl. The Oakland Raiders may have simply forgotten that Jon Gruden created their offense during his time as their head coach. The 18–0 Patriots may have simply run out of gas by the time they reached the Super Bowl. All of that is possible. Yet when taken as a whole, coincidence fails to account for the fact that the outcomes all of these games seemed to go the NFL's way. Too many times it appears that the NFL's best storylines become part of its crown jewel, the Super Bowl. While it's true that nearly every game can be hyped in one way or another, what kind of magic does the NFL possess to make its Super Bowl the most-watched TV event every year? How did the NFL take such a hold of the public's consciousness in just a matter of 40 years? How does the NFL manage to have 17 of its games (all Super Bowls) rank in the top 30 highest-rated TV programs of all time? How can it possess all 10 of the top 10 positions for most-watched TV programs since 2000? Is the game of football really that popular, or is the NFL so well leveraged it can craft itself, its teams, and its storylines to do as it wishes? Has its focus on all things television- and media-related paid off by turning what was once a secondary sport into a show business powerhouse capable of tinkering with play on the field to the extent it can ensure the ball always bounces the league's, the TV networks', and the sponsors' way?

Something, at some point in time, should have occurred that derailed the runaway freight train that is the NFL's success. Criminals in the NFL, drugs in the NFL, gambling in the NFL, manipulation in the NFL, and yet even with all those negatives swirling around the league for the past *50 years*, the NFL's ratings have continually risen and its profits constantly grown.

How is that possible?

CONCLUSION

NOW IS A GOOD TIME TO REMIND YOU THAT EVERYTHING you read in this book is true. Results have not been fabricated nor have statistics been manufactured. Every case regarding athletes committing crimes, using drugs, or gambling is as true as research would reveal. It is not my fault that investigations into these wrongdoings have not disclosed the true depth of what's occurring off the field and behind the scenes. The lenient punishments doled out by the leagues as a result of "athlete indiscretions" are not my doing. Nor do I sign athletes and coaches to multimillion-dollar contracts. I did not create the system that allows every professional sporting league to make a majority of its profit, literally billions of dollars, from television revenues. I wasn't in the executive boardrooms when marketing schemes were designed to maximize storylines and sell athletes as heroes to a gullible public. Every fan out there watching is culpable for allowing that to occur.

It is interesting to note that though the television networks fund professional sports this does not give them ownership of the games they pay to broadcast. The leagues maintain those rights. A person cannot rebroadcast or retransmit a game of baseball without "the express written consent of Major League Baseball" rather than FOX or ESPN. Prior to the start of every NFL game is the statement, "The following is a presentation of the National Football League." A similar message concludes each game. If this is true, then what exactly are fans watching?

Many athletes, coaches, and others associated with professional sports will freely admit sports are entertainment. Unlike any other form of entertainment, however, fans expect each game will follow a certain set of established rules. The funny part is that there is no guarantee that those rules will be followed. Where is it written that a game's officials have to be fair or unbiased? Nothing on your ticket states a game has to be played a specific way. There is no law against cheating. As was pointed out during the trial of the 1919 White Sox, players are not even paid to win. They are paid simply to play, to entertain the gathered crowd by displaying their athletic skills and nothing more. The results, the fact that one team wins and another loses, ultimately does not matter. Another game will be played tomorrow, next week, or next year. The cycle begun decades ago will perpetuate as long as fans watch.

That is what the leagues need more than anything: for people to watch. Is it so much of a stretch to believe games have been fixed to coax fans into stadium seats and mesmerized to TV screens for exactly that purpose? What is there to prevent it? There is no federal law in place to protect the public from this type of fraud. Professional sports are simply assumed to be on the level. When it is well established that the leagues control everything before, after, and surrounding their sport, why is it so wrong to think that what they are truly selling—the games—remain untouched? After all, as Joe Namath learned, it's just show business. ★

WORKS CITED
CHAPTER 1 US AND THEM

FANS

1. Daniel Wann, "The Causes and Consequences of Sport Team Identification," *Handbook of Sports & Media*, ed. Arthur A. Raney and Jennings Bryant (Mahwah, NJ: Lawrence Erlbaum Associates, 2006), 335.

2. Ibid., 342.

3. Vassilis Dalakas, Robert Madrigal, & Keri L. Anderson, "We Are Number One! The Phenomenon of Basking in Reflected Glory and Its Implications for Sports Marketing," *Sports Marketing and the Psychology of Marketing Communication*, ed. Lynn R. Kahle and Chris Riley (Mahwah, NJ: Lawrence Erlbaum Associates, 2004), 70.

4. Ibid., 71–72.

5. Wann, *Handbook of Sports & Media*, 342.

6. Ibid., 341.

7. Ibid., 343.

OWNERS

1. Johan Keri, ed., *Baseball Between the Numbers: Why Everything You Know About the Game is Wrong* (New York: Basic Books, 2006), 221.

2. Jerry Gorman and Kirk Calhoun, *The Name of the Game: The Business of Sports* (New York: John Wiley & Sons, 1994), x.

3. Keri, ed., *Baseball Between the Numbers*, 216.

4. Ibid., 211.

5. Ibid., 209.

6. Ibid., 211212.

7. Ibid., 213.

8. Ibid., 222.

9. Ibid., 218.

10. Ibid., 224.

11. Ibid., 218.

12. Ibid., 220.

13. Gorman and Calhoun, *The Name of the Game*, 44.

14. Keri, ed., *Baseball Between the Numbers*, 217.

15. Roger G. Noll and Andrew Zimbalist. *Sports, Jobs, and Taxes: The Economic Impact of Sports Teams and Stadiums* (Brookings Institution Press, 1997).

CHAPTER 2

ATHLETES

1. Congressman Tom McMillen with Paul Coggins, *Out of Bounds* (New York: Simon & Schuster, 1992), 101.

2. Bill Romanowski with Adam Schefter and Phil Towle, *Romo: My Life on the Edge: Living Dreams and Slaying Dragons* (New York: William Morrow and Company, Inc., 2005), 6.

CRIMINALS

1. Jeff Benedict and Don Yaeger, *Pros and Cons: The Criminals Who Play in the NFL* (New York: Warner Books,1998), x.

2. Jeff Benedict, *Out of Bounds: Inside the NBA's Culture of Rape, Violence, & Crime* (New York: HarperCollins, 2004), 20.

3. Keith Law, "Baseball needs a backbone regarding DUIs," espn.com, March 27, 2007. sports.espn.go.com/espn/page2/story?page=law/070327&sportCat=mlb

4. Mike Freeman, *Bloody Sundays* (New York: William Morrow and Company, Inc., 2003), 184.

5. Matt Mosley, "Steelers' double standard?" sportsillustrated.cnn.com, March 21, 2008.

DRUGS

1. Ron Suskind, "Deadly Silence: How the Inner Circles Of Medicine and Sports Failed a Stricken Star," *Wall Street Journal*, March 9, 1995.

2. Ibid.

3. McMillen with Coggins, *Out of Bounds*, 162.

4. Phillip Smith, "High in the NBA," alternet.org, March 6, 2001. www.alternet.org/drugreporter/10555/

5. Ibid.

6. Associated Press, "Stern: NBA holding steady financially," espn.com, February 15, 2009. sports.espn.go.com/nba/news/story?id=3908026

7. ESPN.com News Services, "Former relief pitcher Howe killed in car crash," espn.com, April, 29, 2006. sports.espn.go.com/mlb/news/story?id=2425900

8. Associated Press, "NASCAR says Mayfield again tests positive for methamphetamine," July 15, 2009.

9. Ibid.

10. Jenna Fryer, "France defends NASCAR's drug policy," abcnews.com, July 3, 2009. abcnews.go.com/Sports/wireStory?id=7996063

11. Ibid.

12. Lawrence Taylor with Steve Serby, *LT: Over the Edge: Tackling Quarterbacks, Drugs, and a World Beyond Football* (New York: HarperCollins, 2003), 48.

13. Ibid., 91.

14. Robert Huizenga, *"You're Okay, It's Just a Bruise"*: *A Doctor's Sideline Secrets About Pro Football's Most Outrageous Team* (New York: St. Martin's Press, 1994), 325.

15. Ibid., 209.

16. Freeman, *Bloody Sundays*, 183.

PERFORMANCE ENHANCERS

1. Len Pasquarelli, "NFL adds amphetamines to banned substances list," espn.com, June 27, 2006. sports.espn.go.com/nfl/news/story?id=2501680

2. Bernie Parrish, *They Call It a Game* (New York: The Dial Press, 1971), 71.

3. Ibid., 69.

4. Taylor with Serby, *LT: Over the Edge*, 72.

5. Romanowski with Schefter and Towle, *Romo: My Life on the Edge*, 82.

6. Unknown, "NHL drug testing," drugfreesport.com, 2006. www.drugfreesport.com/newsroom/insight.asp?VolID=36&TopicID=4

7. Tom Haudricourt, "Drug Policy Working; Selig happy with amphetamine ban," *Milwaukee Journal Sentinel*, July 12, 2006.

8. Jose Canseco, *Juiced: Wild Times, Rampant 'Roids, Smash Hits, and How Baseball Got Big* (New York: Regan Books, 2005), 135.

9. Ibid., 133.

10. Mark Starr, "Glimpses of a Golden Age," *Newsweek*, March 31, 2008.

11. Canseco, *Juiced*, 149.

12. Buster Olney, "Sources: Forthcoming Mitchell report will be 'huge story,'" espn.com, October 13, 2007. sports.espn.go.com/mlb/news/story?id=3060689

13. Jayson Stark, "A-Rod answers questions, raises more," espn.com, February 17, 2009. sports.espn.go.com/mlb/spring2009/columns/story?columnist=stark_jayson&id=3914265

14. Bob Nightengale, "Giambi: Baseball's apology needed over steroid issue," usatoday. com, May 23, 2007. www.usatoday.com/sports/baseball/al/yankees/2007-05-17-giambi-steroid-issue_N.htm

15. Charles Chandler, "Medical records of ex-Panthers reveal ill effects, multiple refills leading to Super Bowl," *Charlotte Observer*, August 27, 2006.

16. ESPN.com News Services, "Sources: Chargers' Merriman suspended for steroids," espn.com, October 23, 2006. sports.espn.go.com/nfl/news/story?id=2635475

17. Charles Chandler, "Medical records of ex-Panthers reveal ill effects, multiple refills leading to Super Bowl," *Charlotte Observer*, August 27, 2006.

18. "NFLPA to accept HGH testing," sportsillustrated.cnn.com, January 31, 2008.

19. Romanowski with Schefter and Towle, *Romo: My Life on the Edge*, 7.

20. Ibid., 7.

CHAPTER 3 GAMBLING

1. Richard O. Davies and Richard G. Abram, *Betting the Line: Sports Wagering in American Life* (Columbus: Ohio State University Press, 2001), 2.

2. Ibid., 19.

3. Ibid., 53–54.

4. Dan E. Moldea, *Interference: How Organized Crime Influences Professional Football* (New York: William Morrow and Company, Inc., 1989), 252–253.

5. Davies and Abram, *Betting the Line*, 6.

6. Dan Gordon, *Beat the Sports Books: An Insider's Guide to Betting the NFL* (New York: Cardoza Publishing, 2005), 33.

7. Ibid., 25.

8. Gregg Easterbrook, "TMQ's annual Bad Predictions Review," espn.com, February 10, 2009. sports.espn.go.com/espn/page2/story?page=easterbrook/090210

9. ESPN.com News Services, "Goodell: 'We have to educate our players ...'," espn.com, February 2, 2007. sports.espn.go.com/nfl/playoffs06/news/story?id=2752126

10. Chris Mortensen, *Playing for Keeps: How One Man Kept the Mob from Sinking Its Hooks into Pro Football* (New York: Simon & Schuster, 1991), 171.

11. Ibid., 171.

12. Michael Franzese, Interviewed by Jim Rome, The Jim Rome Show, February 15, 2006.

13. Ibid.

14. Ibid.

15. Moldea, *Interference*, 53.

16. Davies and Abram, *Betting the Line*, 67.

17. Ibid., 72.

18. Biography of Bobby Layne, profootballhof.com. www.profootballhof.com/hof/member.aspx?PlayerId=126 (accessed October 26, 2009)

19. Moldea, *Interference*, 84.

20. Hornung, *Golden Boy*, 151.

21. Moldea, *Interference*, 91.

22. Alex Karras with Herb Gluck, *Even Big Guys Cry* (New York: Holt, Rinehart, and Winston, 1977), 162.

23. Ibid., 159–160.

24. Hornung, *Golden Boy*, 152.

25. Karras with Gluck, *Even Big Guys Cry*, 160.

26. Ibid., 158.

27. Hornung, *Golden Boy*, 150.

28. Ibid., 112–113.

29. Ibid., 132.

30. Ibid., 116.

31. Ibid., 157.

32. Moldea, *Interference*, 85.

33. Ibid., 183.

34. Larry Merchant, *The National Football Lottery* (New York: Holt, Rinehart, and Winston, 1973), 223–224

35. Davies and Abram, *Betting the Line*, 113.

36. Robert Cherry, *Wilt: Larger than Life* (Chicago: Triumph Books, 2004), 14.

37. Armen Keteyian, Harvey Araton, and Martin F. Dardis, *Money Players: Days and Nights Inside the New NBA* (New York: Pocket Books, 1997), 60.

38. Associated Press, "Thomas is named in betting report," *New York Times*, June 17, 1990.

39. Michael Y. Sokolove, *Hustle: The Myth, Life, and Lies of Pete Rose* (New York: Simon & Schuster, 1990), 199.

40. Ibid., 206.

41. Ibid., 205.

42. Associated Press, "Investigation found no gambling on baseball," espn.com, April 26, 2005. sports.espn.go.com/mlb/news/story?id=2046549

43. David Halberstam, *Playing for Keeps: Michael Jordan and the World He Made* (New York: Random House, 1999), 317.

44. Keteyian, Araton, and Dardis, *Money Players*, 191.

45. Ibid., 117.

46. Ibid., 196.

47. Halberstam, *Playing for Keeps*, 321.

48. Keteyian, Araton, and Dardis, *Money Players*, 191.

49. Ibid., 196.

50. Michael Leahy, *When Nothing Else Matters: Michael Jordan's Last Comeback* (New York: Simon & Schuster, 2004), 101.

51. Michael Jordan, Interview on *60 Minutes*, October 23, 2005.

52. Freeman, *Bloody Sundays*, xxvii.

53. Jeremy Roenick, ESPN's "Outside the Line Nightly," February 8, 2006.

54. Rick Westhead and Ken Campbell, "Gambling allegations shake hockey world," *Toronto Star*, February 8, 2006.

55. ESPN.com News Services, "Coyotes' Tocchet to be arraigned in 7-10 days," espn.com, February 9, 2006. sports.espn.go.com/nhl/news/story?id=2323292

56. Ibid.

57. Associated Press, "Tocchet avoids jail, gets two years probation," espn.com, August 17, 2007. sports.espn.go.com/nhl/news/story?id=2978637

58. Ibid.

59. Chad Brown and Alan Eisenstock, *Inside the Meat Grinder: An NFL Official's Life in the Trenches* (New York: St. Martin's Press, 1999), 76-77.

60. Associated Press, "Umps angry over background checks," sportsillustrated.cnn.com, January 30, 2008.

61. Wayne Drehs, "Numbers indicate unlikely outcomes in games Donaghy officiated," espn.com, July 24, 2007.

62. Ibid.

63. ESPN.com News Service, "Attorney drops bombshell accusations, argues for probation for Donaghy," espn.com, May 20, 2008. sports.espn.go.com/nba/news/story?id=3404607

64. Associated Press, "Disgraced ref's lawyer says NBA scandal goes much deeper," afp.google.com, May 20, 2008.

65. ESPN.com News Service, "Attorney drops bombshell accusations, argues for probation for Donaghy," espn.com, May 20, 2008. sports.espn.go.com/nba/news/story?id=3404607

66. Chris Sheridan, "NBA to revamp ref gambling rules; Jackson, Nunn see roles reduced," espn.com, October 26, 2007. sports.espn.go.com/nba/news/story?id=3079309

67. Ibid.

68. Ibid.

69. Stevin Smith, ESPN's "Outside the Line Nightly," February 8, 2006.

CHAPTER 4 TELEVISION

1. McMillen, *Out of Bounds*, 182.

2. Parrish, *They Call It a Game*, 126.

3. Dan Brown and Jennings Bryant, "Sports Content on U.S. Television," *Handbook of Sports and Media*, ed. Arthur A. Raney and Jennings Bryant (Mahwah, NJ: Lawrence Erlbaum Associates, 2006), 85.

4. Gorman and Calhoun, *The Name of the Game*, 60.

5. Ibid., 70.

6. McMillen, *Out of Bounds*, 185.

7. Ibid., 185.

8. Gorman and Calhoun, *The Name of the Game*, 70.

9. Ibid., 61.

10. Ibid., 82–83.

11. David B. Sullivan, "Broadcast Television and the Game of Packaging Sports," *Handbook of Sports and Media*, ed. Arthur A. Raney and Jennings Bryant (Mahwah,

NJ: Lawrence Erlbaum Associates, 2006), 136.

12. Ibid., 136.

13. Ronald Grover, "The NFL's Big Score," BusinessWeek.com, November 17, 2004. www. businessweek.com/bwdaily/dnflash/nov2004/nf20041116_3284_db011.htm

14. Brown and Bryant, Handbook of Sports and Media, 87.

15. Ronald Grover, "The NFL's Big Score," BusinessWeek.com, November 17, 2004. www.businessweek.com/bwdaily/dnflash/nov2004/nf20041116_3284_db011.htm

16. Parrish, They Call It a Game, 122.

17. Keteyian, Araton, and Dardis, Money Players, 233.

18. Associated Press, "Browns sued by TV station after team cuts ties," espn.com, July 26, 2006. sports.espn.go.com/nfl/news/story?id=2530067

19. "News Broadcasters Slam New NFL Policy," imdb.com, April 3, 2006. www.imdb. com/news/ni0093419/

20. Ibid.

21. Stephen Dinan and Jerry Seper, "NFL rejects Border Patrol ad," Washington Times, February 14, 2007.

22. Karras with Gluck, Even Big Guys Cry, 3.

23. Don Weiss with Chuck Day, The Making of the Super Bowl: The Inside Story of the World's Greatest Sporting Event (Chicago: Contemporary Books, 2003), 15.

24. Ibid., 312.

25. Parrish, They Call It a Game, 111.

26. Davies and Abram, Betting the Line, 46.

27. Leahy, When Nothing Else Matters, 2.

28. Sullivan, Handbook of Sports and Media, 142.

29. Ibid., 142.

30. Ibid., 141.

31. Joe Namath, NFL Network's "America's Game: The Super Bowl Champions: The Story of the 1968 Jets."

32. Canseco, Juiced, 92.

33. Tim Green, The Dark Side of the Game: My Life in the NFL (New York: Warner Books, 1996), 136.

34. Freeman, Bloody Sundays, 107.

CHAPTER 5 THE GREAT HIPPODROME

1. Weiss with Day, The Making of the Super Bowl, 41.

2. Ibid., 100.

3. Ibid., 100.

4. Ibid., 151.

5. Ibid., 157.

6. Bubba Smith and Hal DeWindt, *Kill, Bubba, Kill!* (New York: Simon & Schuster, 1983), 130.

7. Gerry Philbin, NFL Network's "America's Game: The Super Bowl Champions: The Story of the 1968 Jets."

8. Bubba Smith Interview, *Playboy*, November 1982.

9. Parrish, *They Call It a Game*, 128.

10. Weiss with Day, *The Making of the Super Bowl*, 150.

11. Ibid., 167.

MAJOR LEAGUE BASEBALL

12. Paul D. Staudohar, "The Baseball Strike of 1994-95," *Monthly Labor Review*, March, 1997, 26.

13. Canseco, *Juiced*, 200.

14. Ibid., 180.

15. Ibid., 204.

16. Ibid., 76.

17. Ibid., 199–200.

18. "MLB's revenue tops $6 billion," sportsillustrated.cnn.com, November 15, 2007.

NASCAR

19. "Major Crackdown: NASCAR hands down suspension to Waltrip crew chief," sportsillustrated.cnn.com, February 15, 2005.

20. David Newton, "Waltrip still reeling from Daytona debacle," espn.com, July, 6, 2007. sports.espn.go.com/rpm/columns/story?seriesId=2&columnist=loombdavid&id=2927946

21. Mark Ashenfelter, "Nationwide teams irked by alleged Gibbs Racing team's cheating," espn.com, August 17, 2008. sports.espn.go.com/rpm/nascar/nationwide/news/story?id=3539659

22. "Major Crackdown: NASCAR hands down suspension to Waltrip crew chief," sportsillustrated.cnn.com, February 15, 2005.

23. Robert Lipsyte, "'The Call' is answered in Earnhardt's Pepsi 400 victory," *New York Times*, July 9, 2001.

24. Bob Zeller, "Is NASCAR tinkering around?" *Virginian Pilot*, February 19, 1995.

25. Dave Rodman, "Dale Jr. wins emotional Pepsi 400," nascar.com, July 9, 2001. www.nascar.com/2001/NEWS/07/07/junior_wins/index.html

26. Robert Lipsyte, "'The Call' is answered in Earnhardt's Pepsi 400 victory," *New York Times*, July 9, 2001.

27. Associated Press, "Skeptics question Junior's win," abcnews.go.com, July 9, 2001.

28. Dave Rodman, "Dale Jr. wins emotional Pepsi 400," nascar.com, July 9, 2001. www.nascar.com/2001/NEWS/07/07/junior_wins/index.html

29. Jenna Fryer, "Stewart likens NASCAR to wrestling," sportsillustrated.cnn.com, April 25, 2007.

30. Ibid.

31. Ibid.

THE NATIONAL BASKETBALL ASSOCIATION

32. Percy Allen, "Well, maybe your team should just tank it," *Seattle Times*, April 5, 2007.

33. Associated Press, "Timberwolves assured lottery pick with loss to Grizzlies," espn.com, April 19, 2007. proxy.espn.go.com/nba/recap?gameId=270418016

34. Associated Press, "Wolves' Owner Taylor feels Garnett 'tanked' end of last season," March 18, 2008.

35. Ibid.

36. Ibid.

37. Adrian Wojnarowski, "Boston's empty 'tank,'" yahoo.sports.com, January 30, 2007. ca.sports.yahoo.com/nba/news?slug=aw-celtics013007&prov=yhoo&type=lgns

38. David Stern, CBS Sports Broadcast of 1985 NBA Draft Lottery, June 18, 1985.

39. Pat O'Brien, CBS Sports Broadcast of 1985 NBA Draft Lottery, June 18, 1985.

40. Keteyian, Araton, and Dardis, *Money Players*, 61.

41. Ibid., 8.

42. Ibid., 173.

43. Ibid., 185.

44. Ibid., 7.

THE NATIONAL HOCKEY LEAGUE

45. "The truth behind Gretzky's L.A. trade," cbc.ca, video original broadcast date August 10, 1988. archives.cbc.ca/sports/hockey/clips/6209/

46. Scott Morrison, "Wayne Gretzky traded...California here he comes," *Toronto Sun*, August 10, 1988.

47. Ibid.

THE NATIONAL FOOTBALL LEAGUE

48. Richard Sandomir, "Parity in the N.F.L. is good for ratings," *New York Times*, December 17, 2002.

49. Ibid.

50. Ibid.

51. Thomas George, "NFL entry fee is set at $140 million," *New York Times*, May 26, 1993.

52. R. David Read, "Restoring the Superdome," *Sound & Communications*, Vol. 52, No. 11, November 20, 2006.

53. "Take that, Katrina: Triumphant homecoming for Saints, Superdome," espn.com, September 26, 2006. espn.go.com/nfl/recap?gameId=260925018

54. Ibid.

55. Aaron Kuriloff and Erik Matuszewski, "NFL Broadcast Ratings Rise as Patriots' Perfect Year Lures Fans," Bloomberg.com, December 21, 2007. www.bloomberg.com/apps/news?pid=20601079&refer=&sid=aNMPlyNWp8B0

56. Ibid.

57. "Despite player concerns, NFL backs refs during controversial Pats-Ravens game," espn.com, December 7, 2007.

58. Aaron Kuriloff and Erik Matuszewski, "NFL Broadcast Ratings Rise as Patriots' Perfect Year Lures Fans," Bloomberg.com, December 21, 2007. www.bloomberg.com/apps/news?pid=20601079&refer=&sid=aNMPlyNWp8B0

59. Ibid.

60. Michael Silver, "Special…Delivery," time.com, December 26, 2001. www.time.com/time/magazine/article/0,9171,189912,00.html

61. William Morrow, *Patriot Reign: Bill Belichick, the Coaches, and the Players Who Built a Champion* (It Books, 2005), 240.

62. Bob McGinn, "That defeat still hurts," *Milwaukee Journal Sentinel*, January 31, 2008.

63. Ibid.

64. Brad Biggs, "Holmgren still explaining 'concession' touchdown," *Chicago Sun-Times*, February 4, 2006.

65. Bob McGinn, "That defeat still hurts," *Milwaukee Journal Sentinel*, January 31, 2008.

66. Bill Pennington, "Super Bowl XXXII Notebook: Surprised by Strategy," *New York Times*, January 27, 1998.

67. Ibid.

68. Mike Freeman, "Super Bowl XXXIII; Robinson's Arrest Looms Larger After the Falcons' Defeat," *New York Times*, February 2, 1999.

69. "Sorrowful Time," sportsillustrated.cnn.com, February 1, 1999.

70. CBC News, "Music City Miracle gives Titans win over Bills," cbc.ca, December 20, 2000. www.cbc.ca/sports/story/2000/12/20/titans000108.html

71. "Titans stun Bills in miracle finish," espn.com, January 8, 2000.

72. Peter Lawrence-Riddell, "Controversy thrives in Patriots-Raiders encounters," espn.com, January 19, 2002. a.espncdn.com/nfl/playoffs01/s/2002/0119/1314426.html

73. Ibid.

74. Ibid.

75. Romanowski with Schefter and Towle, *Romo: My Life on the Edge*, 253.

76. Ibid., 253.

77. Freeman, *Bloody Sundays*, 60.

78. Frank Litsky, "McNabb Said to be Ill at End of the Super Bowl," *New York Times*, February 9, 2005.

79. Greg Bishop and Michael Brick, "In Cat and Mouse Game, Patriots Are Central Players," *New York Times*, May 11, 2008.

80. Associated Press, "Opinions on Pats tactics mixed among holdovers from Eagles' NFC title team," espn.com, September 13, 2007. sports.espn.go.com/nfl/news/story?id=3017964

81. Ibid.

82. Ibid.

83. ESPN.com News Service, "Senator wants to know why NFL destroyed Patriots spy tapes," espn.com, February 2, 2008. sports.espn.go.com/nfl/news/story?id=3225539

84. John Clayton, "Walsh, NFL still haven't worked out deal for Spygate testimony," espn.com, April 1, 2008. sports.espn.go.com/nfl/news/story?id=3322568

85. Len Pasquarelli, "NFL will review Holmgren comments," espn.com, February 8, 2006. sports.espn.go.com/nfl/playoffs05/news/story?id=

86. Associated Press, "NFL says Super Bowl 'properly officiated'," espn.com, February 8, 2006. sports.espn.go.com/nfl/playoffs05/news/story?id=

87. Ibid.

88. Len Pasquarelli, "NFL will review Holmgren comments," espn.com, February 8, 2006. sports.espn.go.com/nfl/playoffs05/news/story?id=2322700

89. Associated Press, "Holmgren still feeling Super Bowl pain," foxsports.com, March 30, 2006.

SOURCES

BOOKS

Gutman, Dan. *Baseball Babylon*. New York: Penguin Books, 1992.

Hall, Donald with Dock Ellis. *Dock Ellis in the Country of Baseball*. Fireside, 1989.
Helmbold, R.L. *Have the World Series Been Fixed?* RAND Corporation, 1970.

Holst, Art. *Sunday Zebras*. Lake Forest, IL: Forest Publishing, 1980.

Howe, Steve and Jim Greenfield. *Between the Lines: One Athlete's Struggle to Escape the Nightmare of Addiction*. Masters Press, 1989.

Kelley, Scott W., and Kelly Tian. "Fanatical Consumption: An Investigation of the Behavior of Sports Fans Through Textual Data." *Sports Marketing and the Psychology of Marketing Communication*, ed. Lynn R. Kahle and Chris Riley. Mahwah, NJ: Lawrence Erlbaum Associates, 2004.

Kerkhoff, Blair. *Upon Further Review: Controversy in Sports Officiating*. Lenexa, KS: Addax Publishing Group, 2000.

Morgan, John. *Glory for Sale: Inside the Browns' move to Baltimore & the new NFL.* Bancroft Press, 1997.

Neyer, Rob. *Rob Neyer's Big Book of Baseball Blunders: A Complete Guide to the Worst Decisions and Stupidest Moments in Baseball's History.* New York: Fireside, 2006.

Raney, Arthur. "Why We Watch and Enjoy Mediated Sports." *Handbook of Sports & Media,* ed. Arthur A. Raney and Jennings Bryant. Mahwah, NJ: Lawrence Erlbaum Associates, 2006.

Rose, Pete with Rick Hill. *My Prison without Bars.* New York: St. Martin's Press, 2004.

Rosen, Charley. *The Wizard of Odds: How Jack Molinas Almost Destroyed the Game of Basketball.* New York: Seven Stories Press, 2003.

Shirley, Paul. *Can I Keep My Jersey?: 11 Teams, 5 Countries, and 4 Years in my Life as a Basketball Vagabond.* New York: Villard Books, 2007.

Smith, Robert. *The Rest of the Iceberg: An Insider's View of the World of Sport and Celebrity.* Portland, OR: Inkwater Press, 2004.

Torre, Joe and Tom Verducci. *The Yankee Years.* New York: Doubleday, 2009.

Wood, Chris and Vince Benigni. "The Coverage of Sports on Cable TV." *Handbook of Sports & Media,* ed. Arthur A. Raney and Jennings Bryant. Mahwah, NJ: Lawrence Erlbaum Associates, 2006.

Zimbalist, Andrew. *Baseball and Billions: A Probing Look Inside the Business of Our National Pastime.* New York: Basic Books, 1992.

WEBSITES

www.basketball-reference.com
www.baseball-almanac.com
www.gamblersanonymous.org
www.legendsofhockey.net
www.ncpgambling.org
www.sportsvenues.com
www.thesmokinggun.com
www.whitehousedrugpolicy.gov

ARTICLES

Associated Press, "Two on Royals Admit Cocaine Charge," *New York Times,* October 14, 1983.

Associated Press, "Johnson arrested, charged in altercation with girlfriend," espn.com, September 14, 2005. sports.espn.go.com/nfl/news/story?id=2160514

Associated Press, "Favre angry that NFL turns its back on Robinson," espn.com, October 18, 2006. sports.espn.go.com/nfl/news/story?id=2631221

Associated Press, "Police: Johnson was at club during fatal shooting," espn.com, December 16, 2006. sports.espn.go.com/nfl/news/story?id=2699400

Associated Press, "Jason Kidd filing for divorce," January 10, 2007.

Associated Press, "Barkley admits he has gambling problem," msnbc.com, February 6, 2007. nbcsports.msnbc.com/id/16997600/

Associated Press, "Grand Jury likely getting names in plea bargain," espn.com, March 30, 2007. sports.espn.go.com/mlb/news/story?id=2854555

Associated Press, "NHL: no steroid problem for us." December 14, 2007.

Associated Press, "Baseball Establishes Investigations Unit," espn.com, January 14, 2008. sports.espn.go.com/mlb/news/story?id=3192208

Associated Press, "MLB, Players' Union agree to more frequent drug testing," espn.com, April 11, 2008. sports.espn.go.com/mlb/news/story?id=3341940

Associated Press, "Belichick insists Pats did not try to hide taping of opponents signals," espn.com, May 16, 2008. sports.espn.go.com/nfl/news/story?id=3400028

Associated Press, "NBC sells out Super Bowl ads for record $206M," msnbc.com, January 31, 2009. nbcsports.msnbc.com/id/28951579/ns/sports-super_bowl_xliii/

Associated Press, "Super Bowl ratings down from last year's high," abcnews.com, February 2, 2009. abcnews.go.com/Entertainment/wireStory?id=6786284

Associated Press, "Stallworth released on $200K bail," espn.com, April 3, 2009. sports.espn.go.com/nfl/news/story?id=4036024

Associated Press, "Comcast to run NFL Network amid talks," espn.com, May 1, 2009. sports.espn.go.com/nfl/news/story?id=4120117

Associated Press, "NBA draft lottery marks 25 years," espn.com, May 19, 2009. sports.espn.go.com/nba/draft2009/news/story?id=4175984

Associated Press, "Game 7 most-watched contest since '73," espn.com, June 15, 2009. sports.espn.go.com/nhl/playoffs/2009/news?id=4261434

Associated Press, "Donaghy to serve at halfway house," espn.com, June 19, 2009. sports.espn.go.com/nba/news/story?id=4267658

Associated Press, "Deal extended through '10-11 season," espn.com, July 15, 2009. sports.espn.go.com/nhl/news/story?id=4329779

Bauman, Michael. "The quarterback's challenge - football star Brett Favre's addiction to painkillers." Sporting News, May 27, 1996.

CBC Sports. "Stimulants common in NHL: Quintal." cbc.ca, March 23, 2005. www.cbc.ca/sports/story/2005/03/22/quintal050322.html

CBSSports.com Wire Reports, "Barkley vows to stop gambling," cbssports.com, May 19, 2008. www.cbssports.com/print/nba/story/10833403

Curran, Tom. "Decision makers say prospects' admissions won't hurt them." nbcsports.com, April 18, 2007.

Domowitch, Paul. "NFL Films is taking shots." Philly.com, March 27, 2008.

ESPN.com News Services, "Kidd accused of abusing his wife," espn.com, January 19, 2001.

ESPN.com News Services, "Papers question reasons for resignation," espn.com, July 13, 2004. sports.espn.go.com/nhl/news/story?id=1839352

ESPN.com News Services, "Ex-MLB'er Segui says he's player in FBI affidavit," espn.com, June 18, 2006. sports.espn.go.com/mlb/news/story?id=2489724

ESPN.com News Services, "Report: Panthers ignored risks of 'alarming' steroid use," espn.com, August 28, 2006. sports.espn.go.com/nfl/news/story?id=2563563

ESPN.com News Services, "Court: Feds may use drug testing data from 2003," espn. com, December 28, 2006. sports.espn.go.com/mlb/news/story?id=2709496

ESPN.com News Service, "NBA says that probe of gambling and referees isn't finished," espn.com, October 21, 2007. sports.espn.go.com/nba/news/story?id=3072928

ESPN.com News Services, "Reports: Donaghy bet on more than 100 games he worked," espn.com, May 17, 2008.

ESPN.com News Services, "Reports: Arthur, Chalmers sorry for role in rookie camp incident," espn.com, September 5, 2008. sports.espn.go.com/nba/news/story?id=3570994

Farber, Michael and Don Yaeger. "Capital Losses." *Sports Illustrated*, March 17, 2003. sportsillustrated.cnn.com/vault/article/magazine/MAG1028225/index.htm

Goldaper, Sam. "Jackson, Barkley are fined for bets." *New York Times*, January 12, 1990. www.nytimes.com/1990/01/12/sports/jackson-barkley-are-fined-for-bets.html

Goldstein, Joe. "Explosion: 1951 scandals threaten college hoops." espn.com, November 19, 2003. espn.go.com/classic/s/basketball_scandals_explosion.html

"Hockey's Dirty Linen." *Time*, March 22, 1948. www.time.com/time/magazine/article/0,9171,804494,00.html

Hohler, Bob. "Patriots' Kraft has led winning drive." *Boston Globe*, January 30, 2005. www.boston.com/sports/football/patriots/articles/2005/01/30/patriots_kraft_has_led_winning_drive/

Klein, Jeff Z. "Game 5 of Cup Finals on NBC is Top Saturday Night Telecast." *New York Times*, June 8, 2009. slapshot.blogs.nytimes.com/2009/06/08/game-5-of-cup-final-on-nbc-is-top-saturday-night-telecast/

MSNBC.com News Services, "Artest's agent reportedly to appeal suspension," msnbc. com, July 16, 2007. nbcsports.msnbc.com/id/19762686/

Newton, David. "In light of Mayfield, drivers want list." espn.com, May 16, 2009. sports.espn.go.com/rpm/nascar/cup/news/story?id=4167695

Pugmire, Lance. "Clemens is named in drug affidavit." *Los Angeles Times*, October 1, 2006. articles.latimes.com/2006/oct/01/sports/sp-clemens1

Puma, Mike. "Strawberry's Story One of Unfulfilled Potential." espn.com. espn.go.com/classic/biography/s/Strawberry_Darryl.html

Quinn, T.J. "Failure leaves a testy Barry." *New York Daily News*, January 11, 2007. www.nydailynews.com/sports/baseball/2007/11/15/2007-11-15_failure_leaves_a_testy_barry.html

"Report: Steve Howe had drugs in his system when he died," yahoo.sports.com, June, 28, 2006. sports.yahoo.com/mlb/news?slug=howetoxicology&prov=st&type=lgns

Schmidt, Michael S. "Baseball's Drug Testing Lacks Element of Surprise." *New York Times*, October 31, 2007. www.nytimes.com/2007/10/31/sports/baseball/31testing.html?_r=1

Sheridan, Chris. "NBA declines to fine Blazers for e-mail." espn.com, January 14, 2009. sports.espn.go.com/espn/print?id=3831137&type=story

Silverstein, Tom. "Details of addiction, anger revealed in MVP's book." *Milwaukee Journal-Sentinel*, August 12, 1997.

"Sports People; NHL Drug Inquiry," *New York Times*, May 13, 1986. www.nytimes.com/1986/05/13/sports/sports-people-nhl-drug-inquiry.html

"Sports People; Wilson Apologizes," *New York Times*, November 12, 1983. www.nytimes.com/1983/11/12/sports/sports-people-wilson-apologizes.html

"Stoudamire Suspended After Drug Arrest," cbc.ca, July 8, 2003.

OTHER SOURCES

CBS News: *60 Minutes*, March 30, 2005.

Discovery Times: Doping To Win.

ESPN: Outside the Lines Nightly, February 8, 2006.

NFL's Films: NFL's Greatest Games: The 1958 NFL Championship.

Pedowitz, Lawrence B. *Report to the Board of Governors of the National Basketball Association.* October 1, 2008.

Transcript of both Michael Jordan retirement speeches as published by *Chicago Tribune*.

Transcript of David Stern's press conference regarding Tim Donaghy as published on espn.com, July 24, 2007.

ACKNOWLEDGEMENTS

While the research and initial writing of this book was a solo effort on my part, there are quite a few people who made that possible. First and foremost, I would like to thank my wife Sarah whose self-sacrifice and love made this book a shared effort. This is as much hers as it is mine.

Next in line are my parents, Donna and Jim, who were always there for me when I needed them. They instilled a love of history along with the recognition that what has already occurred will undoubtedly affect the future. I am forever grateful to them both for a lifetime's worth of love and support.

The initial influence for this book came from my brother Kevin whose repeated claims of "this is fixed!" ushered me down the path that ultimately resulted in this work. Without him, this book likely would not exist. A big thank you is necessary for my sister Kathleen, my brother Bill, my sister-in-law Kris, and my nieces and nephews Ryan, Emma, Dylan, and Raquel for their constant support and help. I'd also like to thank the entire Grabowski clan and Cheryl Parsons for not laughing at me when they learned what I was writing.

A wealth of support, advice, arguments, and knowledge came from the following people who (I think) always believed, whether they would admit it or not: Jeff & Sheri Robbins, Todd & Amy O'Brien, Michael & Michelle Schulz, Matt Venci, Don & Ann Fleming, Steve & Val Becker, Scott & Keri Sandberg, Bryan & Libby Quesenberry, Jason & Lexi Fritz, Pete Hopkins, Mike Wagner, Bruce Wolf, Brian Pluemer, Jeff Wurster, Tony & Jo Maze, Tim & Jen Kubly, Peter Wokwicz, Jon Solwald, Bridget & Tom Pinzger, Dionne & Lee Kujawa, Irene & Ki Gillies, and Greg Steplyk. A thanks is also in order for Joellen Dooley, Marion Osenga, Craig Bacle, and the staff of A-major Music for keeping me employed even while my mind was clearly not on my job.

Without the help, aid, and advice of my manager Janet Loftis and her mysteriously silent partner Jim Goldschlager, my writing career may have died out long ago. Thanks for believing and sticking with me for so long.

Thanks to Feral House publisher Adam Parfrey for his great suggestions and editing ideas without which this book may have been a rambling mess. Fine tuning came from editor Dave Wills of The Copy Doctor. A shout-out goes to all the others at Feral House as well for treating me so well.

The original article that served as the backbone of this book and alerted me to the fact that other people were indeed interested in this subject matter was first published in the late, great *Paranoia* magazine. Thanks to Al Hidell and the rest of the staff at *Paranoia* for giving me the break while risking the wrath of the NFL in publishing that piece.

A special thanks goes to Michael Ravnitzky whose help in securing information from the FBI via Freedom of Information Act requests was invaluable to this book. Also, thanks for the lead on the Rand Report concerning the fixing of the World Series.

A tip of the cap goes to the following for believing, supporting, helping, and spreading the word that the fix is in: "The Power Hour" radio program with Joyce and Dave, Henry Abbott of ESPN.com's TrueHoop blog, Patrick Hruby of ESPN.com's Page 2 (you publish that interview with me yet?), Jack McCallum of *Sports Illustrated*, Greg Bishop of the *New York Times*, Elliot Kalb of FOX Sports (you still owe me a book, pal), Gary Baddeley at disinfo.com (this could've been yours), Richard Roeper for "debunking" me then being too afraid to respond to any requests to speak my piece, cracked.com, oddjack.com for labeling me a "crackpot firestarting journalist," Daniel Neiden, Judith Newman, Ron at carolinasucks.com, Lee Mangano, Derek Addams, Bryan Lauritzen, Hussain Habib (keep them kids reading, coach), Christopher Wilhelm, Justin Uselton, Larry "Double L" Blong, and you—for buying and/or reading this book. ★